# PEASANTS IN HISTORY
*Essays in Honour of Daniel Thorner*

Daniel Thorner

# Peasants in History

*Essays in Honour of Daniel Thorner*

Edited by

E. J. HOBSBAWM
WITOLD KULA
ASHOK MITRA
K. N. RAJ
IGNACY SACHS

Published for

SAMEEKSHA TRUST

by

OXFORD UNIVERSITY PRESS

CALCUTTA   DELHI   BOMBAY   MADRAS

1980

*Oxford University Press*

OXFORD LONDON GLASGOW
NEW YORK TORONTO MELBOURNE WELLINGTON
NAIROBI DAR ES SALAAM CAPE TOWN
KUALA LUMPUR SINGAPORE HONG KONG TOKYO
DELHI BOMBAY CALCUTTA MADRAS KARACHI

Printed in India by P. K. Ghosh
at Eastend Printers, 3 Dr Suresh Sarkar Road, Calcutta 700014
and published by R. Dayal, Oxford University Press,
P17 Mission Row Extension, Calcutta 700013

# Preface

In seeking to commemorate Daniel Thorner we have brought together a collection of essays by some of his many colleagues, ad-
mirers and friends. Daniel was in the first instance a student of
India, and above all of rural India. It is therefore natural that the
largest single group of contributions should deal with the agrarian
problems of the subcontinent which was so near to his heart. However, Daniel was far from a narrow regional specialist. His strength
lay in the capacity for seeing agrarian India as a particular case both
of economic development and of peasant agriculture. As Fernand
Braudel reminds us, in the last decades of his life he made a world-
wide impact as an analyst of the peasant economy in general, that is
to say, the peasant economy in the context of historical transformation and economic development. Hence we chose 'Peasants in
History' as the general theme of this commemorative volume. The
subjects of the papers range widely both in time and place, but the
general theme, we trust, provides the cohesion which Daniel would
have welcomed.

The editors regret the long delay in publication. It will not affect
the function of the volume, which is to commemorate a scholar who
could not in any case have seen it, but, though mainly due to factors
beyond our control, still calls for some apology to the patient con-
tributors. One of them, Erich Jacoby, died in 1979, and we take this
opportunity to pay tribute to a distinguished agrarian specialist. We
would also like to express our thanks to Anne Destenay who
translated Fernand Braudel's portrait of our friend and to Clemens
Heller of Maison des Sciences de l'Homme in Paris, which sub-
sidized three other translations. We hope that the eighteen papers
collected here will demonstrate how much agrarian and peasant
studies and historians of development owe to him.

Finally, the editors gratefully acknowledge the assistance rendered
to them by Alice Thorner in putting this volume together.

E. J. HOBSBAWM
WITOLD KULA
ASHOK MITRA
K. N. RAJ
IGNACY SACHS

# Contents

# Daniel Thorner

## FERNAND BRAUDEL
*Maison des Sciences de l'Homme, Paris*

WHO will one day sum up everything that Daniel Thorner, who no doubt knew India better than almost anyone else in our day, must have combined within himself in order to attain such heights and impose his mastery of his subject? Immense knowledge, a thorough apprenticeship in many different domains (in particular an outstanding grasp of the vast field of political economy) and above all, intelligence, for which there is no substitute, and passion which is indispensable for great achievements.

Others have spoken and will speak of his successful career and the importance of his writings. I shall not mention these, as I am not qualified to do so. I shall speak of Daniel Thorner himself, as I remember him throughout our long friendship.

We met in 1960, at the start of his brilliant career at the Ecole des Hautes Etudes in Paris, and became friends immediately without wasting any time; he was always smiling or rather laughing his huge laugh, and at the same time he was straightforward, intelligent, impassioned and always master of himself. He had to say what was on his mind and try out his ideas on someone, and this often led on to a lively discussion about the affairs of the world, which never ceased to preoccupy him. The conversation never centred on himself, or on his own passing difficulties, or on what he had been, or on the things in his own past which did him most credit in our eyes. Vanity was not his strong point.

All who knew and liked him, like myself, felt as though they knew him already before meeting him: he must always have been himself. The illusion is strongest when I read the excellent biography of him that Alice Thorner has written as a preface to the forthcoming collection of his writings, *The Shaping of Modern India*. I feel as though I am with him at Columbia, where he was a student; I meet the great Simon Kuznets, of whom he often spoke to me, whose student and colleague he was, and to whom he owed his education in economics; I also meet W. Norman Brown, for whom he had a special and enduring affection, for he helped to introduce Daniel to India, the talisman, the spring of youth and the joy of his life, which was a series of friendships, fulfilling his constant need to find support in the happiness and confidence of others. So, you may think, he had nothing but friends, lucky man. He was indeed a lucky man and an example to us all. He exorcized his enemies by never speaking of them and scarcely ever thinking of them, and if circumstances brought unpleasant experiences to his mind, he would make a comic face, almost like a child, to rid himself of bad memories. He did not waste his time or his happiness on them.

As I search for the key to his character a picture haunts me with such persistence and clarity that it may well reveal him as he was with others as well as with myself. A door opens quickly, without hesitation. Scarcely over the threshold, he laughs and talks, entering to the sound of music, coming to the point straight away, totally involved in what he wants to say, what he has come to say. Has he prepared his remarks? Certainly not. He simply needs to think aloud, to explain to himself and his interlocutor whatever is on his mind and serves at this particular moment to focus his tempestuous thoughts. One day the whole world assails him; another time he thinks that the entire realm of the social sciences needs reorganizing; on yet another day he is wounded to the quick by a cruel item of news during the Vietnam war, which filled him with horror, or during the war in Bangladesh, which did not allow him a moment of peace.

He then had to talk about it, tell his friends about it and ask for their support. He was to an astonishing degree a born scholar, and at the same time a true citizen of the world and an advocate of every just cause, even—or above all—when it seemed to be a lost cause. Daniel was a man who never stopped on the threshold, at the beginning of what he had to say. It was never worth asking him to engage in a discussion step by step, using all the customary circumlocutions. He could only run. At the Congress of economic history in Aix-en-Provence in August 1962, an illustrious historian took it upon himself to make a rash attack on India; Daniel exploded and the audience suddenly woke up; a storm arose in the somewhat drowsy atmosphere of a hot afternoon in Provence.

Although he did not hunt for chances to surprise people, he was delighted when they came to him. In September 1967 he found out that my wife and I were in Moscow, where he had just landed by plane from India, with the intention to spend a day or two before continuing to Paris. He happened to be in our hotel, on Gorskaia. After a gaily trumpeted announcement by telephone, he appeared in our room laden with messages and presents—he could not come back from India empty-handed.

The last time I saw him he dropped in to see us very early one morning on the top floor of the block where I live, laden with provisions for breakfast for the whole household. His illness was already upon him and he could not sleep, so he would walk the streets of Paris as soon as it was light. On that same morning he brought me books which I have not yet returned to Alice; they are still here, visible from afar, in my bookcase, reminding me of him.

His gifts had a reason behind them. He knew that I was working slowly, constantly looking back and revising, on the earliest phase of modern capitalism. He volunteered help; in his view, I ought to read this or that book, or that particular chapter. I hesitated, so he explained it to me; I did not see his point straight away, so he explained it again. He was one of those rare and exceptional teachers who are always ready to offer help and share their knowledge. In 1960, in an effort to save a reform of the secondary school history syllabus, I wrote a textbook on the *Monde Actuel* ('The World Today'). I mentioned India in it, so Daniel gave me guidance, and still more guidance; he entered into the fabrication of my text as though he were in his own workshop, then realized that it was someone else's and that the shop floor had to be arranged to suit that person. This he was delighted to do, and did the same for various other people too.

Gradually, however, his main interest changed. He may have been influenced by France and Paris; it may have been the result of his astonishing adaptation to the French culture surrounding him. I sometimes thought that he fell into the favourite snare of French thinking when he turned to generalities and began to philosophize on our professions. It may simply have been that he needed to turn once more to the discussions of his youth which he had left behind him like open wounds which, although no longer painful, needed attention, treatment, and above all a cure. He had kept up an unbroken dialogue with Marx, Max Weber whom he admired less, and Veblen, as well as Chayanov, whom he brought out of oblivion and imposed on his French colleagues, as well as setting him up as his own mentor. The time had come to state his own position, to know exactly where he stood with regard to these intellectual predecessors.

In fact no theoretical 'model' gave him full satisfaction; they all (including the systems defined by 'means of production') seemed to him at one point or another to be in disaccord with observable reality. At this stage he wrote an article for the *Annales*, describing the first of his own models, which was intended to be operational. This contribution in itself would have been enough to establish his reputation; I consider it a masterpiece: 'L'économie paysanne, concept pour l'histoire économique' ('Peasant Economy as a Concept in Economic History'). The argument is one of exemplary clarity, beginning with an exact definition. The concept of peasant economy, applied to the whole economy of a given country, must satisfy a number of objective criteria: at least half the production is agricultural; at least half the working population is engaged in the rural economy; there is an organized State; there exist both an urban network and a distinction between town and country; at least half the agricultural production comes from family holdings. The object is clear: it is to bring the concepts of 'subsistence economy', 'feudal' economy and 'oriental' economy (the Asian mode of production) closer to each other by giving to them a content at the same time more concrete and more general; to distil from them a model applicable to the pre-industrial societies of the past and the 'under-developed' societies of today, which 'under apparent diversity' provides a 'common denominator'—in the face of other 'historical structures such as slavery, capitalism and socialism'. There followed examples: Tsarist Russia, Indonesia, Mexico, India, China and Japan, all of which, whatever the differences between them may be, 'are now emerging or have already emerged, from peasant economy'.

This method of argument and comparison in time and space brought Daniel Thorner amazingly close to historians who like myself remain faithful to the ideas of Marc Bloch, and think that every model should be based on empirical observation, completed on a theoretical plane, then re-exposed to the test of real life, just as a boat built on land should be launched on the sea to prove it is able to sail, or else it has no reason for existing.

During the last years of his life, his thinking continued to deepen along these lines. When we met for the last time, he spoke at length of the criticism he was preparing of the criterion of 'means of production', valid in one place but not in another, valid under certain historical circumstances, but inexact or rather inadequate under certain others. He wanted personally to clarify this vital point of Marxist theory, by means of a meticulous construction of comparisons, based on his own experience as a historian, sociologist and economist.

He laughed heartily once again that day as he set out his arguments. And yet his life was coming to an end, unknown to him and to us. How could we believe it? He had so many ideas, so many plans—enough journeys for a hundred years!

This is how he lived, loved and acted. This was how he was at home, in his peaceful house in the rue Guy-de-la-Brosse, the centre of his existence, alongside Alice, also wedded to India, alongside Nicholas, their elder son, wedded in spirit to the immensity of Russia, alongside Phoebe and Joel, both younger, who had adopted France with ease. For his friends, to see him surrounded by his family was to see him at the heart of his happiness. Don't you think so, Witold Kula, Clemens Heller, Eric Hobsbawm, Moses Finley? And in the same setting, Daniel and Alice managed to protect the last months of their beloved elder daughter, Susan, also a victim of the inexorable illness which later struck down her father. I do not know of any more wonderful and moving moral achievement.

# I

# The European Experience

# I

# Scottish Reformers of the Eighteenth Century and Capitalist Agriculture

E. J. HOBSBAWM

*Birkbeck College, University of London*

SINCE the great majority of human beings in the pre-capitalist period lived by agriculture, the relation between agriculture and capitalist development has long preoccupied historians, and has led to extensive discussions, not least among Marxists. The sheer weight of the agrarian sector in pre-industrial societies is such as to make any form of development largely dependent on what takes place, or fails to take place, within it. Conversely, capitalist development necessarily transforms the role and character of agriculture, if only by reducing it to one among many other occupations, and very likely to the historically unprecedented state of a small minority occupation.

There are thus two kinds of questions involved in the problem of the relation between agriculture and capitalist development. What was it about the agrarian sector which, in some but not in other historical contexts, permitted or prevented, encouraged or inhibited, capitalist development in general or in the non-agricultural sector? How was the structure of the agrarian sector itself transformed by capitalist development? The difficulty about both these questions lies in specifying exactly what is capitalist or non-capitalist in agrarian structure, or, if specifications are made, in quantifying them.

A great deal of agriculture over a lengthy historical period can be assigned capitalist or non-capitalist character only, as it were, by its context. If we did not happen to know that, say, the thirteenth century English peasants whose sheep-flocks provided some of the wool for the export market, belonged to a feudal society (e.g. through their status as villeins), we might find it impossible to distinguish their economic activities from those of nineteenth century New

Zealand settlers—forgetting for a moment that the latter would not have been in New Zealand at all but for the existence of a capitalist world economy. The apparent similarity of so much agricultural activity in the periods we retrospectively assign to a feudal, a transitional or a capitalist period, has long led to considerable confusion in the literature.[1]

What is true of pre-industrial and transitional agriculture also applies to capitalist agriculture. Capitalist industry, as a whole, is readily distinguishable from pre-capitalist manufactures as a whole by its characteristic relations of production, namely the dichotomy between a group of private persons or firms which own the means of production and the mass of the labour force which does not own them but works for wages. There is no distinction of equal simplicity in agriculture. The 'agro-industrial enterprise', to use a Peruvian term for the agrarian equivalent of the modern factory complex, is not the norm of capitalist agriculture, but merely one version of it. The unquestionably capitalist farmer, whether owner or tenant of his land, may continue to provide a far larger proportion of labour himself or through his family than even the small nineteenth century industrial entrepreneur. Wage labour, though no doubt crucial, continues to be employed on a far smaller scale than in industry. We may therefore be tempted to seek the specific character of such agriculture simply in specialized production for the market, and it is unquestionably true that capitalist farming, even on mixed farms, is increasingly and essentially commodity production, in which subsistence agriculture plays a diminishing part. However, if mere market production were to be the only criterion, we should be tempted to classify the numerous pre-industrial examples of it as something like capitalist enclaves, or even evidence of the capitalist character of the economy. The temptation has not always been resisted, but, as attempts to prove that seventeenth century Latin American *haciendas* were as 'capitalist' as twentieth century ones show, obscures rather than clarifies.[2]

The present paper seeks to clarify the nature of capitalist agriculture by means of a historical example which has been, somewhat surprisingly, rather neglected in the voluminous literature on this problem: the case of Scotland in the eighteenth century. This small, poor and backward country undoubtedly existed in the context of a European and increasingly a global international capitalist economy, but it would be quite unrealistic to regard even the bulk of the economy of its Lowlands in the late seventeenth century as 'capitalist', still less the clan economy of its Celtic Highlands. Yet by the end of the eighteenth century, Scotland was not merely a part of British capitalism, but—both in its industry and in its agriculture—a pioneer of capitalist development, in certain respects superior to England. The rapidity and the dramatic character of this transformation is reflected in Scottish theory—Scots became the pioneers of political economy and historical sociology—and Scottish literature which virtually invented the 'historical novel'. Yet if fictional literature chiefly reflected, and attempted to come to terms with, this transformation, theory was deeply concerned to bring it about: Adam Smith's *Wealth of Nations* is best read—as his contemporaries read it—as a handbook of development economics at a time when economic development could not but be capitalist. This theory sought to identify not only the nature of the historical process which led to economic development, and of the obstacles that stood in its way, but also the conditions which would allow them to be overcome. Hence there was no sharp line which divided theorists from practical reformers—a fact which makes the literature unusually useful for our purposes.

Two aspects of it make it even more relevant to our discussion. The Scottish writer-reformers saw the problem of their country specifically as one of transition from feudalism to capitalism. (The term 'commercial society', as used by them, is a synonym for competitive capitalism.) Indeed, they probably formed the earliest, and one of the rare, examples of a middle class[3] which saw its objectives and historic function in these precise terms. For it would seem that the very term 'feudal system' and later 'feudalism', as a description of an entire socio-economic as well as legal and political order of society, were invented by Scottish intellectuals in the course of these discussions, though the point of departure for this generalization— first recorded in print in 1757[4]—was the treatment of 'feudal laws' by Montesquieu. The term 'feudal system', rapidly adopted—it is already found in Adam Smith's 1763 *Lectures on Justice* (para 8, pp. 36 ff)—became common currency among agrarian writers and reformers.[5] 'Feudalism' or 'feudism' appears from the 1790s, as writers groped for an even wider generalization, but, though it occurs in Scotland almost a quarter of a century before it does in France (1817) and almost half a century before it does in England— it is first recorded in the O.E.D. for 1839—its use was only sporadic.[6]

It need hardly be added that the Scots reformers were quite clear in their minds that the object of their efforts was to give up the feudal, and embrace the commercial system,[7] i.e. to effect a transition from feudalism to capitalism.

The second relevant aspect of the Scottish discussions is their specific concern with agriculture. Adam Smith himself shows no special interest in industrial innovation, no sign of recognizing the signs of industrial revolution already visible around him, and indeed an attitude towards merchants and master-manufacturers as a separate group which was at best ambiguous and at worst one of suspicion.[8] On the other hand he made it quite clear that the most important employment of capital was that which improved agriculture; a preference natural enough in the era of the Physiocrats. Indeed, in Medick's words 'he may be much more readily regarded as an analyst of the conditions of agricultural progress in the society of his time, than as a prophet of Industrial Revolution'.[9] Indeed, what held back the natural progress of opulence in Scotland in his view was the lag of an agricultural sector compared with the disproportionately rapid development of the commercial and manufacturing sectors. In short, the development of capitalism, historically initiated within the cities, could not proceed to its fullest extent until it also transformed the countryside and agriculture. It is not surprising that economists and agrarian reformers are hard to separate from one another,[10] or that writings on farming often include obvious paraphrases of Adam Smith's arguments.

What, then, did eighteenth century Scots mean by capitalist agriculture? What was required for the transition from 'the feudal to the commercial system'? The answer to these questions cannot but illuminate a discussion which (particularly among Marxists) actually derives historically from their debates and in some ways continues them. This does not mean that we have to accept their views, though as historians we would be unwise to neglect them.

## II

Before attempting to answer these questions, it may be convenient briefly to single out some of the specific conditions of Scotland, other than the merely geographic and climatic,[11] which give the Scottish solutions of our problems a particular character.

First, Scotland was a dual society and economy, in which the tribal Highlands coexisted with the entirely different and far more advanced Lowlands. The struggle for the equivalent of a bourgeois revolution in Scotland was also the struggle between two societies. Its major victories, reflected in revolutionary legislation in 1695 and 1748, were the consequence of military victories of the Whig[12] Lowlands (allied with, and later deliberately merged with, England) against the tribal levies of the Highlands: the revolution of 1688 and the Highland rebellion of 1745. The Scottish reformers, though often aware of the human and moral values of clan society, were militantly hostile to it.

Apart from anything else, this coexistence provided a confrontation of value systems poles apart from one another.[13] Adam Smith himself confronted the paradox—by bourgeois standards—of the Highland chieftain Cameron of Lochiel, who was capable of raising 800 armed men for war or rebellion, though his total rent-roll amounted to hardly £500. The lucidity with which Scots writers saw the problem of rural transformation, the systematic and revolutionary manner with which they confronted it, owed much to the sharpness of this confrontation and the need to liquidate a rival society with dramatic speed.

Second, the legal basis of property was entirely feudal, so that technically *all* land-occupiers with legal as distinct from customary rights were tenants either of the king or of one of his vassals as 'blanch-holdings' or 'feu-holdings' respectively; these being 'the only holdings of modern times', after the abolition of *mortmain* (ecclesiastical holdings) in the Reformation.[14] The form taken by the legal liquidation of feudalism was not the abolition of feudal tenures, but rather their transformation into the equivalent of property or commercial tenancies—leaseholding feudalized[15]—together with the abolition of all legal force for customary rights. Thus no *general* bourgeois property-right was created, so that the actual number of landowners remained quite small: less than 8,000 in all Scotland, consisting of less than 400 with a rental value of more than £2,000 per annum, a little over 1,000 with a rental value of £500–2,000, somewhat over 6,000 smaller properties and 144 corporate properties.[16] The reasons why peasant occupiers did not resist this virtual dispossession more effectively are complex and obscure. The point to note is that legally the solution to the agrarian problem was uniquely favourable to landlords and capitalist tenants, and uniquely unfavourable to the peasantry.

Third, the programme of modernization, as formulated by the group of intellectuals who became its spokesmen,[17] enjoyed the support of the great bulk of the Lowland ruling class, urban and rural, aristocracy, gentry and burghers. The entire Lowland elite, irrespective of any internal differences, faced two problems in common: relations with the Highlands and relations with England. For all of them the future of Scotland, as well as their own, depended on the solution of these two problems, that is to say, as it turned out, on the control and subjugation of the Highlands, and on integration into the 'common market' and Empire of Britain.[18] The effective political community of the Lowlands therefore developed something like a general consensus and national policy, with some exceptions, e.g. on the law of entail, which appear to have caused no major difficulties.[19]

Fourthly, with the removal in 1745 of the last major internal obstacle to capitalist 'modernization', the armed resistance of the Highlands, the Lowlands were in a position to exploit the uniquely favourable European and British *conjoncture* of the later eighteenth century, and enter upon a dramatically rapid period of economic development. The very necessity to remove these obstacles in a revolutionary manner and the speed of the subsequent change, encouraged both a far more systematic analysis of the requirements of economic development and a far more systematic action to bring about development. The Scots were well aware that in this respect their transformation was superior to the more prolonged and less systematic processes of change in England.[20]

### III

What, then, are the criteria of a capitalist agriculture, as the Scots reformers saw it? James Anderson[21] lists the following 'obstacles to the advancement of agriculture':

1. Commonable lands (i.e. common fields and practices)
2. Commons (i.e. lands held in common by the community)
3. 'the minute division of property'
4. 'intermixture of property'
5. Mills (i.e. the seignorial monopoly of the mills)
6. Inadequate size of farms
7. Inadequate security of tenure, improper conditions and restrictive clauses

8. Want of capital among farmers
9. Injudiciously made enclosures
10. Church lands in *mortmain* and entail
11. Indefinite claims upon land
12. Want of easy means of communication
13. Want of markets
14. Injudicious fiscal regulation
15. Want of means of circulating agricultural knowledge among farmers.

Leaving aside mistakes in the application of otherwise legitimate policies (9, 14) these obstacles fall into three overlapping groups. First, there are those standing in the way of adequate bourgeois property or lease-rights, due to peasant custom (1–4), feudal rights and practices (5, 7, 10) or possibly both (11). Second, there are those inhibiting effective capitalist enterprise even with adequate legal conditions, e.g. the formation of productive units of adequate size or shortages of capital (3, 6, 8). Third, there are deficiencies in the infrastructure, notably in transport and communications (12, 13, 15).

It is at first surprising that the problem of an adequate market does not seem to be seriously considered, except in the minor physical sense of the absence of *places* for buying and selling (13). Of course, the Scots reformers took it for granted that agricultural capitalism implied a growth of the proportion of farm-output exchanged through the market and consequently a growing complexity of the social division of labour, which found its expression precisely in the exchanges between buyers and sellers:

It is certain that the servants and other persons employed by the farmers of Berwickshire, now spend more money yearly in the shops of Berwick, and the small towns scattered over the country, than the landed proprietors, farmers and cottagers, in short the whole population of the country, expended in that way, in 1755, before the introduction of improved husbandry. At that more remote period, almost every family manufactured the coarse, homespun articles of clothing which they required. Almost every person is now more profitably employed in labouring for the farmers, either directly or indirectly; and now purchase, from the excrescence of their farming wages and other gains, what they were formerly obliged to make for themselves, or were unable to obtain. In every town and village, saddlers, carpenters, plough and cart wrights, mill-wrights (for threshing machines and fanners), masons, bakers, and butchers, now abound, where such trades before hardly existed.[22]

Indeed, the increasing elaboration of such division of labour is a convenient indicator of agricultural commercialization in its key (domestic) market; for agricultural exports, at least in earlier periods of capitalist development, affect only a minority of specialized or unusually well-situated locations and products.[23] At one extreme reformers observed with sorrow the backward Hebrides where 'The common articles of living cannot be obtained, or at least with great difficulty, by any persons who do not possess land. Hence labourers, mechanics, manufacturers, fishers and traders, find it impossible to support themselves by their occupations.'[24] At the other extreme, they hailed the transfer of population from countryside to settlements as a solution of the problem of backwardness through increasing division of labour: 'The population is not only increased, and the land rendered more productive, by the establishment of well-regulated and industrious villages; but labourers are at hand, in the time of need, and artificers, of various denominations. . . . Villages afford also, a ready market for whatever the farmer has to sell.'[25]

Nevertheless, the extent to which the Scots reformers equated economy and market has one disadvantage for the historian. It led them, in spite of an enthusiasm for numbers which caused authors to describe themselves as 'landed proprietor and a friend to statistics', to neglect the quantitative importance of the subsistence sector in agriculture, and hence to measure its decline. Where this decline was dramatically visible, it was noted in passing; where it was not, its failure to decline might be observed and deplored. Fundamentally, it was of no interest. The feudal survival of *thirlage* (the obligation to grind corn at the seignorial mill) was widely criticized, but, as the economist Anderson thought, it did little harm where, as in the progressive county of Midlothian, convention reduced it 'to mean nothing else than that the farmer must grind the oats and pease which are to be consumed in his own family only', leaving him free to sell the rest.[26] On the other hand what worried him was the *scale* of market sales, for where the market was dominated by peasants or excessively small farmers, petty trading stood in the way of real commercial development.[27]

The major reforms necessary were clearly in the field of property rights. What was required was to transform the land into a commodity. This in turn implied (*a*) the freedom to sell or mortgage land without restraint, and (*b*) its transformation into property units suitable for bourgeois enterprise, i.e. disentangling the owner's or lessee's right to dispose of it from the multiplicity of collective or individual obligations in which peasant customs and the 'feudal system' had enmeshed it. The programme was utterly revolutionary,[28] and the reformers were quite aware of this. It required either the forcible abolition of older systems of property right from without, or their erosion from within, by the conversion of a sector of the old agrarian population to the advantages of bourgeois property, or both. To judge by the literature it seems that, with one exception, the resistance of feudal landowners looked easier to overcome than that of the traditional peasants, who clearly formed the main obstacle. The significance of this point will be discussed below. In short, the rulers of the 'feudal system' could be more easily converted into beneficiaries of the 'commercial system' than its subjects.

Lords, it was argued, would admittedly have to abandon the non-economic advantages of lordship, but in return would receive spectacular improvements in their economic position which, in a bourgeois society, reinforced or replaced social power. The ideal solution, though admittedly one which is 'perhaps a departure from the natural prejudices of the landlord',[29] would be to lease the land only to capitalist entrepreneurs capable of producing the maximum rent: 'a steady determination on the part of the landowners to let their farms to none but tenants of approved skill and industry, and real capital'.[30] This means that the lord must give up all rights to the tenant's non-economic dependence (and all sense of non-economic obligation to him) other than the cash-nexus of an economically determined rent; but the landlord must realize that he purchases 'that dependency at a considerable diminution of his yearly income'.[31] He must, in effect, choose between feudal or tribal lordship and poverty on one hand, and bourgeois aristocracy and wealth on the other. It was confidently expected that most would make the second choice, consoled perhaps by the fact that though 'the better sort of principal tacksmen [have] become more indifferent about their inferiors', 'the impression of attachment to their natural superior is not totally effaced':[32] the peasant would still feel loyalty to his lord.

The argument was evidently effective, except where seignorial monopoly was an obvious source of profit, as in the lords' control of the mills, and where the proposed changes appeared to affect the very existence and permanence of the nobleman's family, as in the question of entail. The only two specifically 'feudal' obstacles on Anderson's list are control of mills (5) and entail (10). It is admitted that 'it gratifies the pride of a proprietor to be able to preserve and to hand down his name through a long line of succession; and, as it encroaches on the commerce of the land, it enhances its value'.[33] Nevertheless, while the reformers did not waver in their hostility to a form of inheritance 'which, in all stages of its progress, has been detrimental to the public interest, as well as inconsistent with domestic happiness, and which in the last stages of its career (to which it is fast approaching) may be attended with more serious and aggravated evils',[34] they acknowledged that its worst evils could be mitigated. The Act of 1770, for instance, allowed an owner to undertake long-term improvements, charging most of the cost on his future heirs, and making possible certain exchanges of land for the purposes of economic improvement—benefits which legal ingenuity had extended so as to 'render the latitude of the act tolerably sufficient for all purposes of profitable exchange'.[35]

Fortunately it was also practicable to rely for improvements on tenants rather than landlords, and the act made certain that in long leases—the only sensible way to exploit entailed land rationally—the tenant was obliged to pay for enclosures himself 'on the well-grounded forethought that, if not executed at his expense, there was but little probability of their being executed at all'.[36] Entail—which had been granted without limit to landowners in 1685—was part of the price paid to the feudalists for their support of capitalist agricultural development. On the whole, considering the advantages, they were content with the bargain.

That is, all except the more backward tribal chieftains of the Highlands. Their resistance was broken by force of arms after 1688, 1715 and, most ruthlessly and finally, in and after the Rebellion of 1745. Feudal right was therefore formally abolished after the Rebellion by Act 20 Geo. II c. 50.

No similar bargain could be offered to the peasantry as a whole. Indeed 'so intractable are the generality in regard to *meum et tuum*, that a compulsory law was found necessary', in the words of the Rev. C. Findlater of Newlands, Peebles, one of the many writers confirming, at least in Scotland, the link between Calvinism and capitalism.[37] Two Acts of 1695 dealt with both commons and common fields by permitting *any* proprietor to force a division of common lands, and by providing for open fields to be 'disentangled into distinct continuous masses' from intermingled strips. The landless could not lose common rights; but they could not convert them into land either. The measure did not affect lords, since in Scotland the lord of the manor as such possessed no seignorial right over commons. There seems to have been little use of these statutes until after 1746,[38] but thereafter enclosures became rapid and general. As noted above, the statute of 1746 formally deprived custom ('use and wont') of all legal force in land tenancy.

It was quite clear that these measures attacked the poorer peasantry as such. Anderson observed that common rights and practices were due largely to single peasant holdings being sub-economic.[39] The measures to make property bourgeois were designed to clear a large part of the peasantry from the land, on the grounds that minifundism even on the best principles of bourgeois property-right would not create capitalism in agriculture. It wasted a large proportion of the land on subsistence plots, and immobilized on it an uneconomically large labour force, which could be employed elsewhere to greater profit. As the Rev. C. Findlater put it:

Before the extension of trade and manufactures afforded so many outlets to profitable occupation, it is probable that, upon the death of the farmer, his children, having no other profitable occupation in view, would continue the possession; either agreeing to manage it, without division, as a common concern; or dividing it amongst them into minute separate possessions.[40] Upon the former scheme, their management would be subject to every cause of inefficiency . . . ; upon the latter scheme, to all the inconvenience and expence of keeping, in a constant state of preparation, a *reservoir* (so to speak) of labour, to effect what could never pay for it: to which may be added, too, the temptation, or even the necessity, of forcing corn to grow (for maintenance of such superabundant population), in considerable despite to nature, and at such disproportionate expence of the labour of men and horses, as, in other occupations, or more favourable situations, might have produced a tenfold greater profit.[41]

Quite apart from their inability to afford improvements, the small peasants 'generally, at least in the West of Scotland, indulge a large portion of hereditary pride and indolence, which disqualifies them for the pursuits of profitable industry',[42] and the subdivision of lands reduced them to beggary. Indeed, unless forcibly shaken out of his traditional ways, even the potential capitalist peasant-farmer was likely to remain inefficient.[43] The Rev. Mr Dickson of Dunse in his 'Treatise on Agriculture' argued against rent in kind on these grounds. The small farmer, having few wants, would just produce enough for subsistence and to deliver his rent. When his crop falls short, there is nothing for him to do: 'his spirits must sink and inactivity and indolence become habitual.' He will not improve and 'it can scarcely be supposed that he will leave the track that his fathers have walked in before him'.[44] Conversely, even the notoriously progressive and enterprising farmers of the Lothians had first to be propelled out of their torpor: 'a change of system has brought the small farmers to embrace a line of conduct which nothing short of necessity could have compelled them to do' or to 'reconcile them' to the destruction of the system of peasant farming.[45]

Efficient capitalist agriculture therefore required both economic concentration and farmers willing to modernize. Improvement, thought Andrew Wight—a practical farmer and protégé of the great Lord Kames, though not himself much of an ideologist—'can only be executed by substantial and enlightened tenants, whereof there are but few'.[46] On the one hand 'it is obvious that such patches [of subdivided land] stood a better chance of being improved, by falling into the hands of an opulent landholder or of a tenant possessing capital, and occupying a sufficient breadth of land, to encourage him to vest that capital in effective improvements'.[47] On the other, minifundism deprived the capitalist farmer of labour, because of 'the facility of getting small plots', though the population was 'too numerous for the necessary purposes of agriculture', according to yet another capitalist-minded Calvinist minister, the Rev. John Bethune.[48]

There was the usual debate about whether agricultural improvement led or ought to lead to actual rural depopulation, but none about 'the diminished number of tenants', though it had to be admitted by 'philosophy and common sense' that this was in the short run accompanied by 'imaginary ills and temporary inconveniences', and its 'ultimate benefits' could therefore not be judged 'from the first appearances'.[49] However, in fairness to the reformers we ought to note that almost all of them seem to have been highly critical of the forcible 'clearance' of Highland crofters to make room for sheep, which eventually took place. Wight disliked the policy of the Commissioners of Annexed Estates (the lands confiscated from the rebellious Highlanders and other supporters of the Stuarts) who wanted 'to enlarge the farms and employ the superfluous hands in manufactures and in day labour' on the ground that men were the finest crop of the Highlands. Sinclair concluded: 'It is not by feeding black cattle nor sheep, in the Highlands, that the country can be improved, but by the introduction of arts and agriculture.' And the Englishman Marshall took a most sensible and prophetic view:

The argument which has been held, about whether the Highlands should be inhabited by the human species or by sheep, can have no sufficient ground, until the country be rendered fully productive, and fit for the support of either . . . and certainly the proper time for retrieving it from a state so disgraceful to a civilized nation is, while there are people in it. [For] should the Highlands of Scotland be once depopulated, it might be found difficult to repeople them.[50]

And yet, the reformers were faced by the fact that the bulk of the peasantry simply did not want to behave like capitalist entrepreneurs; not to mention the fact that, if they all did, farms would be on average of uneconomic size.[51] For they distinguished carefully between the thrift and greed of peasants whose profits in the past came 'from habits of parsimony and from frequent transactions in buying and selling cattle' and the desirable modern farmer, who operated in a different manner.[52] Often, one feels, the modernizers were on the verge of despair. Sinclair did not think that any good factors (estate administrators) could be found among the local population in the backward North of Scotland. Wight, writing of Renfrewshire, complained of the 'mean, miserable tenantry, satisfied with bare subsistence, and unwilling to do better, for fear of having rents raised on them' and saw the only solution in patience. In time businessmen would retire from city to countryside and bring their business habits with them. And Sir George Stewart Mackenzie Bart. had given up all hope for his counties of Ross and Cromarty in the Highlands. With few exceptions, he thought, 'all our native farmers have proved themselves totally unfit for occupying land'. 'A considerable number of farmers from different parts of Scotland have settled in Ross and Cromartyshires; and from the improvements they have made, it is probable that ere long the whole arable of the counties will be possessed by farmers from the improved districts of Scotland.' In short, total expropriation of the indigenous peasantry seemed the only solution.[53]

Nevertheless, a small part of the peasantry would benefit, if they turned themselves into rural bourgeoisie, a task to which the reformers devoted a great deal of attention. Given that the tenant-farmer had to provide the income of the landowner also,[54] he had to be a substantial entrepreneur. This meant that he had to be provided with a sufficient incentive to prevent him, as a good capitalist, from shifting into more profitable activities: 'they can be induced to devote their skill and property to agriculture, only by the fair prospect of an adequate recompence', to quote Whyte and Macfarlan. In Anderson's words: 'To do all this requires a very large capital: and a man who has a large capital, has a right to expect, and he must have, a comfortable subsistence for himself and his family, or he will abandon that occupation.'[55]

A striking illustration of this tendency to separate out the rural bourgeoisie from the rest of the peasantry and labourers is the construction of farmhouses. The classical house of the rich peasant of the Lothians on the eve of agricultural change was a two-room building of roughly 30 by 14 feet, the 'but and ben'. The 'but' was used as kitchen, servants' quarters, dining room, and sleeping quarters for the maid-servants and the daughters of the house; the 'ben' was the private quarters of the 'gudeman', where he slept with his wife and younger children and entertained guests of equal or superior standing.[56] The 'gudeman' was clearly much better off than poorer folk, but though he may have enjoyed 'rough plenty' he lived essentially in the same manner as they. And indeed, the transition was perhaps slower than the reformers allowed. Even in 1802 the Edinburgh *Farmers Magazine* noted that, though better off, many 'continue to be mostly supplied with necessary maintenance from the produce of their farms, and to be clothed by their own manufactures', though by this time few did not purchase some luxuries such as butcher's meat, shop-bought Sunday clothes and, naturally, tea.[57]

Agrarian improvers thought of his life in very different terms. Somerville considered it essential for the house on a 300–500 acre farm to have two good sitting rooms, 4–6 bedrooms, closets, garrets for the servants and a kitchen behind the house. He considered that building it should require the equivalent of a year's rent (£300–400).[58] Donaldson, writing of the much more remote county of Elgin, estimated that £200–300 would be necessary for farm-buildings—though this doubtless also included stables and the like.[59] Admittedly even the cottages were now improving. In East Lothian few new ones were said to be smaller than 20 by 17 feet, but the difference between farmers' and cottagers' accommodation was now immense: the reformers' estimates allowed perhaps £10–15 for the building of a cottage as against £300–400 for 'housebuilding'.[60] And as the farmer was encouraged to turn himself into a rural bourgeois, he adopted the corresponding values. Fife farmers abandoned physical labour, according to the 'survey' of that county, to concentrate on

their chief business [which] is to superintend. The operative and servile part is committed to others: but the master's presence and direction are everywhere to conduct and forward various necessary operations. . . . These requisite attentions, together with the business of the counting-room, and his attendance on markets . . . are surely much more conducive to his interest than holding the plough, thrashing the grain, or filling and driving his own dung-cart.[61]

Yet if this new class of bourgeois agricultural entrepreneurs, and the landowners who stood behind them, were to maximize their profits, this required not merely the rational use of the factors of production as then available, but above all initial, and preferably continuing, 'agricultural improvement'. And this improvement necessitated investment. In the discussion of what constitutes capitalist agriculture it is too often forgotten that it was, among other things, an agriculture which required capital. Indeed, whatever had been the case earlier, by the early nineteenth century 'want of capital' was listed as the first of the obstacles which still stood in the way of progress in Peebles (1802), in Renfrew (1812), and for all of Scotland (1814).[62] The literature, which calculated costs with a tenacious Scottish appreciation of money, makes it clear that the sums involved were very large, by the rural standards of a notoriously poor country. Without rent and any initial improvements (drainage, enclosure, major constructional work, bringing new land into cultivation, etc.) the mean cost over the whole country per Scots acre (slightly larger than the English acre) of arable was reckoned at about £8.5.[63] Major improvements could at least double this, since it was stated that in Moray the tenant's initial investment was halved if the landlord constructed the buildings, and enclosed the fields. Thus a tenant of a 120 acre arable farm (probably Scots acres) on loamy soil in Dumbarton would need to be able to put his hand on almost £1,800 before he could think of his first harvest: £1,060 for livestock, fertilizer, seed and 'implements' and the remainder for rent and labour.[64] In fact, in Fife it was estimated, according to Sinclair, that the initial capital required *without* major preliminary improvements was between two and half and five times the annual rent, free of debt and excluding running expenses and rent itself, but major improvements might well require more, though Whyte and Macfarlan's detailed calculations for various sizes and types of farms in Dumbarton suggest an average of four times the annual rent for a tenant's initial year. Such sums required credit (which in turn required security) and substantial profits. A farmer, thought Sinclair in the light of his surveys, 'ought to gain 15 per cent on the capital he laid out' which would enable him to pay 5 per cent interest on his loans. Fourteen per cent was 'hardly equal to that to which a farmer is justly entitled'.[65] In short 'without stock to begin upon, very few ever get above the world', as a minister observed in remote Caithness, contemplating the backwardness of the local peasant agriculture.[66]

The Scottish model of capitalist agriculture therefore required the destruction or transformation of feudal lordship and its associated structure of rights in property and domination. The Scots reformers did not seek the *abolition* of landlordism, partly no doubt because they were political realists, but mainly because they were confident that pre-capitalist landlords would find it advantageous to transform themselves into capitalist ones (i.e. maximizing rent through maximizing their tenants' profit), and because their control over the selection of tenants provided a powerful mechanism for revolutionizing the pattern of rural life and economy. The model did not *exclude* latifundism or large-scale estate agriculture, but the reformers, following Adam Smith, were strongly opposed to it.[67] A rural middle class was their chosen instrument. However, the landlord was undoubtedly envisaged as a possible source of investment and credit for his tenants, since this would help to maximize his rent.[68]

At the same time the model required not the transformation but the destruction of the traditional peasant economy and its associated set of communal and family structures, rights and practices. Though a minority of peasants could and must become rural bourgeois entrepreneurs, the requirements of an agricultural production, maximizing profit, output and productivity, must make the majority of peasants redundant as such, if only because it required a drastically changed ratio of productive labour to land: i.e. a large increase in the size of the average farm, and a large reduction of the number of people previously maintained on the same area as agriculturalists. Opinions differed as to whether this process led to depopulation or not. Though absolute depopulation was not required in the rural sector—expanding agricultural production and the growth of the division of labour might well raise total agricultural and non-agricultural employment even in the countryside—it certainly did not surprise observers.[69] Certainly the optimal solution, which the Scots reformers attempted to implement ruthlessly and, in their opinion, successfully, was the abolition of the peasantry. Opinions, and doubtless local experiences, differed on the question whether the rural bourgeoisie developed spontaneously, converting its landlords to the possibilities of rent-maximization, or whether its creation required prior institutional and legal changes and incentives or selection by 'rational' landlords. Clearly both developments played their part, though in unusually prosperous areas such as Berwickshire, the Lothians, Fife and Clydesdale the initiative, once the legal possibilities of 'improvement' existed, may have come mainly from the tenants.[70]

Lastly, agriculture needed to become more capital-intensive. It is interesting that, unlike some later writers, the Scots reformers did not stress production for the market or of cash crops in itself— witness their comparative lack of statistical interest in subsistence production. They rather fixed their attention on the reorganization of rural landed structure and production (i.e. the relations of production and their equivalents in legal and property rights) along capitalist lines, together with the techniques of agricultural improvement. They were thus against 'feudal' agriculture whether or not it happened to produce for the market to any extent. Of course they were concerned about market problems, but chiefly in so far as technical difficulties, e.g. of transport, or defects in the distributive mechanism, hampered its development.

It only remains to observe that the actual 'agrarian revolution' in Scotland followed the lines suggested by the reformers. Thus in Ayrshire between 1755 and 1800 it has been described as consisting mainly of (*a*) enclosure of farmland previously wholly open, (*b*) the abolition of surviving co-tenancies and feudal servitudes and their replacement by modern individual leases, (*c*) consolidation and enlargement of many holdings, (*d*) the reduction or elimination of cottagers and (*e*) the general adoption of liming.[71]

## IV

Though the Scottish model in some respects reflects the specific historical conditions of the country, it is clearly designed as a *general* model of capitalism in agriculture. This underlines the difficulty created by its insistence on the elimination of the peasantry. There is no doubt that the model requires this elimination in one way or another—essentially, leaving aside the role of the landlords, by the concentration of most of the land in the hands of a smallish bourgeoisie of 'farmers' and the expulsion from it of the rest.[72] However, other modes of elimination are not excluded. The argument for this was not merely on grounds of agricultural efficiency. Adam Smith himself was aware of the obstacle constituted by traditional agriculture to the capitalist growth of the economy as a whole. For not only were the possibilities of the division of labour more limited here than elsewhere, as he pointed out at the outset of his book, but also agriculture could 'support itself under the discouragement of a confined market, much better than manufactures' because 'each person in it must require little more than the custom of one, two, or, at most, four such families as his own, in order to dispose of the whole produce of his labour'.[73] It follows that the larger the peasant population, the smaller the incentive to expand the market.

Yet we know that the 'classical' roads to capitalist agriculture which eliminated the peasantry in various ways—the Scottish, English and what Lenin called the 'Prussian' and 'American' models—remained exceptional even in the developed world until well past the middle of the twentieth century, i.e. for most of the history of capitalism so far. The bulk of total agrarian production, outside a few areas and a few special cash-crops and products, continued to come from peasants, because, mainly for social and political reasons, they could not be eliminated, and because even many of those who would have been eliminated from agriculture for economic reasons, maintained themselves in the countryside, or in regular contact with it, by a combination of sub-marginal or subsistence farming with other occupations. Only since the 1950s has the percentage of the agricultural population declined so dramatically, especially in the 'developed' countries, that we appear to be within reach of the Scottish ideal of an agriculture from which all but the bourgeois entrepreneur (in the form of the commercial cultivator) and the hired labourer have fled.

The Scottish analysis would lead us to infer that the survival of the peasantry must have been an obstacle to the development of capitalist agriculture and the capitalist economy in general, and that the surviving peasantry resisted its development. It is indeed plain that peasants as a class have supported the opponents of Adam Smith's kind of capitalism, whether from right or left, much more often than its proponents, and it has been plausibly argued that, at least in the sixteenth to eighteenth centuries, peasant success in resisting elimination slowed capitalist development.[74] On the other hand it would be difficult to prove that the development of *world* capitalism has, since say 1850, been seriously held up by the survival of the peasantry —though a case for particular countries can be plausibly made; and it would be even more difficult to argue that the long survival cf a peasant-based agriculture in patently industrializing countries such as West Germany, Belgium, or the Scandinavian ones, has been a serious obstacle to capitalism there.

Does this imply that there is an alternative 'peasant road to capitalism', based not on the elimination of the peasantry from, as it were, 'outside', but on its internal transformation—through economic and social differentiation—into the components of a capitalist agrarian economy? Possibly it does, though always with the proviso recognized insufficiently or not at all by early Marxist analysts that there is no close similarity between the development of agrarian and non-agrarian capitalism, notably in the matter of concentration. However, though examples of such endogenous transformations of a traditional peasantry into a capitalist agriculture based on family farms, can no doubt be found—perhaps in the Low Countries between the sixteenth and nineteenth centuries, in nineteenth century Denmark, in wine-growing regions, etc.—on the whole they seem at least as exceptional, in their fully developed versions, as is, historically speaking, the radical elimination of the peasantry. If this is so, an important political conclusion may follow incidentally. Much of the agrarian policy in many socialist countries has, following early Russian debates, been based, at least initially, on the assumption that a socialist economy was incompatible with peasant agriculture based on family cultivation, because this would endogenous'y generate or regenerate (rural) capitalism. The fear of a small socialist island destined to be submerged in the surrounding sea of a peasant-generated capitalism, undoubtedly haunted the early Bolsheviks. If there is no *general* tendency for a peasant economy to generate capitalism, this fear turns out to have been groundless, though there may still be other reasons for supposing that such an agriculture is incompatible with a socialist economy. This question need not be discussed here.

Nevertheless in *some* way peasant agriculture had to be made compatible with and subservient to the capitalist economy; otherwise it would almost certainly have stood in the way of the development of such an economy on a large scale, as the Scots reformers argued.

The obvious way is through the extension of the market, for the sale
of a surplus in a market for varying prices is sufficiently familiar
even to most subsistence peasants to provide a convenient transition
to agriculture as essentially commodity production. Historically
Lenin was quite right in arguing that 'the change that is the essence
of the problem' was that 'the small farmer becomes a commodity
producer, whether he wishes to or not'.[75] It is certain that the development of a capitalist market outside agriculture must increasingly
transform and subordinate agricultural production, and to this
extent the Marxists were right as against the Narodniks. On the
other hand it now seems impossible that even by 1917 much of
Russian peasant agriculture could be described as 'capitalist' or that
the consequent class differentiation and class conflicts within the
village had reached the point of no return.[76]

We may, of course, with Wallerstein, define as 'capitalist' *any*
agriculture functioning within an economic system whose global
structure is determined by its capitalist sector, but this is hardly
more than an evasion of the problem by redefining terms, unless it
helps us to identify and measure the actual changes within peasant
agriculture which are the result of its integration into a global
capitalist system. That, of course, is what Marxists tried to do in the
crucial decades of their first major debates on 'the agrarian question',
say 1894–1914[77]—debates which arose precisely out of the recognition that it was not enough simply to state that capitalism dominated
the development of agriculture, but that the ways in which this
domination affected its internal structure had to be specified. Yet,
while these debates demonstrated clearly enough that peasant farming was being eroded and transformed by capitalism, they also
demonstrated that politically socialists did not quite know what to do
about the large body of peasants in developed countries who could
be classified neither as rural bourgeois nor as rural proletarians or
quasi-proletarians except in those cases where a traditional, and
almost by definition non-capitalist, peasantry could be regarded
more or less as a collective revolutionary mass, and appealed to
accordingly.

A peasant economy so adapted to capitalist development is not
analogous to other internally non-capitalist sub-economies integrated
into a global capitalist economy, such as slave and serf estates. In
one sense it is less sharply distinct from capitalist agriculture than
these, inasmuch as the commercially-minded large peasant, working

with family labour supplemented by hired hands, can often be distinguished from the capitalist farmer only by economic and technological context, the one can insensibly be transformed into the other, and finally, as mid-twentieth century western capitalism has demonstrated, economically marginal or sub-marginal agrarian enterprise in developed countries can disappear leaving agriculture confined, for practical purposes, to little more than its capitalist sector. In another sense, it is more sharply distinct. While the slave-plantation is the actual creation of world capitalist development at a certain stage, and the classic export-oriented serf-estate in large parts of Eastern Europe[78] is a modification of previous structures of domination so drastic as to amount to novelty, the peasant economy, where it resists class or state pressure, remains much more independent of the capitalist world market and therefore undergoes no equally dramatic structural transformation during the equivalent historical period. Conversely, slave and serf estates, just because of their greater dependence on the capitalist system which has given rise to them, are (paradoxically) far more specialized and extreme versions of non-capitalist relations of production, much as the attempt to achieve the speeds of transport of an industrial age by means of sail produce a far more specialized kind of sailing ship than before. In turn, their adaptability is increasingly limited. Whatever the arguments about the 'profitability' of slavery and serfdom as a form of business enterprise, there is no denying the fact that beyond a certain point the development of large agrarian capitalist enterprise has been based on the revolutionary transformation of coerced-labour estates through the formal *abolition* of slavery and serfdom.[79] The adaptation of the peasant economy is more gradual, partly because some of it imposes more obstacles to capitalist developments and partly because some of it imposes fewer such obstacles.

How far this adaptation of peasant economy to capitalism amounts to its transformation into capitalist agriculture cannot be determined *a priori*, but only in the light of concrete situations, varying from one country and historic period to another. The only situation when we can claim with some confidence that such a transformation has taken place on a national scale is the one when the peasantry as a class has been virtually eliminated both by the social differentiation within the agrarian population and, more important, by its dramatic reduction to a small minority of the economically active population—in short, when the prospect envisaged by the eighteenth century Scots reformers is becoming a reality; e.g. in France between 1921 and 1969 with its reduction from almost 40 per cent of the economically active population to barely 13 per cent,

Between the time when the bulk of the peasantry, i.e. the bulk of the pre-industrial population, exists largely outside the capitalist market, and the time when the bulk of the surviving agricultural population can be regarded as 'capitalist', there is a long period when we can claim no more than that the peasantry adapts itself to the dominance of a capitalist economy, as it might, under other circumstances, adapt itself to the dominance of a non-capitalist economy. For the 'peasant economy' is not hegemonic but subaltern; at most it is independent, namely where the economic and socio-political mechanisms for extracting its surplus are too weak to establish effective domination through the market or otherwise.

The Scots reformers of the eighteenth century were aware of two things. They knew that the dominance of the capitalist economy had to be imposed and what economic and politico-legal changes this implied. They also believed that rapid 'modernization', the leap from backwardness to a vanguard position in capitalist development, could not, except in a few favoured localities, wait upon the gradual adaptation and transformation of the peasantry. They therefore opted for its virtual abolition, and the specific historic circumstances of eighteenth century Scotland allowed them very largely to carry out their programmes. Yet what makes them interesting to historians and analysts of the transition to capitalism is not their practice, but the lucidity with which they recognized and analysed their historical task, the obstacles which stood in their way, and the nature of the capitalist agriculture they sought to establish.

## NOTES

1. Indeed, the fullest discussion of the relations between capitalism and agriculture by Marx, the well-known chapter on the genesis of capitalist ground rent in *Capital*, III, is largely concerned with the fact that at first sight, and without careful analysis, capitalist and non-capitalist forms of rent may be impossible to distinguish by their actual *form*.
2. E.g. A. Gunder Frank, *Capitalism and Underdevelopment in Latin America*, Penguin, 1971, pp. 59–61, 158.
3. '... men who have been educated in the middle and inferior ranks of life, who have been carried forward by their own industry and ambition ...'

(Adam Smith, *Theory of the Moral Sentiments*, I, II, II, pp. 92 f, cited after Hans Medick, *Naturzustand und Naturgeschichte der bürgerlichen Gesellschaft*, Göttingen, 1973, p. 279.

4. In John Dalrymple, *An essay towards a general history of feudal propriety in Great Britain*, London, 1757, and Henry Home, Lord Kames, *Historical law-tracts*, London and Edinburgh, 1758. Dalrymple was a follower of Kames, perhaps the most important influence on these discussions both as a thinker, a lawyer and, not least, drafter of a type of lease which became the model for capitalist tenancies. For the early history of the term see Franco Venturi, 'Tra Scozia e Russia: un dibattito settecentesco sul feudalesimo', *POCCA— Russia*, vol. I (1974), pp. 9–40. For Kames, see William C. Lehmann, *Henry Home, Lord Kames, and the Scottish Enlightenment*, The Hague, 1971, and Ian Simpson Ross, *Lord Kames and the Scotland of his Day*, Oxford, 1972. For the impact of his leases, see James Anderson, *General View of the Agriculture . . . of the County of Aberdeen*, Edinburgh, 1794, pp. 155 ff; and for his practical influence, Andrew Wight, *Present State of Husbandry in Scotland*, 4 vols., Edinburgh, 1778–84.

5. Cf. *Farmers Magazine* (Edinburgh), vol. I (1802), p. 191: 'The feudal system, which was not abrogated in Scotland till 1748, enervated the faculties of the farmer, and kept him in a state of the most abject dependence' etc.

6. The earliest example, to my knowledge, is in J. Morison's description of the parish of Canisbay, Caithness, in 1794 (*First Statistical Account*, vol. VIII, p. 148): 'the monster Feudalism is hiding his head in shame.' For other attempts to form similar words, which did not establish themselves, see Robert Heron, *General View of the natural circumstances of . . . (the) Hebudae or Hebrides*, Edinburgh, 1794, p. 78 ('feodism'), and George Chalmers, *Caledonia, or a Historical and Topographical Account of North Britain* (1807), new edn. Paisley, 1888, vol. II, p. 843 ('feudism').

7. *General Report on the Agriculture of Dumbarton*, Glasgow, 1811, p. 301.

8. Cf. R. Koebner, 'Adam Smith and the Industrial Revolution', *Economic History Review*, second series, vol. XI, no. 3 (1959), pp. 381–91.

9. Medick, op.cit. p. 278.

10. Thus James Anderson, described and cited by Marx as 'the real discoverer of the modern theory of ground rent (Rententheorie)', was also, as Marx notes, 'a practising tenant-farmer and an important agronomist in his time' (*Capital*, III, *Werke*, vol. XXV, p. 633). Marx observed correctly that his theory of differential rent was developed incidentally, in the course of writing a variety of essays 'directly destined for a public of farmers and agriculturalists' (*Theories on Surplus Value*, II, *Werke*, vol. XXVI, ii, p. 103). We may add that Marx, unlike many of his followers, was evidently well acquainted with the Scottish theorists of the eighteenth century.

11. The poverty, remoteness and relatively unfavourable agricultural conditions of most of Scotland did not prevent the transformation of its Lowland farming into one of the best and most technically progressive in Europe. These factors alone therefore did not play a decisive role, except perhaps in providing Scots farmers with an unusually cheap labour force, strong and healthy though fed on little but oatmeal porridge, on which Scots 'improvers' never failed to congratulate themselves. Perhaps it also underlined the

importance of relatively heavy initial capital investment for agricultural improvement.

12. The word 'Whig' was originally derived from a term of abuse directed against ultra-Calvinist Scottish Lowland rebels against the Stuart kings.

13. 'It was thought then disgraceful for any of the sons of these wadsetters, to follow any other profession than that of arms and agriculture; and it is in the remembrance of many now living, when the meanest tenant would think it disparaging, to sit at the same table with a manufacturer' ('Statistical Account of Boleskine and Abertarf', *First Statistical Account*, vol. xx (1798), p. 23).

14. 'Burgage' by which town burghers held of the king, did not extend outside the property of burghers in (royal) burghs, and was therefore negligible. For a lucid discussion of the legal situation, see Sir John Sinclair (ed.), *General Report on the Agricultural State and Political Circumstances of Scotland*, Edinburgh, 1814, vol. I, chapter 2, Appendix 1.

15. Sinclair, loc. cit. pp. 188–9.

16. Sinclair, *General Report*, vol. III, Appendix, p. 4.

17. For the emergence of this group, see N. T. Philipson, 'Culture and Society in the Eighteenth Century Province: The Case of Edinburgh and the Scottish Enlightenment', in L. Stone (ed.), *The University in Society*, Princeton, 1972; also N. T. Philipson and R. T. Mitchison (eds.), *Scotland in the Age of Improvement: Essays in Scottish History in the Eighteenth Century*, Edinburgh, 1970.

18. On the role of wealth accumulated by Scots in war and India, as capital for agricultural 'improvements', see *Scotland and Scotsmen in the Eighteenth Century. From the MSS of John Ramsay*, ed. Alexander Allardyce, Edinburgh and London, 1888, vol. II, p. 247. Ramsay died in 1814.

19. Largely because of the so-called Montgomery Act of 1770 (10 Geo. III, c. 55) to improve lands under entail, for which see below.

20. Cf. e.g. James Anderson, *Essays relating to Agricultural and Rural Affairs*, Edinburgh, 1796, vol. III, pp. 19–20, 27. Also James Anderson, *General View of . . . Aberdeen*, Edinburgh, 1794, pp. 150–2.

21. Anderson, *Essays*, loc. cit.

22. Sinclair, *General Report*, vol. I, p. 605.

23. Sir Archibald Grant, Bart. (*A Dissertation on the Chief Obstacles to the Improvement of the Land*, Aberdeen, 1760, p. 29) probably expressed the common view that the fortunes of farming depended on the home market: 'When traders and manufacturers are few, and do not increase in proportion, the farmer must seek a foreign market which is precarious, and agriculture stops and languishes.'

24. John Walker D.D., *An Economical History of the Hebrides and Highlands of Scotland*, Edinburgh, 1808, vol. II, p. 340. Cf. also Macdonald's *General View of . . . the Hebrides*, Edinburgh, 1811, p. 535: 'The effects of commerce upon agriculture have been but faintly and partially experienced in the greater part of these isles.'

25. James Robertson D.D., *General View of . . . the Southern Districts of . . . Perth*, London, 1794, pp. 65–6.

26. *General View of . . . Aberdeen*, pp. 45–6.

27. Ibid. p. 58. Cf. also Sir John Sinclair, *General View of . . . the Northern*

*Counties and Islands of Scotland (including the Counties of Cromarty, Ross, Sutherland, Caithness and the Islands of Orkney and Shetland)*, London, 1795, pp. 122–3, where it is noted that grain cannot be sold advantageously in small quantities.

28. 'What we call land is an element of nature inextricably interwoven with man's institutions. To isolate it and form a market for it was perhaps the weirdest of all the undertakings of our ancestors' (K. Polanyi, *Origins of our Time*, London, 1945, p. 179).

29. Sinclair, *General Report*, vol. I, chapter 2, Appendix 1, p. 219.

30. The Rev. Andrew Whyte and Duncan Macfarlan D.D., *General View of ... Dumbarton*, Glasgow, 1811, p. 301.

31. Sinclair, loc. cit.

32. 'Boleskine and Abertarf', *First Statistical Account*, vol. xx (1798), p. 33.

33. Sinclair, op.cit. p. 207.

34. Ibid.

35. Ibid. pp. 234–5.

36. Ibid. pp. 233, 235.

37. Ibid. p. 230.

38. Ibid. p. 100.

39. Anderson, *Essays*, vol. III, pp. 19–20.

40. Anderson, op. cit., suggested primogeniture to avoid such parcellization.

41. *General View of ... Peebles*, 1802, p. 52.

42. Whyte and Macfarlan, *General View of ... Dumbarton*, p. 20.

43. 'The farmer, in ancient times, seldom reared any crop but oats, a little barley, and peas. ... Hence, a small farm rendered him hurried in time of seed and harvest, and the manufacturing it occupied his whole labour during winter. In summer he was literally idle! In these enlightened times the farmer is ploughing, sowing and reaping, every month of the year' ('Kilmadock or Doune', *First Statistical Account*, vol. XX, pp. 68–9).

44. Cited in J. F. Erskine, *General View of ... Clackmannan*, 1794, p. 23.

45. Robert Somerville, *General View of ... East Lothian*, London, 1805, pp. 52–3.

46. Andrew Wight, *Present State of Husbandry in Scotland. Extracted from the Reports made to the Commissioners of the Annexed Estates*, Edinburgh, 1778–84, vol. I, p. 53.

47. Whyte and Macfarlan, op. cit. p. 20. See also Findlater, *General View of ... Peebles*, p. 52.

48. 'Dornoch', *First Statistical Account*, vol. VIII, pp. 16, 18. John Walker D.D. thought they should all become labourers, available for the occasional peak demands of the farmers (*An Economical History of the Hebrides and Highlands of Scotland*, Edinburgh, 1808, vol. I, p. 86); but Whyte and Macfarlan (op. cit. pp. 248–50) felt that the availability of cheap but inefficient migrant labour from the neighbouring Highlands discouraged farmers from improving as rapidly as they might do.

49. Somerville, *General View of ... East Lothian*, p. 52.

50. Wight, op. cit. vol. v, pp. 140–51; Sir John Sinclair, *General View of ... the Northern Counties*, pp. 136, 162–4; Marshall, *General View of ... the Central Highlands of Scotland*, London, 1794, p. 52.

51. This is discussed by James Anderson, *General View of ... Aberdeen*, pp. 50–2.

Also Sir George Stewart Mackenzie, *General Survey of . . . Ross and Cromarty*, London, 1810, pp. 140–1.

52. John Wilson, *General View of . . . Renfrew*, Paisley, 1812.

53. Wight, op. cit. vol. III, pp. 319–20; Sinclair, *General View of . . . the Northern Counties*, p. 166; Sir G. S. Mackenzie, op. cit. pp. 138, 140–1.

54. In the oft-cited words of Alexander Wedderburn, *An Essay upon the Question 'What proportion of the produce of arable land ought to be paid as rent to the landlord?'*, Edinburgh, 1770, he had to earn three rents: one to cover his costs, one for the landlord and one for his profit.

55. Whyte and Macfarlan, op. cit. p. 300; Anderson, *Essays*, pp. 79–80.

56. For a good description, see T. C. Smout, *A History of the Scottish People, 1560–1830*, London, 1969, chapter 13, I.

57. *Farmers Magazine*, vol. I (1802), p. 288.

58. *General View of . . . East Lothian*, pp. 36, 41.

59. G. V. Donaldson, *General View of . . . Elgin or Moray*, Edinburgh, 1794, p. 37.

60. *General View of . . . Midlothian*, 1795, pp. 41–2.

61. Cited in *Farmers Magazine*, vol. I (1802), pp. 287–8.

62. Findlater, *General View of . . . Peebles*, p. 252; Wilson, *General View of . . . Renfrew*, pp. 347–8; Sir John Sinclair, *General Report*, vol. III, pp. 374–7.

63. Sinclair, *An Account of the Systems . . .* , p. 63; for more detailed information, ibid. pp. 63–9.

64. Whyte and Macfarlan, pp. 54 ff.

65. Sinclair, op. cit. pp. 71, 80.

66. 'Wattin', *Statistical Account*, vol. X (1794), p. 270.

67. *The Wealth of Nations*, bk. V, chapter 2 (1921 edn., ii, p. 359): 'If the land-lords should, the greater part of them, be tempted to farm the whole of their own lands, the country (instead of sober and industrious tenants, who are bound by their own interest to cultivate as well as their capital and skill will allow) would be filled with idle and profligate bailiffs whose abusive manage-ment would soon degrade the cultivation, and reduce the annual produce of the land.'

68. E.g. R. Douglas, *General View of . . . Roxburgh and Selkirk*, Edinburgh, 1798, pp. 27–8: landlords grant tenants a sum equivalent to a year's rent to undertake stipulated improvements; or more usually supply material and labour to the tenant who feeds and assists these workers.

69. Thus local depopulation was said to be due to 'the principal tenants extending their farms and removing their cottagers' (Gartly, Banff), 'enclosures' (Cameron, Fife), 'the improvements of land and the junction of farms' (Airly, Forfar), 'the expulsion of cottagers by farmers' (Dunnottar, Kinkardine), 'partly to the growing extent of farms' (Wattin, Caithness), 'chiefly by the monopoly of farms' (Oxnam, Roxburgh), 'the natural consequence of the union of farms' (Demino, Fife) etc. (*Statistical Account*, vol. X (1794), pp. 140, 198, 210, 221, 261, 317, 357n).

70. Cf. Anderson, *Essays*, vol. III, pp. 133 f; *General View of . . . Clydesdale*; but see *General View of . . . East Lothian*, pp. 52–3, cited above.

71. J. H. G. Lebon, 'The Beginnings of the Agrarian and Industrial Revolution in Ayrshire', in *Ayrshire at the Time of Robert Burns*, Ayrshire Arch. and Nat. Hist. Soc., Kilmarnock, 1959, pp. 158–9.

72. Thus the proportion of peasant householders to total population in a typical old-style parish (Dunnett, Caithness) was 1:7, but in a typical 'improved' parish (Eccles, Berwick) 1:32 (*Statistical Account*, vol. X (1794), pp. 239, 253).
73. *The Wealth of Nations*, bk. IV, chapter 9 (1921 edn., ii, p. 201).
74. On this last point, see R. Brenner, 'Agrarian Class Structure and Economic Development in Pre-industrial Europe', *Past and Present*, vol. LXX (1976), pp. 30–74.
75. 'New Data on the Development of Capitalism in Agriculture', *Selected Works*, London, 1938, vol. XII, p. 275.
76. See T. Shanin, *The Awkward Class*, Oxford, 1972.
77. Cf. H. G. Lehmann, *Die Agrarfrage in der Theorie und Praxis der deutschen u. internationalen Sozialdemokratie*, Tübingen, 1970.
78. The question whether all the 'second serfdom' of Eastern Europe—in fact most of it was, for that region, 'first serfdom'—is to be ascribed to the effect of the world market, need not be discussed here. Cf. Wallerstein, op. cit. pp. 90–6; Perry Anderson, op. cit. vol. II, pp. 196, 203–12.
79. The point about the decline of the 'first serfdom' in western Europe, and its transformation into agrarian relations which, in some countries, evolved into agrarian capitalism, is that it occurred *before* the formation of a global capitalist system and as a consequence of the breakdown of the earlier economy which made the large seignorial estate viable. Nor was it immediately or recognizably transformed into 'capitalist agriculture'. The well-known Dobb–Sweezy debate, in so far as it is about 'What came after feudalism in Western Europe?', turns on this point (P. M. Sweezy in *Science and Society*, Spring 1950, pp. 134–67). The debate on *The Transition from Feudalism to Capitalism* has most recently been reissued (ed. R. H. Hilton, London, 1976; Monthly Review Press, N.Y., 1977).

# 2

# Money and the Serfs in Eighteenth Century Poland

## WITOLD KULA
### University of Warsaw

In the Middle Ages the agrarian system in Poland was based on the rent paid annually by peasants to their landlords. The rent was paid mainly in cash, but it also included certain payments in kind produced on the peasants' holdings, and a certain amount of compulsory labour. The scale of the latter was small since the home-farm of the manor was small. The contributions in kind might also be small, since they were meant primarily to feed the landlord's household, which was not large. In addition to agricultural work on the home-farm, compulsory labour was utilized for the construction and maintenance of public works (roads, bridges, dikes, etc.).

Such an agrarian system both relied upon and resulted in the existence, within a reasonable distance, of a market in the form of a town with its periodic fairs and market-days. The produce that was left to the peasants after paying the small amount of dues in kind to their landlords and after consuming a considerable portion in their own families, had to be taken to the market in the nearby town and sold; the proceeds in cash had in part to be passed on to the landlord as rent, and in part to be spent by the peasants on certain consumer and producer goods.

In this way, nearly the whole product was produced by the peasants and on peasant holdings. Nearly the whole product left after satisfying the immediate peasant needs used to pass through the market, and thus affect the prices shaped there. The prices in turn determined the amount of the money received by the peasants. A peasant, by himself, had a minimal impact on the price paid to him but he had complete control over the manner in which he spent the money obtained at the market which remained with him after the payment of the feudal rent. Obviously the way the money left at the disposal of the peasants was actually spent depended upon customary tastes and the prevailing scale of values, but that is a separate issue.

The network of market-towns which this system required had to be dense in order for everyone to have access to a town. The towns could, or rather had to, be small, because the quantity of marketable product was small and the radius of accessibility of a town was short. In those times the division of labour between town and country was far from complete. Town-dwellers often kept poultry and pigs; many of them owned gardens and orchards and made use of the land around the town. Nevertheless, they were not in a position to provide for themselves all the food they needed.

As the estates held by the magnates, and especially those held by the king and the clergy, gradually expanded, owners of these estates did not hesitate to rearrange the network of towns so as to suit their own convenience. Thus, for example, a new town might be created in the centre of a group of villages belonging to a single estate.

The agrarian system in Poland underwent a basic transformation in the second half of the fifteenth century and the first half of the sixteenth; in fact, the process began earlier and continued much later. The number, and especially the area, of the feudal manors increased as a result of incorporating and bringing into cultivation barren land or land which had been only partially exploited (e.g. natural pastures), and also of taking over lands which had previously belonged to peasants. Large peasant holdings, on which the peasants produced the entire indispensable product and nearly all the surplus product, were gradually transformed into small ones, on which only the indispensable product was produced. The surplus came to be produced on the land of the greatly expanded home-farms (the Polish term being *folwark*, distorted from German *vorwerk*). Thus surplus was created by the compulsory labour of the peasants, who were now able to furnish it since their own holdings, which had been reduced in size, required less work. In the average case, the peasant had to till the same area of land as before, the difference being that now a large part of that land belonged to his seignior, and was tilled by the peasant only because he was forced to do so.

Polish scholars have discussed the problem on many occasions, trying to explain the entire process, and especially the fact that the peasants did not rebel against these changes (the reduction of the average size of peasant holdings and the imposition of compulsory labour) which were so unfavourable to them. Many explanations have been suggested. Several of them pointed to factors that could, and probably did, operate simultaneously. Such explanations must accordingly be treated as not mutually exclusive.

Thus, it is likely that the peasant tolerated these changes just because they were tolerable. As has been said, the area of the land to be tilled by one peasant did not necessarily increase, and the product available for use by the peasant and his family did not necessarily decrease. The prevailing inflationary trend accounted for the fact that the peasant, even though he had less to sell, could do so under terms of trade that were now more favourable for him. The only difference was that it was now known which plot would yield the harvest to be deposited in the peasant barn, and which the harvest that could go into the lord's granary.

The indispensable product went into the peasant barn, and the surplus into the lord's granary. The peasant no longer had to sell his product on the market in order to devote part of the proceeds in cash to paying the rent due to his lord. It was now the lord himself who sold the product wholesale. There was now little contact between the peasants and the town market, and only a brief possession of cash by the peasants (if at all).

The schema, as outlined above, is, of course, simplified in the extreme. The changes referred to were neither violent nor sudden. They took place gradually over a long period of time. This was the factor which, at least in part, disarmed peasant resistance. Nor was the peasant cut off from the town market completely and, as it were, by one stroke. This was so, above all, because the cash rent specified in the medieval privileges continued in most cases as an obligation on the part of the peasants. But, since the nominal amount remained the same, the burden had become small as a result of long-term inflation. Small as it was, this rent had to be paid; and in order to pay it, the peasant had to sell some of his product. Further, some taxes imposed by the state authorities (in small amounts) and some fees due to the Church were traditionally paid in cash. Thus the peasant would sell a little on the town market, and would buy even less.

He did not have much to sell, and from the proceeds he had to pay the rent and occasionally a tax or Church fee. When it came to the remainder (if there was a remainder at all), he did not have many options. He had to cover certain expenses that were socially or even physically indispensable. Sometimes, salt and articles made of iron (for instance nails) would be all he would buy.

The problem of salt is significant in this connection. Salt is needed universally, being indispensable for the human body. At the same time, the consumption of salt does not depend on an individual's likes and dislikes. One can partake to excess of alcoholic beverages, but any excessive use of salt is unlikely, even if we consider the needs of animal husbandry and of conserving certain products for the winter. The gentry had long acquired the right to obtain salt gratis, and often used to pass on salt to the peasants, *not* gratuitously, of course. This was quite easy because the production of salt was possible in only a few places, which could easily be controlled (the royal monopoly, etc.). Forcing the peasants to buy the salt which the gentry obtained for nothing made it possible to drain peasant purses of those small amounts of cash which remained after the payment of the rent, the state taxes, and the Church fees.

At that point the peasant purse should have been empty. But it was not. Why? Because, despite the efforts of the lords of the manors, the contacts between peasants and the town market were more durable than the landlords would have preferred; these links with the town market were so important to the peasants that they were ready to do without certain amenities in order to preserve them.

Where were the traces of these contacts visible? Essentially in two spheres: Firstly, we find evidence that peasants had in their possession articles which they were in no position to produce themselves. This applies, for instance, to window panes and iron nails. The author of a late eighteenth century handbook for the production of glass remarks that glass is a commodity 'without which no peasant would be satisfied'. A Renaissance poet, when describing in a long Latin poem the territories which today constitute the Western Ukraine, gives vent to his astonishment upon noticing that various objects are made in that region without the use of nails, a technique which had long been forgotten in historical Poland. The production of glass and iron was not so highly concentrated as was the production of salt, but it nevertheless remained beyond the possibilities of individual peasant holdings. If peasants owned objects made of glass or of iron, they must have bought them. Or probably it was their fathers or forefathers who had bought them, if we consider how meticulously the peasants handled every nail and every piece of broken window pane. The iron parts of agricultural tools and implements (spikes of harrows, blades of spades, ploughshares, etc.) are the most important items among the objects listed in last wills.

Secondly, we find that peasants used to consume certain items which they did not produce on their holdings; the two most important of these were salt and alcoholic drinks. Salt has been discussed above. Vodka (previously beer) was also an almost constant element of peasant diet. Unlike salt, vodka can be made at home. Numerous conflicts between the gentry and the peasants arose in connection with the prohibition of home distillation of vodka. Conflicts also turned on the drinking by peasants of vodka in an 'alien tavern', i.e. in a tavern situated in the nearby town or belonging to the owner of another manor.

Iron, glass, salt, and vodka, possession of which by peasants has been confirmed, all prove that peasants retained contacts with the market, either directly or indirectly. To obtain these items the peasant had to sell something. In the case of a window pane or nails, the peasant had to sell some of his product to one townsman and to use the cash thus obtained for buying window glass or nails from another townsman. Thus the money did not stay long in the peasant's purse, which served mainly to transfer money from one townsman to another. When it came to vodka, beer, and often salt, the first stage remained the same: the peasant would sell his product to a townsman for money; but the second stage was different: the peasant would hand over the money to his seignior, and not to another townsman.

In the eighteenth century various attempts were made by the owners of large estates to intercept the money paid by peasants for iron, glass and similar products. Estate owners set up factories to make textiles, glass and metal products for sale to the peasants. If, despite the best efforts on the part of his seignior the peasant still has money which he spends at the town market to buy manufactured goods or articles made by craftsmen, let him buy those things from his seignior. But the factories set up for this purpose were in most cases short-lived. The landowners' hopes usually failed to materialize, despite the fact that such factories often had access to free raw materials, free labour, or water installations which could provide hydraulic power. They also enjoyed certain extra-economic privileges, such as monopolies (the imports of certain articles from other estates or from abroad being banned).

Large-scale development of factory production (of felt, linen cloth, iron, and glass) undertaken by the magnates to satisfy the needs of the town population and, above all, the peasants in eighteenth century Poland were more a matter of intentions than of accomplishments. But they were interesting in that they illustrated the aspirations of the owners of large estates, on the one hand, and of the peasants, on the other. Since the peasants succeeded in preserving their links with town markets and with money—links which the gentry hoped to cut—the gentry tried to drain the peasants of their money. They succeeded in doing so to a varying degree; in the case of vodka they succeeded marvellously. The astonishing fact which requires further study is how the peasants managed, despite the logic of the system, to retain enough money so as to enable the gentry to drain large sums from them by means of their monopoly of the sale of alcoholic drinks.

We have so far discussed the peasants' opportunities for having contacts with money. But a distinction must be made between physical contacts with money, when money is passed from hand to hand in the form of physical objects, i.e. coins, and contacts with money as an intellectual category. Money in the sense of an intellectual category makes it possible to evaluate everything, to add different qualities to one another, to find a kind of common denominator for all things, and to express everything in the form of price.

Money in the sense of physical objects does, of course, have certain properties which other physical objects lack. Coins are handled carefully and examined scrupulously before being accepted in payment. The indentations on the rim are checked. Money has the same structure as society: gold for the gentry, silver for the townspeople, and copper for the peasants. Coins used to be hoarded as treasure by being buried under carefully remembered trees—to please the archaeologists, as it were.

A special ritual was observed in monetary transactions. In rural court cases, the sum which was the subject matter of contention was expected to be physically deposited on the judge's table. The person to whom the sum was adjudged had to raise it up with customary gestures to indicate that he was satisfied by the decision and would not make any further claims.

But did the peasants, or, to put it more broadly, the rural population, think about money in terms of a mental category and not just in terms of physical objects? There are various clues as to the answer, but they are subject to different interpretations. In rural courts, money was more frequently treated as a mental category than as physical objects deposited on the judge's table. And fairly large sums might be involved. The facts are as follows.

Family and economic relationships among peasants living in a given village were extremely intricate. Marriages were usually concluded within the village, and so in most cases were loans. The mortality rate was high, the average lifespan short; hence the number of widows and widowers was large. Since a widow or a widower was unable to take care of his holding singlehanded, people had to remarry. Both spouses often had children by their previous marriages. Loans of a horse for ploughing or a bushel of grain in the period before the harvest were often superimposed on family relationships. All this accounted for the fact that legal acts such as wills used to be extremely intricate. Provisions in a will could be of various kinds: which child would have the heifer and which would have two pigs, which daughter would have her mother's wedding dress, who would be entitled to a free lifelong residence, and who would be obliged to feed the small orphans.

The variety of such obligations was such that one might cancel out another; although the total value might be large, the final settlement could involve a fairly small net sum. To arrive at that final balance was extremely difficult: the peasant mentality was unable to apply the concept of money to all the objects and rights involved, the more so as these included consumer goods of short duration, such as food, and of long duration, such as buildings, as well as privileges such as the right of free residence or the right to receive annuities. The settlement to be reached in the court (usually prepared before the court session) was based on bargaining in terms of indivisible magnitudes (a cow, a room, etc.), without any common denominator —'I take this, you take that, and let him be given something else.'

The qualitative variety of the elements of such a settlement was usually so great that to reduce them all to a common denominator would not surprisingly seem absurd to the parties for whom the settlement was an important matter, and who wanted to understand every element of it.

On the other hand, evaluation in terms of money of certain damages suffered by peasants on account of actions by administrators or superior tenants is quite often found in the petitions submitted by peasants to their lords in the eighteenth century. But this method was applied only in certain cases, precisely those in which the evaluation was fairly easy (for instance, a horse which had been recently bought for a specified sum and which died from having been overburdened upon orders of the administrator). It never happened that all the damages suffered were evaluated in terms of money, nor, which is equally important, were the items thus evaluated summed up. Money was still far from being considered a common denominator.

The sphere in which the existence or non-existence of the concept of money as a common denominator or value can best be observed is that of the relation between the peasants and the lord of the manor. What was considered at that time the obligation of the peasants to the seignior? A number of specified items and services or a total considered as having a given value? In reports of inspection of estates held by the Crown we often find the formula: 'they do not furnish them because they do not have them'[1] with reference to certain dues in kind, such as honey, sheep, and pigs. This indicates that in the opinion of both the peasants and the inspectors (hence the gentry in general), the peasants were obliged to supply specified items or to perform specified operations. If they did not have bees, sheep, or pigs, they obviously could not supply them. We do not come upon the idea that they should provide instead some other items 'of the same value'. Such a substitution, in fact, would not be easy to carry out. The peasant would have to take some of those products of which he had a surplus (that is, over and above his needs *qua* consumer and *qua* producer) to the nearby town, to sell them, and to meet his obligations from the proceeds. But what would be an equitable amount? And who would determine this amount?

The practical impossibility of evaluating obligatory labour in terms of money proved the greatest obstacle to the emergence of the concept of money as a common denominator of value in relationships between the peasants and the lord of the manor. In the eyes of the serf, as the direct producer, a day of labour to be furnished to the manor was not a unit which could be added or subtracted. According to the season, a day of labour differed in value both for the peasant and for the lord of the manor. The point was not that one day would be worth more than another, although sometimes this was actually the case. The point was that one day of labour was different from another day and did not correspond to it in all respects. According to the season, one day was longer than another. The economy of the manor required both the long and the short days, though not in the same number. These differences were, as a rule, reflected in statutory provisions which specified how many days of labour were to be furnished in winter, how many in summer, how many in periods of urgent field work, etc. Peasants very often complained about the refusal of their labour by the lord of the manor, who, even though the peasants duly appeared in the morning, preferred to exact their labour in a peak period. The peasants protested and refused to comply with such demands. For them, one day of labour did not necessarily equal another day of labour, and their contention was justified. To exact a day of labour in the summer instead of a day of labour in the winter meant effectively to increase the burden on the peasant who had to furnish that labour.

There were interminable controversies over the ratio between a day of labour worked on foot and a day of labour worked with draught animals. It was commonly assumed in the rules of the manors that two days on foot equalled one day with draught animals. Yet the prevailing opinion among the peasants was that one day with draught animals was worth more than two days on foot. But how much more? No single answer was possible. Yet the peasants often commented on the issue, not in words, but in deeds. In many cases peasants tried to rid themselves of draught animals in order not to have to furnish draught labour. If we consider that the draught animals owned by peasants served to till not only the fields of the demesne but the peasant holdings as well, we can understand how dramatic was the decision to rid oneself of draught animals in order to evade the duty of furnishing draught labour. In effect, a basic element of the productive forces of the manor was thus at the mercy of the peasants. Theoretically, the provision by the peasants of draught labour for the demesne was expected to function in a reasonable way: the peasants would take good care of their draught animals because these served to till their own holdings as well. It did function in this fashion over long periods. But, when the oppression of the peasants exceeded a certain limit, rather difficult to define, the peasants used to let their draught animals die in order not to have to furnish draught labour.

Thinking in terms of money encountered a fundamental obstacle in the fact that there was no common measure for products and labour. In the feudal economy, the labour furnished by the serfs and the cash rent did not have any common measure. If they had, the conversion of serf labour into money payments would not have posed any problems. But the manorial economy based on serf labour could not function if the serfs could choose between furnishing their labour and paying a sum of money. In a manorial economy a given day of serf labour must be worked *hic et nunc*. If a meadow belonging to the manor has to be mowed on a certain day and if the serf, instead of coming in person with his scythe, sends 15 Gr (Gr stands for *Grosz* or *Grossus*; in the period under consideration 30 Gr equalled 1 zloty), the farming needs of the manor would not be satisfied. Lords of manors often fined peasants for not supplying serf labour, but such a fine was essentially a punishment and not a means for obtaining the equivalent of the lost labour.

Consider, for instance, the following text. 'The villages of Kosmala, Zedrman and Osieck complain that, as a substitute for their labour which is not required, they have to pay a rent of 52 zloty each instead of 38 zloty. Their complaint is groundless, because the [administration of the] castle of Rabsztyn, while it needs much serf labour for tilling and repairs to the building of the district office, does not hire labour. Only in cases where a peasant does not furnish any serf labour at all . . . does he pay 15 Gr for each day of foot labour. Similarly, when the castle needs serf labour, it pays to the village 15 Gr per day for foot labour.'[2]

The functioning of the manor sometimes required that an equivalent for labour be fixed in terms of money. As we have seen, a day of draught labour was generally taken as equalling two days of foot labour despite the prevailing peasant opinion that the true ratio was more than two to one. This ratio was sometimes reflected in the documents. In the province of Plock in 1765, a day of draught labour was calculated at 15 Gr and a day of foot labour at 6 Gr.[3] When the manor required hired labour in addition to serf labour, various tariffs developed, probably following various controversies. The day's pay might depend, for instance, on the nature of labour. 'When required, they should work for the manor, being paid 19 Gr for one day of work during the harvest of winter crops and 15 Gr during the harvest of spring crops; mowing of meadows to be paid at 1 zl 3 Gr per day and raking of hay at 12 Gr.'[4] These differences are related to the degree of effort involved. Sometimes the duration of work was also taken into account. We find the following entry with regard to the village of Wilkow: 'Hired labour, when the manor needs it, is to be paid 24 Gr for one day of foot labour in summer, and 15 Gr for one day of foot labour in winter.'[5]

These prescriptions are taken from reports of inspection of estates held by the Crown; hence they are regulatory in nature. It is only occasionally that we are able to penetrate more deeply and to discover the actual facts. For instance, we find a reference to the village of Korabiewicze: '[they make us] build dikes, clean rivers, cut grass, harvest crops, and they pay us 15 Gr per man per day, to which we have to add 1 zl per day for each man whom we have to hire.'[6] From this statement a simple calculation indicates that in the province of Rawa in the late eighteenth century when there was urgent work to be done in the fields, one day of hired labour was worth 45 Gr.

But we have to bear in mind that the overwhelming bulk of the days of labour utilized in agriculture in the course of the year did not influence the formation of this price. For the major part of the work required on the demesne, this price had no significance since the manor had at its disposal the unpaid labour due from the serfs. We do not know whether a serf had to hire labour for the cultivation of his own holding, and if so, on what terms he could hire it. In any case, no large amount of labour was involved, and probably it was paid only partly in cash, the rest of the payment being in kind. In this case the cash rate of 45 Gr per day would not apply.

Medieval Polish agriculture did not involve full employment during the greater part of the year. There was a reserve of manpower which could not be employed for technological or social reasons. But during short periods, which were of essential importance from the agricultural point of view, there was a shortage of manpower. It was the amount of labour which was required during the peak periods which was the subject of clashes between the manor and the peasants. In slack periods the manor would waste the serf labour to which it had a claim, but when there was urgent work to be done in the fields, it tried to squeeze more labour out of the serfs than that which it could rightfully claim.

It is against this background of social relations that the basic process of the penetration of money into the rural areas took place in the form of commutation of labour services and compulsory paid labour.

Commutation of labour services, observable almost exclusively in South Western Poland, resulted from situations in which the manor had the right to more serf labour than it could rationally use. The lord of the manor could then try one of two solutions: (*i*) he could sell a certain amount of serf labour (calculated on a person-per-day basis) to one of his neighbours, which was considered both immoral and illegal; or (*ii*) he could resort to commutation of labour services, i.e. he could demand payment by the serfs for the labour he did not claim from them.

Compulsory labour was introduced when the lord of the manor needed more labour than he had the right to claim, and forced the peasants to work on the manor for payment. Commutation and compulsory paid labour were methods which directly resulted in the birth of the labour market. But that was the next stage in the process.

## NOTES

1. In 1564, the Diet decided that the estates held by the Crown would be inspected, and that such inspections would be repeated periodically. This series of inspections yielded a vast amount of documents, which have been published for a number of years. The statement quoted here is drawn from the report of the inspection of the estates of the Crown in the provinces of Ruthenia in 1661–5, cf. *Lustracja wojewedztwa ruskiege, 1661–1665*, part III, Ossolineum, 1976, p. 14 *et passim.* (Cited hereafter by province, year, part (if indicated), and page.)
2. Cracow province, 1789, I, p. 196.
3. Plock province, 1765, p. 118.
4. Rawa province, 1789, p. 150.
5. Rawa province, 1789, p. 83.
6. Rawa province, 1789, p. 125.

# 3

# Drink in Old Russia

R. E. F. SMITH

*University of Birmingham*

WHEN Vladimir, prince of Kiev, considered abandoning paganism, he rejected Islam as an alternative because, he said, 'Rus' loves to drink, we cannot be without it.'[1] At this period, before the Mongol invasions of the thirteenth century, mead was probably a common alcoholic drink in Russia. The term *med* means both 'mead' and 'honey'. Usually in the sources of this period it refers to drink, but sometimes there are unequivocal references to honey used as sugar would be nowadays.[2] Mead was drunk by the nobility in the tenth century, to judge by the chronicle's account of O'lga's revenge for her dead husband in 945 A.D.[3] From the thirteenth century the Novgorod princes had their mead-makers.[4] The Slavs, however, were essentially forest people exploiting the resources of their environment by a combination of gathering and cultivation; the gathering of honey from wild bees in the forest was the source of the raw material for mead. Thus it seems probable that mead was made throughout the whole area occupied by the Rus' and at all levels of society, even though there is no direct evidence for this.

The other common drink of Kievan times was *kvas*, a lightly fermented beer, sometimes flavoured with fruits or berries. There is, for example, early evidence for apple *kvas*.[5] A twelfth century manuscript mentions 'much drink, mead and kvas'.[6] Beer, too, is mentioned in the documentary sources, one of which implies it was a usual drink even for the sick: 'he should take as much as he can of food and beer.'[7]

In the period following the Mongol invasions mead and beer remained the commonest intoxicating drinks, but there may gradually have been a change in their relative importance; at least there seems no adequately clear basis for the blunt statement that, 'as formerly, the basic drink was mead'.[8] It is true that the Nomocanon of the thirteenth century permitted three cups of mead a week to be drunk during days of abstinence and on fast days allowed one cup to be drunk if fish was eaten.[9] In addition, there is chronicle evidence for the consumption of mead and for the plundering of mead from lords' cellars.[10] The Moscow prince had extensive bee forests from at least the fourteenth century and an administrative department was developed to deal with them.

However, the sewer, the man responsible for drinks in a great lord's household, was called *sytnik*, from the term for honey water (*syta*).[11] It thus seems that in the centuries immediately after the thirteenth century Mongol invasion, mead became increasingly a lord's drink.[12] Colonization and cultivation disturbed or destroyed the wild bee population and made honey a luxury consumption item.[13]

Most charters which use the term *med* seem to refer to honey, often as an item of produce rents and measured by weight. In 1378, however, troops beyond the river P'yana (i.e. Drunk) found 'mead and beer, they drank themselves very drunk, of a truth they were drunk beyond the Drunk'.[14] In fact, the relatively little evidence we have suggests that beer was a common, if not the commonest, intoxicating drink from the fourteenth century. A charter of 1391 noted that monastic peasants had to grind malt and brew beer.[15] Probably beer grew in importance for the mass of peasants as mead was increasingly restricted to consumption by lords. For the late fifteenth century there are many references to the consumption of beer by peasants. The Grand Prince in 1455–62, for instance, laid down that 'the servants and court investigators (*dovodchiki*) of my Bezhets representatives, and also the boyar people and anyone else uninvited, shall not go for beer to their monastery people [i.e. dependants], whoever may live under them in that village and the hamlets'.[16] A similar prohibition was issued against the Grand Prince's dependants who 'go uninvited for festivals, feasts and fraternities (*bratshiny*) and do them [the metropolitan's peasants] violence, take mead, beer and ale (*braga*) from them by force'.[17] Ale was sometimes liable to tax in the sixteenth century.[18] That beer was still commonly brewed in the late sixteenth century seems implied by the vagueness of the rule on a monastic estate that 'if anyone has any beer, the steward is to have a gift'.[19]

*Kvas* does not appear to be mentioned in the documents of this time; it undoubtedly continued to be made, but perhaps because of its very low alcoholic content it is unlikely to have produced the problems connected with intoxication which would feature in the documents. This was probably the day-to-day drink of most peasants.

All the drinks so far mentioned might be hopped. In parts of north European Russia wild hops were found.[20] They were also cultivated on special hopfields.[21] Hopfields sometimes evidently belonged to the settlement rather than to individual tenements.[22] The Law Book of 1589 laid down that hopfields and orchards were not available for redistribution in certain circumstances.[23] In some areas hops were a regular item of produce rents at least from the fifteenth century.[24] Sometimes such payments might be commuted.[25] In Novgorod and Pskov hops were a regular item of trade from the thirteenth century; prices fluctuated considerably, and this suggests that demand at times outstripped supply.[26] Monasteries consumed considerable quantities of hops; one in Vladimir was allowed to purchase annually, tax free, 40 puds of honey and 50 puds of hops.[27]

Hopped drinks were especially intoxicating; in the mid-fifteenth century the Venetian Iosaphat Barbaro commented that Russian mead and ale were hopped and that 'a drink results as stupefying and intoxicating as wine'.[28] Such hopped drinks, being able to be kept longer, might have a higher alcohol content. Paolo Giovio, basing himself on information supplied by a Russian interpreter in 1525, noted that the people 'drink mead which they make from honey and hops. It will keep for a long time in caulked barrels and acquires value with age.'[29] It is, thus, understandable why the term for hops (*khmel*') also meant 'drunkenness' and the related adjective 'drunken'.

Brewing mostly took place for special occasions. A late fifteenth century document refers to the preparation of mead, the brewing of beer and ale 'for St. Boris's day or for some lord's festival, or for a wedding or birth, or for Easter week'.[30] The Grand Prince's officers were to be informed and the man could then hold a drinking party 'for three days. But between those festivals he is not to keep drink by him. Nor is he to keep mead, beer and ale for sale.' Herberstein, who was in Moscow in the early sixteenth century, noted that 'drinking mead and beer is forbidden to the common folk save at certain times of the year, at Christmas, Shrovetide, Easter, Whitsun and a few other fixed seasons. They celebrate on these occasions more on account of the drink than from reverence.'[31] These were the occasions when there were 'feasts and fraternities' in the villages and hamlets of estates.[32] At this stage, though, there is usually no mention of any special place or building for such festivities. The lack of any such establishment no doubt made the efforts of the Grand Prince's officers to control drinking somewhat uncertain.

There was a long-standing problem, at least in the eyes of authority, of both personal and social behaviour at such festivities. According to the Metropolitan's Justice, a document dated about 1390–1430, if a wife went to a feast 'with other people', this was ground for a divorce.[33] Charters stress that violence might occur at these festivities; if loss was caused by intruders they were liable to a fine, frequently a double one, without more ado. To judge from the numerous fifteenth and sixteenth century documents dealing with intrusions by neighbouring peasants, and, especially, officials, the feasts and fraternities were regarded as opportunities not merely for free drink, but also for extortion and recruitment of labour by officials.[34]

Perhaps the resulting conflicts between officials and celebrating peasants gave rise to the aphorism that 'an uninvited guest is worse than a Tatar'. In 1504, for example, the Grand Prince gave an extensive list of intruders: the officials and court investigators of his Moscow representatives and volost heads, other people of the representatives and the volost heads, then his own manorial people, and finally boyars' slaves and serfs and the dependants of monasteries.[35] Other documents add grooms and kennelmen to the list. Apart from drink there would, of course, be food at such festivities, though the definition of military provisions of bread, beer and something to go with them (*vologa*) 'as for a feast' does not imply great luxury.[36] We have already seen that women also attended.

In the central areas of the Moscow state, then, drinking took place within the home, either by the family or by a larger group who formed a fraternity for the purpose of sharing both costs and enjoyment. There is little evidence in the first centuries after the Mongol invasions of special drinking houses and little if any attempt to control drinking, at least in the core of the emergent Russian state; in fact, we have much evidence of concern to avoid interference, especially by officials, with drinking in people's own homes. The only limitations were regulations aimed at limiting the right to brew intoxicating liquor to certain specific times of the year, or occasions, and to obtain income from the declarations made.

In areas more subject to influences from the Baltic region we find a somewhat different pattern. A section of a Pskov law book which is believed to date from the early fourteenth century laid down that: 'The prince's people are not to hold strong liquor (*korchma*) in their tenements, neither in Pskov, nor in the subject towns; nor are they to sell mead by the bucket or scoop nor by the barrel.'[37] Here, too, it appears that at this stage sales of liquor took place from dwellings. Later the term *korchma* came to mean 'tavern', a place where drink and food were to be had (but not one operating a state monopoly of alcoholic drinks). Even in the late fifteenth century, however, the term retained its meaning of 'strong liquor'. 'The German merchant is not to trade in Pskov in strong liquor or beer, but apart from strong liquor and beer any good may be freely taken into Pskov....'[38] Spirits in the late fifteenth century were evidently imported from Riga and Derpt (Yurevets). The tavern, then, was at first a dwelling place where food and drink were available for sale; sometimes it became a specialized institution. It was found mostly in the Baltic (Pskov), West Russian (Smolensk) and southern areas, but was unimportant in the central areas of Russia.[39]

A major change took place with the growth of the power of Moscow; this resulted in increased attempts to control social life and these took many forms. Among them were a series of measures against taverns, accompanied by a public outcry on the part of certain publicists. According to the testimony of foreigners in the late fifteenth century the brewing of beer, the making of mead and the use of hops were forbidden. 'Seeing that the people there, owing to drunkenness, abandon work and much else that would be useful to them, [the Grand Prince] issued a prohibition on the making of ale and mead and the use of hop flowers in anything at all.'[40] 'They are great drunkards and are exceedingly boastful of it, disdaining those who do not drink. They have no wines, but use a drink from honey which they make with hop leaves. This drink is not at all bad, particularly if it is old. However, their sovereign does not allow everyone to prepare it freely, because, if they were free to do so, they would be drunk every day and would kill one another like beasts.'[41]

Herberstein, who was in Moscow in the early sixteenth century, claimed that the Tsar, Vasilii Ivanovich (1505–33), built an establishment where his servitors could drink beer and mead 'because other Russians are prohibited from drinking mead and beer, save for a few days in the year'.[42] In 1544 Ivan IV sent an official to establish eight tavern houses (*korchemnykh dvorov*) in Novgorod.[43] These presumably were houses operating the Tsar's monopoly of drink; they led to such drunkenness that the archbishop of Novgorod, Feodosii, protested against taverns and, on 27 December 1548, the Tsar ordered the taverns and drinkshops (*pitie kobattskoe*) in Novgorod to be closed;[44] 'the reeves of the town quarters and streets, 30 men, were given two barrels of beer and six buckets of mead and one and a half buckets of bitter [*sc.* strong?] wine as an allocation'.

In the 1540s or possibly the early 1550s Ermolai-Erazm proposed taverns should be closed in Pskov and all the Russian towns. 'But if the taverns are not removed ... there shall be retribution for this on those who grow rich thereby.' He added that 'if, in the world's custom, men and women indulge in intoxicating drink, then certain sacrilegious persons will come, playing psalteries, viols, drones and drums and other devilish games, and playing pranks before the married women, leaping and singing ribald songs. Seeing this, the wife, who is already seated as if overcome by drunkenness, has lost the strength of sobriety and is prey to the desire for satan's game; her husband has also weakened, his mind is inclined to other women and he glances here and there with his eyes and caresses them; and each man gives a drink and kisses another's wife; and then there will be embraces accepted and insidious speeches woven and devilish mating.'[45]

The Tsar's policy, however, had both moral and financial aspects. The Tsar himself made this clear when he raised issues 'about the taverns granted in towns and in dependent towns and in volosts; they have been granted from of old, but now any representatives and those holding livings should set aside the ale-due from those lands, and there should be no tavern at all, since great harm is done to the peasants by the tavern and destruction to their souls.'[46]

What was this 'great harm'? It was in part the dangers of drunkenness and the 'immorality' which Ermolai-Erazm and others disapproved. But there were additional reasons for the hostility to drink and the attempts to control its use especially in social contexts. The mid-sixteenth century was a disturbed period in the Moscow state; there was much crime and brigandage on the roads. In a society with a low average density of population, and that population scattered for the most part in very small settlements of only three or four tenements, any focal point acquired particular importance in the social communications network. It was reasonable in such circumstances for the authorities to look on taverns as centres not merely of immorality, but also for the dissemination of unorthodox and hostile views and for the rallying of criminal oppositionists. This was the basis on which the attempt to establish a new institution took place. This institution was the drink-shop (*kabak*) which sold state-produced or licensed liquor; it was run either directly by state officials or was farmed out in return for a money payment. It is first clearly mentioned in the mid-sixteenth century.[47] The organization of the *kabak* had far-reaching implications. Domestic brewing, of course, long continued; for example, a Dvina customs farm charter of 1560 mentions hops on a par with grain in trade.[48]

Concern for state control of social and even private drinking is demonstrated by such documents as the charter for a number of volosts in the region of the Northern Dvina. 'If any people on the Penezhka and the Viya and on the Sura begin to keep a tavern the favoured heads [three names] and their fellows, ten persons, shall hold the tavern securely—so that on the Penezhka and on the Viya and on the Sura the volost peasants keep no drink for sale.'[49] Any peasant found with drink for sale was liable to heavy penalties: 2 roubles to be paid to the Grand Prince and 2 to the volost people; those drinking were to pay a quarter rouble. If anyone wished to celebrate a festival, to commemorate parents or so on, he could be allowed to do so 'for five days or a week' provided he made the necessary declaration.

Even closer control was imposed when in 1571 on Friday of Easter week, the privy clerks Semen, son of Fedor Mishin, and Aleksei Mikhalov Staroi rode in to Novgorod and forbade the boatmen to ferry people over the Volkhov; they ordered them to cross by the Great Bridge. They also forbade the dealers in spirits to trade and set up a check point on the Great Bridge; and if they caught a dealer with spirits on him or a man who was drunk, they ordered him to be beaten with the knout and cast into the water from the Great Bridge.[50]

In the mid-sixteenth century there was, thus, an attempt to control public drinking, both that involving sales and that by kin, friends or neighbours (who might, as we have seen, form a 'fraternity' for a celebration at common expense). Officials now had exclusive rights to keep and dispense alcoholic drinks and paid the Treasury for this right. At least, this was the situation on paper; but it is hard to believe that the domestic brewing of beer and ale and, where honey was available, the making of mead, did not continue.

The question of spirits is different. It is believed by some that vodka, i.e. a distilled alcoholic drink, reached Russia in the late fourteenth century.[51] It seems unlikely, however, that alcoholic products would reach Moscow from the Genoese colonies on the Black Sea coast (as has been suggested), since the Tatars had been converted to Islam in 1389.[52] Indeed, even the rare and costly imported wines ceased to come by this route.[53] A more likely route was via the Baltic; there were close relations between the Teutonic Order and Pskov, the Hanseatic League had a yard in Novgorod and there were other links. The import of strong drink by this important trade route was evident at least from the 1470s.[54]

Paolo Giovio noted that, apart from mead, the Russians drank 'beer [*birra*] and ale [*ceruisia*], as we see among the Germans and Poles; these drinks are made from wheat and rye or barley and are offered at every feast'.[55]

It is only in the late sixteenth century that there is more widespread documentary evidence for spirits produced in Russia. In 1588 a fine of 4 roubles was exacted in the St. Joseph Monastery, Volokolamsk, from those who had distilled its grain.[56] In 1597, significantly enough in Easter week, a survey official rode into a hamlet on an estate of the Patriarch and 'tormented the peasants and Mikhailo demanded from them beer and wine (*vino*) and food for himself and for his horse'.[57] At this date *vino* meant not only wine, but also spirits. A document of 1600 makes this clear. A complaint was made by a monastery that some junior boyars were continually making beer and wine and their slaves, peasants and labourers were selling it. An instruction was issued that 'you are to observe closely that the junior boyars Osip Ostrenev and his brothers, and other junior boyars in the Kurmysh uezd, are to distil wine and brew beer for themselves in the tenements. But the slaves in their tenements, and the peasants in their hamlets, are not to make beer and wine for themselves, nor to keep a tavern nor to sell wine to be taken away. If any junior boyar begins to keep a tavern or to sell wine to be taken away, you are ordered to take from them the drink and the stills and to impose a penalty on them. If drink for sale is taken for the first time, you are ordered to have a penalty of five roubles from each man and are

4

ordered to imprison him for one month. If anyone sells a second time, you are ordered to have a penalty of ten roubles, and the offenders are to be beaten in the market place with the knout, and cast into prison for half a year.'[58]

The class implications of drink were clear to foreigners at the end of the sixteenth century. 'Large tubs of sweet mead and beer were set for the people in different places in the Kremlin and each one was able to drink. Drinking beer and mead is the greatest pleasure [for Muscovites], especially when they are able to drink as much as they wish, and in this they are masters; most of all [they love] vodka which is forbidden all of them except the gentry and merchants' stock.'[59] In 1611 a prince was accused of various abuses against some monastic peasants. Among other offences the prince's men had ordered the peasants to 'distil wine and brew beer and prepare all sorts of provisions from their peasant grain'.[60] This material agrees closely in date with the earliest known Russian manuscript on distillation which is after 1542 and may be early seventeenth century.[61] By the late seventeenth century internal customs books record triple and quadruple stills.[62]

In the early seventeenth century the drinking habits of the invading Poles and Swedes no doubt impressed themselves on at least some levels of Russian society and encouraged some limited demand for spirits and imported wines. In general, though, the mass of the people continued whenever possible to brew and drink their domestic mead or beer, as they had done for many centuries. A monastery regulation of 1602 still laid down that 'if any peasant brews beer, a declaration is to be made and the payment is a denga a quarter of beer. But if any peasant brews beer and makes no declaration, he is liable to a fine of two roubles to be paid to the monastery. And they are to be ordered to drink quietly, so there shall be no fighting and violence and no criminal activity whatsoever.'[63] Quiet drinking, in fact, does not seem always to have taken place.

The authorities continued their efforts to control drinking and also to extract income from drinking by farming out the right to keep drink-shops through local officials.[64] By the middle of the seventeenth century 'in Moscow and in free settlements around Moscow many people making a living by trade and farmers of drink-shops live'.[65] This continuing reliance on the authorized drink-shop (*kabak*) meant that, in official language, the old word for tavern (*korchma*) had come to mean prohibited, secret or illegal drinking establishment. An instruction of 1618 states that 'the prohibited drink is ordered to be removed and given to the drink-shop official to be sold to the drink-shop; those dealing in prohibited drink and those consuming it are to be liable to exactions in accordance with the Sovereign's former order.'[66]

Evidently strong drink continued to be imported in the seventeenth century. A charter of 1636 mentions that 'they bring spirits (*vino goryachoe*) and all sorts of fine German drink from the sea coast to Solovki monastery'.[67] In 1639 a search of villages belonging to a monastery in Suzdal', remote from the coast and not directly on major trade routes, disclosed that 'Russian people and Germans and all sorts of foreigners keep by them prohibited drink which is for sale, spirits, beer and mead, also tobacco, raw and ground, and they trade and make a living by that prohibited drink.'[68]

The last chapter of the 1649 Code of Laws attempted to regulate such matters in detail. Severe penalties, both heavy fines and physical punishment and imprisonment, were to be imposed on those keeping taverns and similar penalties, but without imprisonment, applied to those drinking. Torture was to be used to establish the facts. There was a continuing class differentiation in the legislation. 'If anyone's people [i.e. slaves] or peasants [i.e. serfs] or yard-slaves are brought in and, when questioned, those people brought in tell them to whom they sold the spirits they had stolen from their boyars, those people brought in are to be tortured about selling the spirits, whether their boyars knew about that.'[69]

The production of spirits, because of the equipment and capital required, thus seems to have been largely in the hands of lords, presumably not always on a legal basis. This is evident from another section of this law which lays it down that 'the ten-men are to look and watch carefully in their tens [i.e. their districts] that, if any gentlemen and junior boyars whom anyone shall set up in tenements have spirits in accordance with declarations, those gentlemen and junior boyars shall have no extra spirits above what is in the declaration and shall not let anyone into their tenements without a declaration.'[70]

This control of strong drink was one means by which in the course of subsequent centuries lordly and state exploitation of the enserfed peasantry was realized. In the eighteenth and nineteenth centuries landlords with surplus grain converted it into spirits which found a constant legal market in the state monopoly; state income from the excise farm or from direct exercise of its monopoly became a major item, sometimes the largest item, on the income side of the state budget. An item of domestic production and consumption was converted into an instrument of exploitation.

Thus, by the mid-seventeenth century, when serfdom was finally legally imposed on the Russian people, they were also virtually deprived of the right in law to produce any domestic alcoholic drink.The increased availability of spirits was more easily controllable and the central authorites used this to attempt to impose a monopoly and to extract considerable income in the process. The New Office, one of the central state administrative departments, was the responsible body; it had a section known as the Drink-shop department. The usages established in Moscow by this department provided the basis for the 1649 legislation and were extended from Moscow to apply to other towns.[71]

## NOTES

1. *Povest' vremennykh let*, I, 1950, 60 (986).
2. The *Kievo-Pecherskii paterikon* mentions that boiled wheat was mixed with honey and served at table.
3. *Povest' vremennykh let*, I, 1950, 41–2.
4. *Gramoty Velikogo Novgoroda i Pskova* (hereafter *GVP*), no. 1 (1264). These officers are mentioned in the later contracts between town and prince.
5. I. I. Sreznevskii, *Materialy dlya slovarya drevnerusskogo yazyka*, I, 1203. *Novyi i polnyi rossiiskoi khozyaistvennoi vinokur*, II, 1802, 144–5, gives recipes for apple and pear kvas. D. A. Korolev, *Russkii kvass*, 1963, 4, writes that at the present time 'wild apples, pears, cranberries, red whortleberries, cloudberries, strawberries, blackcurrants and raspberries' are chiefly used.
6. Sreznevskii, loc. cit.
7. Sreznevskii, op. cit. II, 930 (c. 1100).
8. A. V. Artsikhovskii in *Ocherki russkoi kul'tury XIII-XV vekov* (hereafter *ORK*), I, 302.
9. *Russkaya istoricheskaya biblioteka*, VI, 1.122.
10. *Polnoe sobranie russkikh letopisei* (hereafter *PSRL*), IV, 85 (1328).
11. D. Galton, *Survey of a Thousand Years of Beekeeping in Russia*, 1971, 12.
12. A. L. Khoroshkevich, *Torgovlya, Velikogo Novgoroda s Pribaltikoi i zapadnoi Evropy v XIV-XV vekakh*, 1963, 328, notes that costly imported honey was sold mostly to lords.
13. J. Krizanic, *Politika*, 1663, I.3 noted how potash production interfered with the gathering of honey.
14. *PSRL*, IV.73.
15. *Cambridge Economic History*, I (revised), 540. The charter is translated in full in R. E. F. Smith, *The Enserfment of the Russian Peasantry*, 39–40.

16. *Akty sotsial'no-ekonomicheskoi istorii severovostochnoi Rusi* (hereafter *ASEI*), I, no. 264. Cp. nos. 356 (1467–74), 462 (1478–82); II, nos. 127 (1448–70), 386 (1470) and many others.

17. *Akty feodal'nogo zemlevladeniya i khozyaistva XIV-XVI vekov* (hereafter *AFZ*), I, no. 146 (1425–62). Cp. nos. 147 and 148 (1464–73).

18. *AFZ*, II, no. 129 (1534).

19. *AFZ*, II, no. 391 (1591).

20. *ASEI*, I, nos. 196 (1447–55); 373 (1467–74); *AFZ*, I, nos. 12, 32, 33; 100 (9 December 1525), 101 (15 November 1525); *Sbornik gramot Kollegii ekonomii*, no. 51 (1519–20); *GVP*, no. 122 (fifteenth century), 120.

21. *ASEI*, III, no. 56 (c. 1462–69).

22. *SGKE*, I, no. 61 (24 April 1528).

23. *PRP*, IV.434.

24. *Novgorodskie pistsovye knigi* (hereafter *NPK*), III, 738; cp. 682–3; V, 579–80; *ASEI*, I, no. 221 (second half of sixteenth century).

25. *NPK*, I, 439–41.

26. *GVP*, nos. 1 (1264), 2, 3, 6, 7, 9, 10, 14, 15, 19, 22, 26 (11 July 1471); *Pskovskaya 2-ya letopis'*, 163–4 (1467).

27. *ASEI*, III, no. 92 (22 October 1623). The pud is 16.38 kg or 36 lb.

28. *Viaggio alla Tana*, in *Barbaro i Kontarini o Rossii*, 1971, 133, 158.

29. Gerbershtein, *Zapiski o Moskovitskikh delakh*, Iovii Novokomskii, *Kniga o moskovitskom posol'stve*, ed. A. I. Malein, SPb., 1908, 272.

30. *AFZ*, II, no. 124 (1462–1505). St Boris's day was 2 May or 24 July, Old Style.

31. Sigmund von Herberstein, *Description of Moscow and Muscovy 1557* (ed. B. Picard), London, 1969, 93.

32. I have unfortunately not been able to consult A. Popov, *Piry i bratchiny*, Moscow, 1854.

33. *ASEI*, III, no. 8.

34. *ASEI*, I, no. 264 cited above. See also, Smith, *Enserfment*, 62.

35. *AFZ*, I, no. 70. Cp. no. 124; III, I, nos. 11 (1564), 14 (1567), 37 (1599), 48 (1605); III, Suppl. No. 5.

36. *Pskovskaya 2-ya letopis'*, 60 (1480).

37. *Pskovskaya sudnaya gramota*, in *Pamyatniki russkogo prava*, II.301.

38. *GVNP*, nos. 78 (13 January 1474), 134. Cp. *Pskovskie letopisi*, II.196; *PSRL*, IV.248–9.

39. I. Pryzhov, *Istoriya kabakov v Rossii*, 1868, 34.

40. Barbaro, *Viaggio alla Tana*, in *Barbaro i Kontarini o Rossii*, 133, 158. See note 31 above.

41. Contarini, *Viaggio in Persia*, ibid. 204–5, 328–9. Contarini was in Moscow in 1476–7.

42. Gerbershtein, *Zapiski*, 99.

43. *PSRL*, 30.205.

44. *PSRL*, 30.151.

45. *Letopis' zanyatii Arkheograficheskoi kommissii* (hereafter *LZAK*), XXXIII, 198.

46. Number 4 of Ivan IV's questions to Metropolitan Makarii, February 1550, *PRP*, IV.577–8.

47. See note 44 above; also Sreznevskii, *Materialy*, I.1169 (1563).

48. *LZAK*, XXXIV, 201–2.

49. *PRP*, IV, 194–5 (1570s).

50. *PSRL*, 30.158.

51. Pryzhov, *Ocherki*, 196; J. H. Billington, *The Icon and the Axe*, 1966, 86, 660–1.

52. Billington, loc. cit.

53. *ORK*, I, 304.

54. See note 38 above. Khoroshkevich, *Torgovlya*, 323–32 does not mention spirits, only wine.

55. Gerbershtein, *Zapiski o Moskovitskikh delakh*, 272. Malein's Russian translation mistakenly renders *ceruisia* as 'vodka'.

56. *Slovar' russkogo yazyka XI-XVII vv.*, vyp. 2, 183.

57. *AFZ*, III, section 2, no. 109.163.

58. *AFZ*, III, Section 1, no. 43 (27 October 1600).76. These penalties are the same as those in the Code of Laws (1649), chapter xxv, para. 1, where there are some additions.

59. Isaak Massa, *Skazaniya*. 65, referring to 1599.

60. *AFZ*, II, No. 428, 484.

61. N. A. Bogoyavlenskii, *Drevnerusskoe vrachevanie v XI-XVII vv.*, 1960, 74.

62. S. I. Sakovich, *Iz istorii torgovli i promyshlennosti Rossii kontsa XVII veka* (Tr. GIM, vyp. 30), 1956, 40, 83.

63. *AFZ*, III, 1, no. 44 (1602).

64. *Akty Moskovskogo gosudarstva*, I, 219–20.

65. *Akty Arkheograficheskoi ekspeditsii* (hereafter *AAE*), IV, 45 (1648). See also the 1649 Code of Laws, chapter xviii, paras. 21, 23.

66. *AAE*, III, 129.

67. *AAE*, III, 390.

68. *Akty yuridicheskie*, 101.

69. *Sobornoe ulozhenie 1649g.*, xxv, para. 6.

70. Op. cit. xxv, para. 20.

71. S. B. Veselovskii, 'K voprosu i sostave i istochnikakh XXV glavy Ulozheniya tsarya Alekseya Mikhailovicha', *Russkii Istoricheskii Zhurnal*, 1–2, 1917.

# 4

# The Kolkhoz and the Russian Muzhik

*(Private plots of the Soviet Kolkhozniki and their social impact)*[1]

MOSHE LEWIN

*University of Pennsylvania*

THE story of the private family plots farmed by members of the kolkhozy is, on the face of it, the story of a simple rural pastime or hobby, at best a means to vary the diet and earn some pocket-money on the city market by selling a few eggs or potatoes. What else would one expect from a sown area amounting to less than 4 per cent of the total, and distributed to the peasant families in small allotments of a maximum of half a hectare?

However, a closer look at these privately farmed plots shows that they are much more than a hobby. In fact, we are facing here one of the anomalies and paradoxes of Soviet social and economic life, rich in unexpected contradictions, and the consequences of these extend far beyond the apparently insignificant scale suggested by the figures on sown area.

The official views seem, at the first approach, to minimize the importance of the phenomenon: the privately farmed plots are but a subsidiary and only temporary activity of the peasants whose main efforts and interests lie in their membership and work in the kolkhozy, those large-scale, highly mechanized and modern socialist enterprises. But there are also other arguments in the official views, appeals for vigilance and numerous campaigns organized by the government about and against these plots, which raise some questions in our minds. The energy displayed by these campaigns betrays the government's awareness that the phenomenon may have been far more significant than is suggested by the idea of its transient and 'subsidiary' character.

The history of these plots—the way in which it all began in the winter of 1929–30 with an all-out collectivization drive and the virtually wholesale expropriation of peasant cattle, including small animals,[2] and then further zigzags of policy and stubborn peasant resistance—was certainly dramatic, violent and often led to bloodshed. Much of it revolved around the plot, the unwillingness to part with the horse, but especially the cow—the family's mainstay and the peasant women's *sine qua non*. The first years of 'collectivization' were full of massive and persistent riots of the womenfolk which were caused by what Stalin later called 'our minor misunderstanding' with the kolkhoz women 'about the cow'[3]—certainly an understatement trying to play down what really amounted to a major social contest between the peasantry and the State. The problem consisted of more than just these types of riots—but those were among the most direct and violent acts of opposition to the government during the first years of collectivization.

By 1935 the government seemed to have learned the lesson and have reached a decision to compromise with the peasants by legalizing the plot fully, and guaranteeing in the new status of the kolkhoz the right to a certain number of cattle to be kept on the family farm.[4] Though this status was not openly challenged after that, the problem was far from over. The government kept a constant watch over this activity and engaged in counter-attacks alleging the abuse by the kolkhozniki of the plots and accusing them of pursuing private commercial gain at the expense of the collective sector of the kolkhozy. One of the fiercest of such attacks occurred under Stalin just before the war (there were several more after the war and under Khrushchev), when a stern law of 27 May 1939 signed by Stalin and Molotov claimed that the peasants, with the connivance of kolkhoz managements and local authorities, surreptitiously enlarged the plots and the number of cattle, minded their private interests and tended to shirk in the kolkhozy. A vociferous campaign was instigated clamping down on the plot owners with new taxes and procurement quotas. Special government controllers were created to check the size of the plots and the economic activity on them, and a huge network of committees was set up to measure the plots, cut down the unlawful extra and return it to the kolkhozy.

The campaign was presented in the propaganda channels as an anti-capitalist drive and it had at least two important results. First, as figures disclosed in the 1960s showed, the whole activity was one of the numerous exercises in aberration quite characteristic of Stalin's Russia; on the whole, the kolkhoz peasantry did not even fully use its statutory limits in terms of number of cattle and the legal size of plots.[5] Only 10.4 per cent of the kolkhoz households might have eventually overstepped the limits by small amounts[6] and much of the land confiscated from these transgressors was very poor or otherwise unusable and the kolkhozy who got it 'back' had no use for it.

The second factor was no less important: the clamping down on the plot caused the numbers of cattle to fall—something the country just could not afford in view of the tense situation with food supplies and the war already on the doorstep. Such blows to popular consumption and welfare were the constant and predictable result of every campaign against the plots.

It is not difficult to see why. According to one estimate, in 1938 about 45 per cent of total farm output was produced on the 3.9 per cent of sown area which was worked privately by the peasant families (0.49 ha. per household). The kolkhoz family derived from this plot half of its money income, almost all of its animal foodstuff and most of its potatoes and vegetables, while the kolkhoz supplied them mainly with grain.[7] The family plot, apart from producing 52.1 per cent of the kolkhozy's potatoes and most of the fruit and vegetables, maintained over half of the country's cattle and most of the cattle available in the kolkhozy,[8] and they produced 71.4 per cent of the milk, 70.9 per cent of the meat and 43 per cent of all wool.[9] At the same time these tiny enterprises, through sales to the city population on kolkhoz markets, contributed the impressive share of some 20 per cent of all marketed food supplies[10] and supported friends and relatives in the city with gifts. They also provided the government with procurements and contracts, which became particularly exacting in 1939.[11] This performance was achieved through something like 6 per cent of the labour input of adult males and 33.6 per cent of the women's labour.[12] Not unexpectedly, as became clear very soon to the government's experts, the kolkhoznik earned more from the plot than from the kolkhoz,[13] and his workday on the plot gave him, in 1937 and again in 1938, twice as much as the day's work on the kolkhoz.[14]

This is not the whole story but it is enough for us to conclude that the small plot fed the peasantry and contributed decisively to the country's agricultural output and to the food supplies. It was, despite its small scale, a major economic branch and an indispensable producer. It was also, as Soviet writers admit today, a factor sustaining not only the country but the whole kolkhoz system as well. Such facts bring us far away from the official image of an auxiliary and transitory activity. The private small enterprises look rather like a 'giant dwarf', an important and vital producer, and this is why whenever the government tampered with it beyond a certain point, a worsening of the country's food situation followed automatically.

But why should the government have indulged in warfare against the plots? An exhaustive answer to this question will not be attempted here. However, the whole problem will get into proper focus if the general situation of the country's agricultural production is presented. During the years of the First and Second Five-year Plans, till the bumper crop of 1937, agricultural production kept falling, animal foodstuffs and grain alike. Only the figures for the three and a half years of the pre-war, unfinished Third Five-year Plan showed an improvement. After 1934 the numbers of cattle stopped falling, and together with grain production began slowly to increase. But, as corrected official figures published after Stalin's death have shown, there was no reason for jubilation. By 1940 the country produced less animal foodstuffs than in 1916, a war year. It did produce somewhat more grain than in Tsarist Russia, though not much more than in NEP, and this was achieved through an enlargement of sown area without any significant qualitative progress. The average yields were only 7.7 quintals per hectare, still no better than under the pre-collectivization system, and still extremely low despite the vaunted benefits of modern large-scale organization, of kolkhozy and sovkhozy, with their hundreds of thousands of tractors and combines, with numerous ministries and so on.[15] It was against the background of such poor results—in view of the growing number of mouths to be fed many would agree that they were indeed catastrophic—that the performance of the private plots in this overall output looked so outstanding. They were more efficient, more reliable than the kolkhozy and sovkhozy, and without them the peasants and the country would have starved. Thus the country needed this sector of private peasant activity.

But the government was not ready to interpret these facts as manifestations of a failure of its policies and an expression of the need to accept an open and frank compromise between the two sectors for the benefit of both: grain and industrial crops on the kolkhoz fields, cattle and vegetables on the private farms with state help in fodder, agronomy, supplies. Instead, a 'rotten compromise' prevailed, unacknowledged and vociferously denied, which helped to transform eventually complementary activities on plots and in the kolkhozy into competing and contradictory, alien forces. State policies and ideology preferred it that way.

The kolkhoz system, as it emerged by 1933, represented a combination of three sectors, locked in an uneasy, antagonistic coexistence. First, there was the large kolkhoz with its administrations. Second, the state-owned Machine and Tractor Stations were given work on kolkhoz fields in accordance with a contract signed with the kolkhoz. Finally, the third sector was formed by the multitude of private plots. On the face of it, a symbiosis was supposed to reign between the three. In fact, as has been said, the picture was less idyllic: in each of the three sectors there were serious discrepancies between ideological and constitutional statements, and reality. The kolkhoz, being in theory a co-operative, was supposed to be run by administrations freely elected and supervised by the general assembly of its members. In fact, kolkhoz leaders were superciliously watched by local administrations and the police, and were summarily dismissed and appointed at will. The co-operative principle was thus no more than a fiction.

The MTS, state agencies that were created in theory to service their client kolkhozy and to do for them the job they wanted for a reasonable reward, were in fact the real bosses on the fields, geared to squeeze grain out of the kolkhozy, to 'plan' and control them, and to exercise political and police supervision. This bureaucratic organization was created because the kolkhozy could not afford, or rather, the government felt, could not be trusted with agricultural machinery. The MTS were inefficient organizations, often in conflict with and frequently mishandling the kolkhozy, which had little recourse against them and their power.

The plot, the most efficient producer of them all, was in theory a small supplementary device. But, at the same time, the ideologists and the politicians magnified it into something quite unusual: its very existence was seen as a result of 'survivals of a petty-bourgeois mentality', its activity was basically motivated by the peasant's lust for private gain and his commercial spirit, and the whole sector was presented as an alien body in socialist society. Thus the peasantry as plot owners were ideologically illegitimate, deeply immoral, and barely tolerated for the time being.

The whole so-called collectivized agricultural organization thus resembled a peculiar awkwardly shaped cart with two huge wheels and one small, one big wheel dragging the peasants not too willingly into a pseudo-cooperative, the other supplying them with machinery over which they had no say, and the small third one feeding them. At the same time the three disproportionate wheels, instead of really pulling in one direction, were badly co-ordinated, and all too often blocked each other, each of them operating under different constraints and a different, often contradictory system of motivations. Without massive state coercion nothing of this kind could have existed for long in such a form. It did of course continue to exist, but the results of such husbandry, not unexpectedly, were extremely disappointing.

The government, frustrated by the weakness of what it had hoped would soon become a superior social and economic form, and seeing it easily beaten as producer by the dwarf plots, tended to present the plots and peasant greed as the main culprit of the poor results of the new agricultural system. It claimed therefore that the main problem consisted in 're-educating' the peasant and changing his mentality.

*En attendant*, the system did not look like a very 'pedagogic' institution. It could not have been one with this kind of ideological attitude which distorted reality and produced faulty analysis. The problem with the plot was not so much a 'backward mentality', but its simple economic necessity. The branch was not subsidiary or auxiliary, but indispensable. The labour put into it was hard and honest and the motivations legitimate and fully comprehensible. To present this labour as somehow 'immoral', suspect etc., was the result of the ideologist's own distorting mirror that prevented him from seeing things as they were. The conflict with the peasants was imposed on them by political constraints and ideological predilection which were no more than an expression of an attempted rape of social realities. Moreover, the principles the government set out to inculcate were not the ones of co-operation, solidarity, and economic progress. Rather, they involved the imposition with iron gloves—anything else would not do—of the very different principle of absolute priority and superiority of the interests of the State over the interests of the producers. In practice, it amounted therefore to a system where state procurement, rather than production became the central axis of the relations between the State and its kolkhozy, with a third or more of the output being extracted from the kolkhozy for no more than a nominal price which covered only a small part of their production cost. This was the central principle from which stemmed all the other traits of the system. 'Material responsibility' instead of 'material stimulation'—such is the highly critical verdict of a modern Soviet author even though he uses, for obvious reasons, quite guarded terms.[16]

It all ended up in a system which could not be a rational economic proposition. Not surprisingly, terms like cost, profitability, material interests and material incentives were excluded from official thinking. Forced deliveries, forced minima of workdays to be spent on kolkhozy fields, detailed production plans imposed from above—a whole system, in fact, forced from above—justify the assessment by a western scholar that the kolkhoz became 'a system of forced labour'.[17] Shadows of the past could be seen in this situation, ever more reminiscent of what was abolished in 1861. The peasant reacted by, as it were, splitting his personality as producer and employing two measures according to two different types of motivation. One when working 'for them', the other when working for his family. This was similar to what happened in the system of serfdom when there was nonchalance and neglect on the fields of the *pomeshchik*, and hard work on his own farmland. Behind the *pomeshchik* stood the might of the State, behind the kolkhoz and the MTS stood the State too; but it had a more difficult task now than the old State, namely, to 're-educate' not only the peasants but the kolkhoz administrations as well.

The disquieting parallel with serfdom runs even deeper when it is realized that the kolkhoz regime under Stalin strait-jacketed the peasantry into an economic and juridical system which discriminated against them in more than one way. Peasants had to suffer not only from the 'normal' disadvantages of rural backwardness (which are still at work today)—bad schools, few cultural amenities, bad roads —but they were also declared an inferior class and treated accordingly. Their remuneration for labour was based on the 'residual principle' without the guaranteed income which other classes enjoyed.[18] There was no social security system for them, no help for housing, a system of state duties to which nobody else was subjected, special higher prices to pay for goods, the denial of passports in order to control their mobility, and an elaborate and heavy system of taxation directed against their private plots.[19] The fact of having to run their plots could also be construed as a handicap, rather than some kind of privilege.

Thus the State, awaiting the abolition of classes in a very next historical stage, 'told' the peasants quite firmly that they were a suspect and inferior class. The peasants knew it anyway. As the State stood over their heads and forced on them its 'first commandment'—this was the biblical term actually employed—'supply the State first', the peasants responded quite audibly: 'supply yourself and your family first.' The lesson they learned from experience taught them, in essence, that 'if you don't take care of your family nobody will, it will starve'. This was a fact of life which is freely admitted today by some Soviet authors. In this situation a deep and basic clash of interests was bound to develop: the State perceiving the peasant as dangerous to the foundations of the regime, and the peasant viewing the State as a menace to the survival of his family.

Only in the 1960s did it become possible in the Soviet Union to state some of these truths as well as the paradoxical fact that, despite the economic and ideological warfare conducted by the government against the plots during those years, 'the private plot was in fact the only stimulus to participation in social production',[20] and thus the system's saviour *malgré soi*!

Nevertheless, for over a generation Soviet agriculture found itself locked in a vicious circle which did not allow it to advance this branch—a problem that is far from being resolved satisfactorily even today. In terms used by a Soviet author, kolkhoz production does not grow because productivity of labour does not grow and this happens because the kolkhoznik is not interested in working in conditions of very low income. 'But improving his income is impossible because production does not grow.'[21] This author has in mind some of the backward kolkhozy in the 1960s. In fact, this diagnosis applies well to the whole system in the past as well as, to an important degree, the present.

In this situation of stagnation in agriculture, the position the peasantry found itself in—the position of an 'estate' discriminated 'from above'—was strongly reinforced and perpetuated 'from below' by the activity of the kolkhoz families on their private plots. Both factors, the State and private enterprise, helped to shape the social realities of the Soviet countryside in an unexpected way. The traditional peasantry was supposed to become 'modernized' in the process of collectivization and industrialization of agriculture, to the extent of actually withering away and changing its social substance. In fact, the kolkhoz system developed a quite different tendency in relation to those peasants who remained on the land. They showed no signs of withering away. Quite the contrary.

As we have said, the State created a situation in which it laid a priority claim to what the kolkhozy produced. But the peasants were supposed to run this system themselves, although it neither fed them nor offered them any guaranteed income. In addition to labouring in the kolkhoz they were supposed to take care of their families and much of the rest of the country as well. Their perception of the reality in which they found themselves reminded them of the duality experienced by their ancestors in serfdom and they responded with the traditional diffidence towards the State—as was the case with peasants for generations. An old tradition was here simply continued and was fully reflected in the consciousness of a class identity shaped by conflicting forces.

To be sure, there was no longer an oppressive landowning class. Instead a new social force emerged: the bureaucracy of an industrializing state. But while the state rushed ahead into the age of machines and mass communications, its peasants were socially 'frozen' in an earlier stage, if they did not actually move backwards. There were, of course, tractors and combines on kolkhoz fields, but even with these there was a problem: this technology was implanted without enhancing the country's agricultural production for at least a generation. The factory system, where the machine does not belong to the worker, was a source of immense rise in productivity and this was the case with the soviet system too, despite difficulties and impediments to innovation and technical progress. The kolkhoz, on the other hand, unlike the factory, was not the result of an organic development. It was 'invented' and imposed by the State, and here the main means of production were expropriated. It was to become a botched up transplant, with clear elements of rejection. For a long time massive evidence pointed to the fact that kolkhoz fields were a cemetery for tractors. Peasants broke them, misused them, were not interested. And as far as the plot was concerned, this big machinery was entirely irrelevant. The activity of the plot was entirely outside the technological age. It consisted in the most old-fashioned, archaic, physical work.

But however small and technically backward the plot was, it was still a manifestation of a full-fledged, small-scale, private entre-preneurship. The dependence of the peasant family on the plot for its livelihood—which sometimes made the income from the kolkhoz look 'subsidiary' rather than the other way round—gave a powerful incentive to work with zeal on the plot and to seek out other private sources of income whenever available, and to do the unavoidable minimum in the kolkhoz. This forced the government to undertake action against mass shirking by imposing legal minima of workdays, coupled with penalties for failure to do so.[22] What was at stake, as the peasant understood it, was the survival of the peasant's household and of the family. In order to solve the problem the peasant resorted to his traditional form of economic activity: using and reinforcing the family as a unit of economic activity. It is immediately obvious that such an outcome ought to have had important consequences for the outlook of the Soviet peasantry.

Since the plot was a crucial economic sector, it served as a basis for the perpetuation of the traditional behaviour and attitudes of the peasantry. Deprived of social security and a guaranteed income, the homestead and the plot and the efforts of the family became the only sources of such elementary and basic needs. The peasant hut offered lodging, and the farm offered support for the elderly and milk for the kids. Behind the hut were the cowshed and other farm buildings, the form and substance of an old peasant household (*dvor*), with its sense of cohesion and mutual dependence. The position and role of women and children as well as the elderly continued as ever on the old lines, maybe even increasing the burden on women who became the main factor in running the plot as well as doing work in the kolkhoz. This involved also the tedious and time-consuming business of travelling, often every day in suburban areas, to carry small amounts of eggs, meat, butter or vegetables to the markets—the most important source of family cash.[23] But the trading on markets, apart from being a waste of time which modern methods of organization could have avoided, perpetrated an old dimension characteristic of the life of the peasant family: its dependence on and vulnerability to market fluctuations, Gosplan notwithstanding.

The serious activity on the plot thus added a burden of working hours which other classes did not share, and deprived the peasant of many opportunities to broaden his cultural horizons. Modern Soviet sociologists have grasped the full implications of this factor. Some have pointed out that the private plots of even the sovkhoz and industrial workers, still widespread and economically quite important, influence the outlook and mentality of those involved.[24] The much bigger peasant plot is an even weightier economic and social factor. Although indispensable in order to bring the peasant's income to the level of industrial workers, it has in fact retarded the much-heralded fusion of social classes by perpetuating many classical traits of the peasantry,[25] and maintaining it as a family-based agricultural entrepreneurship. Moreover, the conditions in which this entrepreneurship has been exercised have impeded agricultural progress and encouraged the most archaic methods: primitive physical labour, rather ridiculous conditions of commercialization, and a very low level of consumption. In fact, well into Khrushchev's days the mass of peasants still suffered from underconsumption.[26] Thus, precarious economic conditions, characteristic of small peasants in many regimes, which left no energy for long-term calculations and risk-taking, made family survival dependent simply on the next crop. The psychological traits which such a situation produced in the peasant mentality are notorious: conservatism and sticking to routine, fear of change, opposition to technology, distrust of the cities and of city dwellers, and alienation from the State with its officials, judges, policemen.

In other words, the social effects of the functioning of the kolkhoz system, for a generation at least, consisted in reproducing backward Russian *muzhiki* instead of the modern co-operative industrialized farmers. If anything, these Soviet muzhiks might have become more interested in private property and private farming than they ever were before. Until 1906 the Russian peasants had a very vague concept, if any, of private property,[27] and the well-known efforts of Stolypin and his reforms between 1906 and 1910 were necessary to inculcate in them a degree of dedication to this concept. This was a conscious, not fully successful effort. One may ponder over the possibility that in its Stalinist stage collectivization, although aiming at uprooting such attitudes, went in fact a long way towards reinforcing and developing them.

There was nothing new for the muzhik when official Russia did not recognize his labour for what it was, when it was seen not as hard and honest, but as some kind of a nuisance. This was an insult which the muzhik could take. He was used to being at the bottom of the social ladder and tried to make the best of it, which had significant, sometimes incalculable, effects on the country's destiny. Here was a

5

manifestation of what Russian writers called, approvingly or dis-approvingly according to their ideological predisposition, the old 'muzhik might' (*muzhitskaia sila*).

This vague concept had, nevertheless, a powerful content behind it, expressing the economic, social and cultural influence of old rural Russia and its effect on the behaviour and mentality of Russian society as a whole in the process of becoming an industrialized and urban country. On the one hand powerful forces eroded large sec-tions of the peasantry by absorbing them into non-rural employ-ments; on the other hand, contradictorily, other forces reinforced and reproduced the muzhik. As long as this was true, the old *muzhitskaia sila* was bound to continue and mightily influence the nation and the state system. The fact that these influences and interests of the peasantry were not allowed open forms of expression, through literature or other free channels, did not prevent the opera-tion of deep-seated trends. The moralizing propaganda against petty bourgeois mentality and *melkosobstvennichestvo* or, for that matter, against religious beliefs, would fill out the editorials and speeches, but real cultural and social processes would of course go on un-abated, forming widespread subcultures and distinct modes of beha-viour. The dictatorial method of *zagoniat' vnutr'*, instead of letting interests and ideas out into the open, had a distorting effect on national development, with many subterranean streams of un-acknowledged force quietly taking over the minds of masses of people away from the official clichés, though not always in the most palatable directions. But such considerations bring us far beyond the scope of this study.

To reiterate briefly the gist of our argument. The private plot had a paradoxically disproportionate influence: it was an economically restricted, but a socially powerful force in the shaping of a class. It made the social history of Russia under Stalin, as well as after him, a more complex affair than appearances and clichés would suggest. It entailed the preservation of a rather backward peasantry in an other-wise very dynamic setting. But this was only one instance of a broader phenomenon in Stalinism, in which the dynamism of in-dustrial development and social restructuring went hand in hand with the baffling phenomenon of perpetuation and recreation of much of the imperial past.

# NOTES

1. This paper deals mainly with the period up to about the mid-fifties or, roughly, the period of Stalin's rule. Since then many changes have occurred in the ways Soviet agriculture works and in the position of the peasantry, but it is assumed that many important traits of the past still persist. Some of the problems of the later period are covered in the paper by Prof. Kerblay.

2. Soviet researchers published in the sixties material from the archives showing that although a special high ranking body appointed by the Central Committee in November 1929 to decide about how to collectivize and what to do with the richer peasants recommended the preservation of private plots and especially letting every family keep a cow in private possession, such provisions were simply deleted from the proposed decree by Stalin and Molotov, causing havoc to Soviet agriculture. See V. P. Danilov (ed.), *Ocherki po istorii sel'skogo khoziaystva v soiuznykh respublikakh*, Moscow, 1963, p. 19, and B. A. Abramov, in *Voprosy Istorii KPSS*, 1 (1964), p. 40.

3. Stalin spoke about this 'minor misunderstanding about the cow' on the first Congress of Kolkhoz shock-workers in 1933. See *Na agranom fronte*, 2–3 (1935), p. 9.

4. The statute of the kolkhozy became law in February 1935. It allowed the family a plot of one-fourth to half an hectare, at least one cow, calves and specified numbers of sheep, pigs and unlimited numbers of fowl.

5. The Law 'Concerning measures to safeguard socialized land from embezzlement' is in *Sobranie uzakonenii*, 34 (1939), § 235. For an assessment showing that peasants did not actually fully use the norms for land and cattle ownership, see Iu. V. Arutiunian's article in *Voprosy Filosofii*, 5 (1966), pp. 51–61.

6. V. B. Ostrovskii, *Kolkhoznoe krest'yanstvo SSSR*, Saratov, 1966, p. 69; and *Kolkhozy vo vtoroi stalinskoi piatiletke*, statistical handbook, Moscow, 1939, pp. 11–12.

7. See Karl-Eugen Wädekin, *The Private Plot in Soviet Agriculture*, Berkeley, Los Angeles, London, 1973, p. 57; M. A. Vyltsan, using material from the archives in *Voprosy Istorii*, 9 (1963), p. 27.

8. These figures for 1937 are in Vyltsan, ibid. pp. 17, 19.

9. Ostrovskii, *Kolkhoznoe krest'yanstvo*, p. 91.

10. G. I. Shmelev, *Lichnoe podsobne khozyaistvo i ego svyazi s obshchestvennym proizvodstvom*, Moscow, 1971, pp. 110–11.

11. Ostrovskii, *Kolkhoznoe*, p. 131 for the year 1940; but we should add that youngsters and the elderly also worked.

12. This was admitted already by D. Lurye, in *Bolshevik*, 22 (1934), pp. 36–7.

13. Wädekin, *The Private Sector*, p. 197—but not after 1964 any more. A Soviet author, V. A. Morozov, in *Trudoden', den'gi i torgovlya na sele*, Moscow, 1965, assessed for the year 1964 that one hour's work on the plot produced 2–3 times more income than one hour in the kolkhoz.

14. Some of the relevant figures from Soviet sources are used in my 'Taking Grain' in S. Abramsky (ed.), *Essays in Honour of E. H. Carr*, London, 1974, pp. 305–10. It also contains the relevant information on procurements and prices paid to producers—referred to later in the article.

15. Morozov, *Trudoden', den'gi*, p. 9.

16. Cf. V. V. Gusev, *Kolkhoz kak samoupravlyaishchayasya sistema*, Moscow, 1971, p. 31.

17. Wädekin, *The Private Sector*, p. 18.

18. This meant that the kolkhoznik was paid only from what remained after the kolkhoz paid its debts to the state and deducted material and financial means to its own production funds. Sometimes not much remained. The kolkhoznik did not know what he could expect till the end of the year and he had not much influence on this 'residual'. Morozov, in *Trudoden', den'gi*, p. 113, calling this *ostatochnyi rezhim* exclaimed bitterly: 'in truth, how could one speak of cost accounting and profitability in the kolkhoz if any mismanagement in it can be covered up by the expense of just curtailing the pay for the kolkhoznik's labour.'

19. Shmelev complained about these taxes as exactions, in *Lichnoe podsobnoe*, pp. 111, 112, and lists them as: direct procurements, market tax, milling tax, compulsory insurance of cattle and crops, voluntary contribution to culture-cum-lodging fund which became a normal obligatory tax. All are abolished today. But let us note that these were, except the last, levied from peasants only.

20. Morozov, ibid. p. 176.

21. Morozov, ibid. pp. 172–3.

22. N. Aristov, in *Planovoe Khozyaistvo*, 11 (1939), p. 94, explains the reasons for those minima and other disciplinary measures by the fact that millions of kolkhozniks tended to do nothing in the kolkhoz.

23. *Problemy Ekonomiki*, 3 (1940) devoted an article to the problem of time spent by kolkhozniki in reaching markets and trading on them. The article somewhat embellished the situation, but the fact remains that millions of working days went into it.

24. L. S. Bliakhman, O. I. Shkaratan, *NTR, rabochii klass i intelligentsiya*, Moscow, 1973, p. 210.

25. Arutiunian, in *Voprosy Filosofii*, 6 (1966), p. 57.

26. By 1940 about one-third of the kolkhoz family had no cows. There were 18.5 million homesteads in kolkhozy and only 12.5 million had cows. Some of them might not have wanted cows, but on the whole cowlessness was a traditional Russian syndrome of poor peasants.

27. Michael T. Florinsky, *The End of the Russian Empire*, New York, 1961, p. 180.

# 5

# Peasant Family Economy in the
# USSR today

## BASILE KERBLAY
*Université de Paris*

ALTHOUGH the stir caused by A. V. Chayanov's theories on the specific features of peasant economy provoked heated discussions in the 1920s, by the 1950s it had largely subsided; in fact, it was all but forgotten. Naum Jasny, pioneer of the history of Soviet agriculture, was one of the few authors to quote Chayanov.[1] The latter's name was not unfamiliar to me when, in 1961–2, Daniel Thorner asked me to collaborate in his research on the concept of peasant economy.[2] But little did I suspect the import and originality of this Russian economist whose *magnum opus* was still unknown to me. Thanks to Daniel Thorner's untiring enthusiasm, a patient search in public and private libraries in the United States as well as in Europe enabled us to reconstitute the greater part of the corpus and to publish, under the auspices of the American Economic Association, the translation of *Organizatsiya krest'yanskogo khozyaistva* (1925).[3] This volume also presents the main points of the debate on the nature of transformations in peasant economy between Marxist economists and economists of the organizational school led by Chayanov, to which the publication of his book in the USSR at the end of the NEP gave rise.

Our aim here is to try to establish what is left, after fifty years of collectivization in the USSR, of the family economy which appears under all regimes, regardless of their level of development, as a universal characteristic of rural society.

Certainly peasant family economy is no longer a dominant sector in the USSR, and for this reason the Soviet authorities refer to it as *auxiliary economy* (*podsobnoe khozyaistvo*). It is no longer the family's main source of income. Moreover, activities in this sector are strictly regulated by the statutes of the *kolkhoz* or *sovkhoz*.

## Dimensions and evolution of the family economy

In 1970, 34 million Soviet families profited from an auxiliary economy (a small plot of land and in some cases a few heads of livestock). This number included not only kolkhoz families—15.5 million households—but also 14 million rural non-kolkhoz households, of which 7.5 million were sovkhoz households.[4] In addition 4 million urban industrial and office workers had access to plots. Thus the total greatly exceeded the number of families and individuals living in the countryside.[5]

The importance of this auxiliary sector is not the same from one socio-professional group to another, not only because of differences in income, but also because the size of farms allowed by the legislation varies according to family categories and rural regions. Furthermore, a distinction must be made between what belongs to the family (the *dvor*, i.e. the house and farm, the cattle and poultry, the implements and small tools[6]), and what the family is allowed to use: the plot adjoining the house (*usad'ba*) or the allotment outside the village (*uchastok*).

In the kolkhozy, a family need have only one active member to benefit from the right to cultivate a piece of land not exceeding half a hectare, as stipulated by the model statute currently in force (December 1969). However, this limit is rarely reached since the actual average is about 2,500–3,000 square metres if we do not include certain grazing and mowing concessions on communal land.[7] Since the decree of 6 March 1956, kolkhoz assemblies alone have the right to determine the size of individual allotments taking into account the collective work carried out in the kolkhoz. This is a threat to those who might be tempted to neglect their duties; a legal minimum of work in the kolkhoz was instituted in 1940; it varies according to age and sex.[8]

As for livestock, the 1969 statute allows the republics to establish norms in accordance with local traditions. As a general rule, the kolkhoz family farm can have a cow and its calf, a sow and its piglets, three sheep and their lambs, but no draft animals, about thirty fowls and a few hives. Exceptions to this rule are allowed in republics where stock-farming is a tradition: for example, the possession of a horse or a greater number of cattle, especially among the

Buryat, or of a small herd of reindeer among the peoples of the far North. Donkeys are more generally tolerated because of their frugality: they can survive on a few thistles and some salt in the Caucasian and Asian regions, where they are indispensable on the mountain trails. In fact, livestock statistics show that less than 60 per cent of rural families have a cow or a pig; on the other hand, 80 per cent of the goats are in private hands, probably because this 'poor man's cow' is much easier to feed.[9]

In the sovkhozy, family farms, where they exist, are only on sufferance. They are not guaranteed by legislation: quite the contrary. Allotments may not exceed 1,500 square metres, except in sovkhozy recently constituted from kolkhozy, where the old norms have been retained. *A fortiori*, other categories living in rural areas can only hope to obtain a plot within the limits of the available land reserves by applying to the executive committee of the rural soviet which is responsible for their use. In all cases, the enjoyment of an individual plot can be questioned if the interested party, whether a member of a kolkhoz or not, uses it for commercial ends, or if he leaves it uncultivated for more than two years. The agricultural tax on private incomes is doubled when the legal norms for the possession of livestock are exceeded.[10] Regulations concerning the commercialization of agricultural surplus and its sale on the markets also have the effect of maintaining the auxiliary character of the family farm and of preventing it from degenerating into a profit-making enterprise.

The various limitations imposed on private agricultural activities, the difficulties in obtaining fodder, and the growth of monetary incomes, have not however led to a significant decrease in absolute terms of the private sector (see Table i). It is true that in comparison with 1940, the decrease in area under private cultivation has been considerable, in particular for cereals. But as a basis for comparison, 1940 is rather exceptional, since in this year sizeable regions characterized by non-collectivized agriculture (i.e. Eastern Poland) were absorbed into the Soviet Union. Between 1953 and 1972, the decrease in livestock and in area under private cultivation follows a curve which corresponds to the decrease in the rural population. In relative terms, on the other hand, as a result of the progress of collective agriculture, the proportion of family-produced vegetables and animal products has clearly decreased: one-third of the total production of milk and meat in 1972 as compared with more than 70 per cent in

1940. With regard to the cultivation of potatoes and fruit more than 60 per cent remains in private hands, but this now represents only one-third of the commercialized production. The evolution in the collective production of eggs is even more remarkable—11 per cent

TABLE I

EVOLUTION OF THE FAMILY SECTOR IN SOVIET AGRICULTURE

|  | 1940 | 1953 | 1972 |
|---|---|---|---|
| *Rural population* (millions) | 131 | 107 | 102.5 |
| *Area under family plots* (millions of hectares) | 19.7 | 6.9 | 6.7 |
| of which: cereals | 10.9 | 1.6 | 1.0 |
| vegetables and potatoes | 5.3 | 4.6 | 5.1 |
| area per family (sq. metres) | 3,600 | 2,500 | 2,600 |
| *Hours worked* (annual units in millions) |  |  |  |
| kolkhoz families | 6.7 | 6.6[a] | 0.9[a] |
| other families | 1.8 | 2.9[a] | 4.7[a] |
| all families | 8.5 | 9.5[a] | 5.6[a] |
| *Private herds* (millions) |  |  |  |
| bovines | 31.1 | 23.3 | 24.6 |
| milch cows | 21 | 14.9 | 14.7 |
| pigs | 16.1 | 15.1 | 13.3 |
| sheep | 33.7 | 14.6 | 27.7 |
| goats | 8.7 | 11.4 | 4.5 |
| *Gross production* (millions of tons) |  |  |  |
| potatoes | 47 | 52.3 | 48.5 |
| vegetables | 6.5 | 5.5 | 7.1 |
| meat (carcass weight) | 5.4 | 3 | 4.5 |
| milk | 26.1 | 24.5 | 28.8 |
| eggs (billions of units) | 11.5 | 13.7 | 22.4 |
| wool ('000 tons) | 650 | 360 | 870 |
| *Marketed product* (millions of tons) |  |  |  |
| potatoes | 7 | 7.9 | 5.6 |
| vegetables | 1.1 | 1.2 | 1.9 |
| meat | 1.4 | 0.9 | 1.3 |
| milk | 5.5 | 5.1 | 3.0 |
| eggs (billions of units) | 4.3 | 4.0 | 5.1 |
| wool ('000 tons) | 31 | 23 | 70 |

[a] Figures in the second column correspond to the year 1955, those in the third to 1970.

of the market in 1953, 86 per cent in 1972—since the recent advances in industrial poultry breeding.

In all, in 1970 the family economy represented 28 per cent of the gross agricultural production (but this percentage falls to slightly less than 20 per cent if one subtracts the value of fodder supplied to the private economy by the collective economy) and about 12 per cent of the commercialized production. This last figure would seem to confirm the traditional function of the family sector: to meet the needs of home consumption.[11]

## Home consumption and income

When questioned in a 1971 survey on the reasons for their attachment to the family farm, 35 per cent of the respondents indicated that in the first place it supplied them with almost all their food requirements, 30 per cent invoked its role as a source of additional income, and 12 per cent its value as a leisure occupation. To this should be added the satisfaction of owning one's *own* house and being master in one's own home.[12] The very low level of food purchases per inhabitant in the countryside—41 per cent of the average per town-dweller—confirms that for the same consumption and income structure, rural families provide in kind for more than 70 per cent of their needs (excluding the expenses of buying drink, especially vodka). This contribution of the family farm was estimated at an average of 623 roubles per kolkhoz household in 1961 (RSFSR). More recent figures—260 roubles per member of the family in 1971[13]—show that there has been no decrease in absolute terms. In relative terms, on the other hand, because of the increase in agricultural wages and state allocations, the share of family income derived from private plots has fallen from 43 per cent in 1960 to 27–33 per cent in 1972, while that of remuneration received from the kolkhoz has risen from 25 per cent in 1960 to 43 per cent in 1972 (see Table II).

In sovkhoz families, the contribution of the family farm is much smaller; in 1971 it amounted to only 20 per cent of the overall income (as opposed to 23 per cent ten years before), i.e. an average of 465 roubles per family per month. For families of industrial workers the private plot counts for only 4 per cent of total income. The relative position of the average monthly receipts of these different categories in 1973 can be shown by their respective index numbers when the average salary of all workers is taken as 100. As against this standard the income index for industrial workers was

## TABLE II

### Sources of Income of Families of Workers and of Kolkhoz Members

| | Percentage distribution | | | |
| --- | --- | --- | --- | --- |
| | workers' families | | kolkhoz families | |
| | 1940[bc] | 1972[c] | 1940[c] | 1972[c] |
| A From family economy: | | | | |
| home consumption[a] | | | | |
| market sales | 6–9 | 1 | 48 | 27 |
| miscellaneous | — | 2 | 1 | 2 |
| B From collective economy: | | | | |
| wages and salaries | 71–78 | 74 | — | — |
| kolkhoz earnings | — | — | 40 | 43 |
| C Money payments from the State: | | | | |
| pensions, scholarships, allowances | 20 | 22 | 5 | 20 |

[a] Home consumption is estimated to account for about ten per cent of the income of Soviet families, taken as a whole. It is not taken into account in this distribution.

[b] *Narodne Khozyaistvo SSSR 1922–1972*, p. 303 (industrial workers in Moscow, Leningrad, Kharkhov, Gorki, Sverdlovsk, Ivanovo, Donbas).

[c] *Ekonomicheskaya Gazeta*, no. 4 (January 1974).

108 for 280 days of work; for sovkhoz workers the figure was 86 and for kolkhoz workers 63 for 215 days of work. The lot of the kolkhoz workers has definitely improved since 1967, when it was decided to substitute a minimum monthly wage for the old form of participation in profits at the end of the year in proportion to the number of days of work recorded.

The income in kind of the family sector generally serves as a supplement to the money income of the least well-paid categories, in particular that of old-age pensioners.[14] A survey conducted in 1969 in Lithuania brings out the negative correlation between income obtained from work on the kolkhoz (collective income) and income derived from the family plot (private income) (see Table III).

However, the family economy does not in all cases play the role of levelling up the lowest incomes and thereby reducing the spread.

## TABLE III

### HOURS OF WORK AND STRUCTURE OF AGRICULTURAL INCOMES
### VILNIUS DISTRICT, LITHUANIA: 1969

| Collective income per family in roubles | Percentage of families in each income group | Number of hours worked per family member | | | | Income per family member (in roubles) | | |
|---|---|---|---|---|---|---|---|---|
| | | on kolkhoz | in the home | on private plot | total | collective | private | total |
| 0– 600 | 33 | 350 | 170 | 330 | 850 | 105 | 480 | 585 |
| 601–1200 | 40 | 571 | 179 | 289 | 1039 | 304 | 435 | 739 |
| 1201–1800 | 16 | 469 | 151 | 210 | 830 | 464 | 425 | 889 |
| 1801 and over | 11 | 555 | 141 | 234 | 930 | 722 | 391 | 1113 |
| Total | 100 | | | | | | | |
| Average | | 462 | 180 | 288 | 930 | 296 | 443 | 739 |

*Source:* V. Churakov, *Aktual'nye problemy ispol'zovaniya trudovykh resursov sela*, Moscow, 1972, p. 225.

In a certain number of regions, particularly in the Baltic republics, the advantages offered by the family farms serve to complement high incomes received from collective or state enterprises.[15] On the other hand, peasant production entails expenses as well as bringing in income. Even with the help of neighbours or relatives, maintenance of farm buildings, transport and ploughing involve outlay which other social groups do not have to assure. For example, 6 per cent of the budget of rural families as against 2.5 per cent for urban families, is spent on housing. To these material expenses must be added the hours of work spent on the family farm: on an average, a total of 160–70 days' work per year by one or another member of the family.

## Intensity of work and productivity of plots

Soviet economists estimate that activities of the auxiliary sector take up 31.2 per cent of the time-budget of a kolkhoz worker.[16] The degree of participation in these activities depends on sex and age. Out of a total of 268 workdays a man spends, on an average, 36 days a year on his private plot; a woman spends 108 days out of a total of 292, i.e. 4 hours daily in addition to the $7\frac{1}{2}$ hours worked on the kolkhoz.[17] A survey (in the RSFSR in 1967) has shown that during their active years, men supply 13 per cent of the overall time to the family sector, women 52 per cent, and those who are no longer in their active years 35 per cent (among the old people, 96 per cent are women). When able-bodied men work on the plot, it is only on a temporary basis: young people just out of school or military service who are waiting for a job, or visiting members of the family. In other words, the family economy relies essentially on work done by women (see Table IV).

The data given in Table IV emphasize the considerable difference in the use of leisure hours between town and country, and between the sexes. Farm and family duties require kolkhoz women to work an average of 46 hours per week during the month of June, in addition to their work at the kolkhoz.[18] Those who have a cow (15.1 million in 1972) are obliged to be on hand every day, or to arrange for a substitute; in other areas, it is the cultivation of market vegetables which eats up the spare time. The principal obstacle here is not so much the insufficiency of incomes as the necessity for a family to provide for its own needs when the supply of food products in the countryside is not regularly assured.

## TABLE IV

Use of Time by Families of Workers and of Kolkhoz Members in Average Number of Hours per day During One Week

| | 1963[a] | | | | 1967 | | | |
| | Workers' families | | Kolkhoz families | | Workers' families women only | | Kolkhoz families women only | |
| | men | women | men | women | week-days | off-days | week-days | off-days |
|---|---|---|---|---|---|---|---|---|
| **Time at work** | | | | | | | | |
| Regular job | 5.8 | 5.8 | 7.6 | 5.5 | 5.2 | 0.0 | 6.5 | 3.5 |
| Associated activities | 1.4 | 1.2 | 0.9 | 0.8 | 1.1 | 0.1 | 1.0 | 0.5 |
| Domestic work and associated activities | 2.1 | 4.5 | 3.0 | 6.6 | 5.4 | 6.2 | 6.3 | 7.5 |
| **All other time** | | | | | | | | |
| Care and education of children | 0.3 | 0.5 | 0.1 | 0.5 | | | | |
| Physiological needs (sleep, meals) | 9.6 | 9.0 | 9.0 | 8.4 | 9.1 | 10.7 | 8.3 | 8.8 |
| Leisure activities (cultural, social, sports) | 4.5 | 2.7 | 3.0 | 2.0 | 2.9 | 6.5 | 1.4 | 2.9 |
| Miscellaneous | 0.3 | 0.3 | 0.4 | 0.2 | 0.3 | 0.5 | 0.5 | 0.8 |
| Total | 24 | 24 | 24 | 24 | 24 | 24 | 24 | 24 |

[a] 1963 averages are calculated for all seven days of the week, including non-working days.

*Sources*: V. Patrusev, *Sotsiologicheskie issledovaniya*, no. 1 (1974), p. 89; Petrosyan (G.) quoted in *Problèmes politiques et sociaux*, nos. 31–2 (1970); Perevedentsev, *Nas Sovremnik*, no. 3 (1974).

In the USSR, one does not yet find the liberation of peasant women visible in certain agricultural regions of France where cattle-raising is abandoned and a battery of electrical appliances has reduced the tedium of domestic chores. It is true that little by little certain domestic chores such as baking bread or making butter are no longer current. All depends on how well the countryside is supplied; very often keeping a family cow is the only means of providing milk for the children.[19] The insufficiency of permanent nurseries in rural areas is a cause of absenteeism and is given as the reason by 32 per cent of the women of working age who remain at home. In 1968, only 29 per cent of the children under 7 could be accommodated in nurseries or kindergartens.[20]

Since man has lost his prerogatives as head of the farm, and is now, just like his wife, a worker or an employee of the kolkhoz or the sovkhoz, he has also lost the prestige attached to the status of master (*khozyain*). Nevertheless, he is still indispensable to the orderly functioning of the family farm, for without him how could the cartloads of hay or firewood necessary to everyday life be brought in?[21]

In the common effort which the running of a farm entails, it is not always possible to clearly define each person's contribution. All the more so is the family property—the house, cow, etc.—indivisible. This explains the fact that today, as under Tsarist law, the ownership of the dvor is the *communal property* of the family and not the property of the head of the household.

The extraordinary intensity of family farming on these microfundia which has more to do with horticulture than agriculture, for the plot is regularly watered and abundantly manured, is the secret of its astonishing success. A mere 3 per cent of the area under cultivation supplies 20 per cent of the gross product. But the family economy is still dependent for fodder upon the collective farms.

## Complementarity and contradictions between family economy and collective agriculture

The large mechanized enterprises—kolkhoz and sovkhoz—almost entirely monopolize the production of cereals and industrial crops (sugarbeet, cotton, etc.). For the last ten years they have attempted to industrialize their stock-farming (poultry, baby-beef). The private sector, however, still plays a significant role in making up for the insufficiencies of the collective production in the supply of vegetables, fruit and items of farm produce which require regular attentive care. Thus a certain division of work between family and collective agriculture has emerged.

For a long time, this complementarity was imposed by the compulsory deliveries which rural families had to make to the State procurement agency. Since January 1968, however, these levies in kind have been abolished. The deliveries, which have now become voluntary, are carried out on a contractual basis: growing tobacco for the State monopoly, fattening piglets on the family farm for the kolkhoz. Nearly 12 million calves are turned over each year to the collective farms, which then hand them on to the State as contractual deliveries. In fact the proportion of sales to the State in the marketed product of the family economy has not diminished: 24 per cent in 1970 as against 20 per cent in 1950.

In the other direction, the peasant family still depends on the kolkhoz for the cereals which it does not produce (or produces only in insufficient quantities) and for fodder. Private livestock could not survive without these external supplies.[22] The cattle graze, as always, on the common land under the supervision of a kolkhoz shepherd, who in pre-revolutionary days was at the bottom of the social scale, but now enjoys special attention, since he is entrusted with the cow, a family's most important asset.

Despite this complementarity, the existence, in the heart of a large-scale farm, of a family sector based on a different principle cannot but create problems. A peasant woman cannot be at work both in her own home and outside. In practice, this contradiction is resolved by very long hours, particularly in certain occupations such as that of milkmaids, but also by frequent absenteeism at times when the harvesting of perishable crops on the home-plot cannot wait upon the goodwill of the kolkhoz administration.

A second factor of perturbation has to do with agricultural prices. The freely-negotiated prices on the kolkhoz markets are, depending on the time of the year, from 20 per cent to 100 per cent (sometimes even 200 per cent) higher than the official retail prices, which are already higher than the procurement prices. These differences serve as an incentive to family work. In 1970, a day's work on the kolkhoz brought 3.90 roubles (a Soviet average which includes earnings in kind), while a stint of eight hours on a private plot could produce an income of 4.80 roubles.[23]

In the neighbourhood of big cities, the profitability of carrying produce to sell in person in urban markets tends to increase absenteeism.[24] In order to reduce the number of trips into town, direct individual sales of milk were halted. Surplus milk had to be pooled in collection centres, which arranged commission sales in the form of contracts between the peasants and the urban consumers' cooperatives. Thus few families have the opportunity to sell regularly on the urban markets; others often pool their surplus so as to make only one or two trips a year to the town which they believe will give them the highest returns and where they will be able to buy items not available in the provinces.

For the time being, the existence of the family sector is not threatened as long as its aid is required to supply the needs of the inhabitants of small towns and the countryside. Even the rural schoolmaster cannot manage without his plot. In short, until the collective economy is able to take over the function fulfilled by the family farm, the objective reasons for its survival remain.[25] In the past, restrictions imposed on private agricultural activities generally worked out to the disadvantage of the city-dwellers. In addition to the operation of purely rural factors, this helps to explain the vitality of the family sector which has so far survived all the upheavals of history.

Its existence, however, remains fragile. It is always dependent on decisions which could be taken by the authorities acting through the collective assemblies. In the end, the State is the sole employer, the sole distributor of land and fodder.[26] It alone fixes the level of wages and pensions. In the long run, family economy is also threatened by the young people's lack of enthusiasm for the strenuous work involved in farming. Moreover, the plans for rural urbanization which envisage more compact housing arrangements with only from 100 to 400 square metres of garden next to each house, constitute a direct threat to the existence of family economy in its traditional form. In other words, the future of the family farm will depend, as in the past, on its relationship with the community—village or collective farm—to which it belongs.[27]

## NOTES

1. N. Jasny, *The Socialized Agriculture of the USSR*, Stanford, 1949.
2. Daniel Thorner, 'L'économie paysanne concept pour l'histoire économique', *Annales, Economies, Sociétés, Civilisations*, no. 3 (May–June 1964), pp. 417–32.
3. Daniel Thorner, Basile Kerblay, R. E. F. Smith (eds.), *A. V. Chayanov, on the Theory of Peasant Economy*, Homewood, Ill., Richard D. Irwin, Inc., published for the American Economic Association, 1966.
4. This implies that more than two-thirds of the rural population live in individual houses, and that in most cases these houses are the personal property of the occupants.
5. In 1970, the census counted 24.7 million rural families, of which 6.5 million had members belonging to different socio-professional groups; the division between peasant and worker families is therefore fairly arbitrary in 25 per cent of the cases.
6. Lorries and tractors are not allowed to be privately owned.
7. In irrigated areas, the ceiling is fixed at 2,000 square metres; the effective average in central Asia is 1,900 square metres as against 5,800 square metres in the Baltic regions.
8. The same decree has generalized the payment of monthly advances on the income in such a way as to encourage collective work.
9. In 1971, 89 per cent of rural families possessed a cow in Lithuania and in Azerbaidjan, but only 12.6 per cent in Moldavia and 49.7 per cent in the Ukraine; the regions of central Asia and Kazakstan, which contained 18 per cent of the Soviet rural population, accounted for 3 per cent of the pigs and 40 per cent of the sheep in private ownership. The land under family cultivation amounts to 3 per cent of the cultivated area in the USSR, but goes up to 7 per cent in the Ukraine, 9.2 per cent in the Baltic republics and 21 per cent in Georgia.
10. The agricultural tax on private income is determined by taking into account the situation of each household.
11. Semin, *Preodolenie sotsial'no-ekonomicheskikh razlitchii mezhdu gorodom i derevni*, Moscow, 1973. According to other Soviet sources, only 20 per cent of private production is destined for the market; for certain products such as meat and eggs the percentage is higher (*Vestnik Statistiki*, no. 10 (1966), p. 8).
12. Survey made in 1971 in the province of Novossibirsk (*Izvestija Akadem. Nauk, Sibirskovo otdeleniya*, no. 11 (1974), p. 39).
13. The available estimates of family income differ widely depending on whether or not the total is calculated to include State subsidies (scholarships, pensions) and social benefits (free education, public health service, etc.).
14. The superannuated in the kolkhoz have long suffered under a handicap since their pensions varied according to the wealth of the kolkhoz. It was only in 1964 that the pensioners in the kolkhozy were partially taken over by the State social security; the average pension is now around 20 roubles per month.
15. Wädekin, *Soviet Studies*, January 1975. Elsewhere Ju. V. Arutiunian, *Opyt sotsiologicheskogo izucheniya sela*, Moscow, 1968, has shown that within the

same village family economy was not necessarily a factor of equalization between the different social categories. In this particular case it contributed to reinforcing inequalities.

16. These estimates of time spent in family economy are based on the norms used for calculating labour input in collective agriculture, a procedure which is somewhat questionable.

17. *Ekon. Sel. Khoz.*, no. 3 (1964), p. 11; confirmed by *Kopanka 25 let spustya*, Moscow, 1965.

18. *Sotsiologiya v SSSR*, Moscow, 1963, vol. II, p. 222. This source specifies that husbands also spend 40 per cent of their free time on the private plots (p. 219).

19. Abramov, *Novyi Mir*, no. 2 (1960), p. 17; Solochin, *Kaplya Rosy*, Moscow, 1961, p. 406–7.

20. *Vestnik Statistiki*, no. 8 (1969), p. 22.

21. A. Solzhenitsyn, *The House of Matriona*.

22. These indispensable payments in kind show that part of the earnings of the kolkhoz members are still not monetarized: 50 per cent of the total of the remuneration in 1956, 10 per cent in 1968 (Wädekin, *Revue de l'Est*, no. 4 (1972), p. 12).

23. Semin, op. cit. p. 148.

24. For example, the kilo of potatoes bought for 6 kopeks by the State can be sold for four times that price in town markets at certain periods of the year.

25. For the year 1980, the Council for the Organization of Productive Forces (SOPS) estimates that the share of the auxiliary sector (family) in the total agricultural production will be 24 per cent for milk, 27 per cent for meat, 28 per cent for fruit, 37 per cent for vegetables, and 41.5 per cent for potatoes (*Geografiya SSSR*, no. 11 (1972) ).

26. The price at which fodder is supplied to kolkhoz families exerts a decisive influence on the evolution of private farming. In the month of August 1969, it was decided to evaluate fodder at production price, since the practice of supplying it at retail price tended to discourage families from raising their own animals and had the effect of increasing the purchases of meat products in State shops.

27. B. Kerblay, 'Le village en URSS: permanence et changements', *Sociologia ruralis*, vol. XVI, no. 4 (1976), pp. 258–78.

# 6

# Measuring Peasant Capitalism

*The Operationalization of Concepts of Political
Economy: Russia's 1920s—India's 1970s*

## TEODOR SHANIN

*University of Manchester*

## I. A PROBLEM AND A HISTORY

THE operationalization of concepts finds its significance and its
limitations in the problematic posed. By those standards, our topic—
measuring peasant capitalism—lies at the heart of the major concerns of contemporary social science. It has to do with capitalism as
a process; it relates the understanding of the origins of our time to
the characterization of the essential tenets of the global system we
live in.[1] It is both central and controversial, for, while different
schools multiply argument and terminology, none have managed to
avoid the issue of peasant differentiation and structural change. The
basic concepts of classical and Marxist political economy as well as
those of the mostly neo-classical economics—the contemporary
academic discipline—have been created to explore and to explain
capitalism. All of them took shape outside peasant economies and
societies. All the schools accepted, at least originally, Plekhanov's
crisp contention that, 'historically speaking', the peasantry does not
exist, implying the rapid global spread of capitalism in its 'classical'
sense and the assumption that capitalism equals de-peasantation.
Consequently much of economic theory disregards peasants entirely.
Otherwise these analytical paradigms focused on the dual process of
the peasantry's disappearance and capital formation.

Within the perspective of political economy, and especially in the
various Marxisms of our time, three related issues are central. First
is the process of differentiation of peasantry, confidently expected to

produce or reinforce the basic social classes of capitalism—the capitalists and proletariat. Secondly there is the problematic of 'primitive accumulation', i.e. the exploitation and destruction of the mostly peasant modes of production and livelihood, which makes for the necessary pre-conditions for capital formation and capitalist industrialization—accumulated surplus, 'free' labour and an expanding market.[2] Finally, and on the whole, rooted in the last generation's experience and analysis, there is the question of the ways by which the world capitalist system can actually stabilize, reproduce and even extend peasant economies and societies via their exploitative integration or marginalization.[3]

Of these three only the first will be discussed here, and we consider here the literature on Russia's 1920s, for possible insights into the so-called 'developing societies' of today. This date (the 1920s) and place (Russia) limit the discussion to the problematic of socialists arguing over the realization of their ideals. Within those circles the conceptual characteristics of the issue of peasant differentiation make it of high ideological relevance. Indeed many radical movements have divided and split, predicted and planned, consolidated and purged in accordance with the way questions concerning the peasantry's differentiation were answered. Basic political strategies and class alliances have been treated and anticipated accordingly.

Indeed, no less than the very creation and existence of the proletariat as the major political actor are at stake—hence the extent of the debate and the powerful emotional undercurrents. When such confrontations increase, dictated by the turns of political and economic history, leaders and militants turn into (or turn to) social scientists. Some of them stay at the level of deductive elaboration of categories and programmes, but others proceed to look at relevant data, leading to greater awareness of complexity and of ambivalence of 'simple facts' as well as to greater analytical sophistication. It is usually a sign of maturity when the bridge between theory and *empeiria* comes into focus. The differentiation debate becomes, in part, an operationalization debate.

The translation of the 'algebra' of theory into the 'arithmetic' of field notes or the statistics of censuses and vice versa are, at the best of times, the major difficulty of the social sciences—the more so within a problematic loaded with conceptual ambivalence and a politically tense situation. The numerous ways of avoidance testify to these difficulties, e.g. the ever-increasing tendency to pepper 'pure'

concepts with a few 'empirical' examples. The central problems here
are those of a meaningful quantification and comparison of diversity
within the peasantry, as expressed in peasant wealth, mobility,
patterns of exploitation, capital formation and structural transformation.

It was in Germany that, for the first time, leaders of a socialist
mass movement had to confront the fact of the peasantry as a major
component of their society, and of central importance in any political
strategy they were to design. It was therefore not surprisingly the
place where the differentiation debate took shape.[4] Russia was a
natural next-in-line, the attitude to peasant differentiation forming
dividing lines between the main revolutionary movements as well as
between the main factions of every one of them.[5] Russia was also
the place where those involved most deeply were given the opportunity not only to use statistical data collected by officials and official
academics, but also to undertake field studies on their own.[6]

Those opportunities blossomed fully in the 1920s when the new
revolutionary regime stimulated massive and representative studies
of peasant differentiation while opening the field wide enough to
adherents of different approaches to facilitate debate. Consequently,
while in Germany the interest in problems of operationalization was
limited, it became central in Russia. To proceed, the next socialist
mass-movement and major country in which original analyses of
differentiation within peasantry developed were China's CP and the
writings of Mao. His conceptualization has found a rather underdeveloped operational appendix in the works of Chen Po-ta—the
head-to-be of the Academy of Sciences of post-revolutionary China.[7]

Most recently, India's radical academics took their turn at the
differentiation debate. It goes without saying that no 'discovery of an
issue' is claimed; Marxists of various hues and other students of the
peasantry have discussed it all often enough—the overspill of debate
within the Third International would be enough to provide for that.
All the same a 'break in continuity' since 1970 was evident in the
intensification of the debate, in the new suggestions offered and, to
an extent, also in the new terminology applied. The issue has been
posed in terms of the characterizing modes of production within
India's agriculture.[8] A number of 'specifically Indian' problems like
that of the Colonial Mode of Production have formed part of the
discussion. All the same, while no debate repeats itself in entirety,
the essential structure and problematic of the peasant differentiation

debate of the past is being reproduced. With the debate growing sharper the consideration and reconsideration of data is increasingly coming into focus. The differentiation debate is turning into an operationalization debate.

Such a stage of development offers an opportunity to improve our knowledge of the issue in hand, but there is also the danger of going into a blind alley of a few academics duelling over words and struggling over prestige. One of the ways to 'up the odds' is to broaden the debate by indicating a comparison, the fruitfulness of which was proven often enough.[9] I am referring to the achievements of the Russian scholarly community by the late 1920s and how their analyses relate to the India of the mid-1970s.

## II. INDIA'S 1970s

Comparisons are always tricky and to make this one less abstract let me refer to a specific text. Utsa Patnaik's 'Class Differentiation within Peasantry'[10] is relevant here as a major effort at operationalizing the growth of capitalism and of the class divisions specific to it within the Indian peasantry. There are things besides that in the article, but we shall focus only on the issue chosen.

To recapitulate the relevant part, the paper suggests a labour exploitation ratio $E$ as the empirical approximation and methodological tool to pose and quantify class analysis of the peasantry. In the author's words 'use of outside labour in relation to the use of family labour' is 'the most reliable single index of categorizing peasants' (p. A–84). There are said to be two main ways to exploit labour in the Indian peasant context (similar to China of 1930 but different from, say, Russia of 1910). These are the direct hiring of labourers and the indirect exploitation through leasing out land (p. A–87). This labour–land equation of exploitation 'does not give an exhaustive coverage of all agrarian relations, but only those arising directly in the production process' on the rationale that 'other relations such as those between the trader and money-lender on the one hand and different classes within the peasantry, are themselves conditional upon the existence of class differentiation arising in the production process' (p. A–90). The non-incorporation does not however stop there. There is no way to calculate leasing out in labour days equivalence, and therefore the actual $E$ is limited to the balance of labour hired in as against labour hired out (pp. A–92, A–84). In other words, while the leasing out of land is identified as a major component of class characterization and typified in Tables 3, 3A and 4, it is not incorporated on the scale of quantification, even though the possible contradictory cross-cutting of the two types of categories is mentioned. A single scale of mutually exclusive groups based on the labour balance within every specific household unit then follows (Tables 2, 6), putting households into classes on the assumption that 'from statistical point of view the $E$ criterion simply represents the translation of economic class in agriculture into an empirically applicable form' (p. A–91).

As it stands Patnaik's discussion is important, significant but, at the same time, insufficient or not quite sufficient. Its importance lies in the very issue discussed. It is enhanced by a sophisticated discussion of relations between theory and operational categories. It is significant because labour exploitation index is doubtless central to any attempt to understand the structure and the dynamics of capitalism within peasant agriculture. In this sense it will doubtless 'work', i.e. offer a way to identify peasant classes in a way relevant to the major issues raised. At the same time it is insufficient or not quite sufficient for the following reasons:

(1) It lacks a workable common denominator to quantify ratios of exploitation, even in so far as its two declared major components are concerned. Labour time cannot operate as such a common denominator, despite a variety of attempts in the past. Nor is an alternative way offered to integrate major empirical aspects of rural exploitation in an unequivocal way. The $E$ ratio translates 'class in agriculture' but does not do it 'simply'. Indeed, the resulting reduction to a single index necessarily means a considerable inbuilt mistake. To avoid this one must have a multiplicity of indexes, or else again composite indexes of several components. When these indexes or components clash, arbitrary solutions necessarily follow.

(2) It leaves out major casualities of the processes of rural exploitation, capital accumulation and the peasantry's disintegration (called rather vaguely 'agricultural relations'). As it stands, such a strategy would seem particularly unsatisfactory at delimiting the entrepreneurial/rich end of the scale of $E$ proposed. To study a peasant community without a money-lender and a trader and their impact, is to disregard what every peasant knows to be central and also to omit some of the very springs of change one tries to understand (and

can leave out only *after* establishing their secondary or dependent character). Not to do so within Marxist analysis because of its being Marxist is to me a caricature of Marxism as a major tool of thought and action. Those who doubt the Marxist propriety of such an eclectic realism should go back to the first pages of *The Class Struggle in France* (and many other pages besides). The primary nature of relations of production as against those of circulation, declared by Marx, does not translate into disregard of the latter when class relations are considered. An operationalization within which the richest trader-usurer of a village (and a capitalist farmer in a year?) can be delineated as Middle Peasant is 'insufficient or not quite sufficient'.

(3) It accepts by default the core of the existing methodology concerning data collection and analysis, although introduced and crystallized in considerable conceptual distance from any concern with peasant differentiation and exploitation. It is barely possible that the problematic of peasant differentiation and exploitation can be fully discussed without relating it to alternative methods of empirical study. At the very least such a position cannot be left implicit.

The fact that the labour theory of value forms the core of Marxist economic theory does not necessarily make labour time sufficient to index classes and exploitation within a specific context. Nor is it sufficient to study accumulation of capital, despite its doubtless relevance to it. And so on. Clearly much additional work on operationalization is still pending, even in so far as the specific issue of indexes of exploitation is concerned.

Instead of asking if there is anything useful one could learn from the Russian analyses of similar problems half a century ago after five decades of accumulation of data and expertise, let us instead go to those whom the Russians themselves would accept as experts at the time when the relevant analysis reached its peak, i.e. the late 1920s.

### III. RUSSIA'S 1920s

The 'peasant differentiation debate' within Russia had commenced by the middle of the nineteenth century and was to reach a new stage in the Populist/Marxist debate at the century's end. It proceeded unabated, rapidly increasing in sophistication, to reach a new and final height in the official 1926 debate conducted by the Soviet

Agricultural Academy. It was the last time that important exponents of major theoretical schools within the USSR crossed swords in an attempt to understand the differentiation processes within the Soviet countryside—neo-classical economists, neo-populists, Marxists of different shades. Nor was the discussion limited to that debate, for relevant books and articles published in the late 1920s ran into many dozens.[11]

The operationalization debate within Russia came at the end of the nineteenth century. It took place mostly among the so-called rural statisticians (who were in fact also economists and socio-logists by our own disciplinary standards), largely employed by the Zemstvos, the Russian regional authorities established in 1861. The outspoken commitment and the ideological heterogeneity of this group facilitated lively debate. Much of it took place within the national congresses of rural statisticians, spilling over often enough into the public press and party argument, especially on the left. A number of methodological queries found their final resolution via consensus within this manifold group. For example, the peasant household was accepted as the main unit of analysis, a resolution less self-evident than it seems today. More 'technical' issues (e.g. the 'optical statistical mistake' in which some usage of samples results in a mistaken appreciation of differentiation) would also belong there.[12]

At the very centre of this debate lay the issue which bridged the pre-revolutionary and the post-revolutionary concerns and related them both to our times. It is the issue of empirical representation or at least approximation of peasant socio-economic differentiation, i.e. the issue of capital and capitalist class formation within the Russian peasant society.[13] To put it differently these are the problems of relevance and validity of the operational definitions and categories used to express, to analyse and to refute conceptual claims and theoretical constructs within the peasant differentiation debate.

At the core of this issue are two related questions. Firstly, what is the way to establish an empirically meaningful scale of categories and/or classes into which peasant households can be divided? Secondly, there was a quest for a workable methodology to monitor and explain relevant socio-economic processes, e.g. polarization, in a more satisfactory way than the ordinary census could do. While the first of those methodological problems seemed about to be solved by the late 1920s, the second had been resolved to a considerable degree during the earlier three decades by the so-called

Dynamic Studies and Budget Studies. Let us review those questions in turn.

Attempts to apply to Russian peasant communities a pure Marxist typology of classes under capitalism (as defined by the ownership and the use of the means of production) had failed empirically often enough to be abandoned by its early Russian proponents with few exceptions, e.g. Sukhanov. The heuristic value of an operationalization in which nearly every unit finds itself in the middle category of 'petty bourgeoisie' was next to none. While consequent recategorization was taking place (e.g. 'poor peasants' increasingly replacing 'rural proletarians' in most Marxist writings), those 'in the field' adopted land sown and horses owned as the major indexes of differentiation by wealth of the peasant household. Marxist analysts, Lenin included, have usually accepted those empirical categories (at times 'under protest', pointing out their limitations). The rationale of these indexes was that agriculture was highly grain-centred with no mechanization to speak about, and also that accountancy was easier within these categories. The limitations were very considerable, however. Major aspects of production and exploitation were left outside the main typological scale of empirical studies. An attempt to tackle those aspects and to double-check results was made through multiplication of indexes to incorporate more than 'land and horses'. Both quantitative and qualitative indexes were experimented with accordingly, reaching a new stage of sophistication at about 1910. For example, Khryashcheva's 1911 study in Tula used simultaneously five indexes in which the 'two greats' were supplemented by those of family labour, cows owned and land owned.[14] Baskin's 1913 study in Samara introduced qualitative categories of wage labour usage, non-agricultural income and enterprises-ownership together with land sown to establish a scale of mutually exclusive categories of peasant households: (1) entrepreneurial; (2) part-exploitative; (3) family farming; (4) trading and craft-producing; (5) poor and proletarian.[15]

The 1917–21 Revolution and Civil War led to a considerable levelling within the Russian peasant villages. It also aggravated operational problems of the Russian statisticians. Private land ownership was abolished, land holdings were massively re-divided, 'surplus horses' were requisitioned by the army, and so on. The new egalitarian policies of the state and its tax collectors made old indexes, as recorded, less reliable. Under the circumstances the land sown and horses owned categories used by the state planning and statistical authorities were highly suspect of hiding rather than revealing the actual extent of differentiation. Worse still, even the extent of wage labour did not any longer express the diversity clearly, because in the context a rich peasant was increasingly hired together with his equipment and horses by his poor neighbour.

The possible elusiveness of peasant differentiation to the scrutiny of the operational tools used was debated mostly by the Marxists. The somewhat acrimonious debate between the two Bolsheviks, Khryashcheva and Kritsman, could provide here an example. The issues could not be settled by the usual reference to Lenin's own writings, which offered little guidance in matters of operationalization. While the ignorance of the Russian language in the Anglo-Saxon realm and its dependencies overseas turned volume III of Lenin's *Collected Writings* into a never-ending source of quotations concerning peasant differentiation in Russia, the sources used there, e.g. Postnikov, are methodologically prehistorical. By the time the Russian operationalization debate reached its final peak, Lenin was long gone from the realm of the living.

During the 1920s Kritsman of the Agrarian Section of the Communist Academy was a persistently severe critic of the operational methods used by the Central Statistical Board. In 1928 a team headed by him published a massive re-study of peasant households in accordance with three indexes simultaneously and comparatively used—(*a*) land sown, (*b*) the 'strength' of the household, defined by the extent of cattle owned and the type of equipment used, and (*c*) the use of wage labour. The aim of this analysis was explicitly set out as identification of the classes among the 'pseudo-neutral' majority of peasant households 'defined negatively', i.e. as neither wage employers nor wage employed, and usually referred to as 'middle peasants'.[16] By 1928 a number of Kritsman's associates, like Gaister, had begun to produce field studies in which peasant households were classified by capital and income in monetary terms.[17] Their opponents did not fail to open fire, pointing out the considerable difficulties of estimating such categories in a partly monetized economy, and expressed doubts about a classification which disregarded land held following both the nationalization law and the strictly Marxist interpretation of capital. Alternatives and alternative indexes were suggested. The air was thick with methodological suggestions and experiments—the last blossoming of a social world and a scholarly community destined for instant oblivion.

At this stage there came the intervention of a bright young man from the provinces. His name was V. S. Nemchinov, born in 1894, graduated in 1917, and by 1926 head of a regional statistical department in the Urals (and due in 1928 for the Chair of Statistics in the Agricultural Academy—one of the highest tokens of academic appreciation then available). In his general outlook Nemchinov was a Marxist who, while finding much in common with Kritsman's criticism, offered somewhat different solutions to the problems under debate. In particular he accepted a number of contentions of those Kritsman argued against. Nemchinov set out to establish a satisfactory index of exploitation by which Russian peasant households could be empirically classified to enable study of capitalist accumulation and class creation, exactly the problems discussed in India fifty years later. In a number of ways a new peak in the relevant Russian methodology is reflected in Nemchinov's work and suggestions.

In 1926 Nemchinov published locally a paper which commences with a comparison of eleven variants of methodology used or suggested in so far as the empirical studies of differentiation of Russian peasantry were concerned.[18] These included methodological suggestions by Baskin (one), Khryashcheva (three), Kritsman (one), Gaister (one), Groman (three) and himself (two). Nemchinov proceeded to synthesize all of the qualitatively specific categories and relations, referred to as 'topological groups'. This synthesis is presented in Table I.

### TABLE I
#### CONDITIONS AND MEANS OF PRODUCTION WITHIN A PEASANT HOUSEHOLD

| Means of production | In own household | | In other households |
| --- | --- | --- | --- |
| | owned by others | self-owned | self-owned |
| A. Land | a. En | e. In | i. De |
| B. Fixed capital | b. De | f. In | j. En |
| C. Circulating capital | c. De | g. In | k. En |
| D. Labour | d. En | h. In | l. De |

*Note:* (En) Entrepreneurial, (De) Dependent, (In) Independent.
*Source:* Based on Nemchinov, *Izbranve Proizvedenia*, vol. I, p. 48.

Nemchinov suggested the definition of every peasant household in accordance with the basic topological categories expressing its input in monetary terms divided into the entrepreneurial component $(a + d + j + k)$, the dependency component $(b + c + i + l)$ and the independent operation component $(e + f + g + h)$. (It goes without saying that this division is specific to its historical context, for renting in land was 'entrepreneurial' there but can be (and is) a representation of 'dependency' elsewhere.) In cases in which both the entrepreneurial and the dependent component existed, a balance of both was to be used. Estimates and averages were to be used to establish annual input. Relevant 'price tables' were worked out empirically by Nemchinov's statistical outfit for their own district. The category 'land' $(A)$ was represented by the actual rents of land in the area. Fixed capital input $(B)$ was represented by estimates of amortization. Actual average prices as established were used for circulating capital $(C)$ and labour $(D)$. Every peasant household of the sample was then to be characterized in percentages which can be represented by a formula

$$\frac{En - De}{\text{Total input}} \times 100$$

Table II explains this with an actual example.

TABLE II

AN EXAMPLE OF A PEASANT HOUSEHOLD ESTIMATE
(in roubles of input)

| Means of production | In own household | | In other households | Total |
|---|---|---|---|---|
| | owned by others | self-owned | self-owned | |
| A. Land and meadows | a. 127.25 | e. 176.85 | i. 21.10 | 325.20 |
| B. Equipment & livestock | b. 10.25 | f. 104.60 | j. 35.50 | 150.35 |
| C. Seeds and fodder | c. — | g. 289.70 | k. — | 289.70 |
| D. Labour | d. 251.00 | h. 365.00 | l. — | 616.00 |
| Total | 388.50 | 936.15 | 56.60 | 1381.25 |

*Source:* Nemchinov, op. cit. pp. 49–56. Figures realistic for the period and the area (a rich household).

In this case the entrepreneurial component would be 413.75 roubles and the dependent component 31.35 roubles. The total input being 1381.25 roubles, the results in terms of the formula used would be

$$\frac{413.75 - 31.35}{1381.25} = 27.7\%$$

i.e. the household shows an entrepreneurial component of 27.7 per cent. In cases of trading and similar activities outside agriculture Nemchinov suggested adding their input to the entrepreneurial component of the present household (op. cit. p. 50).

To try it out, Nemchinov proceeded to re-study one of the sample areas of the national annual census within his region. It consisted of 835 peasant households which did not undergo 'substantive changes' within the 1924–5 period (i.e. did not partition, merge, emigrate or liquidate). For every peasant household a balance of basic components of input was prepared in accordance with the programme presented above. All of the peasant households were then divided into six strata/categories. Table III gives the results.

TABLE III

THE DIFFERENTIATION OF 835 PEASANT HOUSEHOLDS IN
TROITSKII AREA, 1925 (per capita terms)

| Category | Percentage |
|---|---|
| Dependency above 50% | 9.70 |
| „     15–50% | 13.05 |
| „     2.5–15% | 9.70 |
| Up to 2½% of either entrepr. or dependency | 52.93 |
| Entrepr. 2½% to 15% | 12.10 |
| „    above 15% | 2.52 |
| Total | 100.00 |

*Source:* Nemchinov, op. cit. p. 58.

This stratification was subsequently compared to, and cross-tabulated with, the groupings of the same households by the 'natural' indexes of land sown, horses owned, etc. The same households were also regrouped once more in accordance with the estimates of value of constant capital in each of them. A number of analytical conclusions was then drawn, reflecting both the content of Table III and these others. For example, Nemchinov concluded that any attempt to delineate 'kulaks'—a major concern of those times—must take into consideration both the 'social characteristics' as defined on the scale in Table III *and* the fixed capital as estimated. (In his studies he divided households into three basic categories of rich, middle and poor.) The consequent analytical operation showed as kulak eight households in his sample (0.96 per cent), taking only those units which appear in the top category of both scales under consideration. Further, he was able to demonstrate that within the independent producers category about one-third of the households was poor by the standards of value of capital, while about one-tenth was rich. The typical 'middle peasant' in terms of both the scale of 'social characteristics' and that of wealth would consist thereby of only 43 per cent of the households studied.

At the beginning of 1927 Nemchinov presented his methodological suggestions in two 'theses' presented to the All-Union Convention of Statisticians. Much of Nemchinov's contribution simply re-stated systematically the essentials of his methodological attempt in the Urals. A class delineation of peasant households was stated to be its aim, expressed in its classical terms as the process of alienation of means of production from the direct producers and the expropriation of surplus value via control of means of production. The issue of modes of production was mentioned but deliberately put aside in view of the 'total lack of suitable statistical characteristics dividing the pre-capitalist mode and the other ones' (p. 63). Nemchinov suggested that his new categories were to be used simultaneously with those of land sown within a section of the national sample selected for more intensive study. The earlier attempt at categorization was extended by incorporating a broader review of pre-revolutionary works of rural statisticians, adding Rumyantsev and Shlipovich to those already named. From what we know, the 1927–8 dynamic census was to incorporate Nemchinov's methodological suggestion. It was caught up in the collectivization upheaval and never published.

That is not all, for Nemchinov's work in the Urals was directly related to specific methodologies designed to study peasant differentiation as a process. While his work on the expression of exploitation was no doubt original, by the time he entered the scene the other methodologies referred to had already been established as a solid achievement of Russian scholarship. Consequently, they had been incorporated into, and were at the very centre of, the work of the state statistical board and planning outfits in the 1920s. As the head of a regional statistical board, Nemchinov participated in all that work; his insights and his very professional knowledge formed in close relation to them. These studies, specifically designed to approach peasant differentiation and the operation of peasant households as a process, fell into two major types referred to as Dynamic Studies and Budget Studies respectively. By the end of the 1920s both were carried out annually on samples representative of all of the regions of the USSR. (The size of the annual sample was by 1926 about 500,000 peasant households for the Dynamic Studies and up to 30,000 households for the Budget Studies.)

Dynamic Studies were introduced first at the turn of the century out of dissatisfaction with conclusions drawn about a process of socio-economic mobility from a census—to everybody's view a spurious procedure yet often used for lack of any better data. Much of what was and still is presented as empirical analysis of a process is actually very much akin to guessing from a snapshot how a ballerina dances—an attempt to look at processes through an inherently static reflection. The author of the Dynamic Studies, Chernenkov, claimed that even a study of two consecutive censuses of samples drawn from similar area must hide much of socio-economic changes and mobility involved, by showing only the residuum of upward and downward mobility and disregarding non-quantitative changes which occurred. What was needed was a re-study which went back specifically to every peasant household in the sample initially studied to represent the totality of changes statistically. Such an analysis enables one to single out substantive changes, i.e. the rate at which peasant households of every peasant stratum transform or disappear via partition, merger, emigration and disintegration; and to grasp the full scope and direction of socio-economic mobility within every chosen stratum and category of peasant households. His results were revealing enough for the methodology to be adopted by five more major studies before the Revolution and to be incorporated into the core of the basic data and annual report by the Central Statistical Board as from 1920.

To exemplify the potential insights of the Dynamic Study, Nemchinov's work on the period of 1924–5 revealed in addition to a 'class map' also the fact that the peasant households with a high rate of dependency were highly unstable, 16 per cent of them disappearing within one single year, mostly through self-liquidation and merger (p. 56). Other dynamic studies monitored the extent of upward and downward mobility within different peasant strata and specific groupings, e.g. those deeply engaged in craft and trade, etc. And so on. Instead of 'statistical snapshots' or a sum total of residuum, Soviet scholars established a system of analysis and a body of data annually reviewed, reflecting the sum total of mobility and structural transformation within the countryside.

Russian Budget Studies developed on a tradition essentially borrowed from the West mostly via the works of F. le Play.[19] Its use for the study of peasant households and its 'modern' form were established by Shcherbina in the Zemstvo of Vorenezh during 1887–91. By moving its focus from families as consumption units to the peasant household, i.e. a production–consumption unit, the whole character of this methodology was transformed. It came to consist of systematic input–output analysis of representative samples of peasant households for the whole of an agricultural year. This information plus the amount of labour, land and equipment available for every peasant household were then presented and analysed statistically in strata defined in terms of wealth. Such a study enabled the explication of specific characteristics of different strata and categories of peasant households in terms of typical production techniques, productivity, consumption patterns, income, accumulation and so on. Despite considerable technical and methodological difficulties, the Russian scholars persistently developed Budget Studies, turning them into a basic tool to monitor and reveal actual processes rather than to assume them on the basis of the empirical studies of their results only, if that.[20]

The considerable conceptual achievement of these Russian scholars cannot be understood at all without an awareness of their major methodological achievements which put them ahead of anybody else in so far as empirical data available and its analysis were concerned. In the words of one of them, 'the Zemstvo statisticians constructed a tool, unique of its kind, for studying the life of the peasantry, such as no other country has at its disposal'. He has also pointed out that it 'substantially diverged in almost every respect from West European models'.[21] For once we do not deal here with a

7

typical display of Russian boastfulness. The claim was true and became even more so while methodological thinking in the 1920s gathered momentum. It still remains true in 1977.[22]

### IV. HERITAGE AND USAGE

What are the possible uses of the Russian methodological heritage for the resolution of contemporary problems? Specifically, what can one learn from it to facilitate gathering an analysis of empirical evidence concerning exploitation and class formation within the Indian peasantry?

Following the chosen path of methodological comparison, I shall not refer here at all to the relevant aspects of the issue of modes of production, to be taken up elsewhere. At 'the other end' of the conceptual spectrum numerous technical and methodological 'tips' of immediate interest can be culled from Russian experience and put to work anew. Yet, it is the way comparison helps to formulate the problematic, which is to my view most important. In so far as the issue of indexing exploitation and stratifying peasant households accordingly is concerned there seem to be three stages of necessary procedure. Each of them represents an answer (or a cluster of answers) to a question crucial for the setting out of those issues in a language directed to field work. These are the questions of types, of the common denominator and of categorization, or scales. The whole range of specific projects in Russia, India and elsewhere is definable in terms of the resolution of these questions. Moreover, the way such a question is resolved narrows down the possible choices further within the sequence.

(*A*) Contemporary peasant societies present a complex network of relations and determinations relevant to the issue, i.e. patterns of exploitation and class formation. To typologize them is to establish a qualitative list of different categories ('topological' in the Russian professional jargon). Within such a taxonomy every peasant household can be defined by a set of binary yes/no answers or else by being placed on a scale of more/less. For example, a peasant household in a sample can be categorized by answering the questions: (*a*) does it employ wage labour on the farm (yes/no)?, (*b*) what equipment does it use (simplest/also a drill/also tractors)?, (*c*) does it also own non-farming enterprises, i.e. a shop, a truck, or a workshop (yes/no)?

A household $X$ employing wage labour on the farm, owning a drill but not a tractor as well as a truck may be then defined accordingly (into, say, the group of the well-to-do and to be watched for possible transformation into a capitalist farm). Such an example brings out clearly enough both the gratifying, if relative, simplicity of usage as well as the limitations of such an attempt using qualitative characterization only. To begin with, there is no direct way to compare relatively the significance of each of these categories. An attempt at further specification rapidly increases the number of the theoretically available slots, making the whole system unwieldy. (There are 12 such possibilities in the example offered above, while a list of this kind actually discussed at the Statistical Convention of 1926 in the USSR included 45 such groups.) While some of the analysts stop at that stage, the validation of many of the major conceptual questions necessitates a further step—the meaningful integration of these categories.

To be truly effective, such a 'step forward' must begin with a satisfactory clarification of the full 'list' of the relevant qualitative categories of rural exploitation and a reasoned decision in so far as consequent selection for usage is concerned. This decision will necessarily dictate subsequent procedure.

(*B*) An attempt to integrate and represent nominal 'topological' categories established can be expressed as the problem of a common denominator. To begin with, for such a need to arise the number of relevant categories must be large. The least unequivocal solution would then be to use simultaneously a number of scales and to trust to either some arbitrary rules of procedure or else the analyst's intuition (when results on different scales contradict each other). A half-way solution, developing further the idea of 'rules of procedure', is to establish multi-variable indices, as for example in defining as middle peasant households all those which have *either* ten acres of operational landholding and two bullocks, *or else* seven acres of operational landholding and four bullocks, etc. An optimal solution would consist of a formula and a 'common currency', enabling integration via meaningful quantification of all of the qualitative aspects of the issue in hand. One index and one quantitative scale only would result.

(*C*) The definition of peasant households in terms of quantified expression of exploitation, empirically recognizable, is not the end of the matter. At the centre of studies of peasant differentiation stands the problem of comparison between specific peasant households and their grouping into conceptual categories rooted in theoretical analysis. In operational language it must involve expressing the empirical results on a scale of peasant groups/categories. Proceeding once more from the least satisfactory, such a scale can consist of categories which are arbitrary (e.g. placing a household of ten acres and two bullocks above a household of seven acres and three bullocks). More satisfactory would be a *quantitatively integrated* scale with arbitrary cutting-off points (e.g. from 5.1 per cent to 10 per cent, from 10.1 per cent to 15 per cent, etc.). The ideal would be a scale translatable directly into the language of social classes, dividing most of the population exclusively into owners of means of production as against proletarians, with very little else. Peasants are not civilized enough to offer such solutions to the purist, but a delineation of optimal solutions is useful for illuminating directions of advance and realistic possibilities at hand. More importantly, any solution to such queries must be closely related to the dynamics, which cannot be 'thrown in' here without a more specific methodological conclusion. We shall turn to it shortly.

A lengthy epistemological discussion of the relations between aims and tools of empirical study could begin here, easily stretching into several volumes. Instead, I shall simply say that I accept most of what was said by those referred to above about the complexities of the matter and the fact that operational solutions can only approximate concepts, not match them. Also, any questions and/or answers would be subject to its context, both social and conceptual as well as related to what can be defined as subject/object relations involved. In this sense different indices can and should be used to illuminate different aspects of a problem and to throw additional light on each other's results. It goes without saying that making use of different indexes does not mean their equality in some eclectic sense, but must be seen in hierarchies of significance defined by the conceptual structure of the question posed. All that accepted, it is still the attempt to push closer the conceptual to the empirical which is the focus of operational debate, past and present.[23] Let us return to that.

The strategies suggested for the class analysis of peasantry can be placed in relation to the sequence of questions/stages suggested. Patnaik's position is to fasten on wage labour and land rent as the main categories. She then declares the impossibility of a common denominator between these categories and subsequently settles for a quantitative scale of one of them, to which a qualitative lessor/ lessee category of exploitative relations is added, the operational relation between which is not (not yet?) fully worked out. Its limitations and strengths as well as my reasons for believing in its qualified usefulness were set out above. As it stands, it should probably be referred to as *LER* (labour exploitation ratio), rather than an *E* one. The different Russian approaches can also be defined via diverse combinations of characteristics, different ways to solve the problems of integration and differences of scale.

Nemchinov's approach reviewed above seems to offer the advantage of high flexibility at this stage (*B*) in its openness to extension and change in the list of qualitative categories without a collapse of integration in the scale used. With a few adjustments (e.g. fertilizers instead of fodder, etc.) it can probably be put to an immediate use in most of the contemporary developing societies, India included. The value of extending the list of exploitative relations relevant to peasant societies must be set against 'the other side of the coin', i.e. the more eclectic nature of the categorization. But it is worth the trouble for it keeps 'in the picture' channels of rural accumulation, exploitation and control. However, such problems cannot be usually solved by pure deduction. An experiment will doubtless be beneficial.

It is important not to treat Nemchinov as a new and final master key. His main importance is in providing a lesson in thinking for oneself, for every social scientist must be also his own methodologist. Both general approach and actual usage must be adjusted to local circumstances. Once more let us see an example of how to build on Nemchinov's scheme by developing new indices. A concept of Net Conventional Income (*NCI*) as developed and defined within Russian studies of peasantry as the sum total of a peasant household's income less all of its input with the single exception of family labour will be used. It will be used, in monetary terms, as a common denominator. The study would commence with a consideration of the basic dimensions of exploitation and capital formation within the relevant peasant society. These could then be categorized to establish two lists of types of income typical of the entrepreneurial/capitalist households (*EI*) on the one hand and the proletarian/poor ones (*PI*) on the other. For example, the *EI* group would include renting out bullocks, renting out land, moneylending, business income, income resulting from use of wage labour at the farm*, etc., while the *PI* group would include wage labour, income from land rented*, etc.

In both groups the last item, marked (*), presents a problem which can be resolved by further analytical work, as long as one remembers that approximation rather than absolute exactitude is sought. Entrepreneurial income resulting from use of wage labour at the farm (*EI**) can be, for example, estimated as the percentage of wage labour within total labour multiplied by the Net Conventional Income from farming. The income from land rented by a poor household (*PI**) can be estimated likewise as the Net Conventional Income with the price of rent incorporated in input. A formula can then be used to define every peasant household, so permitting classification of the sample in terms of the extent of the entrepreneurial self-producing or proletarian tendency within each household, according to the formula

$$\frac{EI - PI}{NCI} \times 100.$$

The longer the list of components, the more difficult the task of empirical estimates and their integration. A balance will have to be struck in such cases. Nor must the choice be arbitrary or purely deductive. Budget Studies can be used as guidance to locate within praxis the most decisive dimension and directions of development of exploitation. In all probability work of lesser depth on large samples and more intensive study of smaller samples will proceed simultaneously.

The paragraph above does not carry a 'better' suggestion, but exemplifies possible ways to extend procedures. The actual job must be left to the practitioners of the work itself. Field work is not conducted by telegrams from abroad. Nor for that matter can it be structured in advance by brilliant deductions from a study room within the 'native' campus, often as far removed from villages as the moon itself.

Finally, a short comment about the second cluster of issues referred to in Section III—the methodology of studying differentiation *as a process*. Once again it is the formulation of the problem which is decisive, and here we can directly benefit from comparison with work of the Russian scholars. The principles established by them by the late 1920s were straightforward enough. To study a *process* one must establish methodology directly relevant to change, i.e. to overcome both the inherent static bias of the ordinary census and the inbuilt descriptive narrowness of monographic studies. All those cannot be simply high abstraction. The Dynamic Study and Budget Study offered a methodological tool to do it at a level which could be, and was, operational and indeed put to use in work on massive empirical data. There is no way to present it here over and above the one-sentence definitions of Section III. The only way is to refer those interested to the basic sources and either make them overcome linguistic idleness or else, 'to take a leaf' out of Thorner's book, get further translations going. Russian Dynamic Studies and Budget Studies are not the last possible word and further methodological development will still be necessary. Before that begins, one should first try to climb up 'the shoulders' of 'giants' for a look ahead.

Which is the moment to bring it all to a close and also back to its beginning by a reminder. The operationalization of concepts finds its significance and its limitations in the problematic posed.

## NOTES

1. For elaboration see, 'The Third Stage: Marxist Historiography and the Origins of Our Time', *Journal of Contemporary Asia*, vol. VI, no. 3 (1976).
2. E. Preobrazhensky, *The New Economics*, Oxford, 1965.
3. J. R. B. Lopes, 'Capitalist Development and Agrarian Structure in Brazil', Cebrap, 1976 (MS.).
4. The debate between Kautsky and David etc. in German Social Democratic Party.
5. For discussion see T. Shanin, *The Awkward Class, Political Sociology of Peasantry in a Developing Society: Russia 1910–25*, Oxford, 1972, chapter 3.
6. For example, Khryashcheva, a Bolshevik, Groman, a Menshevik, and Kushchenko, close to the populists in his outlook, have directed, before the revolution, Zemstvo rural censuses in Tula, Mokshan'sk and Surazh respectively.
7. Chen Po-ta, *A Study of Land Rent in Pre-Revolution China*, Peking, 1966.
8. D. McEachern, 'The Mode of Production in India', *Journal of Contemporary Asia*, vol. VI, no. 4 (1976).
9. The impact of a single translation of Chayanov into English has been indicative enough since Daniel Thorner initiated it. See A. V. Chayanov, *The Theory of Peasant Economy*, AEA, 1966.
10. U. Patnaik, 'Class Differentiation Within the Peasantry', *Economic and Political Weekly*, September 1976.

11. A word-by-word report of the debate was published in *Puti Sel'skogo Khozyaistva*, nos. 4–9 (1927). A great number of relevant articles was also published in *Na agrarnom fronte* of the relevant period.

12. See note 21.

13. See E. Volkov, *Agrarno-ekonomicheskaya statistika rossii*, Moscow, 1923.

14. A. Khryashcheva, *Krest'vanskoe khozvaistvo po perepisyam 1899–1922*, Tula, 1916.

15. V. S. Nemchinov, *Izbrannve proizvedeniya*, vol. I, Moscow, 1967, pp. 71–2.

16. L. Kritsman *et al.*, *Materialy po istorii agrarnoi revolyutsii v Rossii*, vol. I, Moscow, 1928.

17. A Gaister, *Ressloenie sovetskoi derevni*, Moscow, 1928.

18. Nemchinov, op. cit. pp. 44–62.

19. See, for example, A. Chayanov, *Byudzhetnye issledovaniya*, Moscow, 1929.

20. Volkov, op. cit.

21. Quoted from the item 'Zemstvo Statistics' in the Russian encyclopaedia, *Novyi entsiklopedicheskii slovar*, Brokgauz and Efron, vol. XVIII, 1913.

22. For elaboration and examples in English see Shanin, op. cit., which also carries references to the main Russian sources. For alternative review of material available in English see Chayanov, op. cit., and, much more limited, in P. A. Sorokin, F. F. Zimmerman and C. J. Golpin, *Systematic Source Book in Rural Sociology*, Russell and Russell, 1965.

23. Those who would like to challenge my views on that matter should first read T. Shanin, op. cit. chapters 3–7 or T. Shanin, *The Rules of the Game: Cross-Disciplinary Essays on Models of Scholarly Thought*, Tavistock Publications, 1972, etc.

# II

## India, Indonesia, China

# 7

# The Indian Village: Past and Present

ANDRÉ BÉTEILLE
*Delhi School of Economics*

THE Indian village has been a subject of scholarly interest for over a hundred years. In the nineteenth century the studies by Sir Henry Maine and B. H. Baden-Powell stand out as landmarks. In more recent times a large number of investigations have been made by anthropologists, sociologists and economists, so that we now have descriptions of literally hundreds of villages spread through the length and breadth of the country. Perhaps the very weight of this empirical material tends to deter people from attempting to make clear statements about the basic features of the Indian village and the changes taking place in it.

The Indian village has not only been a subject of scholarly interest, it has also occupied an important place in the Indian consciousness. This has clearly been the case since the end of the last century. Both Gandhi and Tagore, the two most influential thinkers of modern India, gave to it a central place in their design of Indian society. They both believed that the village was the principal locus of social life in the past and that the future vigour of Indian society would depend, more than anything else, on the successful reconstitution of its villages.

Clearly, the village itself, as well as the idea of the village as a particular kind of community, is of considerable antiquity in Indian civilization. The historian Niharranjan Ray has emphasized the high value attached to it in the Dharmashastras.[1] Other currents in Indian civilization, particularly in its medieval phase, gave prominence to the town or city, but the village continued to be a basic unit of social organization throughout. The point to bear in mind is that the importance of the village within Indian civilization is to be understood not simply in demographic but also in normative terms. The village was not merely a place where people lived; it had a design in which were reflected the basic values of Indian civilization.

Observers of the Indian village in the twentieth century have been struck, almost one and all, by the many changes taking place in it. If we are to understand what these changes signify, we must have some idea of the earlier design which they are now eroding, and ask what kind of new pattern is emerging in its place. It is not easy to answer such questions, if only because there is no natural watershed which divides the past from the present.

What was the design of the Indian village in the past? How are we to identify this design? Historians are often irked by the tendency among sociologists to look upon the past as undifferentiated and unchanging. Indeed, much misconceived discussion has taken place about the unchanging character of the Indian village. Wars, conquests, migrations, colonizations, and land revenue policies of successive governments have clearly affected the lives of individual villagers and social arrangements in individual villages throughout the ages; such changes deserve the attention which historians are increasingly paying to them. It is another question altogether how significantly they have affected the basic design of the village as a locus of social life.

Among the more stimulating contributions to our understanding of the Indian village are the writings of N. K. Bose who sought to combine in his work the perspectives of ethnography, Indology and social history.[2] Bose maintained that the Indian village had in the past a distinctive design which reflected closely the basic values of Indian civilization. This design had crystallized more or less during the classical phase of Indian history. Many changes were introduced into Indian society during its medieval phase, but these did not affect the basic design of the Indian village. Muslim rule brought in a few new crafts, some new elements were introduced into the population through settlement or conversion or both, but it did not produce any new design to replace the old one. The new groups, whether they practised a new craft or professed a new religion, were fitted into the existing social arrangements without altering their basic character. In other words, these changes were organizational rather than structural.

The nineteenth century, however, saw the emergence of forces which, in Bose's view, were contradictory to those which had ensured the continuity of the basic design of the Indian village for two thousand years. This was not a question simply of a new type of land revenue administration. What was at issue was something far more fundamental—the basic values by which economic life in the village had been governed in the past.

It is obvious that there were variations between villages in the past, as there are at present. Ecological and demographic factors alone would make for considerable variation. In fact, Bose spoke of two polar types of villages, the 'tribal' and the 'Brahmanical', which may perhaps be understood best in terms of the contrast between core and periphery. Villages in the core areas reflected most closely the basic design with which we are here concerned; those in the periphery tended to be smaller, more homogeneous and less stratified.

The contrast between core and periphery has, of course, a geographical dimension, but it cannot be understood in purely geographical terms. The geographical limits of core and periphery, considered separately, fluctuated over time, but their mutual relations had a certain stability. The importance of villages in the core areas cannot be understood simply according to the numerical proportion of such villages, but has to be seen in terms of a cultural model to which a certain value was attached through the ages. Such villages were to be found most commonly in the heartland of Indian civilization, along the banks of the great rivers, near pilgrim centres, and in the environs of imperial cities.

It is in this light that one is likely to be a little disappointed in Baden-Powell's monumental work on the Indian village, despite its wealth of empirical material. For it fails to show how the village captured in its organizational design the distinctive values of a complex civilization. In Baden-Powell's perspective on the Indian village, it is the tribal mode of organization that looms large. More than half way through the book we are told that 'while tribal villages are sufficiently numerous and important to demand a separate chapter, we shall also have to devote another chapter to an *almost* equally large class of non-tribal villages'.[3]

Now, in what follows I shall have little to say about tribal villages, however numerous they might have been in Baden-Powell's time or earlier. I shall present an ideal-typical characterization of the traditional Indian village as a basis for understanding the kinds of changes that are now taking place in it. I do this even though there are obvious dangers in comparing present realities with a conceptual model of the past. Clearly, we will never know the realities of social life in the Indian village in as great detail for the past as for the present.

The ideal-typical village of the past may be characterized by three interrelated features. Firstly, it was a system of multiple gradation, associated with an elaborate division of labour. Secondly, there were in it innumerable vertical ties of a diffuse and enduring nature between families and between persons. Thirdly, there was a general acceptance of hierarchical values among the different members of the village. When changes take place in all these features, as they appear to be doing, the social organization of the village corresponds less and less with its characteristic design.

The gradations in the Indian village may be seen most easily in terms of its arrangement of castes. It was typically a multi-caste unit in which there were not only a top and a bottom, but also a number of intermediate layers. Monographic studies by anthropologists show that a single village might have between twenty and thirty, and sometimes as many as forty or more, castes and sub-castes. It may be argued that these villages are not representative examples, and that there has been a bias among anthropologists in favour of large villages with many castes. But this would probably mean no more than that the anthropologist has been interested more in the typical than in the average.

Social life in the village was based on an economy of land and grain. In addition to agriculture, which engaged the largest number of people, the village also made provisions for a variety of crafts and services. It is in the relations between agriculture, crafts and services that we see most clearly the distinctive design of the Indian village, and, when these relations change, the design itself becomes eroded.

There are two features of village crafts and services that are noteworthy: (*i*) their number and variety, and (*ii*) their association with self-recruiting specialist groups. (It would be tedious to reproduce the lists that we have of the crafts and services—twelve, fifteen, or even more—that the village was supposed to have.) Now, I do not believe that this general preoccupation of the villagers with self-sufficiency in agriculture, crafts and services can be simply dismissed with the argument that few villages, if any, had the full complement of crafts and services required by its inhabitants. The actual number of specialist groups in a village varied considerably, there being more in the core and fewer in the peripheral areas. What is important is that people had a conception of an ideal or a proper village, comprising different categories of people, and they tried to make their particular village correspond as closely as possible to this ideal.

This is seen in the manner in which new villages were set up until as recently as the nineteenth century: the landowners or peasants did not go alone, but took with them, or settled shortly after the village was set up, families of priests, barbers, washermen, blacksmiths, carpenters, potters, scavengers, and so on. In the right kind of village the right people did the right work, and villagers naturally strove to ensure that they did not have to depend too much on outside help for meeting the multifarious needs of their everyday existence. These needs were more various in the core areas than in the peripheries.

As has been pointed out time and again, everyone in the village, including members of specialist groups, might make a living from agriculture, and indeed land was the most valued reward for any kind of service. But participation in agriculture was elaborately graded. Thus, while the scriptures as well as local custom allowed both Brahmans and scavengers to make a living from agriculture, their roles in the productive system were very different. Some lived off the rents from their land; others supervised the work on their farms; and yet others did various kinds of manual work either on their own land or on land not owned or controlled by themselves.

It might be a little misleading to apply the concept of ownership in its exact contemporary sense to the villages of the past. What needs to be understood, on the other hand, are the gradations in (*i*) the rights over the land and its produce, and (*ii*) the obligations of service. It was through the multiplicity of these gradations that the Indian village maintained its distinctiveness in the past. In this scheme of things a high value was in general placed on pursuits which did not involve manual work. Within agriculture, the dominant productive activity, one sees clearly the inverse relationship between the extent of manual work performed and the degree of control over the land. There were some sections of the village whose members were required by custom to abstain from all manual work on the farm; there were others who were required by custom to perform the most onerous form of manual work; there were yet others whose customs allowed the men to work on the farm, but not the women.

In the past there were strict limits beyond which people might not interchange their economic roles in the village. Members of specialist groups might become agriculturists, but not vice versa. It was not for just anyone in the village to become a priest, a barber, a washerman, or even a blacksmith, a carpenter or a potter. To some extent this was true also of the differentiated roles within agriculture. Brahmans, no matter how poor, could not themselves till the land; Untouchables, no matter how enterprising, could not become substantial landlords. In other words, the distinctions between the different grades in the agrarian hierarchy were at one level structural, and it would be quite misleading to view all their members as peasants, comparable to 'so many potatoes in a sack of potatoes'.

No doubt there were shifts in individual fortunes within the village, but one must emphasize that these shifts could take place only within certain limits. Clearly, demographic fluctuations must have had some consequences for the economic conditions of individual families, but these consequences were probably of a different kind in the Indian village than in villages elsewhere. For one thing, elsewhere demographic fluctuations could to some extent be taken care of by a two-way flow between agriculture and the crafts. In the Indian village, on the other hand, one might move from craft to agriculture, but not quite as easily in the reverse direction.

Among those engaged in agriculture, while there would no doubt be a certain amount of movement between large, medium and small peasants, probably of a cyclical nature, the movement from peasant to landlord, and, even more so in the reverse direction, would be of a different order. In a nutshell, landlords would lose caste by becoming peasants, for the landlord belongs typically to a caste whose men did not wield the plough and whose women did not work on the land, whereas peasants, by definition, cultivate their own land. It is not as if people did not lose (or gain) caste in the traditional system, but the time cycles and the adjustive mechanisms involved would be quite different from those involved in fluctuations between small, medium and large peasants in a village consisting only of peasants.

The gradations in the Indian village rested thus on a combination of economic inequalities and inequalities of status, and found their concrete expression in the institution of caste. It would be wrong to believe that each caste was economically homogeneous, or that all the castes in a village could be placed in a linear order, or that no changes took place in the mutual positions of families of the same caste or even of different castes. It would be equally wrong to ignore the extent to which the population of the village was divided and subdivided, and the distinctive manner in which the institution of caste protected the boundaries between these divisions and subdivisions.

Typologically a village with many gradations has to be distinguished, on the one hand, from a peasant village, and, on the other, from one which is dichotomized into opposed classes. The Indian village of the past is often described as a peasant community. My argument is that it was too far differentiated and stratified to suit that label.[4] Further, the differentiation and stratification cannot be seen simply in terms of variations or fluctuations around a certain mean; it has to be understood in the light of a design which is basically different from the design of a peasant community.

All this is not to deny that many Indian villages of the past might in fact correspond fairly well to the peasant type of village. This would clearly be the case with villages in the peripheral areas, whether in the interior hill and forest tracts, or in the frontier tracts. Villages among tribals practising settled agriculture, such as the Santals, Oraons and Mundas, would be very close to this type. But even here one notices the influence of what may be called the 'dominant' model. For instance, among the Mundas one would find in the nineteenth century the population of the village being divided into *khuntkattidars*, Mundas of lesser lineages, and a few low-ranking artisan and servicing 'castes' such as basketmakers, weavers, blacksmiths, and so on.[5]

Nor is it easy to see the traditional village with its many gradations in terms of a simple dichotomy of 'landowning' and 'landless' classes (or castes). The absence of ownership in the strictly contemporary sense does not of course preclude the conflict of interests among people occupying unequal positions in the system of production. At the same time, groups acquire the character of classes to the extent that the conflict of interests between them becomes polarized. What evidence we have of this kind of polarization comes more readily from the present than from the past.

Those who have written about the Indian village have generally been struck by the prominent part played in it by vertical ties of every kind, ranging from the formal and elaborate pattern of *jajmani* relations to the informal and variable relations between patron and client. The prominence of these vertical ties, particularly in the past, should itself put us on our guard against applying either the 'peasant' model or the 'class' model to the Indian village. For a peasant village is a community of equals, or near-equals, and vertical ties, though

8

they may be present in such a community, can hardly be a defining feature of its structure, as they were of the Indian village in the past. Again, the presence of diffuse, enduring personal ties between superiors and inferiors is precisely what keeps in check the polarization of a community into mutually opposed classes.

We get a detailed picture of the Hindu *jajmani* system at the village level from Wiser's study of Karimpur, near Agra in Uttar Pradesh.[6] Wiser describes the system in terms of the exchange of services between the twenty-four castes in the village, noting that there were only three specialist groups lacking (in 1932) to make the village more or less self-sufficient. He takes pains to highlight the institutional basis of these relationships, quoting from both classical and modern writers to support his argument.

Wiser, like many others before and after him, stresses the interdependence involved in the system, although he makes it clear that there was gradation in both services and payments. In many cases, though by no means all, the terminological counterpart of *jajman* is *kamin*, and the *jajman* is clearly the superior and the *kamin* the inferior. It is difficult to account for the inequalities inherent in *jajmani* relations in terms of a single underlying principle. There seem to be at least two different, though interrelated, principles involved, related to gradations in control over land on the one hand, and, on the other, to gradations in types of work on a scale of purity and pollution. What seems to be clear is that the *jajmani* system was not one by which a class of landowning or otherwise privileged people were linked directly to a class of landless or underprivileged people. Rather, it consisted of a series of links, often vertical in nature, between families occupying various positions in a graded system.

It is important to stress the enduring nature of *jajmani* ties, and the pivotal position occupied in the system by families controlling the land which were usually of superior status, although they might not always enjoy the highest position in the formal ranking of castes even within the village. The *jajmani* system as a full-blown institutional order did not exist everywhere; we do not have even a broad idea of its distribution. But if we regard enduring vertical ties between persons and between families as important ingredients in the system, these clearly had a very wide distribution in the past.

M. N. Srinivas has drawn attention repeatedly to the crucial importance of the vertical ties between landlord and tenant, between master and servant, and between creditor and debtor.[7] Relations of this kind, unlike *jajmani* relations in Wiser's sense, were not necessarily channelled along the lines of caste. They took the form either of dyadic relations or of social networks which might to some extent cut across the structure of caste. Indeed, what kept the vertically arranged layers of the village in their place were the many networks running up and down—and laterally—through which individuals and families were linked together.

Srinivas uses the phrase 'patron–client relationship' to cover the different types of vertical ties just enumerated. Patrons might have clients in their own caste as well as in other castes. Patron–client ties served to bridge the cleavages between castes. Patrons belonging to the same caste (or the same economic level) might be rivals, in which case they would use the ties with their respective clients in their contest with each other. Patrons depended on their clients for their power as well as their prestige; clients might in their turn count on the support of their patrons in difficulty or distress.

In the small world of the village the patron—whether as landlord or as master or even as creditor—had some personal involvement in the well-being of his clients. The relations between the two were typically multiplex in character, even though they might not be equally durable in every case. In some cases these relations might be transmitted from generation to generation, while in others the patron might exercise a degree of choice in discarding old clients and attaching new ones. But even the lowliest could turn for protection to someone, who in turn might enjoy the protection of someone else higher up.

In contemporary perspective the relations between landlord and tenant, creditor and debtor, or master and servant appear clearly exploitative in character. On the other hand, this perspective itself was significantly different in the past from what it is today. In the past the social world of the village was permeated by hierarchical values. Not only were different people unequally placed, but each knew where he belonged, and was in a large measure reconciled to his place in the total scheme of things. This contributed to the stability of the design that was distinctive of the village in the past.

Hierarchical values are a familiar feature of pre-industrial civilizations in general, yet one cannot but be impressed by the extent to which they were elaborated in India. Here all sections of society were permitted, even encouraged, to maintain their identities by pursuing distinctive styles of life; at the same time, they had to acknowledge their inequality of condition. What was true of society as a whole was true also of the village. Particularly among the Hindus, the twin concepts of *dharma* and *karma* served to relate the hierarchy of the village to that of the universe.

It must be admitted that a study of the normative texts of classical Hinduism does not provide a full understanding of the values actually held by people at different levels of the village hierarchy. It is unlikely that the hierarchy would appear in the same light from the top as from the bottom, and the texts by and large give us a view of it from the top. But while it is true that we shall never fully know what *dharma*, *karma* and like concepts actually signified for the Untouchable labourer in the past, it is also true that these concepts were widely, if not universally, recognized and acknowledged. Perhaps hierarchical values were actively espoused only by those at the top, while those at the bottom were merely reconciled to them.

Hierarchical values were most clearly expressed through the traditional arrangement of castes, but they had some significance for every type of social arrangement involving superior and inferior positions. Thus, not only Brahmans and Untouchables, but also landlords and labourers were in some ways considered as destined to play unequal roles in life.

It is in the context of these hierarchical values that we have to examine the relations between caste and land control, and between caste and the division of labour. A landlord was more than a mere landlord when he was also of superior caste; conversely, the landless were doubly deprived when they were also Untouchables. Priests, barbers, washermen and scavengers were unequally ranked not by virtue of their work alone, but also because the castes to which they belonged were unequally ranked. Custom, law and religion combined to sustain a moral environment in which hierarchy was considered to be a part of the natural scheme of things.

If we look at the Indian village today, we will find clear evidence of the erosion of the three features that I have described in the preceding section. Once again, it is not essential to know exactly how many villages in the past displayed all these features in their full form. What seems evident is that villages today show less and less the properties which I believe were constitutive of the design of a certain type of village which prevailed in the past. Clearly, there will be differences between one village and another in the extent to which the old design is still manifest, depending upon differences in initial conditions and in their exposure to the forces of change.

The number of gradations in the village is being reduced, and their significance altered. There is in this sense a certain simplification of structure. Now, this simplification might lead in one of two directions. Either the upper and the lower layers become reduced and merge with the middle, so that the village comes more and more to resemble the model of a peasant village. Or, it becomes split through the middle, and landowners and landless become progressively differentiated, so that the village begins to correspond more and more to a bipolar or two-class model.

At the time of independence there was perhaps some hope that Indian villages, battered for two hundred years by the forces released by colonial domination, could be reconstituted into peasant communities of a sort. Land reforms, co-operatives, community development were all thought of as possible means to that end. These and other means have been tried in the three decades since independence, but there is little indication of the village acquiring the kind of social homogeneity that is typical of the peasant village. The basic mistake lay probably in the assumption that the typical Indian village ever was a community of peasants.

There is, on the other hand, considerable evidence of polarization, although the evidence is mixed and by no means easy to interpret. Landowners and landless stand in sharper contrast today than they did in the past. This has come about partly through the erosion of the many intermediate grades—in landholding as well as services—that were a conspicuous feature of the village in the past.

Influences of diverse kinds—land reforms, market forces, population pressures—have simplified the structure of land control in the village. Intermediary tenures have been abolished, and the types of tenants reduced in number. Landowners are now owners in a much fuller sense of the term, without having to share their rights with a variety of intermediaries who in the past might stand between them and the actual tillers. Variations no doubt remain, but it appears that the non-cultivating owner is being replaced increasingly by persons who play a more direct role in cultivation.

If the land reforms succeeded in eliminating or at least in reducing the role of non-working landlords, they certainly failed to do away with the landless. Landless labourers are very much a part of the

Indian village today, and their numbers have grown both absolutely and relatively during the last couple of decades. This growth has been partly a result of demographic pressures, but other factors have also contributed to it. Tenants of various kinds as well as village artisans in varying numbers have been reduced to the condition of landless labourers.

The growth in number of landless labourers is probably the most significant feature of the Indian village of the present. Along with this there are changes in their character and consciousness. In the past the agricultural labourer often combined his work in the field with a number of other services for his master and for the village as a whole. This is now changing. Agricultural labourers are probably becoming increasingly homogeneous in their economic activity and source of livelihood. Here one has to be careful, because there are enormous regional variations, and it is not uncommon, even in areas with high proportions of agricultural labourers, to find that the same person is agricultural labourer, sharecropper and owner of a dwarf holding, all at the same time.

Of considerable significance to the change in the character and consciousness of the growing body of agricultural labourers is the erosion of the kind of vertical ties that were so distinctive of the Indian village in the past. The old ties of patronage are losing their significance for both landlords and labourers, although for different reasons. Landlords prefer a more contractual type of arrangement where they find the traditional obligations to their dependents economically burdensome. Labourers, in their turn, find the demands traditionally made on them by their masters oppressive and exploitative.

The whole edifice of *jajmani* relations, with its complex balance of rights and obligations, has collapsed. We do not know when this process began, but there is not a single account of *jajmani*, from Wiser onwards, which does not describe it as being more or less a thing of the past. Other relationships, of a more diffuse nature, between landowner and tenant, master and servant or creditor and debtor have weakened or been redefined. This redefinition tends to give such relationships a more instrumental character. The easy extension of ties across the village makes it possible now to manipulate relationships which in the past were more binding in nature. All this makes for a greater awareness among the landless of their common interests, and of the conflict of interest between them and their employers.

This new awareness is in turn advanced by the erosion of hierarchical values. It is not easy to measure the changes taking place in the values of village people, but there is no dearth of evidence for this kind of change. Those at the bottom of the village hierarchy, whether as Harijans or as landless labourers, are now less prepared to accept their inferior condition as part of the natural scheme of things. Often the most striking indication of this change is the difference in mood that one encounters between the younger and the older generation of Harijans in the same village.

The difference between the normative order of the past and of the present is clear. In the past, custom, law and religion combined to support the existing pattern of inequality. Today law and politics, at least, proclaim the virtue of equality. This is not to say that inequalities have disappeared or even that they have been reduced, but only that they now exist in a changing moral environment. This changing environment, together with the change in their objective conditions, tends to make the underprivileged, whether as landless or as Harijans, increasingly conscious of their deprivations.

I have in this section merely indicated certain tendencies which have been at work in the countryside during the last hundred years, and increasingly so during the last two or three decades. These tendencies have definitely altered the past character of the Indian village which, I argued earlier, had a distinctive design. Now, while one sees all this, it is by no means easy to show that a new pattern has emerged to replace the old.

There is evidence of polarization, but, as I have said, this evidence is by no means clear. Neither the landowners nor even the landless are today economically homogeneous categories. There are landowners with holdings of small, medium or large size; landowners who themselves cultivate the land, and others who do not; among cultivators, households in which both men and women work in the field and those in which only men but not women do such work; landowners or cultivators who employ wage labourers regularly and others who do so only occasionally or rarely. Among the landless there are tenants, sharecroppers and wage labourers of various kinds. Thus the structure of economic interests is not the same in every village, nor is it always stable in any particular village.

Even where economic divisions are relatively stable and clear-cut, they do not always coincide with the divisions of caste. These latter are everywhere important at one level at least, that which separates the Harijans (and Adivasis) from the 'clean' castes. There are many social distinctions between the Harijans and the clean castes, and in the village the demarcation between the two is clear, being often reflected in the settlement pattern. Indeed, villages today show two tendencies towards polarization, between landed and landless on the one hand, and between clean castes and Harijans on the other, and these two do not necessarily converge.

Again, while vertical ties are changing their character, they have by no means disappeared. New conditions create new needs for people at the different levels of village society. The rich need services and the poor need security. The ties of patronage continue to run up and down village society despite the cracks that are appearing across it.

Finally, while the hierarchical values which gave stability to the village in the past are losing ground, we cannot ignore the role in the present of the coercive apparatus of the state in keeping polarization within politically manageable limits. In the past the state was a remote presence so far as the maintenance of order within the village was concerned. This is no longer the case. Any major crisis in a village today is known at once to the world outside, and the state has increased enormously its capability for decisive intervention.

## NOTES

1. Niharranjan Ray, *Nationalism in India*, Aligarh, Aligarh Muslim University, 1973, pp. 143 ff.
2. See, in particular, N. K. Bose, *The Structure of Hindu Society* (translated from the Bengali with an introduction and notes by André Béteille), New Delhi, Orient Longmans, 1975; first published in 1949.
3. B. H. Baden-Powell, *The Indian Village Community*, Delhi, Cosmo Publication, 1972, p. 226 (italics added), first published in 1896.
4. See André Béteille, *Six Essays in Comparative Sociology*, Delhi, Oxford University Press, 1974, chapter 3.
5. Ibid. chapter 4.
6. William H. Wiser, *The Hindu Jajmani System*, Lucknow, Lucknow Publishing House, 1936.
7. M. N. Srinivas, 'The Social System of a Mysore Village', in M. Marriott (ed.), *Village India*, Chicago, University of Chicago Press, 1955; see also his *The Remembered Village*, Delhi, Oxford University Press, 1976.

# 8

# Village India and its Political Economy

## K. N. RAJ

*Centre for Development Studies, Trivandrum*

IRUVELIPATTU is a village in the South Arcot district of Tamil Nadu. It is situated between the Pennar River, which runs north of it about a mile and a half away, and a tributary of the same river flowing by the side of it in the south. Some imaginative mind in the obscure past saw these two rivers as two fences, *iru veli*, protecting and cutting off the village from the world beyond, and so it came to be called Iruvelipattu, the name by which it has been known ever since.

This was the village that Professor Gilbert Slater chose to visit first, in February 1916, soon after he took charge of the new Department of Economics of the University of Madras. The visit had an objective and it was simple in conception. He wanted students of Economics in the university to look upon the subject, not as 'a series of unintelligible theories to be learnt parrot fashion from Marshall's *Principles*' as they were inclined to, but as one which had 'as its central object of study the causes of and remedies for Indian poverty'. This, he believed, could be achieved if the attention of students could be directed towards the study of particular villages. To decide what questions to focus attention on in such studies, Professor Slater felt the need to visit a few villages himself. Iruvelipattu came his way only because one of his students was a native of this village.

Though the selection of Iruvelipattu was as accidental as that of the students associated with Professor Slater's project, it was evidently as good a choice as one could have made for a study of the kind visualized. Some of his observations about the village at the time are of relevance even now.

For instance, Professor Slater noted that about 400 acres of the 656 acres of cultivated land in the village were owned by one man (who had also another 200 acres in adjoining villages). Half of this

land in the village was directly cultivated drawing on the labour of
40 *padiyals* (bonded labourers who had fallen into hereditary dependence on him through debt), and the rest, about 200 acres, leased out
to tenants who were reported to be generally small holders cultivating
the land with their own labour. A *padiyal* was in effect a serf and was
generally required to work from dawn to dusk; but he enjoyed one
important privilege, namely the right to receive from his master a
regular amount of paddy (or other grain) all the year round, whether
or not he was fully employed. This guaranteed wage, tied to what
could perhaps be described as rather over-full employment, was in
itself quite meagre: it was just over one kg of paddy per day, a
quantity which, as Professor Slater observed, a man would be
'probably able and willing to eat himself without assistance from his
wife and family', in fact about the same as the prevailing ration at
the time for a prisoner doing hard labour in jail. However, a tenant
cultivator who lived on one acre of leased-in land could not have
been very much better off, since the average yield of wet land was
probably not more than about 900 kg of paddy per acre and even the
fixed rents payable in money (which were generally lower than the
share rents payable in kind) seem to have been equal in value to over
350 kg of paddy per acre. Compared to the residual income of about
550 kg of paddy from such a small tenant holding, the annual
guaranteed wage of a *padiyal* at the time—a little over 410 kg of
paddy—does not appear excessively low.

The inferences that Professor Slater himself drew from his observations in Iruvelipattu are interesting. English arable land, he noted for
instance, would bear a crop of wheat only once in four years, while
paddy land in the Carnatic region of South India could produce one,
two and sometimes three crops of rice a year (not to mention other
profitable crops). Nevertheless, he pointed out,

the Indian worker earns very low wages, has a very low standard of
expenditure, and attains a very low level of efficiency, and these three
characteristics of Indian life are so inter-connected, that it is impossible to say which is cause rather than effect. Indian employers
do not believe in the Economy of High Wages; and as yet only faint
beginnings of trade unionism are to be found among Indian manual
workers.

The obvious implication of this observation was that the weak
bargaining power of labour was in part responsible for the inefficient
use of the available land.

Twenty years later Iruvelipattu received academic attention once again when it was decided to re-survey the villages investigated by Professor Slater and his students. The re-survey, guided by Professor P. J. Thomas and a colleague in the Department of Economics, was somewhat more systematic and detailed, and provided additional information on certain matters that had been only briefly touched upon earlier.

In the two decades between 1916 and 1936, several changes had taken place. The population of Iruvelipattu had slightly declined, by about three and a half per cent. Following the Great Depression of the thirties, the price of paddy had fallen to nearly one-half of what it used to be. Apparently in response to these developments, but perhaps also in part due to shortage of water, there was some decline in the area cultivated in the village, particularly of paddy land that was being earlier double-cropped. The gross area sown with paddy (i.e. including the area double-cropped) was reported to have fallen by nearly one-fourth between 1920–21 and 1935–36, and the gross area sown with other crops by over two-fifths. The total output, employment and income in the village must have therefore declined significantly during the period.

There is however no way of determining how precisely the incidence of such decline was distributed within the village society. We can gather from the re-survey that well over a half, in fact nearly three-fifths, of the net cultivated area in the village was under tenancy in 1936; and that the rent on such land was in the range of 310 to 490 kg per acre (depending on the fertility of the land and on whether the rent payable was on a fixed or share-cropping basis). Tenants whose rents were fixed in terms of money were probably affected very adversely. There appears to have been also some deterioration in the terms and conditions of work of the *padiyals*, but, apart from seasonal migration to adjacent regions, no agricultural labourers are reported to have left the village permanently. We are altogether in the dark about the fate of the landlord who had 400 acres of land in the village in 1916, as there is no reference at all to him in the study.

Such loss of a promising trail of enquiry is indeed frustrating, but, thanks to a fortuitous circumstance, some of the threads can be picked up again for a later period. The two surveys conducted in 1916 and 1936 had stimulated enough interest for a scholar from the Agricultural Economics Research Institute at Oxford, Miss Margaret Haswell, to undertake still another investigation of Iruvelipattu in

1961. Though the published findings of Miss Haswell are much too fragmentary, and no study of the village seems to have been attempted since then, they help to fill a few significant gaps in our knowledge, more particularly of its fortunes after India won political independence and embarked on planned programmes of development.

The first decade of planned development brought Iruvelipattu at least two sources of great potential benefit. One was electricity which came to the village in 1958; the other was in the form of land legislation passed in the State in 1960, fixing a ceiling of holdings (pegged at no more than 12 standard acres for a family of not more than five members). The full story of how the two together, electricity plus land reform, affected Iruvelipattu cannot be told yet, at any rate not until someone is stimulated enough to study it over again. Miss Haswell's findings give us however some glimpses of what was changing and what was not, of the direction of change, and above all of the difference between the form and content of the changes that were taking place within this village between the 'two fences'.

The population of Iruvelipattu in 1961 was about 10 per cent higher than in 1916, but the total cultivable area had risen only very marginally. More significantly, there had taken place a sharp decline in the net sown area because the dry land in the village (i.e. land dependent solely on rainfall), which accounted for about a fifth of the total cultivable area, was not being cultivated at all in 1961. Judging from the earlier assessments of land revenue, it is of course clear that the net product from an acre of dry land in the village was perhaps only as much as one-quarter of that from an acre of irrigated (wet) land. Nevertheless, when the pressure of population on land was still high, and a large segment of the villagers could hardly secure their minimum subsistence needs, one would normally expect an increase rather than a decrease in the cultivated area.

The explanation for the apparently perverse trend is to be found mainly in the use of the newly-available electricity for installation of pump-sets, 17 of which were in operation in 1961 and made possible double-cropping of about two-fifths of the net sown area. Those who commanded enough finance to be able to apply more fertilizers along with irrigation could secure more than 1,400 kg per acre of wet land. Presumably, in this way, the new technology made so much difference to returns at the margin that it was no longer worth their while to cultivate with hired labour any of the dry land in their possession.

Leasing it out to tenants was perhaps not attractive enough, in view of the lower rent obtained from dry land and the risks associated with such leasing out.

When these effects of the change in technology ushered in by electricity are considered along with the impact of the land reform legislation the probable direction of the changes in the village economy since then becomes easier to visualize. For, according to Miss Haswell's findings, the direct descendant of the landlord who owned about 400 acres in Iruvelipattu in 1916 was not only very much there but had increased his holding to 500 acres by 1961 and was in the process of 'further increasing his estate' by purchasing land from small cultivators in debt. Since a standard acre had been defined in the ceiling legislation as an acre assessed to land revenue at the rate of Rs 10 to 15 per annum, this holding of 500 acres was the equivalent of only 123 standard acres. Still it was more than 10 times as high as the ceiling fixed. 'His method of evasion', Miss Haswell explains, 'was to register his "surplus" land in the names of others.'

Half of this large holding was under lease to tenants as before. The average yield on tenant-cultivated holdings was only about 1,000 kg of paddy on the average, but the rent payable was no less than 400 kg per acre. Landless agricultural labourers were receiving a wage equivalent to about three and one-third kg of paddy per day; but they were estimated to have on the average only a little over 130 days of work, and could therefore secure no more than about 440 kg of paddy, which was only marginally higher than the annual income of just over 410 kg of paddy for a *padiyal* reported in 1916. It would therefore appear that, even if a labourer was no longer a *padiyal*, freedom from bondage implied no significant increase in income for the landless except in the form of leisure (whether preferred or enforced). Also, as in 1916, tenants with small holdings could not have been very much better off than the landless. On the other hand, one may safely surmise that, of the total paddy output of possibly around 540 tonnes from the village in 1961, the equivalent of at least 200 tonnes accrued to one landowner in the form of rent and profits.

What happened in Iruvelipattu over the period 1916 to 1961 cannot of course be regarded as typical of trends in other villages, either in India as a whole or in Tamil Nadu. In fact, the information available for the rest of the villages covered by the three surveys shows clearly that it was not. On the other hand, Iruvelipattu cannot be dismissed wholly as a freak either. There are several landowners even now in this region who have in effect holdings of irrigated land of a hundred acres and more in size, nominally registered in different names in order to escape the ceiling legislation, receiving a disproportionately large share of the benefits bestowed by rural development programmes.

For instance, one such programme, currently in the process of being implemented on a high priority basis since early this year, is reported to be in Kapistalam in Thanjavur district where one family is known to have owned several thousand acres some time ago and still has substantial holdings in different names (including some in the names of temples and trusts managed by the same family). Not only does the political and administrative apparatus of the government overlook the evasions of the law in respect of ceilings, particularly when the persons concerned are loyal supporters of the regime, but it is at present actively engaged here in getting the drainage and irrigation network in this area re-done in an integrated manner covering several blocks of fields and villages, making new tractorable roads into the fields, and experimenting with soils, paddy varieties, fertilizers, etc. for raising substantially the productivity of this land. Presumably all this is being done as part of the Fifth Five Year Plan and the Twenty-Point Programme.

The rationale of development programmes based on such gross inequality in the distribution of wealth and income is of course well known. Apart from the possibility of a higher rate of saving being realized, the marketed surpluses of foodgrain would be certainly much larger than if ownership of land and the income from it were more equally distributed. In the case of Iruvelipattu itself, as much as one-half of its total paddy output was probably being marketed in 1961. The rural poor may continue to remain poor, or even be reduced to greater destitution, but the more articulate and politically explosive sections of the urban population can be kept content if large enough foodgrain supplies are ensured to them at stable prices.

There are however considerable socio-economic differences between villages and one cannot be sure whether, even if one were to brush aside more basic questions such as of equity, and whom development is for, what appears an easy option in Iruvelipattu would be equally so elsewhere. For, if the ownership of land were less unequal, and if the pattern and intensity of use of resources is found to vary a great deal with other institutional dimensions such as the terms and conditions on which land is leased out and hired labour is available, other alternatives may be open which could appear no less practical and attractive.

This range of issues cannot of course be explored very far with the material available from the few village studies initiated by Professor Slater and followed up by others. The villages covered by all the surveys and re-surveys conducted in 1916, 1936 and 1961, while unique in that they cover nearly half a century, are only five in number. The method and scope of the investigations also vary so much that the data available are to a large extent not comparable. These studies are, however, very useful in helping us to see some of the socio-economic differences between villages and how conventional analysis may fail to capture important consequences arising therefrom.

In fact, there is an important set of issues that economic theory has not squarely faced but which one cannot escape when dealing with Indian village economies. It concerns the role of power and social values in determining what choices are open to whom and how far they can go in exercising them. In the days when it was common to describe the subject as Political Economy, the power exercised by different classes of society and their social values were recognized explicitly as important factors governing both resource utilization and income distribution (as is to some extent reflected even in the observations of Professor Slater on Iruvelipattu). But such non-quantifiable and otherwise inconvenient dimensions have not received similar attention since then and, as more rigour and scientific respectability were sought, they have come to be treated merely as exogenous elements, more or less on a par with, say, climate.

The method of analysis now generally adopted is, therefore, to take into account the resource endowments of each category of owners; try to specify in some general form, given the technical constraints as well as the characteristics of the market, what options are available for each of the relevant products and factors of production, and, by using one or the other of the usual maximization criteria, derive the implicit returns to the respective owners and the probable pattern of resource utilization. This kind of analysis has been used even to explain some features of agrarian economies such as tenancy, share-cropping, and rural under-employment.

In one such recent exercise, attempting to explain variations in the extent and forms of agricultural tenancy in India, a number of interesting hypotheses have been advanced and declared as consistent with the available empirical evidence. One hypothesis is that the percentage of area under tenancy will be higher in areas where the land improvement factor is larger (i.e. soil fertility, rainfall, irrigation etc. is better); another is that the larger the extent of unemployment facing the landless households the higher the extent of tenancy. Similarly, it has been suggested that the percentage of area under share-cropping will be higher in the case of more labour-intensive crops, higher in areas with larger unemployment facing the landless families, but lower in areas with a high differential interest rate that the landless share-cropper has to pay over that paid by those with land of their own, and so on.

Let us consider briefly how far some of these propositions are consistent with the information available to us through the village surveys stimulated by Professor Slater. Compare, for instance, the land–man ratio, area irrigated, the productivity of land, etc. with the extent of tenancy in the village of Dusi in North Arcot district and in Palakkurichi village in Thanjavur district in 1936.

Dusi, inhabited by 294 families (total population, 1316), had 485 acres of wet (irrigated) land and 231 acres of dry land under cultivation; while Palakkurichi, with only 208 families (total population, 869), had under cultivation 977 acres of wet land and only 73 acres of dry land. The land revenue assessments of the time indicate that the net product per acre of wet land in Dusi was nearly twice as high as in Palakkurichi, while that of dry land in the former was only about half as much as in the latter. Thus, while both were extensively irrigated villages, the advantage of 'the land improvement factor' was evidently greater in the former.

There was apparently no great difference in the crops grown in the two villages, with paddy dominant on wet land and groundnut and inferior cereals like ragi on dry land. Data on the extent of unemployment among landless households are not available, but there is one important piece of evidence which suggests that they are likely to have been very much more in number in Palakkurichi than in Dusi. For there were no *padiyals* at all in Dusi, while there were 95 families of *padiyals* in Palakkurichi forming nearly one-half of the total number of families in the village.

If one were to go by the hypotheses stated earlier one would expect the tenancy to be more widespread in Palakkurichi than in Dusi, or, even if it were not quite the case, the difference to be not very large; one would also expect the incidence of share-cropping to be greater in that village. Yet the available evidence is quite to the contrary.

In Dusi the entire cultivated area was under tenancy in 1916; and three-fourths of it was on share-cropping basis, with the share of the landowner as high as five-sixths of the gross produce when all inputs other than labour were provided by the owner. The extent of tenancy had fallen by 1936, and the fixed rent system had become the dominant form of tenancy because many of the landowning families had migrated out of the village and they preferred the fixed rent system which did not call for direct supervision; but the area under tenancy was still nearly three-fourths of the total cultivated area, and even the fixed rents were reported to be more than 1,000 kg per acre (presumably on double-cropped land which accounted for well over 80 per cent of the wet land in the village).

In Palakkurichi, on the other hand, all except five of the landowners are reported to have been directly engaged in cultivation in 1916, and less than a quarter of the total cultivated area was under tenancy. The extent of tenancy appears to have fallen still further to about 10 per cent of the cultivated area by 1936. Moreover, land was being leased out mainly on fixed rent basis. The report on the 1936 survey points out also that, while fixed rents (which ranged from 500 to 650 kg of paddy per acre) were meant 'to give the tenants an opportunity to improve the land and profit by the increased yield', the reverse was the case in practice because they had generally no capital to meet the initial costs of cultivation and the short period of the lease (usually for one year) acted as a disincentive.

The explanation for the sharp contrast between what one might expect on the basis of the theoretical hypotheses and the actual facts as reported from these two villages lies perhaps mainly in the difference in their social structure. In Dusi, all the land was reported in 1916 to be owned by Brahmin families, who formed about a fourth of the total population of the village. Though about one-third of them had migrated from the village by 1936, there is no report of any large sales of land by them, only of changes in the form of tenancy from share-cropping to fixed rent basis. The report on the 1936 survey makes it also clear that over 60 per cent of all the families in the village were Naickers, who, as a community, are known for their willingness to be directly involved in cultivation. This, along with the absence of a plentiful supply of *padiyals*, was in all probability responsible for tenancy being so extensive.

In Palakkurichi, however, most of the land was owned by Nayudus,

9

who formed about one-sixth of all the families in the village. The report on the 1916 survey stated that 'their individual holdings are fairly large'; that they were not only agriculturists 'by custom and instinct' but 'pride themselves upon the thought that agriculture is the noblest, the least harmful and the most independent of all professions'; but that they were extremely conservative, clung to the security offered by the joint family system, lacked individual initiative and enterprise, and therefore remained economically backward. At the same time there was the vast reserve army of *padiyals* in the village, for whom the daily wage in 1916 was stated to be less than 1 kg of paddy (though there were also some extra payments for them over the year) compared to the prevailing rate of 2 kg per day for the free labourer. It is not therefore surprising that direct cultivation with hired labour was preferred to tenancy. But, for the reasons already indicated, the extent of involvement of the owners in raising productivity does not appear to have been very great. The report on the 1916 survey points out that 'about half the land can yield two crops per annum but many cultivators are too indolent to grow two crops'; and that 'the whole village was for generations in the hands of large landlords who did not take any interest in maintaining the full productivity of the soil, and who consequently did not manure adequately'.

A related aspect of resource utilization, one which goes beyond questions of tenancy, becomes evident when one studies the findings from another village, Vadamalaipuram in Ramnad district, which appears to be very different in characteristics from all the other three villages referred to so far. The wet land in this village was but a small proportion (about 6 per cent) of the total cultivated area of 911 acres in 1936, but it had no less than 166 families (with a total population of 668). To judge from the land revenue assessments of the time, the net product per acre of dry land was itself only about as high as in Dusi and Iruvelipattu. It is therefore clear that the per capita availability of land in the village, when reduced to a standard acre basis, was very much lower in Vadamalaipuram than in the other villages surveyed.

The landowners in the village, however, were mostly Naickers, a community with, as noted earlier, no inhibitions about being directly involved in cultivation. Not surprisingly, therefore, the report on the 1916 survey points out that 'all the owners of the land are cultivating landowners'; that 'it is no uncommon sight to see even the richest

ndowner shouldering a plough and walking to his field in the early
orning followed by his workmen, or the owner of the land driving
e bullocks round and round on the threshing ground threshing the
ain, whilst his paid workmen attend to other business'; and that
ere was no sub-letting of land at all in the village. Moreover, not
ly did most of the villagers own some land, but those who did not
d worked as 'permanent labourers' would appear to have been
uch better off than their counterparts in the better endowed villages
ferred to earlier; these labourers got three meals a day in their
aster's houses and, in addition, were paid wages equivalent (at the
evailing prices) to about 450 to 540 kg of paddy per annum.

Another remarkable feature of this village, which partly explains
s achievements, is that a co-operative society had been formed as
rly as 1909. According to the report based on the 1916 survey, the
ciety had come to be accepted as 'a model by the other societies
rrounding it'; loans were being extended by it to members on
ersonal security at a rate of interest of no more than 9 per cent per
nnum; and a number of improvements had also been made in the
llage by construction of a road, drains, and sinking of wells and
bewells. The society had however to be liquidated in 1932 for a
umber of reasons (including mismanagement); this, together with
ilure of seasonal rains for four years continuously, had serious
nsequences on agriculture in the village, and the total cultivated
ea in 1936 was as a result only about half of what it was in 1916.
he report based on the 1936 survey mentioned nevertheless three
teresting facts about the village: (*i*) there was not only an ele-
entary school in the village but a resolution had been passed by the
anchayat to enforce compulsory primary education and a land cess
f 1 to 3 pies in the rupee) had been levied to finance it; (*ii*) there
ad been a progressive fall in the birth rate in the village 'due perhaps
the later age—even 20—at which girls in this village have been
arried'; and (*iii*) 'it must be said to the credit of the villagers that
spite of all difficulties they have the same zeal and enthusiasm for
mmon improvement of the village and for reviving the activities
hich they were forced to give up'.

It is not therefore surprising that, by the time Miss Haswell came
the village in 1961, the village had succeeded in having an electric
mping station installed on the river Arjuna flowing by its side
vhose irrigation potential had been brought to the notice of the
vernment by the villagers as early as 1923). In addition, 45 wells

had also been equipped with electric pump-sets. All this, tak
together, made it possible for the entire land under the control of t
owners in 1916 to be brought under cultivation once again.

Some further observations of Miss Haswell, reproduced by h
after the 1961 re-survey, are perhaps better quoted than summarize
For instance:

The 1958 pilot scheme which provided electricity for a river pumpi
station, and the equipping of wells with electric motor pump-se
has greatly increased the range of choice of product and the tir
pattern of crop production. 'Dry' lands provided work for only 2
months of the year, but irrigation has given a physical producti
advantage. The availability of water throughout the year has result
in more intensive practices, and a fairly constant demand for labou
10 per cent of the net sown area was double-cropped in 1961 co
pared with only 4 per cent in 1936. Landless poor families now ha
some bargaining power and have secured a 25 per cent increase
the daily wage rate from 2.7 kg (6 lb) grain to 3.4 kg (7.5 lb) grain .

Attendance [in the elementary school] is compulsory between t
ages of five and ten, and in 1961 15 per cent of its total intake we
Harijan untouchables . . .

The Panchayat is fairly representative of the village community
which we have noted has a long history of absence of rigid ca
structure—and includes a Harijan untouchable among its me
bers . . .

Acceptance by the community of direct taxation, and the relati
absence of caste, permits considerable flexibility in the econom
and clearly demonstrates that it is in the historical perspective ov
the span of at least a generation that the development planner shou
seek for criteria which will promote rapid economic response in lo
income rural areas.

These and other findings from the various villages whose study w
initially promoted by Professor Gilbert Slater lend support to a vie
put forward by some economists, namely that several crucial assum
tions underlying general equilibrium analysis are simply not val
within the framework of traditional agrarian economies and that t
use of such analysis for interpreting the functioning of these ec
nomies could be misleading. The theoretical limitations of this ki
of analysis when applied to village societies have been clearly point
out by Professor Krishna Bharadwaj. Not only are market and soci
power in these societies generally exercised by a very small minori
but the members belonging to this minority often occupy domina

ositions in a number of factors and product markets simultaneously, ith the result that these markets are interlocked by price as well as on-price links. Thus, when a landowner is both leasing out land nd engaged in trade in the produce of such land, the terms of lease ay not only be more stringent than otherwise, but have specific ipulations as to what crops the tenants can grow and the mode as ell as terms of repayment. These conditions would naturally restrict onsiderably the choices open to his tenants. Similarly, if a landlord ossesses land 'under personal cultivation', it is not unusual to tract under-paid or unpaid services from agricultural labourers as ell as tenants. Transactions in the market for credit offer similar ope for manipulation in other markets.

The main point is that, when markets are interlocked in this way rough price or non-price links, the differential bargaining positions the participants in any particular market cannot be fitted into the nventional models of monopoly or monopsony and absorbed into e framework of general equilibrium analysis. At the same time, as ofessor Bharadwaj has observed, 'such interlocking of markets creases the exploitative power of the stronger sections because, ile there could be limits to exploitation in any one market—due traditions or conventions, or due to economic factors—the inter- netration of markets allows them to disperse exploitation over the fferent markets and to phase out exploitation over time'. What is erefore missed out is something very important, indeed crucial, to e understanding of agrarian economies.

There is another aspect of the problem, noticed by many others, which again Professor Bharadwaj has drawn pointed attention in is connection. It is that the objectives of production themselves pend on the economic status of the individuals and groups con- rned, and that they cannot be defined *a priori*. It is not certain in e first place that members of village communities are maximizing ything in particular. Or, even if they are, it is not clear whether it gross output, or 'farm business income', i.e. gross revenue net of tually paid out cost, gross profits, or something else that is sought be maximized. The very small operators living in perpetual lebtedness might choose to raise as much gross value of output as ssible per acre of land in their possession, and operate land inten- ely even to a point where the additional input costs are more than value of additional output and they are obliged to incur more ot on this account. On the other hand, 'the big cultivators, while

aiming to produce a surplus, may yet prefer not to cultivate the la
intensively for a number of reasons including the existence of oppo
tunities for making profits or for wielding social power through no
farming activities'.

Despite weighty considerations of this kind, it is not clear ho
much impact they have had on the profession and its work in th
area. One has the impression that the majority still find it easier
play the game by the conventional ground rules laid down a
approved of by those who invented the game. The alternative,
course, is to follow the much harder path of first studying empirica
in depth the complex structures and inter-relationships characteris
of traditional agrarian economies, before attempting to advan
general theories and explanations relying on the methods of co
ventional economic analysis. As Professor Bharadwaj has conclud
in her study of Indian agriculture, 'detailed information in historic
specific context about the agrarian economy under study would
required to describe the particular characteristics of its markets, t
nature and extent of the involvement of the different sections of
peasantry and the implications thereof'; and consequently, a mea
ingful analysis of a changing agrarian economy can be carried o
only by such painstaking investigation covering a multitude
villages in different stages of commercialization under diverse co
ditions.

This was no doubt the direction Professor Gilbert Slater was tryi
to give to the thinking of his students through the village studies
initiated. He was at that time going by some hunches, and the surve
he initiated were not as comprehensive and systematic as would
devised if one were to embark on a similar venture now. The villa
studies stimulated by him, including the re-surveys undertaken
1936 and 1961, provide however some very interesting and valual
insights into the political economy of agrarian communities. Th
are a part of the rich heritage of the Department of Economics of t
University of Madras, and it is one on which greater things can
built if only the study and development of economic theory a
closely linked with the study of the environment to which we belo
Theories are now learnt parrot-fashion, repeated, and appli
without an adequate sense of relevance even by scholars in the pi
fession. That such theories are associated with great names in t
literature on the subject does not justify either the habit or t
tradition that is so built up. We must try and revert to the l

spectacular but more rewarding path that Professor Slater was beckoning his students to follow.

# REFERENCES

Gilbert Slater (ed.), *Some South Indian Villages*, Oxford University Press, 1918.

P. J. Thomas and K. C. Ramakrishnan (eds.), *Some South Indian Villages: A Resurvey*, University of Madras, 1940.

M. R. Haswell, *Economics of Development in Village India*, The International Library of Sociology and Social Reconstruction, Routledge & Kegan Paul and Allied Publishers, 1967.

P. K. Bardhan and T. N. Srinivasan, 'Cropsharing Tenancy in Agriculture: A Theoretical and Empirical Analysis', *The American Economic Review*, vol. LXI, no. 1 (March 1971).

P. K. Bardhan, 'Variations in Extent and Forms of Agricultural Tenancy', *Economic and Political Weekly*, vol. XI, nos. 37 and 38 (11 and 18 September 1976).

Krishna Bharadwaj, *Production Conditions in Indian Agriculture: A Study Based on Farm Management Surveys*, Cambridge University Press, 1974.

# 9

# Peasant Classes in Twentieth Century Agrarian Movements in India

## JACQUES POUCHEPADASS

*Centre National de Recherches Scientifiques, Paris*

IT IS impossible to understand a peasant movement in the absence of a notion of the class structure of the peasant population under consideration. The choice of the criteria employed to divide the peasantry into classes is obviously crucial. There is a risk of imposing upon a rural society categories which are not significant, that is, which do not correspond to the lines along which, in fact, this society is divided into distinct groups at a given period. Our objective in this paper is to pass in critical review several attempts at class analysis of the peasant movements which have taken place in India since the First World War.

The sociological approach to agrarian movements is in effect dominated by the classical Marxist analyses of the peasantry. Lenin and Mao Tse-Tung, in particular, divide rural society into five classes: landlords, rich peasants, middle peasants, poor peasants and the rural proletariat—occasionally an even larger number of classes is proposed—on the basis not only of the extent of land ownership but also of the relations of production. These characteristics taken together are seen as determining the revolutionary potential of each class. The degree of support that a particular class is likely to give to the cause of the proletarian revolution decreases, according to the Marxist analysis, with each step upward along the socio-economic scale. The poor peasants are a reliable ally for the revolutionary proletariat, and the middle peasants a possible ally, on condition that they receive a suitable ideological preparation and that they are organized and led along correct political lines. The real class enemies begin with the rich peasants. The principal driving force of the revolution in the countryside, ideologically, if not numerically, is the rural proletariat.

A new interpretation which has recently been proposed on the basis of the same class analysis takes the middle peasants as the driving force, at least in the initial stages, of the great peasant risings of this century. This theory is advanced by Eric Wolf, who presents it as his conclusion after an extensive survey of five major recent peasant wars: the revolutions in Mexico, in the Russian countryside, and in China, the Algerian war of independence and the series of wars in Vietnam. According to Wolf, the poor peasantry and the rural proletariat, in so far as they depend on a landlord for the whole or the greater part of their livelihood, do not possess the necessary base of material security to be able to turn against him, unless they can benefit from the aid of an external force. Only the middle peasant, who holds enough land under a secure tenure so as to be able to feed his family, and who cultivates it with family labour, enjoys the minimum necessary tactical freedom to defy his landlord, and it is he who generally takes the initiative to rebel (Wolf, 1971, pp. 290–2).

A similar conclusion, although arising from different premises, is defended by Hamza Alavi in a comparative essay which deals successively with the rural aspects of the revolution in Russia, the Chinese revolution, and the Indian peasant struggles of the period 1920–50 (Alavi, 1973). According to Alavi, the poor peasants and the rural proletariat form potentially the most revolutionary categories but because of their economic dependence, they are incapable of taking the initiative to begin a movement. The middle peasants, on the contrary, at the start of a movement constitute the most militant element of the peasantry. They supply the initial momentum for the peasant revolution. It is their victories over the higher strata of rural society that serve to free the poor peasants from their inhibitions, and bring them to the fore of the revolutionary movement; at which precise point the middle peasantry begins to waver.

Our knowledge of the principal Indian movements in the twentieth century, although insufficient, has been deepened over the past few years, thanks to a small number of monographic studies focused at the local level, in which the social composition of these movements begins to become discernible. In chronological order, the first of these movements is the *satyagraha* launched by Gandhi in the Champaran district (Bihar) in 1917, against the British indigo planters (Pouchepadass, 1974 and 1975). A detailed study of the Champaran movement has shown that the driving force was made up of rich and well-to-do peasants, usually belonging to high-ranking castes. These villagers had long been the principal opponents of the planters, and they carried along with them the remainder of the peasantry, including the agricultural labourers. The class structure of the second movement, initiated by Gandhi in 1918 in the Kheda district (Gujarat), appears to have been similar. The active nucleus of the movement, directed in this instance against the fiscal demands of the imperial Government, was constituted by rich and middle peasants, whereas the poor peasantry and the agricultural workers remained aloof.[1]

The case of the movements which developed in the United Provinces from 1920 to 1922 in the context of the all-India non-co-operation campaign organized by the Indian National Congress is more complex. Here for the first time rural agitation was initiated and led by the *Kisan Sabhas*, peasant associations set up by members of the young nationalist intelligentsia and rich peasants under the auspices of the Congress. M. H. Siddiqi, who has made the most detailed study of these events, sees in them, at least in the Partapgarh district, essentially a movement of tenant-farmers against abuses by landlords. Participants were recruited among all castes, from Brahmins to untouchable Chamars, with poor and middle peasants predominating, the line dividing these last two categories being difficult to draw (Siddiqi, 1972; Dhanagare, 1975b, pp. 69, 76). In fact the social composition of the movement varied at different points of time and in different districts. The agitation began in Partapgarh district as a movement of tenant-farmers of all levels against abuses by landlords. The situation was similar in the Sultanpur and Rae Bareli districts, where the action consisted primarily in a refusal to pay the rents due to the landlords.

In the next stage, the composition of the Kisan Sabhas of Partapgarh shifted, with landless peasants becoming the majority group in a number of them. In the eastern part of the Fyzabad district which was violently affected by disorders at the beginning of 1921, the agricultural population consisted primarily of poor tenant-farmers and, above all, landless peasants. It was these two elements which dominated the local Kisan Sabhas and led the agitation. They criss-crossed the countryside in bands of 1,000 to 5,000 men, looting the houses of the landlords and rich peasants, and even those of prosperous artisans and shopkeepers. As soon as the Government announced that the agrarian legislation would be modified, and the most notable abuses of the landlords checked, the tenant-farmers lost interest in the agitation, and a great number of the Kisan Sabhas disintegrated. Manifestations of violence on the part of the landless were promptly repressed.[2]

In this movement, something close to Alavi's model seems to have occurred: the late entrance into the movement of the poorest categories of the peasantry, and their immediate radicalization, after the ground had been prepared in the course of a campaign initiated by the less poor sections of the peasantry. But it must be recalled that Siddiqi does not find it possible to distinguish clearly between poor peasants and middle peasants within the class of tenants which constituted, at least in the initial stages, the principal base of agitation.

In the 'non-payment of taxes' movement organized by Gandhi and the Congress in 1928 in the taluk (county) of Bardoli (Surat district, Gujarat), we find essentially the same class structure as in Gandhi's campaigns of 1917 (Champaran) and 1918 (Kheda). The Bardoli agitation, studied in detail by Ghanshyam Shah, appears to have been a movement of rich and well-to-do high caste peasants, principally Patidars, in which the lower classes, the tenant-farmers and the landless peasants, who did not pay land revenue, merely followed their leaders (Shah, 1974, pp. 97–8). The same sort of interpretation seems to be applicable to the campaigns organized from 1920 onwards by N. G. Ranga and his associates in the Andhra delta. From Ranga's own account it is not possible to analyse these movements in terms of class, since he presents them as movements of the entire peasantry, acting as a homogeneous undifferentiated whole (Ranga, 1949, *passim*). But this very fact is symptomatic of movements dominated by the higher strata of the peasantry. A solid sociological analysis of these movements remains to be undertaken. According to the studies which have so far been made on this region, there are good reasons for thinking that the agitation was led by the powerful local middle and rich peasants belonging to the Kamma and Reddy castes.[3] Again, in this case, the agitation was channelled through a network of Kisan Sabhas largely inspired in the initial stages by the Congress ideology. From the end of the 1930s, the peasant movement in Andhra came largely under communist influence. But the class structure of the movement hardly changed, the

Communist Party in this area being dominated by the rich Kamma peasantry (Ram, 1973). With regard to the peasant movement in other parts of south India in the years before independence, we are still too ill-informed, despite the sketch by K. Gough (Gough, 1968–69), to be able to draw well-founded conclusions.

The agitation led by the Congress in the United Provinces in 1930–32, in response to difficulties experienced by the peasantry because of the great depression, represented once again a global movement of tenants against landlords, in the form of a rent-strike. The most active elements were the rich and middle peasants (the principal victims of the crisis), the poor peasants being less severely affected since work for wages, from which they drew a substantial proportion of their income, remained remunerative (Dhanagare, 1975–76).

On the vast Tebhaga movement that broke out in Bengal in 1946, the major source available to us today is the evidence of Sunil Sen, one of the leaders of the agitation (Sen, 1972; see also Dhanagare, 1976). This movement was launched by the provincial Kisan Sabha of Bengal, in the stormy context of the war on the eastern front and the famine of 1943. The Kisan Sabha was directed by Communists of urban middle class origin. The basic demand was for the attribution of two-thirds instead of half of the harvest to the *bargadars* (crop-sharers) by their employers, the *jotedars*, themselves tenants, often quite powerful, of great absentee landlords. In effect this demand went no further than to repeat one of the recommendations of the very official Land Revenue Commission of 1940. Throughout the previous ten years, the Kisan Sabha had consistently set out in this fashion demands which were simple, realizable, and not likely to provoke major clashes with the government or with the jotedars (except, at worst, with the richest of them) (Sen, 1972, p. 23). Among the leaders of the organization there were, together with poor peasants, not only middle peasants but also sons of jotedars. Once the Sabha gave the signal, the movement obtained the massive and spontaneous support of the bargadars, and rapidly became very large. But as it developed, and, by the same token, as the Government replied with repressive measures, the poor peasants became more radical and refused to make a distinction between big and small jotedars (Sen, 1972, p. 49). As a result, while the middle peasants, who made up the bulk of the local leaders of the Kisan Sabha, supported the movement up to the end, hoping that it would eventuate in a full-scale attack on landlordism, the rich peasants progressively detached themselves; in fact, they were closer to the jotedars. A minority of rich peasants remained among the leaders of the organization, but they represented an exception (Sen, 1972, p. 83). The movement was finally broken by the repression of February–March 1947.

The published studies available on the Telengana movement in the eastern region of the princely state of Hyderabad are scarcely more than partisan tracts. It is nonetheless clear that the movement developed in the setting of the post-war economic crisis and under the auspices of a type of peasant organization similar to that of the neighbouring Andhra area; in other words, a Communist-oriented organization dominated by rich peasants of high caste status. At the beginning, in 1946, the agitation developed under the leadership of the rich peasants on a basis of class collaboration, and in response to slogans with very broad appeal directed against the great absentee landlords who were allied to the decadent monarchical order of the State (Dhanagare, 1974). The alliance began to show signs of strain when the poor peasants and the agricultural labourers started to occupy the lands of the landlords, and the wasteland, and to distribute it among themselves. Although the land ceiling fixed by the peasant committees was high, the rich peasants began to waver, and deserted the movement in large numbers after the intervention of the Indian army against the rebels from 1948 onwards. The uprising, which continued nonetheless in the form of a guerilla war, soon mobilized principally poor peasants and agricultural labourers, many of whom belonged to tribes or untouchable castes. Just as in 1921 in the U.P., the sequence of developments in Telengana appears to have followed Alavi's model. But the movement was initiated by the rich and well-to-do peasantry operating as a whole and it does not seem that the middle peasantry as such played a significant role. On the contrary, this category appears to have been comparatively small in numbers in Telengana, and to have had no distinctive political identity (Dhanagare, 1974).

From this rough sketch of the principal peasant movements in India in the period 1917–50, we can see that in most cases the movements developed on the basis of class collaboration. The initiative nearly always came from the upper strata of the peasantry, the elements to which the authors generally refer as 'rich and middle peasantry', apparently without being able to distinguish between these two categories. In a minority of cases, the driving force seems to have come from the lower strata of the peasantry, in particular in certain districts of the U.P. in 1921. Finally, in the last two movements, the Tebhaga agitation and the Telengana uprising, a new phenomenon emerged during a second phase: the development of an antagonism, more or less open, between the poor masses on the one hand and the rich peasantry and even part of the middle peasantry on the other. In none of these three types of peasant mobilization did the middle peasantry play a separate role. In most of the movements, it acted in conjunction with the rich peasantry, but there were also cases in which at least some of its members followed the poor peasants when it was they who took the lead. In the other cases, the middle peasantry played no distinctive role. On no occasion did the middle category *alone* take the initiative in a movement.

Let us now try to explain our conclusions, which run counter to the theories of Eric Wolf and Hamza Alavi. There are three important aspects to consider. First, it is necessary to examine in greater depth the very nature of the middle peasantry as a class. Secondly, the traditional structure of Indian rural society must be explored. The third aspect is historical, and concerns the ideological inspirations of the Indian peasant movement in our period.

It may be worth recalling that in the works of the founding fathers of Marxism, the middle peasantry is generally presented as a class with ill-defined economic boundaries, and given to political vacillations.[4] From Engels to Lenin and to Mao, the class analysis applied to the peasantry always distinguishes clearly between the proletariat on the one hand and the rich peasants and landlords on the other. There are, however, appreciable differences from one author to another, and indeed in different works of the same author, when it comes to determining the nature of the peasant classes between these two extremes, because of the high degree of interpenetration of different types of relations of production. Sometimes the author sets out an elaborate classification, which aims to specify in detail the diversity of class situations.

This is what Lenin did in his 'Preliminary Draft Thesis on the Agrarian Question' prepared in 1920 for the Second Congress of the Communist International (Lenin, 1960–, vol. xxxi, pp. 152–64). He distinguishes three classes between the rural proletariat and the rich peasants, namely the semi-proletarians, the small peasants and the middle peasants. These last are defined as small farmers who are able to produce a surplus, and who are often employers of labour. At other times, on the contrary, the author adopts a looser classification, which slides over the complexity of the actual agrarian situation. But then he often re-introduces subsidiary distinctions in the course of his analysis.

However, Engels, in *The Peasant Question in France and Germany*, published in 1894, distinguishes only two categories above the proletariat: the small self-sufficient peasants, and the vast group of 'bigger peasants', in which are mingled all the intermediary layers between the small peasants and the rich peasant proprietors (Engels, 1968, p. 647). Subsequently, however, he introduces a subsidiary distinction between middle peasants and 'big peasants', without however defining it clearly. The Mao of the 1930s, in a 1933 text entitled *How to analyse the classes in the rural areas* (Mao, 1954, vol. I) and in a handbook written in 1939 for militants, entitled *The Chinese Revolution and the Chinese Communist Party* (Mao, 1954, vol. III), distinguishes two classes between the proletariat and the rich peasants, namely, the poor peasants and the middle peasants. In 1933, he defines the middle peasant as a self-sufficient cultivator who can produce a surplus in good years and who does not employ wage labour apart from peak periods. In fact this definition covers a fairly wide range of varying situations. In the 1939 text, Mao explicitly makes his analysis more precise by introducing into it a sub-category of 'well-to-do middle peasants', counterbalanced by a section of the middle peasantry who, on the contrary, do not have enough land.

These variations in the Marxist definition of the middle peasantry merely emphasize the fact that this class, in contrast to those on either side of it, is extremely heterogeneous. The middle peasants do certainly share an essential characteristic, namely, that they do not work even occasionally for anyone else. The lower limit of the class is thus relatively clear. The upper limit, however, which separates it from the rich peasantry, is on the contrary rather imprecise. Within these limits, this class lumps together a whole range of varying situations with regard to rights in land and relations of production. The middle peasants are landowners or tenants, or both. They cultivate their land with family labour or they hire labour (at least occasionally). Some produce a surplus in good years; others, on the contrary, are indebted and their possessions mortgaged.

The logical consequence of this heterogeneity is that the revolutionary potential of the middle peasantry is uncertain. According to

Mao, this class may be in favour of agrarian revolution and may even accept socialism. It may, however, be hostile to it (Mao, 1954–, vol. III, p. 93), Lenin already insisted on this ambivalence in a speech to the VIIIth Congress of the Communist Party of the Soviet Union in 1919, at a moment when, the Russian rural bourgeoisie having been eliminated, it had become necessary to develop a specific policy with regard to the millions of middle peasants.

We have to determine our attitude towards a class which has no definite and stable position. The mass of the proletariat is in favour of socialism, the mass of the bourgeoisie is opposed to socialism. It is easy to determine the relations between these two classes. But when we pass to a stratum like the middle peasantry, *we find that it is a class that vacillates.* The middle peasant is partly a property-owner and partly a toiler. He does not exploit other toilers. For decades the middle peasant defended his position with the greatest difficulty, he suffered the exploitation of the landlords and capitalists, he bore everything. Yet he is a property-owner. . . . We must most of all refrain from being too hasty, from being clumsily theoretical. . . . Considerable practical ability and knowledge of local conditions is required here. . . . [We have] to work in a way that will introduce the greatest possible clarity into our relations with the middle peasant. This is very difficult, because *this clarity does not exist in reality.*[5]

The political ambiguity of this class is even clearer in Western Europe in the context of the development of capitalist agriculture, which leads to the elimination of the intermediary categories of peasants and toward the polarization of rural society. This tendency to elimination necessarily pushes a part of the middle peasants in the direction of the proletariat. But those who have not yet been touched remain fiercely attached to the idea of private property in land; all the more so is this the case for those who, in the process of polarization, have managed to hoist themselves up into a higher category. All of the peasants would be ready to give their support to a conservative authority which would promise them stability of rights in land (Engels, 1968, p. 647). Thus the heterogeneous composition of this class and the instability of its economic fate make it susceptible to contradictory and fluctuating tendencies. This characteristic is as true of Western Europe during the epoch of triumphant capitalism as it is of Soviet Russia of 1919 or pre-revolutionary China of the 1930s. Nowhere in their writings do Engels, Lenin or Mao envisage that the middle peasantry might spontaneously, as a class, take the initiative to revolt. They conceive only the possibility of converting the middle peasants to the cause of the revolution, and of turning them into reliable allies of the proletariat.

In the context of Indian rural society, other factors in addition to the ones we have just enumerated, make it even more difficult to identify a category of middle peasants with a clear-cut political orientation. First of all, the degree to which kinds of rights in the land and various types of relations of production are layered and entangled appears to be higher in India than anywhere else. Quantitative analysis of village land registers of the British period would reveal in each region, writes K. N. Chaudhuri, the existence of hundreds of different combinations of rights in the land. From the multitude of detailed ethnological studies at the village level, we obtain the same impression as to the complexity of relations of production. The ethnologist knows from experience, says André Béteille, that combinations of family work, wage work and sharecropping are often so complicated as to defy simple classification (Béteille, 1974, p. 32).

When we define a peasant class under these circumstances, what we are doing is, in effect, to isolate one or more characteristics which are common to a given segment of rural society, and to assume that these characteristics constitute a factor of unity which is more significant than the differences which are to be found within the particular segment. In any case, Alavi himself underlines the fact that all of these categories overlap, and that, in order to apply the definitions to a real situation, it is necessary to determine the class alignment of a peasant according to the relation of production from which he draws *the principal part* of his livelihood (Alavi, 1973, p. 295).

We may nonetheless ask whether, at least in certain parts of India, and taking all precautions, we may define a class of middle peasants in such a way as to constitute a significant category. Clearly, the concept of a class of peasants without land or of a class of rich peasants can be applied in a valid fashion in all regions since the particular characteristics which serve to define these classes represent truly major aspects of the existence of these groups, over and above the diversity and complexity of local and individual circumstances. In the case of middle peasants, everything becomes much more vague. First of all, there are regions (where nonetheless peasant movements have broken out) in which the category lying between the rich peasants on the one hand and the poor or landless peasants

10

on the other is numerically weak. This is the case, for example, in the District of Tanjore (Baker and Washbrook, 1975, pp. 22–3, Kumar, 1975, p. 242 and fig. 9); or in the District of Dhulia in Maharashtra, where 75 per cent of the population consists of *adivasi* (tribal) agricultural labourers and crop-sharers, completely dominated by a caste of landowners who have come in from the neighbouring state of Gujarat (Mies, 1976); or, as we have seen, in the eastern part of Fyzabad District in the United Provinces. There are also districts, as for example Champaran and Darbhanga in Bihar, which were, up to the land reform, almost entirely in the possession of one or several very large *zamindars* (landlords), and where there existed practically no peasant proprietors. We find there, true enough, a substantial number of middle-rank tenants. But how can we say of these middle peasants that they enjoy a special degree of security when they are constantly at the mercy of the landlords and their agents, and suffer from many kinds of constraints, social and legal as well as economic, arising from their semi-feudal situation?

In yet other regions, the difficulty arises from the fact that most of the peasant proprietors who hold only just enough land to suffice for their needs nonetheless employ agricultural labourers all year long because of ritual prohibitions against manual labour which affect certain castes of Brahmans. In Kerala and in the Tanjore District of Madras, for example, Kathleen Gough writes that the 'pure' middle peasant is practically non-existent. Most of them employ one or two agricultural labourers on a permanent basis, and engage extra hands in peak season (Gough, 1968–69, p. 529). Those who employ no paid workers at all are, in effect, poor peasants. In these various cases, and probably in others as well, we cannot reasonably consider the category of 'middle peasant' as defined in the Marxist classics to be an operational category, corresponding to a living reality, and thus likely to throw light on the play of forces involved in a peasant uprising. On the contrary, the dogmatic use of this category in a social context to which it is ill-adapted tends to mask the true social composition of the movement under study.

Nevertheless, there is no doubt that there exist in the Indian countryside, in varying proportions according to the region, a certain number of true middle peasants. But in none of the movements which we have discussed does such a group of middle peasants appear to have played a distinct role. In most cases, the authors whom we have cited do not distinguish the middle peasants from the rich peasants in pinpointing the motive force of these movements. In effect, they tend to fall back upon the awkward expression, 'rich and middle peasants', to designate the category which is actually operational in the Indian context at least up until the middle of the present century, that is the *dominant peasantry*.[6]

By *dominant peasantry* we refer to the oligarchy of rich and well-off peasants belonging to a respectable caste who hold either as owners or as tenants the bulk of the land rights in each village. It is to this group that the rest of the village population looks in large part for employment, and often for credit as well. This dominant peasantry serves as an intermediary between the mass of villagers and the administration, or, more generally, the whole of the outside world. The oligarchy exercises authority at the village level by virtue of its economic superiority, of its status as a caste superior to those of the mass of the poorer peasants, artisans and labourers, and of the liberty which it enjoys to employ force. It is important to emphasize that we are not referring here only to the class of genuinely rich peasants but rather to a category which includes the whole group of peasants of respectable caste who hold enough land so that they can supply the needs of their families without having to go out to work for anyone else.

It is within this relatively large category that the moving spirits of the Champaran movement were recruited in 1917. We should insist that it is impossible to define their class origin more narrowly. The same in all likelihood appears to have been the case in the Kheda movement of 1918, in Bardoli in 1928, in the Andhra delta from the 1920s onward, in the United Provinces in 1930–32, and in the initial phase of the Telengana movement. At the village level, the dominant peasantry inevitably consists in large part of families belonging to the caste which is locally dominant in the sense of its land rights rather than its number of families. At the level of a peasant movement as a whole, the dominant peasantry, in the role of a social force, is normally multi-caste. But there are also instances in which movements have been organized on the basis of a particular cultivating caste which constitutes the dominant land-holding group in the affected region; where indeed such a caste exists, which is not everywhere (cf. Mayer, 1958). Thus, for example, the Bardoli campaign was dominated and led at the local level by the caste of *patidars* and their caste association, the *Patidar Yuvak Mandal* (Shah, 1974;

Bhatt, 1970); this organization appears in fact to have played a crucial role in the Kheda movement ten years earlier (Dhanagare, 1975, p. 34). We have already touched upon the important role played by the *Kammas* and the *Reddys* (two cultivating castes) in the movements of coastal Andhra, and also in the Telengana revolt. The mobilizing role of the dominant castes is naturally facilitated by the fact that they are usually represented by experienced and respected caste councils, which are used to dealing with practical questions for the whole of the caste at a regional level. The councils of the lower castes, by contrast, ordinarily confine their activities to ritual matters and to conflicts between individuals in a single village (Elliot, 1970, p. 143; Shah, 1974, pp. 92, 98).

In all of these movements led by a dominant peasantry, it is in effect the traditional pattern of power and authority which operates, but in the context of a conflict at the regional level. The dominant peasantry is nothing other than the group of peasants who, in each village, are spontaneously considered by the villagers as their chiefs, their *maliks*, to use the term proposed by Daniel Thorner (Thorner, 1956), together with their caste-fellows and all those who, more generally, are identified with them. That is why movements launched by the dominant peasantry often develop along lines of class collaboration; the poor peasants and the landless, either of their own will or under constraint, following in the agitation their usual masters, as in Champaran, Bardoli and many other movements. The existence of factional conflicts within the dominant castes, the influence of which upon peasant movements has sometimes been greatly exaggerated, does not alter very much the general picture. There was, for example, in almost every village of Champaran in 1917 a section of the dominant peasants who refused to participate in the agitation conducted by their homologues of the rival faction (Pouchepadass, 1976, chapters 4.3 and 9.2). This did not stop the dominant peasantry from serving as the motive force of the movement as a whole.

These united peasant movements led by a traditional elite approach, in fact, fairly close to the classical model of anti-feudal rebellions frequently described by comparative historians (Mousnier 1971 provides a recent example). We need not be astonished that this type of movement remains predominant in India in a period when rural agitation develops under the aegis of organizations as 'modern' as the Congress, the Kisan Sabhas and the Communist Party. In effect these organizations have almost constantly, at least until the 1950s, followed an implicit or explicit strategy of class collaboration, which left intact the force of the traditional 'primordial loyalties'. In the case of the typically Gandhian movements (Champaran, Kheda, Bardoli), class collaboration was not merely accepted by the political leaders; it was consciously favoured and served as a central element in the ideology. Generally speaking, the absence of clear antagonisms together with the interpenetration of interests and solidarities within the Indian peasantry greatly facilitated the role of such socially amorphous ideologies (Joshi, 1969, pp. 483–5). We will not discuss here Gandhi's well-known ideas with regard to class struggle but will simply note two important characteristics of Gandhian movements. Firstly, the enemy is always exterior to the peasantry: in Champaran it was the British indigo planters, in Kheda and Bardoli it was the colonial government. Secondly, the actual organization of the movement is left to the traditional structures of peasant society, principally the caste councils. As is inevitable in such a case, the political leaders at the head of the movement make speeches; it is the castes of dominant peasants which manage everything at the base.

In the case of the Kisan Sabhas of the 1920s and the 1930s, which were predominantly Congress-oriented, the situation is hardly different. These organizations were led in large part by the dominant peasantry, and the Gandhian ideology prevailed in them. They launched their agitation on a very broad class basis: the key slogan was the unity of all tenants cemented by their hostility to the common enemy, the landlord, or, in the *rayatwari* zone, the solidarity of all the *rayats*, supported by their tenants, against the government. In these categories of tenants and rayats in a wide sense, it was clearly the dominant peasantry which called the tune. This was the pattern of the campaigns undertaken by the Kisan Sabhas in the United Provinces in 1920–22, in the Andhra delta from the end of the 1920s, and in practically all the later agitations. Sometimes in the course of the struggle the Kisan Sabhas became more radical and, once the campaign was well under way, poor peasants and landless labourers played a crucial role. This is what happened in certain Kisan Sabhas in Partapgarh and Fyzabad in 1921. But the leadership as a whole disapproved of these groundswells and took measures to discourage them so that they could develop only in the form of primitive revolts with insufficient organized support; thus they were easily crushed by the governmental repression. (Dhanagare, 1975b refers in this connection to the concept of 'social banditism' put forward by Eric Hobsbawm.)

The moderate broad-based ideology of the early local Kisan Sabhas was reflected in the All-India Kisan Congress (the future All-India Kisan Sabha) which brought them into a national organization from 1936 onward. The new movement officially addressed itself to the entire peasantry of India, that is, to all peasants as distinct from landlords (Rasul, 1974, pp. 5–6). At that time the Kisan organization was aligned with the progressive tendency within the National Congress. The agrarian reform programme adopted by the Congress in its Faizpur session the following year, when the views of the two organizations still coincided, was essentially a call for the removal of abuses to which all tenants were subjected (the text is cited in Ranga, 1939, pp. 9–10). The peasant unity sought by the AIKS extended even to include the landless, although it was clear that they would not be represented within the ranks of the organization itself. This strategy of class collaboration was never to be seriously questioned. Naturally in such a setting it was always the dominant peasantry, which, as in the earlier Gandhian movements, ruled the roost. After 1936 as before, the office-bearers of the Kisan Sabhas were recruited from this category. This pre-eminent position of the well-off peasants was denounced at the Bezwada Congress in 1944 by Swami Sahajanand Saraswati, the radical leader of the provincial Kisan Sabha of Bihar:

[It is] really the middle and big cultivators [who are] . . . for the most part with the Kisan Sabha. . . . They are using the Kisan Sabha for their benefit and gain, while we are using, or rather trying to use them, to strengthen the Sabha till the lower and lowest strata of the peasantry are awakened to their real economic and political interests and needs, and have become class-conscious. (Saraswati, 1944, p. 17)

The AIKS was, nonetheless, dominated at this period by the Communist Party of India. But the CPI itself, after 1936 when it began to work seriously among the peasantry, also advocated almost without exception a policy of class collaboration in keeping with the orthodox anti-feudal strategy. In any case, the directives from Moscow both before and during the second world war did not leave it the choice. Up to the war, the united-front line defined in 1935 by the seventh congress of the Comintern held sway. Again, from 1942 when the Soviet Union had come into the war, the line which prevailed was one of broad national unity behind the allied war effort (Overstreet and Windmiller, 1959, chapters 8 and 9). In the countryside these directives gave rise to slogans for very broad-based actions, conceived as bringing together the whole of the peasantry against only the landlords.

Immediately after the war, in order to rid itself of the anti-national stigma resulting from its support for the British war effort, the CPI tried to get back into the graces of all elements within the rural population by following the same moderate agrarian line. In its election appeal of 1946 the CPI called for the abolition of land-lordism, but pledged 'not to touch the small *zamindar* [landlord] or the rich peasant' (cited in Overstreet and Windmiller, 1959, p. 230). This was the moment when the communist-led Kisan Sabha of Bengal launched the Tebhaga movement. We have seen that this movement was initially supported by the entire peasantry. But the rich peasants became gradually alienated. The communist leadership came face to face with a dilemma. The decision, as announced in February 1947 by Bhowani Sen, secretary of the Bengal committee of the CPI, was that the Kisan Sabha should change its tactic and appeal to a larger base by demanding the abolition of landlordism, that is of the *zamindari* system. This slogan provided a means for restoring the unity of the peasantry engaged in the struggle. But it did not meet the urgent need of the actual situation. As Sunil Sen, one of the leaders of the Sabha, has written:

... the essential pre-condition for building a broader movement was success in the continuing tebhaga struggle, which was faced with severe repression. If the government succeeded in crushing the move-ment, there would be great demoralisation among the peasants. The immediate question therefore was if and how to resist police repres-sion. There was no directive on this question, and the movement was allowed to drift. (Sen, 1972; p. 62)

At the end of the year Bhowani Sen declared: 'We appeal to the peasants not to launch direct action this year as they did last year.' The new government of independent India, he continued, 'must be given an opportunity for fulfilling its promises through legal chan-nels' (cited in Overstreet and Windmiller, 1959, p. 264).

The official attitude of the CPI with regard to the Telengana move-ment was practically identical. There was a tendency on the part of the communist high command in 1946–47 to minimize, almost to ignore, the struggle which was developing in this region. The Telengana communists themselves, although keen to take advantage of a favourable situation for a peasant mobilization, did not in the early stages encourage violent resistance. They limited the demands to the usual very broad platform of struggle against landlordism, a struggle in which the entire peasantry could collaborate. In 1948, however, the radical elements under Ranadive took over the leadership of the CPI; official party support for the Telengana movement was explicitly proclaimed. But the opposition to Ranadive's line rapidly regained its influence within the party. From 1951, when the Indian army had reduced the Telengana guerillas to silence, a constitutionalist line prevailed in the CPI, and the strategy of class collaboration in the countryside once again held sway.

Thus both the Kisan Sabhas and the communists, at least until the 1950s, defended almost without fail a broad-based strategy of peasant action. This permitted the dominant peasantry to play its usual role as a driving force, even in the initial phases of the Tebhaga movement and the Telengana revolt. This same group was still in control of the AIKS in the late 1950s: in 1957, of 51 members of the executive council of the Bengal Kisan Sabha, only 8 were sons of cultivators while 31 were members of the rural 'gentry' (Weiner, 1963, p. 152).

It is, nonetheless, true that the last two movements of our period, those of Tebhaga and Telengana, seem to announce a transition. For the first time, movements launched as ever by the dominant peasantry gave birth to a clear break between the rich peasants and the rest of the villagers. Hamza Alavi, for this reason, was well advised to select these two movements in order to illustrate his thesis. Since the 1950s the transition foreshadowed in these movements has been widely confirmed by the splitting of the communist movement into three distinct parties, and the springing up in all regions of Kisan Sabhas of various tendencies alongside the local branches of the AIKS. In recent years the Indian countryside has harboured innumerable movements organized on a clear and straightforward class basis. It is by no means evident that the middle peasants play a determining role in these conflicts. The different groups within the communist left address their appeals in the first instance to agricultural labourers and poor peasants. It is these categories who seem to have played the leading role in those contemporary movements on which monographic studies have been made in parts of India as different as Kerala, Bihar, the interior of Maharashtra, and eastern Uttar Pradesh (Gough, 1968–69; Prasad, 1975; Mies, 1976; Singh,

1974). To this evidence must be added the fact that, as contemporary development proceeds, the growing polarization of the peasant classes, to use Kathleen Gough's expression, 'knocks down the middle peasants as a significant social category' (Gough, 1968–69, p. 544). Everyone is not in agreement about the reality of this polarization. It is indeed likely that in certain regions agrarian reform, however partial it still may be, may have had the effect of reinforcing the intermediate levels of the peasantry (Singh, 1974, p. 64 gives an example). But the veritable polarization in question concerns not only the extent of land held, but also the emergence of capitalist relations of production in agriculture, which split the middle peasantry once and for all, pushing one part to the side of the mechanized, surplus-producing capitalist farmers, and the rest to the side of the rural proletarians (Saith and Tanka, 1972). That such a process has begun in certain regions can no longer be doubted.

## NOTES

1. Dhanagare, 1975a, p. 41. To know whether Dhanagare's analysis is supported by the conclusions of another recent study, we must await the publication of the thesis of David Hardiman: 'Peasant agitations in the Kheda district, Gujarat 1917–1934', University of Sussex, 1975.

2. Cf. India Office Records, L/P & J/6/1729, File no. 275 of 1921; Report on the Administration of the United Provinces, 1921–22, General Summary, pp. xiv-xix; Proceedings of the Legislative Council of the United Provinces, 15 February 1921, 6 December 1921.

3. See in particular Harrison, 1960; Ram, 1973; Elliott, 1970; Baker and Washbrook, 1975; and the critical review of this last work by Hardiman, 1976.

4. We exclude from this analysis Lenin's pre-revolutionary studies on the peasantry, in particular *The Development of Capitalism in Russia*, 1899, chapter 2; *The Agrarian Question and the 'Critics' of Marx*, 1901 and 1907; *The Agrarian Programme of Social-Democracy in the First Russian Revolution, 1905–7*, 1907. The peasant classes are defined in these works in a very clear fashion, by the use of statistical norms. This quantitative categorization serves only to show clearly the polarization of the peasants as a result of the capitalist development of agriculture. We should not hasten to conclude that Lenin, with naive (and scarcely very Marxist) rigour makes the political potential of each category coincide with the exact limits of his statistical definition. Accordingly, we take into account here only those texts in which Lenin defines the peasant classes in terms of relations of production.

5. Lenin, 1960–, vol. xxix, pp. 198–215 (italics in the original). See also ibid. p. 246.

6. The expression is used notably by Hardiman, 1976, but we assume sole responsibility for its elaboration as a category of analysis.

# REFERENCES

Alavi, Hamza, 1973, 'Peasants and revolution', in Gough, K. and Sharma, H. P. (eds.), *Imperialism and Revolution in South Asia*, New York.

Baker, C. J., and Washbrook, D. A., 1975, *South India: Political Institutions and Political Change, 1880–1940*, Delhi.

Béteille, André, 1974, *Studies in Agrarian Social Structure*, Delhi.

Bhatt, Anil, 1970, 'Caste and political mobilization in a Gujarat district', in Kothari, R. (ed.), *Caste in Indian Politics*, New Delhi.

Chaudhuri, K. N., 1973, *Bulletin of Quantitative and Computer Methods in South Asian Studies*, vol. I, no. 1 (June).

Dhanagare, D. N., 1974, 'Social origins of the peasant insurrection in Telengana (1946–1951)', *Contributions to Indian Sociology*, New Series, no. 8.

—— 1975a, *Agrarian Movements and Gandhian Politics*, Institute of Social Sciences, Agra University, Extension Lecture Series, 1, Agra.

—— 1975b, 'Congress and agrarian agitation in Oudh, 1920–22 and 1930–32', *South Asia*, no. 5 (December).

—— 1976, 'Peasant protest and politics—the Tebhaga movement in Bengal', *Journal of Peasant Studies*, vol. III, no. 3 (April).

Elliott, Carolyn M., 1970, 'Caste and faction among the dominant caste: the Reddis and Kammas of Andhra', in Kothari, R. (ed.), *Caste in Indian Politics*, New Delhi.

Engels, Friedrich, 1968, 'The peasant question in France and Germany' (1894), in Marx, K., and Engels, F., *Selected Works*, Moscow.

Gough, Kathleen, 1968–69, 'Peasant resistance and revolt in South India', *Pacific Affairs*, vol. XLI, no. 4 (Winter).

Hardiman, David, 1976, 'Politicisation and agitation among dominant peasants in early twentieth century India', *Economic and Political Weekly* (Bombay), 28 February.

Harrison, Selig S., 1960, *India, the Most Dangerous Decades*, Princeton.

Joshi, P. C., 1969, 'Agrarian social structure and social change', *Sankhya: The Indian Journal of Statistics*, series B, vol. XXXI, parts 3–4 (December).

Kumar, Dharma, 1975, 'Landownership and equality in the Madras Presidency, 1853–54 to 1946–47', *Indian Economic and Social History Review*, vol. XII, no. 3.

Lenin, V. I., 1960–, *Collected Works*, vol. I–, Moscow.

Mao Tse-tung, 1954–, *Selected Works*, vol. I–, London.

Mayer, Adrian C., 1958, 'The dominant caste in a region of Central India' *Southwestern Journal of Anthropology*, Winter.

Mies, Maria, 1976, 'The Shahada movement: a peasant movement in Maharashtra (India)—its development and perspectives', *Journal of Peasant Studies*, vol. III, no. 4 (July).

Mousnier, Roland, 1971, *Peasant Uprisings in Seventeenth Century France, Russia and China*, London.

Overstreet, Gene D., and Windmiller, Marshall, 1959, *Communism in India*, Berkeley and Los Angeles.

Pouchepadass, Jacques, 1974, 'Local leaders and the intelligentsia in the Champaran satyagraha (1917): a study in peasant mobilization', *Contributions to Indian Sociology*, New Series, no. 8.

—— 1976, 'Planteurs et paysans du Bihar, 1860–1920: spéculation coloniale et résistance paysanne aux origines du mouvement national indien', Doctoral thesis (unpublished), Ecole des Hautes Etudes en Sciences Sociales, Paris.

Prasad, Pradhan H., 1975, 'Agrarian unrest and economic change in rural Bihar—Three case studies', *Economic and Political Weekly* (Bombay), 14 June.

Ram, Mohan, 1973, 'The Communist movement in Andhra Pradesh', in Brass, P. R., and Franda, M. F. (eds.), *Radical Politics in South Asia*, Cambridge (Mass.) and London.

Ranga, N. G., 1939, *Peasants and Congress*, Madras.

—— 1949, *Revolutionary Peasants*, New Delhi.

—— n.d., *Kisans and Communists*, Bombay.

Rasul, A. M., 1974, *History of the All-India Kisan Sabha*, Calcutta.

Saith, Aswani, and Tanka, Ajay, 1972, 'Agrarian transition and the differentiation of the peasantry: A study of a West U.P. village', *Economic and Political Weekly* (Bombay), 1 April.

Saraswati, Swami Sahajanand, 1944, *Presidential address, 8th annual session of the All-India Kisan Sabha, Bezwada, March 1944*.

Sen, Sunil, 1971, 'Dialectics of the peasant movement', in *Society and Revolution: Essays in the Honour of Engels*, New Delhi.

—— 1972, *Agrarian Struggle in Bengal, 1946–47*, New Delhi.

Shah, Ghanshyam, 1974, 'Traditional society and political mobilization: the experience of Bardoli satyagraha (1920–1928)', *Contributions to Indian Sociology*, New Series, no. 8.

Siddiqi, M. H., 1972, 'The peasant movement in Partapgarh, 1920', *Indian Economic and Social History Review*, vol. IX, no. 3 (September).

Singh, Rajendra, 1974, 'Agrarian social structure and peasant unrest: a study of land-grab movement in district Basti, East U.P.', *Sociological Bulletin*, vol. XXIII, no. 1 (March).

Thorner, Daniel, 1956, *The Agrarian Prospect in India*, Delhi.

Weiner, Myron, 1963, *The Politics of Scarcity*, Bombay.

Wolf, Eric, 1971, *Peasant Wars of the Twentieth Century*, London.

## IO

# Whatever Happened to the Zamindars?

ELIZABETH WHITCOMBE

*Dunedin, New Zealand*

No institution of British India so epitomized the imperial presence as did zamindari. The Government of India took pains to demonstrate that it was not content to play the part merely of tax-collector and magistrate; it was as proprietor-in-chief, autocratic but benevolent, that it administered its vast Indian estate. To assist in the discharge of its functions, in which the fiscal, the magisterial and the proprietorial were considered happily to coincide, the Company had taken up the ancient institution of zamindari more particularly in the heartland of its empire in Bengal and the north and refashioned it as enlightened conceptions of Property and the dictates of revenue demanded. The zamindars' hereditary authority as tax-gatherers was enlarged and strengthened by the award of right, title and interest in fixed estates in land; they became landlords and, as such, the literal embodiment of Government's conception of itself. It was therefore hardly surprising that the zamindars should have drawn the fire of the nationalist opposition. By the early twentieth century, the abolition of zamindari dominated the Congress Party's programme of agrarian reforms and the disappearance of these tax-collectors-cum-landlords from those provinces saddled with them—'the garrison of an alien imperialism'—was seen to be virtually synonymous with independence. It was not merely the fidelity with which the zamindars represented the stated aims of the Government of India but the wanton impracticality with which they pursued them which convinced the nationalist reformers, casting a sceptical eye over the agrarian scene and its general wretchedness, that the blame was to be laid squarely at the zamindars' door. 'To our misfortune,' Nehru declared, 'we have zamindars everywhere and like a blight they have prevented all healthy growth. . . . We must, therefore, face this problem of landlordism and if we face it what can we do with it except to abolish it?' Congress was as good as its word. On the eve of independence, in August 1946, it passed a formal resolution to abolish zamindari by the compulsory acquisition, by government, of the zamindars' rights in return for just and equitable compensation. The formalities took six years to complete in Uttar Pradesh. The committee appointed under the resolution to prepare a suitable scheme reported in 1948; a bill was drafted on the basis of its recommendations the following year, and, battered in a series of stormy passages in the Legislative Assembly but not wholly unrecognizable, found its way on to the statute book as the Zamindari Abolition and Land Reforms Act, I of 1951; in May 1952, its constitutional validity was confirmed by the decision of the Supreme Court; the formal vesting of zamindari rights in government took place in June and directions then prepared for the revision of land records in accordance with the provisions of the new law.

The impact of the reform was subtle. Zamindari, as a legal institution, was gone but its abolition had produced no miraculous transformation of the agrarian scene two decades after the passing of the act. In the 1960s the vastness of the Gangetic plain bore a distinct —and to some critical observers distressing—resemblance to the weary descriptions of imperial reports. It was, as it had been for upwards of a century, since public works and the growth of population had driven back the wilderness, 'a level featureless expanse of unenclosed cultivation, densely populated, interspersed with unprofitable cities, field upon field of dust and dullness unspeakable'. District E., and indeed any one of the half-dozen others which collectively accounted for the middle Doab, showed off these unprepossessing qualities to perfection. It also provided, on closer inspection, an object lesson in irrigation and drainage. In a century, canals had compounded the work of the river; it had enhanced the natural advantages of the district's limited complement of well-drained upland but had also accelerated the deterioration of the salt-infested soils of the lowland basins to the extent where, by the late 1960s, they covered an area equal to perhaps a third of the entire district. The zamindars, whose land—the fertile and saline alike—it had been until abolition, were Moslems for the most part, many of the families established for hundreds of years; the district could boast of dynasties settled there in the time of Sher Shah. The history of their landownership read like a textbook of the property law. The zamindar's estate, as defined under the revenue settlements at the turn of the eighteenth century, was a collection of parcels of land, bewildering in its variety of sizes and soil-types and the rights of cultivators who worked it. Within a decade or two of settlement, the original estate had already become unrecognizable, its boundaries distorted by the sale at auction of plots of land in satisfaction of arrears of revenue and civil debt and later by confiscations for complicity in the 'Mutiny'. Later generations took advantage of the windfall of indigo which came with canal irrigation in the last quarter of the century to buy in new parcels of land to be tacked on to the fragments of the old estate while the inheritance laws added their share of confusion. Matters of landed property were justiciable and accounted for the greater part of business in both the revenue and civil jurisdictions, which last administered both the civil law and the personal laws of the indigenous communities; conflict abounded and the district's zamindars rapidly acquired, in proportion to the provision of legal facilities, a fine reputation for litigiousness while their opponents, worsted in the courts, took increasingly to dacoity to resolve their difficulties. Occasionally, at the earnest request of government, a zamindar might indulge in an improvement or two —irrigation, for example and improved seeds from the department of agriculture; but nothing of this description was sufficient to redeem a zamindar's debts. The zamindars, not surprisingly, lost interest in the progress of agriculture. Independence came upon them for the most part presiding ineffectually over the ramshackle empire of their estates; even their once gorgeous corruption had lost its spendour.

Independence, in district E., brought a sharp break with the past. Partition uprooted the zamindars and most removed in 1948 to Pakistan. The axe of zamindari abolition fell therefore for the most part upon the estates of absentees. The law provided for the residuum of their rights to be gathered up into files in the office of the Custodian for Evacuee Property, there to moulder amid much dust while the substance was steadily nibbled away in the prevailing land-hunger. The local well-to-do built literally on the ruins of zamindari. In the town of M., for example, a dusty backwater distinguished by its great antiquity and total absence of redeeming features, only the occasional pile of bricks and rubble remained, by the late 1960s, of the last vestiges of a zamindar's mansion ready for incorporation into the pukka houses of the 'new men'.

Alone of the zamindars in that neighbourhood, Q. sahib had opted to stay. His immediate family, all women, remained closeted in dilapidated grandeur; he himself, in government employment in the north, returned to his ancestral home on occasion to supervise the running of his ex-zamindari. Abolition had greatly simplified the tasks of management. The old estate had run into some hundreds of acres in toto, paying thousands of rupees annually in revenue. The apparent cohesion of the zamindari vanished on close inspection of the rent and revenue rolls: two half-shares in distant villages and literally thousands of plots, many a bare quarter-acre, and of no uniform quality, constituted the bulk estate, scattered amongst villages up to fifteen miles from M. and cultivated by innumerable tenants; two solid blocks of topgrade land, of fifteen and twenty acres respectively, within a mile of M. and separated only by an ancient and opulent mango-grove, completed the records—the zamindar's *sir*, or home farm, in which no tenant right of occupancy could accrue. Under the land reforms, all but this *sir* was acquired by government and dispersed amongst the ex-tenants—amongst perhaps three times as many claimants as there were plots, who were left to their ingenuity and the prospects offered by the consolidation act to make these fragments viable. The ex-zamindar, on the other hand, emerged with exclusive rights to his *sir*, and his mango-grove, and compensation for the lost zamindari with which to embellish them. Two decades after abolition, the thirty-acre ex-*sir* was a showpiece: well irrigated, amply fertilized and ablaze with hybrid vigour. Reduced in size but not in circumstances, the ex-estate, no more than a tenth of the old zamindari, brought in an estimated net annual income of Rs 6,000, ten times the yield of the best years in Q. sahib's father's time.

And this was not for want of a certain struggle towards betterment. The elder Q. sahib had been an improving landlord; in 1940, he had installed a tube-well in his *sir*, one of the first in the district as part of the Gangetic doab hydro-electric scheme and had made good use of the provincial department of agriculture's improved wheat seeds and such fertilizer as he could acquire. But the profits of his improved *sir* were forever swallowed up by the zamindari at large, vast, unmanageably fragmented, charged with commitments to revenue and maintenance of the family which its income could never meet and therefore hopelessly encumbered with debt; in short as ruinous a proposition as it had been for the previous generation. Nearly a

century before, Q. sahib's great-grandfather had found himself heir
to the same predicament and with government's encouragement had
also turned to irrigation, and to the cultivation of indigo which
followed in the wake of the Lower Ganges Canal, opened in 1878,
for rescue from perpetual embarrassment. The astonishing profits
proved true to expectation. They paid the costs of cultivation and
the revenue, and left a regrettably handsome margin for indulgence:
Q. sahib's ancestral residence *inter alia* owed its monumental style
to indigo and the Victorians' seemingly inexhaustible demand for
black crepe. But the boom lasted little more than a generation in
northern India; by the late 1890s, aniline dyes had all but ousted
indigo from the market. Deprived of the profits of indigo, the
zamindar's estate stood revealed for what it was—a representation
of chaos, the directions for which had been laid down with admirable
lucidity in the earliest revenue regulations.

The Company had acted with expediency in meeting the practical
requirements of revenue. It had followed established precedent in
defining fiscal liability and had made its settlements on the formal
basis of its predecessors' revenue-books. But both equity and common sense demanded that those who paid the land revenue must hold
recognized rights to assets in land from which their liability might be
satisfactorily discharged. The Company had thereupon departed from
tradition in redefining the zamindars, the hereditary tax-farmers,
as proprietors; their right to contract for revenue from a given area
was transformed into a proprietary right, title and interest or parcels
of land—an estate—and it entitled the zamindar to collect the rents
of the cultivators, his tenants, while obliging him to pay government
its fixed share. The cobbling of proprietary right on to old revenue
records produced for the most part something wonderfully bizarre
under the head of 'estate'. Claims to villages in entirety were seldom
attested to; a zamindar's rights attached to plots and his estate
emerged as a conglomerate of, let us say, a twentieth of village A, a
sixty-eighth of village B, half of village C, a two-hundred and
twenty-sixth of village D . . . a nine-hundredth of village X, and a
quarter of village Y. A single claim of this nature rarely represented
one zamindar. Zamindari was most commonly held in severalty, by
a coparcenary which ranged in numbers from perhaps a half-dozen
sons and brothers to the multitude of near and distant relatives
making up a *bhaiachara* community. Each segment of the claim was
festooned with cultivators' rights, except for the zamindar's *sir* re-

served for his personal cultivation, an oasis of simplicity in the wilderness of the revenue laws. The zamindars depended upon *sir* and upon the recognized devices of the personal laws restricting alienation to preserve zamindari from following a natural tendency to fall apart. Provision existed for physical partition of family and coparcenary property only in emergency; partition by inheritance was limited for the most part to a formal definition or redefinition of shares.

But the Company had not merely refined coparcenary rights as proprietary rights and fixed them, by successive settlements under Regulation VII of 1822 and Regulation IX of 1833, to a specific area of land: it had also mobilized them, made them alienable in conformity with the new revenue and civil law and in defiance of the old prescriptive rights against alienation. The mobilization of proprietary right was, government argued, a necessity both to satisfy government's legitimate claim to its revenue, in the event of arrears falling due, and to provide for the sound management of zamindars' estates. Improvidence on the part of landlords was to be discouraged. The law of compulsory sales provided the machinery whereby an indebted proprietor might be replaced, legally, by a solvent purchaser. This was a radical departure. Zamindars were accustomed to run their affairs on some form of everlasting credit; the physical and the financial circumstances of their newly-defined estates were such as to make indebtedness virtually unavoidable. With the exception of the occasional model farm after the style of the Begum Sumroo's five parganas of Meerut district, practical management was as much an illusion as the fissiparous estate was a viable proposition. The climate was capricious and agricultural prospects forever plagued by uncertainty; the domestic establishment, overburdened with dependants, was rapacious and the Company's revenue demand, it was later admitted, tended in the earlier, more experimental settlements to err on the side of severity. The hereditary rights of zamindars in groves, in bazaars, over rights of way and river-crossings were all pressed into service to stave off the ruin or at least the auction-purchaser but it was the Company itself which, properly enough, provided the saving grace. Ten or even twenty thousand men from a single district might well be employed in the civilian and military establishment; their contribution, in pay and service perquisites, to the zamindari accounts was incalculable.

11

In 1855, new regulations were passed for the conduct of revenue settlements due for revision; the inaccuracies and inequities of assessment made under the old rules on the basis of vernacular rent-rolls and the settlement officer's suppositions called loudly for reform. Government adopted a new procedure, the physical survey and demarcation of holdings, which was expressly designed to free the settlement officers from the toils of the zamindars' rent-rolls and from the odour of corruption which clung to them. A new passion for accuracy inspired the revenue department. Holdings were to be classified by the quality of the land and the revenue assessments framed from its estimated value. In the course of the next fifty years every cultivated field in the provinces of Agra and Oudh, a total of nearly 30,000,000 acres, was to be surveyed and resurveyed under this 'new model' settlement. The first revisions had been in progress barely two years when the 'Mutiny' broke out. Settlement operations were abruptly suspended, to be reopened in 1858 under new, Crown, management. The annexation of Oudh, formally declared in 1856, was now a reality and the rights of its talukdars and zamindars were subjected to the new pattern of assessment in the course of the following decade. The settlement picture was now complicated by confiscations and the arrival, in consequence, of more auction purchasers on the coparcenary scene. But it was the indirect effects of the 'Mutiny' and its aftermath which told more heavily on the zamindars. The prompt and wholesale disbanding of the 'native' establishment grossly aggravated the problems of upper-class unemployment which was to persist for two generations or more until government reopened the service, to a restricted number of the gentry. Zamindari estates, more particularly in the centre and eastern districts which had traditionally supplied the greater number of the Company's 'native' servants, were at once saddled with a massive increase in the number of direct dependants and deprived of the sustenance of their service income. The writers and sepahis who fell back on the zamindari were full members of the coparcenary. Their rights as such were recognized by the revenue law and their shares in the coparcenary's property were rigorously demarcated under the prescriptions of the revised settlements. As a result, thousands of claimants appeared in the settlement records each with a valid right, title and interest in a thousandth of an acre, or less. The proprietary body of the provinces, battered in the storms of the 'Mutiny' and its suppression, awoke like some great Gulliver to find itself bound down to the land by the measuring-chains and boundary-pegs of the revenue department.

If the state of zamindari was symptomatic of the condition of India at the transfer of power from the Company to the Crown, the zeal expended on the revision of settlements reflected the new government's commitment to rectify it. The Crown government, bent upon Utility, had adopted the Company's policy of 'a selfishness more or less enlightened' and was now to exploit it more ambitiously than its predecessor could ever have attempted. Government expressly acknowledged its responsibility to improve every branch of its administration, civil and military, in its own and its subjects' interest; but it was in public works, above all in irrigation, that imperial policy found its most fundamental means of expression and in Lord George Hamilton its champion of champions. Three decades at the India Office had acquainted him intimately with the exercise of near-total power. There were those who doubted his capacities; 'a small-minded ferret-faced roving-eyed mediocrity', sniffed Mary Curzon, with transatlantic candour; while William Digby heaped sarcasm mercilessly upon him in the dedication to *Prosperous British India*. But no one could justify responsible imperialism and its costs more eloquently than Lord George Hamilton. It was, as he put it,

the special duty of the Indian Government to construct works of general utility and of a remunerative character, for the Indian Government was the owner of the soil of the country and derived a very large revenue from it. They, Government, were much in the position of a landlord who, possessing a large property, determined by opening it out, to increase its value, although aware that the actual tolls on the roads constructed might not compensate him for the cost of their construction.[1]

This enterprise had begun felicitously enough. The Company had admitted, even solicited, private capital for the building of the railways while irrigation, in view of its intimate connection with the land revenue, was considered the exclusive preserve of government. Early successes in this field, in the restoration of the Jumna canals, were achieved rapidly and at minimal capital cost; the profits, in water rates and increment to land revenue due to irrigation, far exceeded expectation and provided government with an incentive and the necessary confidence to step beyond the limits set by the constructions of its predecessors and build new works in a wilderness more or less where none or only the most rudimentary had existed. Costs soared in consequence while profits resolutely refused to appear; the risks inherent in public works policy could not have been more patently demonstrated. The Ganges Canal, for example, the greatest of all nineteenth century innovations, brought in a return of barely 2 per cent on a capital investment of over £3,000,000 borrowed at rates in excess of 6 per cent, six years after its opening in 1854 and offered no prospect of betterment in the 1860s. But government's position was such that it was not merely committed to the construction of irrigation works as the high-minded expression of the duty incumbent upon an improving landlord; it was compelled to invest in them. Finance, as Henry Fawcett rightly insisted, was the key to England's position in India. The Government of India's finances were heavily compromised and works 'of agricultural improvement', designed to be remunerative, offered the best prospect of an increase in revenue sufficient, and sufficiently timely, to relieve the government's embattled budget.

The Crown government had entered upon its tasks with remarkable confidence, given its financial predicament. Its Indian estate had been an expensive acquisition from the start: the purchase of the Company's rights and the costs of the 'Mutiny' had saddled it with a Home Debt which in 1860 already stood at £30,000,000, while the revenues were severely constrained by the inherent inelasticity of demand. The increase in sophistication of methods of assessment introduced by the revision of settlements was matched by an increase in collections—from £33,000,000 to £52,000,000 annually by 1870, of which land revenue provided by far the greatest proportion but this was itself grossly inadequate to narrow the widening gap between income and expenditure. Government itself had limited its own power to hoist its revenue demand. It had fixed most of its settlements either permanently or for a period of thirty years, at a level, in theory if not always carried out in practice, which would guarantee the proprietors an equitable margin and thereby, government hoped, an incentive to improve their standards of production, while the 'Mutiny' had demonstrated the perils of over-taxing the zamindars. Why not cut the costs of government—of law and justice, education, peace and public works—'extravagances!' cried the critics, 'necessities!' cried government: 'If we were not there to give the natives such benefits then we had better telegraph Lord Lytton to wind up the concern and come home. . . . To govern on European principles with an Asiatic revenue is a difficult thing and must from time to time lead to serious difficulties.'[2] The only solution to this impasse which government could seriously consider was to invest in works of improvement which must raise its revenues and the general welfare no doubt along with them, to the desired levels by raising the value of the property from which they were derived, and if the works were not adequately remunerative, steps must be taken to make them so.

Financial necessity demanded the wholesale improvement of Indian agriculture: so much was abundantly clear by the early 1870s. Government was prepared to shoulder the burden directly to the extent accounted for by the construction of public works. For the rest, it was determined to enlist the active support of the landed proprietors to whom its compromised means, slender establishment and an undying faith in the virtues of self-help required that the matter of local improvements be entrusted. Like government, the zamindars were for the most part hopelessly in debt and it was precisely this incontrovertible fact which, although deplorable in itself, provided government, by itself the greatest of all indebted proprietors, with the opportunity for the practical demonstration of how to make good; and the larger the zamindars' debts, the better this opportunity became. Indebtedness was, as we have seen, virtually synonymous with management for the majority of zamindars. It had persisted and even worsened, in spite of the law of compulsory sales which had been intended to remedy it. Auction purchases had proved no solution: they aggravated fragmentation and threatened the stability of government and its revenue in that they displaced, legally but not physically, hereditary proprietors in favour of parvenus from beyond the pale of the proprietorial community who were thenceforward forever at loggerheads with the dispossessed coparcenars. None of this was conducive to good management. In the later nineteenth century government revised its policy and took steps to strengthen zamindari against encroachment and to rescue it from the logical consequences of government's property laws. The turn of official mind was cogently expressed in a series of enactments for the relief of proprietorial indebtedness. These included, *inter alia*, provisions for government's taking over, temporarily, of the encumbered estates of minors under the auspices of the Court of Wards, a manager being seconded from the revenue department to act expressly as landlord whose duty it was 'to leave no method untried by which he can improve the condition of those entrusted to his care'.[3]

Government, and more especially the provincial Board of Revenue, might well have entertained the notion that with its guidance model farms worthy of a Coke of Norfolk-on-the-Jumna might arise from the debt-ridden ruins of the Wards' estates. But in practice this as all other improving enterprises was subject to formidable constraints. There was its budget: average annual allocations ranged from Rs 150,000 to Rs 200,000 to cover a total of more than 200 estates under Wards' management in both NWP and Oudh in any given year. There was the problem of size, and fragmentation of the estates: more than half consisted of shares in tens of villages. There was the problem of the extent of indebtedness. There was the problem of the tenantry, or more particularly of the conflict between zamindar and occupancy tenant, for each of whom investment in the improvement of the estate or the holding frequently constituted encroachment on the other's rights. Inevitably, therefore, the NWP estates, the smallest, most fragmented and most heavily indebted on the Wards' rolls, accounted collectively for a bare 20 per cent of the annual allocation for improvements; Oudh, on the other hand, distinguished by its large, compact estates cultivated largely by tenants-at-will, their proprietors' authority untrammelled for the most part by the complications of occupancy right, regularly took 40 per cent; while for the better part of 10 years from the mid-1800s, the Maharajah of Balrumpur's estate, a not-so-little kingdom in Gonda district, sporting a splendid hunting-lodge for official guests, consumed the remaining 40 per cent.

In short, conditions in something under half of the Wards' estates were such as to permit 'more or less useful work': experiments with local varieties of staple crops popularly reputed to possess some advantage—Jaunpuri maize, Muzaffarnagar wheat, Poona sugarcane—most of which succeeded, and the occasional exotic—English carrots, Cape and Canadian oats—which did not; the addition of the occasional Sindhi cow or a half-dozen buffaloes from Hissar to improve the herd; the digging of earthen and masonry irrigation wells. Improvements, the Board intimated to its officers deputed to management duties, should be confined to those which were 'speedily remunerative . . . the liquidation of debt should receive first attention'.

What was true of the Wards' estates was true of the provinces in general. The same obstacles—debt, fragmentation, the tenancy laws and budgetary constraints—beset the department of agriculture, established in 1874, in its attempts to carry out the directives of the revenue department and coax the provinces, by way of the zamindars, into improvement. The superintendent, the costs of whose establishment accounted for nearly 60 per cent of the department's annual expenditure, was charged with the dissemination of technical improvements designed, in the first instance, to be remunerative; zamindars whose circumstances were sufficiently propitious—those who possessed if not a compact estate at least a block of good-quality irrigated *sir*, were relatively unembarrassed by debts and conflict with occupancy tenants—were selected as the department's honorary local agents and, in a few instances, persuaded to form voluntary agricultural associations. The example set in due course by the improving zamindars was confidently expected to penetrate the interior strata of the rural community, to the mutual benefit of government and society. It was not intended that the department of agriculture should meet more than the costs of the design of improvements. Government was prepared to assist in the business of dissemination with grants from its revenues. The Company had inherited the ancient institution of *takavi* by which loans were made, at interest, from the public treasury for improved cultivation, chiefly the digging of irrigation wells and acquisition of draught stock. By ploughing a portion of its revenues back into the land, government had a creditor's interest in improved agricultural production. But the Company allowed takavi, in all the bothersomeness of its dealings with the zamindars, to lapse. In the 1870s, the Crown government undertook to revive it and duly erected a statutory fence around it to protect it from abuse. As a consequence, the practical limitations on the use of takavi were now formidable. Statutory provisions safeguarded the security of government's revenue but made it prodigiously difficult, and time-consuming given the documentation insisted upon by law, for the provincial authorities to make takavi grants. The annual disbursements recorded in the revenue files were a monument to government's caution: for two decades, to the mid-1890s when recurrent famine forced government into a flurry of relief expenditure, grants under the head of takavi stood annually at an average of one-eight-hundredth of the land revenue receipts. And that eight-hundredth could not but be concentrated, for the most part, on the best of zamindars' *sir*.

To the (occasional) zamindar in practical command of his estate, the benefits made available by government by the 1890s were considerable: there was canal-irrigation in the Doab and official encouragement to cultivate indigo and wheat for export; there were the improved seed schemes of the department of agriculture in which he might well be taking an active part by running a demonstration-cum-seed farm on part of his *sir*; and there was the new concession to proprietors, expressly intended to stem the rising tide of their indebtedness, viz. the reduction of the assessment on *sir* itself. But while *sir* had come to be or at least to resemble an economically viable unit—indeed, more often than not the only solvent component of the zamindar's estate, its solvency could not be relied on to support the entire zamindari, and its cousins and its aunts, without a measure of serendipity; and with the virtual collapse of indigo, serendipity proved hard to come by.

Meanwhile government itself was made increasingly sensible of the precariousness of its finances. In 1896, in an atmosphere heavy with the concerns of famine and its expenses, government resolved on devolution of its responsibilities: the provinces must take more of their share of the imperial burden, which must include a large share in the development and dissemination of agricultural improvement. Government undertook to increase its commitment and at the same time actively to solicit, more intensively than before, the practical co-operation of the zamindars. With the usual concessions to security, in the form of a modest allocation of staff and budget, government presided over the launching of the co-operative movement, to be led and in part financed by the rural well-to-do. The agricultural department received a new lease of life. The first agricultural chemist was appointed; the Director of Land Records and Agriculture, W. H. Moreland, designed and implemented a co-ordinated scheme for the multiplication and distribution of improved seeds by selected zamindars. The report of the (Government of India) Irrigation Commission appeared in 1904, which recommended that a huge zone be demarcated for the development of minor, especially well, irrigation, to be carried out by private means supplemented by technical and financial assistance of government and supplied not by the irrigation but by the agriculture department. Government accepted the recommendation and thus put into operation the first irrigation development not directly determined by land revenue demand but tailored to the scale of cultivation. 1905 saw the foundation of the Imperial Agricultural Research Institute at Pusa, in neighbouring Bihar. Work here proceeded with alacrity under the direction of Albert Howard. The main thrust of its activities was towards the improvement of wheat for export in line with standards set by the British Millers and Bakers

Association and accepted, as virtually a guaranteed market, by government.

Progress in instilling improved principles and practices, beyond the limits of the already converted, was a series of fits and starts. Voluntary agricultural associations made little headway: they 'have no organic life', the agricultural department complained in its report for 1903–4, 'but they can be galvanized into a semblance of activity which however produces no result of permanent value'. Practical work was confined to improved wheat. Government clearly found even this heavy going, and drew encouragement where it could—notably from the Porter Association of Allahabad, dominated by 1908 by the Kunwar Sahib, the very model of the modern improving proprietor: he maintained stud bulls, he imported seed wheat and seed potatoes under government recommendation, he sank no less than 60 wells, he constructed and operated his own sugar factory. Government heaved a sigh over Kunwar Sahib: 'the improvement of agriculture would be a much simpler matter than it is if such an enlightened and beneficent gentleman as the Kr Sahib were generally to be found'. Progress in the formation of associations was itself halting: only two had been started in addition to Allahabad's and attempts at formation had been launched in two other districts. Official policy was hardly a potent stimulus: government was to limit itself to practical advice, 'while abstaining from interference with its actual management'. By 1908–9, there were faint stirrings in districts east of Allahabad, but overall growth was slow in the extreme. By 1910–11, only eight associations had been registered.

The growth in demonstration farms was similarly lethargic: eight only were listed on the department's books by 1909–10, five of them owned by the Honourable Thakur Kushal Pal Singh of Oudh. Government could however point with increasing confidence to the profitability of such farms: to the Raja of Chandapur's conspicuous success with sugar-cane on his Rae Bareli farm and the sales of seed wheat from Babu Ram Chandra Gupta's farm in Muzaffarnagar —Rs. 5,000 in 1908–9, more than Rs 9,000 the following year. A few more years of the desultory recruitment of the rajahs of Oudh to the cause followed. By 1913–14, it was clear that government's efforts to establish the demonstration zamindar were bearing fruit. The number of private farms under departmental supervision suddenly rose from a mere four to forty, the central districts could boast of 14 seed-farms alone. Progressive farming amongst the gentry had become a reality and as such had acquired a strikingly modern appeal to the professional classes: 'some 6 enlightened members of the Lucknow Bar', the department reported in 1915–16, 'have come forward to help in the cause of agriculture.'

But the pattern of growth continued along old lines and the ironies of imperial policy persisted. The bulk of private farms were to be found in Oudh where, owing to the nature of the land tenure, it was easier—as it always had been—to arrange for compact areas. By reason of the restrictions, peculiar to the rent and revenue laws of Oudh, on the growth of occupancy right, the talukdars and zamindars of the province could order matters largely as they wished without overmuch fear of contests in the courts: it was up to them whether they chose to adopt government's suggestions as to the practical management of their estates and their choice, also, as to whether they wished their tenants to benefit. Some did, and the spread of Pusa wheat through parts of the provinces was their doing. Government was optimistic as to the value of the Oudh farms in pointing the way for the development of the masses. 'The owners are men of capital', the department stressed, 'and are in a position to show what can be done on holdings of an economic size, properly cultivated and irrigated. They thus set a standard for smaller men to follow.' It was a hard standard for smaller men. The proprietors of Oudh ranged from the benevolent few to the bone-idle and the bloody-minded, the vast majority whose relations with their tenants verged on the unprintable. Most tenants could not profit from the new agriculture: not so much by reason of the miniscule size of their holdings but because of the insecurity of their tenure. In the NWP, fragmentation and perpetual conflict over the accrual of occupancy right in, and out, of the courts, restricted both the zamindar's and the tenant's attempts to improve. Within the formidable limits imposed by tenurial conditions, however, the scope for improvement was as yet large and government continued to draw satisfaction from the department of agriculture's success. In 1919, the wartime bottleneck in the supply of pumping plants and implements was removed and the numbers of private farms on the department's books shot up, to a total of 202 registered in 1920–1, varying in extent from 10 to 250 acres. Net annual profits ranged from 25 per cent on the smallest to the dizzy heights of 185 per cent and 260 per cent on the more splendid of Oudh's model farms. By 1923–4 the numbers had risen to 405: five years later, the roll stood at 964.

Government continued to express its belief that 'in course of time these farms cannot but make their influence felt on the agricultural practice of the surrounding villages. . . . The UP is pre-eminently a zamindars' province and the best way to reach the masses actually engaged in agriculture is through the zamindars.'

But was it the best way? In its last great public enquiry into the condition of Indian agriculture, the royal commission of 1927–8 under Linlithgow's chairmanship, government shied away from the question. The commission's deliberations were restricted to technicalia; 'it was forbidden to consider the question of land tenure as a factor in agricultural production', one of the best-qualified witnesses called before it, Harold Mann, wrote twenty years later, recalling the deep disappointment he had felt at the decision. Government had good reason to depart from the tradition of its agrarian enquiries, the practice of which had been to investigate exhaustively the condition of the cultivating classes. The relation of landlord and tenant had now become hotly political. 'Agriculture', it was felt, was best and certainly most encouragingly considered from the exclusive standpoint of technical improvement. The Commission made its copious recommendations in this light and the departments of agriculture set out, with budgets enlarged for the purpose by 200–300 per cent, to implement them.

The gentry of Oudh had, as we have seen, always been in a relatively strong position to be able to profit from government's agricultural advances, whilst in Agra there had been problems restricting the department's achievements. The reform of the tenancy law now eased those restrictions. The landed interest, dominant in the provincial legislature, agreed to the principle of statutory rights for the unprotected tenantry and received in return greater facilities for the realization of rents and for the acquisition of *sir*, a longer term of settlement, a limit to the degree to which their revenue could be enhanced and various other concessions. Congress might rage, with its 'no rent' campaign and its anti-zamindari propaganda and not unreasonably so. The zamindars, unimprovers, anti-improvers and improvers alike, all enjoyed a handsome measure of official protection in their freedom of action to choose where and how to seek their profits or whether to seek them at all. With the grace of government patronage, the zamindars in their debt-ridden splendour were thus in a position to cock a snook at Congress and its cry of 'Abolition!'

And, for that matter, at much which was unpalatable in the world at large: at the slump, for instance. By the early 1930s, prices of staple food-grains had plummeted throughout the provinces and a dramatic rise in acreages sown bore witness to cultivators' attempts to make up for the loss in value by increases in outturn, with how much success it is difficult to say: there is no evidence at least to suggest that distress was either widespread or cataclysmic. But the progressively-farming zamindar was on an altogether better wicket. With the collapse of the export market in food-grains, government encouraged the sale of wheat, formerly the prize export staple, on the domestic market. From 1931–2, some 8,000,000 acres annually, nearly one-quarter of the total food-grains area of the provinces, were put under improved wheats. The zamindari farms, 1,240 of them registered with the department of agriculture by 1930–1, supplied the bulk of the seed and thus not merely survived the slump but profited from it.

And then there was sugar-cane. Strictly a tropical crop, its large-scale cultivation in the sub-tropical north is largely an accident of history, an unforeseen consequence of the revival and expansion of canal-irrigation in the western and later the central districts of the provinces in the course of the nineteenth century. The domestic canes of the provinces were markedly poorer in sucrose content than those of southern and western India but reached maturity in 18 months whereas the tropical crop required two to two and a half years. The development of canal-irrigation in the Doab brought about a great increase in acreage, from a few thousand to hundreds of thousands of acres by the turn of the century. Along with indigo, cane had fast become the most profitable crop. Acreages under rainfed cane in the eastern districts also increased but outturn was poor, and became noticeably poorer—the vagaries of rainfall combining with the alkalinity of the soil to depress the yield and cheat the cultivator.

Until the 1920s, government's interest in the technicalities of cane, and the prospects for its improvement, was marginal. The occasional improving zamindar who took to the sugar-manufacturing business did so with a good variety of local cane more happened upon than systematically selected. By the mid-1920s, however, Clarke, the latest in a distinguished line of agricultural chemists in the provincial service, had succeeded in domesticating high-sucrose canes from Coimbatore. The ground was literally prepared: the canal-irrigated tracts of Agra province were conditioned to cane cultivation and were joined, at the beginning of the 1930s, by the thousands of acres in west and southern Oudh opened for irrigation by the Sarda Canal, the greatest of all irrigation schemes in the U.P. and expressly designed for the co-ordination of irrigation and agricultural development, with wheat and sugar-cane as chief staples. Again, it was the domestic market which was to be supplied. Government backed the cane venture to the hilt: it put its weight behind the cultivation of cane, to which the greater proportion of the agricultural department's resources was now devoted, and it undertook to organize the sugar industry: in a radical departure from its previous policy of non-interference, it placed the manufacturing of sugar under controls and committed itself to battle for fair prices to cane cultivators. The co-operative movement in India had been placed on a firm legal footing by the enactments of 1904 and 1912; provincial legislation followed in the next two decades on the lines indicated by model enactments prepared by the Government of India. By the 1930s, the U.P. had some thousands of registered agricultural credit societies but since these, on closer examination, turned out to be a fine rationalization of the status quo, a front more often than not for moneylenders' regular operations (a field in which, again, zamindars were also conspicuous) the progress of the co-operative movement as such cannot be said to have been other than dilatory in the extreme. But co-operation provided government with the framework on which it could proceed to organize the sugar-cane business. In 1934, the first Sugar-cane Co-operative Societies were launched in the U.P. Existing sugar-factories, some fifteen of them, the oldest in the eastern districts, the majority established in the western districts within the previous decade, were made the focal point; cane-growing areas were zoned, so many villages to supply such and such factory, with a fixed quota subject to seasonal review by the interested parties—government, the factory owner and the cultivators. 'Cultivators' was a somewhat misleading term: government adhered firmly to its general policy of agricultural improvement and sought its recruits for the cane co-operatives amongst the prosperous, or potentially prosperous, 20- to 50-acre 'farmers' who were expected to take the rest of the village with them. The proposition was attractive to the improving zamindar, notably in the western divisions of Meerut and Rohilkhand, where cane had a head start. The Agra Tenancy Act of 1926 had assisted, by making it easier for the zamindar, hitherto much impeded by fragmentation, legally to acquire *sir*; irrigation facilities were amongst the best in the provinces and were, in the later 1930s, to be greatly improved in these divisions by the installation of tube-wells under the Gangetic doab hydro-electric scheme. The progress of the co-operatives was, however, slow not so much for any want of rural enthusiasm but because of the often violent resistance on the part of the factory owners to any trimming of their power. Government was in a cleft stick and forced to temporize, unable to drive the factory owners into out-and-out opposition. The Congress party changed matters. The first Congress government, which took office in 1937, was determined to organize the cane co-operatives into a powerful force, and did so: it permitted them legally to refuse supply to factories not keeping to their side—the purchase price—of the bargain drawn up between co-operative and factory owner at the beginning of each cane-crushing season. The co-operatives of the western and to some extent the central districts also were in a strong position. Factories had mushroomed in what was the best cane-growing land of the north, with the result that two or more commonly lay within cart-distance of villages assigned to any one zone. A recalcitrant owner stood to lose his cane to a more compliant competitor and also to the *khandsaris*, small open-pan 'cottage' factories in which, again, it was not uncommon for the local zamindar to have an interest. By the 1940s, factory owners were being driven into compromise with the co-operative leaders. But in the eastern districts, competition and its advantages were rare; factories, the oldest in the provinces, were larger and fewer than in the west and khandsaris, for technical reasons to do with the recovery from rainfed cane, uneconomic. The largest growers, talukdari and zamindari, tended to form alliances of mutual benefit with the factory owners, thus controlling price and profits, and at the same time to exploit the co-operatives at the expense of their tenants, whose names were duly entered by the zamindar in the society's register, swelling the membership and thereby increasing government's allocation of seed-cane, fertilizer and credit to be cornered by the zamindar. By competition or by monopoly, one way or another, the cane-growing zamindar profited from the co-operatives and Congress support; tenants benefited where the zamindar and, especially in the west, occupancy-right, permitted. Cane had thus become the latest manifestation of the ubiquity of zamindari power and that with the blessing of Congress.

But Congress was at the same time unequivocally committed since decades to the formal abolition of zamindari; it was also active in support of the anti-zamindari *kisan* (peasant) movement. A certain ambiguity in its position in no way deterred Congress from pursuing the issue of land reform, by means of abolition, with vigour. Such reform was lamentably overdue. It was nearly twenty years since the Linlithgow commission's recommendations as to the practical means to be adopted for the advancement of Indian agriculture had formally been accepted by government; but, barring the conspicuous successes in the cane fields, few of the improvements devised and found profitable on demonstration farms had been taken up in the provinces at large. As Harold Mann insisted, much of the reason for this failure lay in the problem of the cultivator's relationship to the land and government's persistent refusal to confront it. But Congress was determined to proceed where the imperial government had faltered and to redefine cultivating right more radically than a century of tenancy enactments had attempted. The legal obstacle to redefinition was zamindari; it had therefore legally to be removed. Congress accordingly resolved, in August 1946, on the eve of Independence, to abolish zamindari—equitably, with due regard for the payment of compensation in return for the acquisition of zamindari rights by government. The committee set up under the resolution to prepare a suitable scheme reported to the new government in 1948. In July the following year, the Zamindari Abolition and Land Reforms bill was presented to the legislative assembly.

The zamindars' reaction was predictable. The Congress threat had become reality; zamindars the length and breadth of the provinces were outraged. And not solely in defence of immemorial and hitherto virtually inviolate privilege of status. Sir Jagdish Prasad of Moradabad, big in sugar, put the case bluntly for the progressive interest. What mischief, precisely, was the bill designed to correct? Government in its ignorance and vindictiveness would rather create mischief than remedy it. Government did not know even the basic facts about tenure; it lumped all zamindars together indiscriminately, the progressive with the retrograde. To take zamindari land would in no way solve the agrarian problem; instead the productive, highly capitalized land would be dispersed, while the basic problem of inequality of distribution would remain, unremedied, since zamindari land itself was patently insufficient to meet the demand. Since the measure was doomed by its inherent impracticality to failure, government, in calling for the abolition of zamindari, could be moved by nothing more than pure and unadulterated spite.

Government stood firm. Its confidence perhaps stemmed largely from the realization that while zamindari abolition might not in itself prove to be a sufficient condition for land reform, no reform could in fact take place without it. 'We have not in any way been influenced by any extraneous consideration,' G. B. Pant had said in introducing the bill. 'In fact we have never been hostile to zamindars or for that matter to any other section of the community. We wish to do all that we can for the welfare of every one but all of us have to realize that the good of each individual lies in the good of all and in this new order it is necessary that even for the preservation of individual interests these of the larger whole should not be neglected or underrated.' Seen in the cold light of legal day, the method by which Congress proposed to reconcile the conflicting claims of zamindars and tenants was by no means inelegant. A new system of tenure was to be established, of four classes of tenants—two major (*bhumidars* and *sirdars*), and two minor (*asamis* and *adhivasis*). Zamindars were to become bhumidars in respect of their personal cultivation—*sir, khudkasht* and groves—gratis; government was to acquire zamindari rights in all property not covered under the head of personal cultivation and to pay compensation for them; tenants were to be redefined as sirdars with permanent heritable (but not saleable) rights in their holdings and might choose to become bhumidars, with fully alienable rights, on payment of ten times the annual rent.

Government's intention, consistent with its declared policy of decentralizing the rural economy by reform not revolution, was not to extirpate zamindari but rather to cut it down to size. Defenders of the bill might well argue as did Hukum Singh, the revenue minister, and not without foresight, that abolition might well prove beneficial to the majority of zamindars. Not surprisingly, the zamindars' leaders found this preposterous: an ill-defined promise of solvency, when zamindars had managed without it for centuries, was no consolation for so drastic a reduction in their property and their power. They preferred to pit their strength against the passing of the bill and for the preservation of their estates in entirety, however unworkable. A certain optimism pervaded their meetings throughout the provinces. After all, as Nawabzada Hyder Ali had pointed out to the Sitapur zamindars' conference in January 1947, the zamindars were twenty lakhs strong and if only they organized themselves properly 'no government would dare to ignore them much less crush them'. The British Indian Association led the way and the zamindari associations followed, the kisan movement snapping at their heels. But the goings-on in the countryside played little part in the battle against the passing of the reforms: that battle was fought in the legislative assembly, on government ground, and it was a foregone conclusion that the bill would be carried. It ran the gauntlet of the anti-Congress opposition, peppered by amendments, but survived relatively intact to become law in 1951. It was over a year, however, before its provisions could be brought into effect. The zamindars had a last legal card to play. In actions brought before the high court at Allahabad and at Patna in neighbouring Bihar, they impugned the constitutional validity of zamindari abolition, as contravening the fundamental right to property guaranteed under article 31. The matter was settled by a decision of the supreme court (and the constitutional point clarified subsequently by an important amendment), in favour of the state government in June 1952. On 1 July 1952, zamindari rights were formally vested in government.

Some ex-zamindars took it philosophically. 'The abolition of zamindari ushers in a new era in our country,' Kanwar Guru Narain told the U.P. Praja party. 'We must not give way to despair and shall adjust ourselves to the new situations.' For some, adjustment was out of the question. Partition had decimated the Muhammadan zamindari community, notably of the western and central districts, while the grandest, most splendidly spendthrift of the zamindars and many absentees in towns and cities, long out of touch with anything dignified under the title of 'personal cultivation', faced ruin. But the majority could afford to be sanguine as to their prospects. Abolition had been so long in coming; the last round of litigation had provided a fine opportunity for the strategically-minded to take stock—and in taking stock, the ex-zamindars were greatly assisted by a certain generous imprecision in the newly-enacted arrangements which, in this respect, followed faithfully in the footsteps of imperial precedent. The aim of the legislators was, expressly, redefinition, not redistribution—in short, to rewrite the revenue records in a simpler, more equitable language. Accordingly, the amorphous tangle of zamindari was laid out, theoretically, in neat parcels of ex-*sir*, -khudkasht and groves in which the ex-zamindars, now automatically made bhumidars, had heritable and transferable rights. But what, in practice, *was sir*? The problem of its definition was as old as the revenue law. More than a century of regulations and enactments, of deliberations by the Board of Revenue and settlement officers' estimates, had not

12

solved it. Strict limits had never applied and, by the time zamindari abolition became law, a wholesale enlargement had taken place on innumerable estates, not least by the device of multiple registration amongst family members, in the rush to anticipate restrictions first under the tenancy act of 1939, and then of the land reforms. And what did 'personal cultivation' mean? Something unthinkable which the higher castes could not, or would not, entertain, not least in the knowledge that government would find itself powerless to insist on the observation of the letter of its new law.

It so happened that the manner in which the land reforms were implemented compounded the difficulties of definition and demarcation and thus catered for the ex-zamindars' interests more generously than government had intended. Compensation was given top priority and its assessment, on all land except that personally cultivated, was to occupy the bulk of the revenue establishment till the late 1950s. While government sought to wrap the zamindars' wounds in compensation bonds, it turned a blind eye to the aggrandizement which could not but take place under the head of 'personal cultivation' with the record-keeping establishment so assiduously employed elsewhere. It was, moreover, not merely the compensation arrangements which seriously compromised the integrity of the revenue records at the inception of the reforms. In 1952, fortuitously perhaps, the *patwaris* (record-keepers) came out on strike. Government responded by a wholesale dismissal of the strikers and the recruitment of new officials, newly designated *lekhpals*, in their place. But the lekhpals turned out either to be unqualified, in spite of government's hasty attempts to organize crash courses in record-keeping, or, if qualified, to be the patwaris under another name. The patwaris were after all resident in, especially, zamindari villages; they were the traditional guardians of the records, traditionally dependent on the zamindar's bounty, and their services were literally highly prized. As a result of all this, the records—from 1953 to 1958, at least, after which time the revenue department ceased to make public comment in its annual reports—proved on such inspection as was made to be grossly defective. Revenue officers rarely ventured further, into the thickets of multiple registration of title farmed out amongst brothers, uncles, absentees, servants, even elephants in the ex-zamindari stables. No legal restriction on the size of holdings existed prior to the passing of the ceilings act almost a decade after abolition, in 1960; a certain dilatoriness on the part of the legislators in this respect assisted ex-zamindari families to pool their resources in profitable harmony.

Ex-*sir*, nicely indeterminate, provided the basis for economic viability; compensation, the capital with which to achieve it. Meanwhile the land revenue demand, declining steadily since the 1920s, had fallen to near derisory levels. A large-landholding tax, when introduced in the late 1950s, proved in practice to be nearer fiction than fact and its collection was a fiasco. No agricultural income-tax existed. Debt relief statutes removed the ex-zamindars' hereditary encumbrances. A way paved with assets and cleared of liabilities lay ahead. Congress had made zamindari viable, in theory, by abolishing it. It had solved the root-problem of its fragmentation. The new law divested the ex-zamindar of his plethora of uneconomic fragments; he retained the workable core of the estate while the fragments— hundreds and thousands of plots, many less than a bigha—were parted up amongst as many tenants as could prove legal claim. Some few appear to have emerged from the proceedings with modest to sizable holdings—the ex-occupancy tenants stood to benefit best; but the majority of cultivators whose claims were satisfied found themselves saddled with the zamindar's problem of the unviable fragment and without the zamindar's income. Government went further. It made ex-zamindari viable in practice. In the new capital-intensive agricultural strategy, introduced into the provinces in the late 1960s, the Congress government had the means to realize the imperial dream: progressive farming amongst the gentry. Within a year or two of the programme's inception, virtually every district could field a fine crop of demonstration ex-zamindars—the Rai Sahibs with their 30-, 40-, 50-, 100-acre holdings, their multiplication farms of the latest Mexican wheat and Philippines paddy, their tube-wells gushing out 16,000 gallons an hour, much of it on highly profitable hire, their tractors, their godowns stacked with fertilizer, their cold-stores—and their groves, their rights over fairs and bazaars, their brothers and sons in the civil service and industry, the army and the police sending regular remittances to swell the family accounts in pre-Mutiny fashion . . .; in short, a tenth of the zamindari, but ten times the income.

## NOTES

1. *Hansard*, series 3, 226, (1875) 804.
2. Ibid. 246, (1879) 1171.
3. *Report of the Court of Wards' Estates, NWP*, 1879–80, Appendix D, 47.

# II

# Changes in Land Ownership Pattern: Structural Change in Indian Agriculture

## V. S. VYAS

*Indian Institute of Management, Ahmedabad*

THE agrarian system in a country reflects the main attributes of production units and their mutual alignment. Since these are not independent of each other, factors influencing one aspect of the system also affect other aspects as well. However, those favouring structural changes generally lay stress upon changes in the relative position of different categories of agricultural producers as a precondition for increasing agricultural production. It is recognized that structural changes are not relevant in some cases and other reforms, i.e. organizational changes or policy measures, are more important. It is also understood that, without appropriate supportive measures, gains of structural changes can soon evaporate. While there is substantial agreement on these aspects among students of agrarian systems in this country, there is no such unanimity on processes by which structural changes are brought about. An undue emphasis on legislative or 'extra-constitutional' sources of change is seen in the literature on the subject (Joshi, 1975). Other important determinants, e.g. market transactions and demographic factors, are generally not given due importance. In this paper, we will be examining changes in the structure of land holdings in India during the 1960s, various processes by which the changes have come about, and the underlying causes which could explain these changes.

The structure of production units in agriculture can be classified on the basis of size of land holdings, gross or net produce, value added, capital employed, extent of wage labour, extent of marketable surplus, gross or net worth of the enterprise, and so on, As in other countries, Indian economists are not satisfied with a unidimensional measure of classifying production units in the agricultural sector. The holdings, for example, have been classified on the basis of area covered, in terms of gross product, gross and net worth, and extent of wage labour (Vyas, 1968; Rudra *et al.*, 1969; Patnaik, 1975). Yet the predominant form of classification has been on the basis of acreage. This is partly because data on size (acreage) of the holdings are most readily available and a whole set of information, e.g. land utilization, cropping pattern, yield, etc., is related to the size-class of the holdings. Another reason for the bias towards size of holdings is that, in Indian villages, control over land and control and authority over local level institutions usually go together. Access to other factors of production is largely determined by the size of land holdings (Vyas, 1976). Income differences in relatively homogeneous rural areas can be better explained by the size of land holdings than by other important variables (Repparto and Shah, 1975). No wonder, therefore, that in any scheme of structural reforms in agriculture state intervention is expected, in the first instance, to affect changes in the size pattern of land holdings.

By selecting size as the principal classifying element, comparability between different classes of production units is not automatically ensured. Quality of land, tenurial arrangements, and the intensity of land use may differ significantly for different size-groups. If coverage is large, say, the whole country, one is probably justified in assuming that intra-class differences are statistically less significant than inter-class differences and, hence, changes in the relative position of different classes of holdings can provide meaningful insight into the functioning of the agrarian system. For these reasons, agrarian categories are identified in terms of size-groups of land holdings in this paper.

## Changes in holding pattern

The reports of various rounds of the National Sample Survey (NSS) are the principal source for obtaining an all-India picture of the distribution of land holdings. Under four different rounds of NSS, the landholding pattern in India has been investigated: eighth round (pertaining to 1953–54), sixteenth round (1960–61), seventeenth round (1961–62) and twenty-sixth round (1970–71). For 1970–71, a census of holdings was also conducted as part of the world-wide Agricultural Census, a project sponsored by the FAO to obtain information from its member countries on various aspects of the agricultural economy. The findings of the census, especially on ownership holdings, are not comparable with those of the NSS owing to differences in concepts and methodology (Sanyal, 1976). Partly for this reason, but also because only the NSS provides comparable information over a period of time, we have relied on the data collected in the seventeenth and twenty-sixth rounds of the NSS for our study.

From the viewpoint of agrarian relations the decade 1961–70 is very important for several reasons: (1) By the 1960s, the tenancy reform phase of the land reform programme was virtually over; practically in each state the principle of 'land to the tiller' was incorporated in land reform legislation. (2) Two distinct waves of land ceiling legislation, one more drastic than the other, swept the country —the first in the beginning years and the second, a more stringent one, in the closing years of the decade. (3) Since 1964–65, a new strategy of agricultural development was introduced in the country which yielded bountiful results in some parts of the country. (4) Terms of trade started moving in favour of agriculture since the early 1960s and, by the closing years of the decade, the trend was firmly established. (5) In spite of three 'plan-less' years in the decade, the public outlay in agriculture was fairly large. (6) Several organizational innovations such as Intensive Agricultural District Programme (IADP), rehabilitation of co-operative movement, introduction of *panchayati raj* (the system of democratic decentralization), etc. were introduced with the objective of strengthening supportive systems and ensuring agricultural development.

While these developments were meant to help agricultural growth, the net outcome, judged in terms of production, was not at all satisfactory. The rate of growth in agricultural production was 3.6 per cent a year during the 1950s, which came down to 2.2 per cent a year in the 1960s. Nor could the industrial growth pick up enough momentum to make a dent in rural unemployment and underemployment. While the causes and consequences of the slow rate of growth in agriculture in spite of several favourable factors need careful examination, this paper is restricted to the examination of the nature of changes in land ownership, and only by implication relates some of the developments listed above to these changes.

Use of ownership holdings to highlight aspects of structural change needs some explanation. Land is the most important asset of farmers in India. A change in the landholding status reflects, more accurately than any other index, the relative prosperity or destitution of various classes of Indian farmers. In the production process, the contribution of land as a factor of production is still predominant. Lastly, political power and economic hegemony in Indian villages revolve around land ownership.

Table I gives distribution of land holdings *owned* by households in 1961 and 1971 as revealed by the seventeenth and twenty-sixth rounds of the NSS.* One way to gauge changes in the holding structure is to calculate the concentration ratios for two distributions, i.e. the landholding pattern obtaining in 1961–62 and that obtaining in 1970–71. The calculation of Gini-coefficient shows that the landholding structure had become slightly less skewed (from 0.525 to 0.512)** by the end of the decade compared to the early years. However, the concentration ratio may conceal more than what it reveals. There are various ways in which the value of concentration ratio may increase without in fact meaning an enlargement of the bigger holdings at the cost of the small-sized holdings. For example, medium-size holdings may expand in number and area at the cost of small and large holdings and may thus raise the coefficient of concentration. It will be necessary, therefore, to take a close look at the actual changes in different size-groups of holdings (Dantwala and Rao, 1974).

To facilitate inter-class comparison, we have consolidated the size-groups of holdings reported in NSS rounds into five categories; marginal landowners (those owning less than 1 acre); small landowners (owning land between 1 and 5 acres); medium landowners (5 to 15 acres); big landowners (15 to 50 acres); and large landowners (owning more than 50 acres of land). The following facts emerge from the study of the data for 1961–62 and 1970–71 (see Table I).

(1) The number as well as proportion of households in the marginal holding group has significantly increased.
(2) Acreage under marginal holdings has slightly declined.
(3) The number of small landowners has increased, but their importance in terms of proportion of total number of landowners has marginally declined.

---

*In subsequent discussion, 'holdings' and 'households' are used synonymously. Since the proportion of jointly owned holdings in the NSS sample was very small (Sanyal, 1976), such usage would not vitiate the results.

**Gini-coefficients can vary slightly depending on the exact formula used. In the above calculations, the formula used is that given by Kendall and Stuart. See M. G. Kendall and A. Stuart, *Advanced Theory of Statistics*, vol. I, p. 46.

TABLE I

ESTIMATED NUMBER OF HOUSEHOLDS AND AREA OWNED BY DIFFERENT SIZE-GROUPS OF HOLDING
(All-India)

| Size-group of ownership holdings | | No. of households and area owned | | | | | | |
|---|---|---|---|---|---|---|---|---|
| | | 1970–71 | | | 1961–62 | | | |
| | | No. of households ('000) | Area owned ('000 acres) | Average area (acres) | No. of households ('000) | Area owned ('000 acres) | Average area (acres) | |
| Marginal | (below 1 acre) | 35,640 (43.99) | 4,910 (1.58) | 0.14 | 23,579 (36.84) | 5,062 (1.59) | 0.21 | |
| Small | (1–4.99 acres) | 27,415 (33.83) | 71,158 (22.86) | 2.60 | 22,468 (35.11) | 58,465 (18.39) | 2.60 | |
| Medium | (5–14.99 acres) | 13,564 (16.74) | 112,464 (36.13) | 8.29 | 13,002 (20.32) | 109,703 (34.51) | 8.44 | |
| Big | (15–49.99 acres) | 4,058 (5.01) | 96,856 (31.12) | 23.87 | 4,514 (7.05) | 109,252 (34.37) | 24.20 | |
| Large | (50 acres and above) | 350 (0.43) | 25,856 (8.31) | 73.87 | 437 (0.68) | 35,379 (11.13) | 80.96 | |
| Total | | 81,027 (100.00) | 311,245 (100.00) | 3.84 | 64,000 (100.00) | 317,861 (100.00) | 4.97 | |

*Note:* Figures in parentheses are percentage to total.
*Source:* NSS no. 144, Seventeenth Round, for 1961–62, and NSS no. 215, Twenty-sixth Round, for 1970–71 figures.

(4) Area under small holdings has increased both in acreage as well as in proportion to the total owned area in the country.
(5) In numbers, total area and per household area, medium-sized holdings displayed trends more or less similar to small-sized holdings.
(6) The number as well as proportion of big and large holdings have declined.
(7) Acreage under big and large holdings has declined both in absolute terms and as proportion of total acreage.

Thus, an impression is created that during the 1960s small and medium holdings gained in importance while big and large holding groups, relatively speaking, lost their importance. This is brought out more sharply in Table II, which gives increase (decrease) in number and area of holdings in different size-groups.

TABLE II

INCREASE/DECREASE IN NUMBER OF HOLDINGS AND AREA OWNED BY DIFFERENT SIZE-GROUPS OF HOLDINGS IN 1970–71 ABOVE 1961–62

| Ownership of holding | Difference in 26th Round over 17th Round | |
| --- | --- | --- |
| | No. of holdings ('000) | Area owned ('000 acre) |
| Marginal | 12,061 | −152 |
| Small | 4,947 | 12,693 |
| Medium | 562 | 2,761 |
| Big | −456 | −12,396 |
| Large | −87 | −9,523 |
| Total | 17,027 | −6,616 |

*Source*: Same as Table I.

## Factors underlying structural change

There are various ways by which these shifts in the relative importance of different size-groups of holdings could have come about. And there is no way of knowing precisely how this has happened. There could be a 'ladder' process functioning in an upward direction or in a downward direction. In the positive, i.e. upward, manifestation, it could mean landless workers acquiring land and becoming marginal landowners, marginal landowners acquiring more land and becoming small landowners, and small landowners by the same process emerging as medium landowners. The ladder can work in reverse direction also when medium owners lose land and swell the ranks of small landowners, small owners are pushed to marginal owner category, and marginal owners join the ranks of the landless. At least one carefully conducted study, in Gujarat, has concluded that there is some evidence, howsoever feeble, of a positive ladder from landless workers to small landowner stage (Dantwala and Shah, 1971).

In the absence of similar studies for other parts of the country,* one can examine a few relevant hypotheses with the help of aggregate data and indirect evidence, explaining the changes depicted in Tables I and II. As possible explanations one can suggest (1) purchase of land by marginal and small landowners and sale of land mainly by large and big owners; (2) impact of land reforms and movements of similar nature like *bhoodan*, 'land-grab', etc. resulting in the breaking up of large holdings and allocating of land to small owners; and (3) demographic pressure necessitating division of holdings. These could be identified respectively as market-induced, institutional, and demographic processes.

Before discussing these processes, it needs to be emphasized that inter-class comparisons attempted above may conceal significant intra-class movements as well as information on 'entry' and 'exit' in different size-groups. Lack of relevant information precludes any systematic construction of a transition matrix. However, relative shifts in importance of different size-groups at two points of time as attempted above is an important indicator of structural change in the holding pattern.

*Market processes.* Even in developed countries, market transactions in agricultural land are not numerous. In traditional societies, such transactions are all the more limited because until a dire need arises a peasant would not like to sell his land. Provisions of various laws enacted in recent years also contributed to the 'freezing' of the land market in India, e.g. a scheduled tribe landowner cannot sell his land to a non-scheduled tribe person. In spite of these factors, at least till the mid-1950s there was some evidence of land sold by

* There is a study focused on operational holdings in Haryana, which has concluded that small farmers were losers in terms of *operated* area (Bhalla, 1977). The issue we are discussing pertains to *owned* area.

small and medium landholders and purchased by large and absentee landlords (Rao, 1972). The classical pattern seemed to be: indebtedness due to natural calamities or social ceremonies leading to hypothecation of land with money-lenders (who in many cases were big landowners) and eventual transfer of the land to money-lenders or bigger landlords. During the 1960s this process seems to have come to a halt. I have explained elsewhere the possible reasons for the discontinuation of this pattern (Vyas, 1976). Briefly, the fear of ceiling legislation acted as a brake to further expansion of holdings of big and large farmers. Opportunities for further intensification of farming in several parts of the country lured cultivators with larger liquid resources away from purchase of land. Tenancy legislation in a number of states made the process of buying land by the erstwhile tenants easy, and this process is well documented for the western region of the country (Dantwala and Shah, 1971; Desai, 1974). For similar developments in other parts one has to rely on localized surveys and studies. Available evidence suggests that the land market tended to work in favour of small and marginal landowners rather than against them.

*Institutional changes.* It would be wrong to assume that market forces alone, or in the main, were responsible for obtaining the results noted above. The land market served to supplement the effects of land reforms, which played a much larger role in influencing the ownership pattern. Directly, the imposition of ceiling on holdings and the allotment of surplus land among the landless led to a diminution of the bigger holding classes and the creation of small holdings. It is well known, however, that direct transfer of land was not a quantitatively significant phenomenon, the total area of surplus land redistributed among the landless till the beginning of the 1970s amounting to hardly 1 million acres. Indirect pressure exercised by legislation was more important. In spite of fictitious transfers and other devices employed by large landowners,* enactment of land ceiling legislation led to large scale disposal of land by big landowners, particularly absentee owners, to forestall the effects of legislation. Since tenancy legislation gave the right of purchase of land to the cultivating tenant, this process was further accentuated. However, the process did not unfold in a neat fashion.

---

*A keen observer of rural social scene, V. R. Gaikwad, has maintained that such *de jure* transfers have a built-in tendency to become *de facto* partitions (Gaikwad, 1975).

There were on the one hand a large number of cases of ejection of small tenants, and on the other, numerous cases of acquisition of land by tenants. During the 1950s and 1960s, a remarkable shuffle took place in the countryside. It is yet to be fully documented though there is strong evidence to suggest that, in large parts of the country, small landowners and the landless were net gainers in this process. Small owners were able to retain their holdings against the machinations of large farmers and they, as well as the landless, were the main beneficiaries once the larger farmers decided to dispose of part of their land in order to be on the right side of the law. Movements such as *bhoodan* and land grab in themselves did not benefit small and marginal farmers in a measurable way, but did contribute in creating a climate such that the large farmers thought it wise to dispose of part of their land. Factors which led to a diminution of holding size or encroachment on a poor farmer's land by the rich farmer proved to be weaker than those which were working in favour of small farmers or landless labourers (Vyas, 1962; Dantwala and Shah, 1971; Rao, 1972).

*Demographic pressures.* While the increase in area under small holding groups—and the retention of area in the marginal holding group—could be explained by the market and institutional processes, the increase in their number is basically due to population increase in cultivating households and lack of alternative employment opportunities in the countryside. An expansion of the household or, more commonly, the death of the head of the household, leads to division of holdings among legal heirs. Unfortunately, there are no systematic studies of the household dynamics in rural areas which would give a precise measure of the sub-division of holdings over a period of time due to demographic factors. In the absence of such studies, one can only arrive at a rough approximation of the changes in the number of agricultural holdings which may be attributed to population pressure.

On the basis of what may be considered as realistic assumptions, we have estimated the likely increase (from 1961 to 1971) in the number of holdings in different size-groups due to expansion in the number of households and have then compared it with the actual number as revealed in the twenty-sixth round (see Table III). It may be noted at the outset that, in this exercise, households and holdings are taken as coterminous, i.e. jointly owned holdings are ignored. The estimates are arrived at on the following assumptions:

## TABLE III

### EXPECTED AND ACTUAL NUMBER OF HOUSEHOLDS IN DIFFERENT SIZE-GROUPS OF HOLDINGS

| Size-group of ownership holding | 1961–62 | | Estimated population for 1971 | 1971–72 | | | Difference A – E |
|---|---|---|---|---|---|---|---|
| | No. of households ('000) | Size of household | Population ('000) | Population ('000) | Size of household | Actual no. households ('000) A | Expected no. households ('000) E | |
| Marginal below 1 acre | 23,579 | 3.65 | 86,063 | 104,825 | 4.92 | 35,640 | 21,306 | 14,334 |
| Small 1–5 acres | 22,468 | 5.02 | 112,789 | 137,377 | 5.39 | 27,415 | 25,487 | 1,928 |
| Medium 5–15 acres | 13,002 | 6.31 | 82,043 | 99,928 | 6.69 | 13,564 | 14,937 | –1,373 |
| Big 15–50 acres | 4,514 | 7.35 | 33,178 | 40,411 | 7.73 | 4,058 | 5,228 | –1,170 |
| Large above 50 acres | 437 | 8.73 | 3,815 | 4,647 | 8.96 | 350 | 519 | –169 |
| Total | 64,000 | | 317,888 | 387,188 | | 81,027 | 67,477 | |

*Source:* See text.

(a) the rate of growth in population of different size-groups was the same and was equal to the rate of growth in population in rural areas between 1961 and 1971 as revealed in the 1971 Census;

(b) the size of households for different groups as given in the seventeenth and twenty-sixth round of the NSS for the operational holdings holds true for size of households for ownership holdings in the same size-class (this assumption had to be made since the seventeenth round did not give size of households according to ownership holdings).

Based on these assumptions population in different holding groups was worked out for 1961 by multiplying the number of holdings with the size of household (as given in the sixteenth round). It was projected for 1971 at the rate of 2.18 per cent per annum. Projected population was converted into the number of holdings by dividing the population by the size of households (as given in the twenty-seventh round). This gave the 'expected' number of holdings for each size-group in 1971. The expected number of holdings was compared with the actual number of holdings in 1971.

It is clear from Table III that in the case of marginal holdings the actual number of holdings is more than the expected number of holdings. This means that a large number of *new* marginal holdings were created, apart from those which came about due to the partitioning of households. In other size-groups, the trend was just the opposite, i.e. the expected number of households was more than the actual number, suggesting net migration from other size-groups. The increase in the number of marginal holdings, a substantial part explained by demographic factors, could be either by what we have described earlier as the reverse ladder process or by landless households acquiring small plots of land. From our discussion, the latter seems to be a more plausible explanation. Similarly, a reduction in the number of large and big holdings could be either due to migration of the households, or, more probably, division of land holdings sliding them in the lower size-group. It bears repetition that the synoptic picture presented above conceals intra-size-group changes; it also does not provide an accurate description of the 'entry' and 'exit' from one size-group to another. Its chief merit is in presenting the final position after inter- and intra-size-group changes have been worked out.

*Summing up*

Our analysis as given above in terms of the country as a whole suffers from the fact that it takes no account of the vast diversity of India. Nonetheless certain important conclusions follow from this review of structural changes in the holding pattern. It is suggested that, even in our present system, enough pressures could be generated by legislative and administrative processes to enable small producers in the countryside to hold their own. Impulses released by these reforms could be cumulative. The land market could be induced to function in a way beneficial to small and marginal farmers. The reform measures may also create a climate in which non-legislative redistributive movements could gather momentum. But these rather favourable factors would not prove adequate for raising productivity, generating surpluses in agriculture and triggering off a process of absorption of the additional work force available in the households of small and marginal landholders in gainful non-agricultural activities. The Indian experience of recent years is important inasmuch as it shows that the hegemony of the rural rich can be challenged by a combination of legislative, market-induced, and 'extra-constitutional' moves, but a different approach and strategy is required to enable small and marginal farmers to consolidate their gains.

# REFERENCES

Bhalla, Sheila, 1977, 'Changes in Acreage and Tenure Structure of Land Holdings in Haryana: 1962–72', *Economic and Political Weekly*, vol. XII, no. 13, Review of Agriculture (26 March).

Dantwala, M. L. and Shah, C. H., 1971, *Evaluation of Land Reforms*, vol. I, University of Bombay.

——and Rao, V. M., 1974, 'Inequality in Farm Income—A Comment', *Economic and Political Weekly*, vol. IX, no. 20 (18 May).

Desai, M. B., 1974, 'Changing Farm Production and Organization in Surat', M.S. University, Baroda (mimeo).

Gaikwad, V. R., 1975, 'Agricultural Development Through Community Action: Scope and Limitations', Technical Report no. 98, Indian Institute of Management, Ahmedabad.

Joshi, P. C., 1975, 'Land Reforms—A Trend Report', in *A Survey of Research in Economics*, vol. IV—Agriculture Part II, Allied Publishers, Bombay.

Patnaik, Utsa, 1971, 'Capitalistic Development in Agriculture—A Note', *Economic and Political Weekly*, vol. VI, no. 39, Review of Agriculture (25 September).

Rao, V. M., 1972, 'Land Transfers in Rural Communities—Some Findings in a Ryotwari Region', *Economic and Political Weekly*, vol. VII, no. 40, Review of Agriculture (30 September).

Repparto, R. and Shah, Vimal, 1976, 'Internal Policies for Income Distribution —A Case Study in Rural India' (mimeo).

Rudra, Ashok, Majid, A. and Talib, B. D., 1969, 'Big Farmers of Punjab', *Economic and Political Weekly*, vol. IV, no. 39, Review of Agriculture (27 September).

Sanyal, S. K., 1976, 'A Review of the Conceptual Framework of Land Holding Surveys', *Indian Journal of Agricultural Economics*, vol. XXXI, no. 3 (July–September).

Singh, Harpal, 1976, 'Structural Changes in the Size Distribution of Holdings— A Macro View', *Indian Journal of Agricultural Economics*, vol. XXXI, no. 3 (July–September).

Vyas, V. S., 1962, 'Land Reforms in India—Review of a Decade', in Sinha, M. R. (ed.), *A Decade of Economic Development and Planning in India*, Asian Studies Press, Bombay.

——1968, 'Economic Efficiency in Small Farms of Central Gujarat', in 'Seminar on Problems of Small Farmers', Indian Society of Agricultural Economics, Bombay.

——1976, 'Structural Change in Agriculture and the Small Farm Sector', *Economic and Political Weekly*, vol. XI, nos. 1 and 2 (10 January).

## I2

# Famine Mortality: A Study of the Bengal Famine of 1943*

A. K. SEN

*Nuffield College, University of Oxford*

'THE Secretary of State for India', wrote *The Statesman*, the Calcutta newspaper, on 16 October 1943,

seems to be a strangely misinformed man. Unless the cables are unfair to him, he told Parliament on Thursday that he understood that the weekly death-roll (presumably from starvation) in Bengal including Calcutta was about 1,000, but that 'it might be higher'. All the publicly available data indicate that it is very much higher; and his great office ought to afford him ample means of discovery.[1]

The characteristics of mortality in the Bengal Famine have remained controversial issues, and it is to these issues that this paper will be devoted.

In Section 1, the available evidence on the total size of famine mortality will be examined. In the second section, the relation between famine mortality and epidemic diseases will be explored—a field that has been the subject of some discussion and controversy in recent years in the context of European epidemics (see, for example, Wrigley, 1969; Jutikkala and Kauppinen, 1971; Blix, Hofvander and Vahlquist, 1971; Chambers, 1972; Braudel, 1973; Tranter, 1973; and Post, 1976). Section 3 is concerned with the regional pattern of mortality in the Bengal Famine, while Section 4 deals with the rather scanty information on its occupational pattern. In the fifth section, some general observations are made on the pattern of Bengal Famine

*For extremely helpful comments on an earlier draft of this paper, I am indebted to David Glass. I am also grateful to Robert Cassen and R. H. Gray for some probing questions.

mortality compared with normal mortality in Bengal at that time. There is a concluding section.

## 1. How many?

Sir T. Rutherford, the Governor of Bengal, wrote to the Secretary of State for India on 18 October 1943, two days after the *Statesman* editorial:

Your statement in the House about the number of deaths, which was presumably based on my communications to the Viceroy, has been severely criticized in some of the papers. My information was based on what information the Secretariat could then give me after allowing for the fact that the death-roll in Calcutta would be higher owing to the kind of people trekking into the city and exposure to inclement weather. . . . The full effects of the shortage are now being felt, and I would put the death-roll now at no less than 2,000 a week.[2]

Was this close to the mark?

The Famine Inquiry Commission (1945) noted that 'from July to December 1943, 1,304,323 deaths were recorded as against an average of 626,048 in the previous quinquennium', and the difference attributed to the famine comes to a bit over 678,000.[3] This would make the average weekly death-roll in excess of 26,000 rather than 2,000.

The Famine Inquiry Commission went on to note that 'all public health statistics in India are inaccurate', and 'even in normal times deaths are not fully recorded'. In rural Bengal deaths were reported by the village *chowkidar* (village watchman), in addition to his other duties, and he was 'usually illiterate, and paid about Rs 6 or Rs 7 a month'. During the famine period, 'in certain places the salaries of *chowkidars* were not paid and they deserted their posts to obtain work on military projects and aerodromes', while 'some of them died'.

The replacement of dead and vanished *chowkidars* was no easy matter and several weeks and months might elapse before successors could be found, during which deaths presumably went unrecorded. Further, at the height of the famine thousands of people left their homes and wandered across the countryside in search of food. Many died by the road-side—witness the skulls and bones which were to be seen there in the months following the famine. Deaths occurring in such circumstances would certainly not be recorded in the statistics of the Director of Public Health.[4]

Taking note of all this, the Commission arrived at the conclusion that 'the number of deaths in excess of the average in 1943 was of the order of one million'—nearly all of it in the second half of the year.[5] On this estimate the death-roll in the second half of 1943 would seem to have been around 38,000 *per week*.

No reason was given by the Commission for choosing the particular correction ratio that was used, except the thoroughly respectable one that it was arrived at 'after due consideration of the available facts' (p. 109). To this figure of one million deaths attributed to the famine of 1943, the Commission added the number of registered deaths in the first half of 1944 in excess of the previous quinquennial average without any correction. The reason for this asymmetry stemmed from the Commission's belief that there was 'an unquestionable improvement in the collection of mortality statistics' at the end of 1943 due to efforts made by civil and military medical authorities (p. 109). The excess death registration for the first half of 1944 amounts to 422,371. Adding this to the estimate of one million for 1943, the Commission rounded off the mortality toll of the famine thus: 'about 1.5 million deaths occurred as a direct result of the famine and the epidemics which followed in its train' (p. 110).

Dr Aykroyd, a distinguished nutrition expert, who was a member of the Commission and who in fact made the Commission's estimates of mortality,[6] has recently stated that he now thinks 'it was an underestimate, especially in that it took too little account of roadside deaths, but not as gross an underestimate as some critics of the Commission's report, who preferred 3 to 4 million, declared it to be' (Aykroyd, 1974, p. 77). Who were these critics and how did they arrive at their figures?

The most quoted estimate came from the Anthropology Department of the Calcutta University, based on a sample survey. The following estimates were released on 21 February 1944—much before the Famine Inquiry Commission had even been appointed:

The Anthropology Department of the University of Calcutta has carried out a sample survey of ten of the famine-affected districts of Bengal. The statistics for eight districts have so far been tabulated. They cover eight hundred sixteen family units with a total membership of three thousand eight hundred and eighty. The total deaths in these groups during June–July 1943 and November–December 1943, has been three hundred eighty-six or ten per cent during six months (i.e. 100 per thousand)…. As the death rate for Bengal does not exceed thirty per thousand per annum, i.e. fifteen per thousand for six months, the excess mortality (100−15) of eighty-five per thousand, that is, eight and a half per cent, has to be ascribed to famine and the pestilence that followed in its wake. As some areas in North Bengal were much less affected than Western or Central Bengal or the deficit areas of Eastern Bengal, some reduction has to be made to estimate the total mortality figures for Bengal. It will probably be an underestimate of the famine to say that two-thirds of the total population were affected more or less by it. On this basis the probable total number of deaths above the normal comes to well over three and a half millions.[7]

The applicability of an excess mortality rate of 8.5 per cent to two-thirds of the population of Bengal is, in fact, a piece of pure guess-work, and an illegitimate one at that, since the sample that was surveyed was chosen from the worst affected areas in Bengal. Later the leader of the group, Professor K. P. Chattopadhyaya, himself pointed out limitations of this estimate and proposed a figure of 2.2 million for excess deaths in 1943. Adding the half a million excess deaths taken by the Famine Inquiry Commission for 1944, Chattopadhyaya came to a 'minimum' estimate of 'total excess mortality' equalling 2.7 million.[8]

Between Chattopadhyaya's figure of 2.7 million and the Famine Inquiry Commission's 1.5 million (not to mention the minute estimates in contemporary official statements in London and New Delhi),[9] there remains quite a wide gap. The representative nature of Chattopadhyaya's sample remains totally unclear, and the arbitrariness of the Commission's correction factor makes it difficult to evaluate their estimate also.[10] But in some ways, a more fundamental question concerns the time coverage of the mortality estimates. Both these figures cover up to June 1944. The acute starvation associated with the famine had ended around December 1943, even though 'the death rate remained high throughout the greater part of 1944' (Famine Inquiry Commission, 1945, p. 1). When did the death rate, in fact, return to 'normal'? The Famine Inquiry Commission did not answer this question. It could not have, since at the time the Report was submitted in 1945, the death rate had not *yet* returned to normal. When did it do so? This is clearly one of the first things to ascertain, since the forces of post-famine epidemics to which the Commission refers in incorporating the excess deaths in the first half of 1944 in its total mortality estimate, went on raging for years.

For this and indeed for any other year-to-year study, we have to rely on death registration data with suitable corrections. It is argued in the *Census of India, 1951*, in its report on the 'Vital Statistics of West Bengal: 1941–50', that while there are errors in registration, 'under-registrations are fairly uniform and do not take sudden leaps and bounds from year to year' (vol. VI, part 1B, pp. 1–2).[11] While it seems most likely that the registration ratio did decline in 1943 and improved again in 1944, there seems to be little reason for assuming a radically different proportion of post-1944 registration compared with pre-1943 ratios.

For West Bengal, Jain's use of the reverse survival method yields an under-registration of deaths of 33.9 per cent in 1941–50. This makes the actual mortality 51 per cent higher on the average than registered mortality. I shall use this ratio of correction *uniformly*, though it should be noted that this would tend to *underestimate* famine mortality since registration was especially bad in 1943—the year of the famine and of peak death even in terms of registration data. There is, thus, a downward bias in our estimation of famine deaths.[12]

In Table I numbers of the registered deaths for each year from 1941 to 1950 are given for West Bengal. The time pattern is one of *monotonic* decline except for the one severe jump upwards in 1943. In fact, despite falling each year after 1943, annual mortality did not return to the 1942 level even by the end of the decade. Since the number of deaths had tended to fall each year, the Famine Inquiry

TABLE I

RECORDED DEATHS IN WEST BENGAL, 1941–50

| Year | Deaths | Excess deaths | |
|---|---|---|---|
| | | A | B |
| 1941 | 384,220 | | |
| 1942 | 347,886 | | |
| Average 1941–42 | 366,053 | | |
| 1943 | 624,266 | 258,213 | 276,380 |
| 1944 | 577,375 | 211,322 | 229,489 |
| 1945 | 448,600 | 82,547 | 100,714 |
| 1946 | 414,687 | 48,634 | 66,801 |
| 1947 | 387,165 | 21,112 | 39,279 |
| 1948 | 385,278 | 19,225 | 37,392 |
| 1949 | 372,559 | 6,506 | 24,673 |
| 1950 | 356,843 | −9,210 | 8,957 |

*Source*: Based on death statistics from *Census of India, 1951*, vol. VI, part 1B, Table IV.

Commission's procedure of taking the average mortality in the previous *quinquennium* as the 'normal' mortality may understate excess mortality for the famine years. Instead I have made two sets of estimates: estimate A with the 'normal' being taken to be the average of the deaths in 1941 and 1942, and estimate B with the 1942 death rate being taken as the 'normal'. Estimate B yields, naturally, a higher series of 'excess deaths', which are presented for 1943 to 1950 in Table I. However, even estimate B can be thought to be understating the magnitude of excess mortality, since the relevant comparison is not with the level in the *pre-famine* year, but with the level to which the expected death rates *would have fallen* in the post-famine years *but for* the intervention of the famine.[13]

The numbers of excess deaths under assumptions A and B respectively for each year are given in Table I. The 'excess' becomes negative for A in 1950 onwards and for B in 1951 onwards; this is the consequence of taking a stationary death norm, which, as discussed above, understates the levels of excess mortality.

Adding up until the excess mortality is eliminated yields a total excess mortality due to the famine of 648,000 for assumption A and 784,000 for assumption B. If the turmoil of the partition of Bengal in 1947 and the displacement resulting from it make us reluctant to read the impact of the famine in the excess mortality figures beyond 1946, we can be conservative and count the excess figures only during 1943–46.[14] This yields a total registered excess mortality of 601,000 under assumption A and 673,000 under B.

If Jain's (1954) estimate of under-registration in West Bengal during 1941–50 is applied uniformly, then these excess registration figures would have to be raised by 51 per cent to arrive at the actual excess mortality.[15] This yields 908,000 and 1.016 million respectively under A and B.

All of this relates to West Bengal only. The famine was at least as serious in East Bengal—later East Pakistan, now Bangladesh.[16] Unfortunately, there is no 'reverse survival' estimate of under-registration for East Bengal, comparable with Jain's calculation for West Bengal. I have not, therefore, tried to make an independent estimate of famine mortality in East Bengal. However, the *Census of Pakistan, 1951* reports an estimate, viz. a figure of 1.714 million, 'worked out from official statements, which as explained are largely estimates in the absence of reliable reports'.[17] Added to my estimates for West Bengal this yields 2.622 million and 2.730 million respectively, under

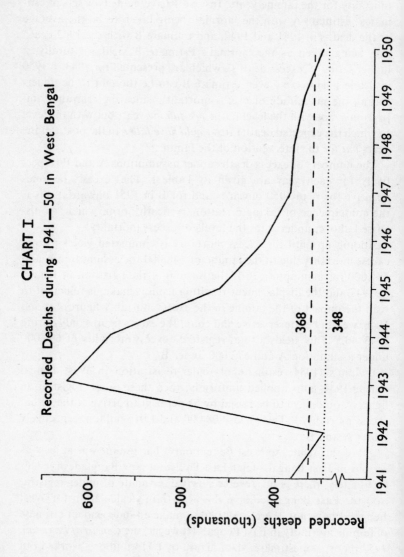

CHART I

Recorded Deaths during 1941—50 in West Bengal

assumptions A and B. Note that the East Bengal figures given in the Pakistan Census take account of deaths only up to 1944, and not up to 1946 as in our West Bengal estimates. Taking note of the facts that, (*i*) the population of what became West Bengal was almost exactly a third of the population of undivided Bengal in 1941, (*ii*) the registered number of deaths in West Bengal tended to be around a third of the total number of deaths in Bengal before 1943, and (*iii*) in the famine year the number of registered deaths in West Bengal was again almost exactly a third of that in Bengal as a whole,[18] if we feel bold enough to treat famine excess mortality in West Bengal to be a third of that in undivided Bengal, then the total Bengal famine mortality works out as 2.724 million and 3.048 million respectively under assumptions A and B.

These figures are put together in Table II. Since the Famine Inquiry Commission and K. P. Chattopadhyaya both gave excess

TABLE II

ESTIMATES OF BENGAL FAMINE MORTALITY

|  | Excess mortality in 1943 (millions) | Total excess mortality due to the famine (millions) |
| --- | --- | --- |
| Famine Inquiry Commission | 1.00 | 1.50 |
| K. P. Chattopadhyaya | 2.20 | 2.70 |
| Assumption A+Pakistan Census |  | 2.62 |
| Assumption B+Pakistan Census |  | 2.73 |
| Assumption A blown up for all Bengal | 1.17 | 2.72 |
| Assumption B blown up for all Bengal | 1.25 | 3.05 |

mortality figures separately for the famine year 1943, the results of our calculation with blow-up for Bengal are shown separately for 1943 also. It is interesting that Chattopadhyaya's overall estimate comes fairly close to those presented here, but the coincidence is accidental, since his figure refers to mortality in 1943 and in the first half of 1944 only. In fact, for 1943 as such the estimates given here are quite close to those of the Famine Inquiry Commission. The bulk of the difference in our respective total estimates arise from (*i*) the longer time coverage in my estimates (using, however, the same logic as employed by the Commission itself in attributing high post-famine mortality to the famine), and (*ii*) continued correction for under-registration of deaths even beyond 1943 (using results of corrections through the reverse survival method).

Since there were several downward biases—as explained—built into the estimates presented here, we may be inclined to pick a figure around 3 million as the death toll of the Bengal Famine. (It has also the merit of being a 'round' number—that arbitrary preference shown by our ten-fingered species captivated by the decimal system.) But what emerges most powerfully from our analysis is not so much the largeness of the size of total mortality, but its time pattern—lasting for years after the famine. This was largely due to the epidemics associated with the famine, and to this issue I now turn.

## 2. How?

In December 1943, Bengal reaped a harvest larger than any in the past. Curiously enough it was also the month in which the death rate in Bengal reached its peak in this century. The famine in the form of starvation had by then come largely to an end—starvation deaths seemed to have peaked around September and October that year. Cholera mortality reached its maximum in October and November. Malaria peaked in December, and continued in its elevated position through the next year and later. Small-pox reached its height in March and April of 1944, and a greater height still one year later. The starvation phase of the famine had given way to the epidemic phase.

Table III presents the yearly time series of registered deaths from some of the principal causes. The sharp jump upwards in 1943 of cholera, malaria, 'fever', dysentery, diarrhoea, etc., can be easily seen. For seasonal reasons the impact of small-pox was not felt until the following year since it hits primarily in early spring. Taking the average mortality in 1941 and 1942 as the 'normal' mortality for each disease separately, 'excess mortality' from each disease has been calculated for the period 1943 to 1946. The last row presents the inter-disease breakdown of excess mortality.

Before discussing the inter-disease pattern of excess mortality, it is worth commenting on the absence of starvation as a major reported cause of death during that great famine. One reason for this peculiarity is that starvation was not typically used as a separate category in

## TABLE III

### DISEASES AND DEATHS IN WEST BENGAL: 1941 TO 1946 REGISTRATIONS

| | Dysentery, diarrhoea, and enteric group of fevers | Cholera | Malaria | 'Fever' (excluding Malaria) | Small-pox | TB | Respiratory diseases other than TB | Total |
|---|---|---|---|---|---|---|---|---|
| 1941 | 25,321 | 15,612 | 85,505 | 109,912 | 9,286 | 7,989 | 34,345 | 384,220 |
| 1942 | 23,234 | 11,427 | 85,078 | 97,764 | 1,023 | 6,734 | 32,847 | 347,886 |
| Average 1941–42 | 24,278 | 13,519 | 85,291 | 104,838 | 5,155 | 7,362 | 33,596 | 366,053 |
| 1943 | 41,067 | 58,230 | 168,592 | 159,398 | 2,261 | 6,830 | 35,140 | 624,266 |
| 1944 | 36,040 | 20,128 | 166,897 | 176,824 | 19,198 | 7,318 | 37,052 | 577,375 |
| 1945 | 24,463 | 8,315 | 123,834 | 122,549 | 23,974 | 6,951 | 33,839 | 448,600 |
| 1946 | 25,651 | 9,774 | 102,339 | 121,391 | 4,971 | 7,227 | 31,926 | 414,687 |
| Excess: 1943–46 | 30,109 | 42,371 | 220,498 | 164,810 | 29,784 | −1,122 | 3,623 | 600,716 |
| Share of total excess (percentage) | 5.0 | 7.1 | 36.7 | 27.4 | 5.0 | −0.2 | 0.6 | 100.0 |

*Source:* Based on current registration data, reported in *Census of India, 1951*, vol. VI, part 1B. Note that the 'enteric group of fevers' figure both under 'fever' and under 'dysentery, diarrhoea, and enteric group of fevers'; but the overlap is quantitatively rather tiny.

reporting deaths. This was partly due to the habit of using traditional categories in reporting causes of death, but also due to the fact that typical starvation deaths show other identifiable symptoms at the final stages, and these *proximate* 'causes' tend to fit well into the traditional categories. For example, it is common to die of starvation through diarrhoea (indeed, 'famine diarrhoea' is a well-known phenomenon) as well as dysentery—partly as a result of eating uneatable objects. Clearly, many of the deaths reported under 'dysentery, diarrhoea and enteric group of fevers' were, in fact, starvation deaths. The same holds for several other categories, including the general category of deaths due to 'fever'.[19]

Excluding 'fever', which is a diverse basket of diseases varying from influenza and measles to cerebro-spinal fever and *kala-azar*, the ranking of the main diseases in terms of their contributions to excess mortality were (in decreasing order): malaria, cholera, 'dysentery, diarrhoea and enteric group of fevers', and small-pox. The nature of these ailments suggests that the explosive outbursts of epidemics during and immediately following the famine were affected not merely by starvation and malnutrition, but also by the impact of the famine on sanitary arrangements, water supply and other civic amenities, exposure to vectors through movements in search of food, as well as inability to receive medical attention thanks to destitution and breakdown of public health facilities.[20] In addition, infectious diseases can spread directly to people who may not have been affected otherwise by the famine. Epidemics do, of course, also have a rhythm of their own.[21] Once an epidemic occurs, its echo effects may last for quite a few years.

The diseases unleashed by the Bengal famine had the dual characteristics of being both (*i*) epidemic diseases associated with previous famines, and (*ii*) endemic diseases in the region. Malaria had been associated with Indian famines at least from the nineteenth century,[22] and epidemics of cholera and small-pox had been observed in many previous famines, including the Bengal famine of 1770. Dysentery and diarrhoea are, of course, 'peculiarly famine diseases'—as the Famine Inquiry Commission described them. The same applies to the mixed bundle called 'fever excluding malaria'. But all these diseases were also endemic in the region. Malaria and fevers, which are sometimes difficult to distinguish,[23] were the biggest killers in the pre-famine days, followed at quite some distance by 'dysentery, diarrhoea and enteric group of fevers', cholera, and small-pox in that order.

In the sharing of famine mortality, the relative positions are not very different, with malaria and fever being followed at a substantial distance by cholera, 'dysentery, etc.', and small-pox, in that order.

There is, however, something of a contrast in the group of respiratory diseases including TB. These diseases killed many more in the pre-famine period than any of the other groups of diseases, with the exception of malaria and other fevers. But, remarkably, mortality from TB and that from other respiratory diseases seem to have been hardly influenced by the Bengal famine (see Table III). This experience is *not* unusual in the context of other Indian famines, in which TB and other respiratory diseases have not typically played a prominent part, but there is something of a puzzle in this in a more general context. The linkage of TB and other respiratory diseases with malnutrition is well established (see Keys, 1950), and seems to be conceded even by those who dispute the influence of starvation as such on other diseases spread through infectious contagion (see, for example, Chambers, 1972, pp. 82–6).

Tuberculosis is, of course, slow to develop and is influenced more by chronic undernourishment than by a short period of severe starvation; this might suggest that the spread of tuberculosis would not be much enhanced by a famine. But famine-induced movements and sanitary breakdowns may help in the expansion of the infection. More importantly, since tuberculosis and other respiratory diseases were already widespread in Bengal, it would be natural to expect that starvation during the famine would convert morbidity into mortality on a substantial scale. That this was not reported as having happened during and immediately after the Bengal famine, thus, does leave one with an interesting and important problem. Attributing this counter-intuitive phenomenon comfortably to an assumed error of reporting is tempting, but this explanation would be convincing only with empirical evidence of the existence of such a bias on a large enough scale. Also, since TB and other respiratory diseases typically had rather undistinguished records in previous Indian famines *as well*, an *ad hoc* explanation for the Bengal famine of 1943 as such is not what is needed.

The Bengal famine killed mostly by magnifying the forces of death normally present in the pre-famine period—a magnifying role that other famines had played in the past. The universality of this endemic-to-epidemic relationship is, however, seriously affected by the apparent inertness of TB and other respiratory diseases. This inertness also seems to contrast quite sharply with the view taken of these diseases in the international literature on famine-induced epidemics (see, for example, Keys, 1950; Foege, 1971; Chambers, 1972).

## 3. Where?

Excess mortality can be estimated separately for each district in West Bengal on the basis of the registration data presented in the *Census of India, 1951*, vol. VI, part 1B. These are presented in Table IV with the 'normal' level of mortality being taken to be the average of the figures for 1941 and 1942. The percentage excesses for the famine year 1943 and for the period 1943–46 are presented separately, and the ranks in the two orderings of excesses are also given. The inter-district variations are quite remarkable, even though for every district the excess is positive both for 1943 as well as for the period 1943–46.

There are some differences between the two rankings. Malda, which ends up as the most affected district overall, was one of the less affected districts in the famine year itself. Similarly, Midnapur which was most affected in the famine year, ends up in a somewhat moderate position for the whole period. The pattern of the epidemics that followed the famine re-ordered the districts in terms of mortality. However, the two rankings are not unrelated, and the value of Spearman's rank correlation coefficient is 0.60, which offers no problem in rejecting the null hypothesis that the two rankings are independent.

What is perhaps of greater interest is the fact that the Bengal Government's diagnoses of the relative severity of the famines in the different districts differed quite substantially from the excess mortality rankings for 1943–46 as well as for 1943 itself. A five-category classification of the subdivisions was issued by the Revenue Department in 1944, and a four-category classification by the Department of Industries also in the same year.[24] Putting together the classification of the subdivisions within each district, I have presented a broad three-class partitioning in Table IV reflecting the two official views of 'degree of incidence of famines'. Both put Malda—ultimately the most affected district—in the lowest category of incidence. The two did the same to Murshidabad and Birbhum, but in fact both the districts had a high incidence of excess mortality in 1943 as well as in the period 1943–46. On the other hand, 24-Parganas, which neighbours Calcutta, and from where many destitutes trekked into Calcutta at the height of the famine,[25] was put in the highest category of

## TABLE IV

EXCESS MORTALITY IN WEST BENGAL: DISTRICT-WISE BREAKDOWN

| District | Average mortality 1941–1942 ('normal') | Excess mortality 1943 | Excess mortality 1943–1946 | Percentage excess 1943 | Percentage excess 1943–1946 (annual) | Excess rank 1943 | Excess rank 1943–1946 | Intensity class according to Bengal Govt.: Revenue Department | Intensity class according to Bengal Govt.: Dept. of Industries |
|---|---|---|---|---|---|---|---|---|---|
| Malda | 8,237 | + 3,080 | + 45,512 | + 37.4 | + 129.0 | 9 | 1 | Slight | Slight |
| Howrah | 18,842 | + 15,832 | + 52,444 | + 84.0 | + 69.6 | 3 | 2 | Moderate | Slight |
| Murshidabad | 32,382 | + 32,691 | + 87,869 | + 101.0 | + 67.8 | 2 | 2 | Slight | Slight |
| Birbhum | 23,007 | + 17,482 | + 51,369 | + 76.0 | + 55.8 | 5 | 4 | Slight | Slight |
| Calcutta | 30,385 | + 21,883 | + 61,588 | + 72.0 | + 50.7 | 6 | 5 | | |
| Midnapur | 52,489 | + 72,250 | + 104,747 | + 137.6 | + 49.9 | 1 | 6 | Severe | Severe |
| West Dinajpur | 10,858 | + 1,600 | + 20,281 | + 14.7 | + 46.7 | 13 | 7 | Slight | Slight |
| Nadia | 21,819 | + 17,021 | + 31,914 | + 78.0 | + 36.6 | 4 | 8 | Slight | Slight |
| 24-Parganas | 54,062 | + 37,151 | + 65,501 | + 68.7 | + 30.3 | 7 | 9 | Severe | Severe |
| Jalpaiguri | 20,171 | + 6,633 | + 21,062 | + 32.9 | + 26.1 | 11 | 10 | Slight | Moderate |
| Hooghly | 21,688 | + 5,808 | + 18,299 | + 26.8 | + 21.1 | 12 | 11 | Moderate | Slight |
| Burdwan | 35,401 | + 12,057 | + 26,382 | + 34.1 | + 18.6 | 10 | 12 | Moderate | Slight |
| Bankura | 26,212 | + 13,958 | + 15,953 | + 53.5 | + 15.2 | 8 | 13 | Moderate | Slight |
| Darjeeling | 10,495 | + 763 | + 1,779 | + 7.3 | + 4.2 | 14 | 14 | Slight | Moderate |

*Source:* Based on *Census of India, 1951*, vol. vi, part 1B.

incidence in both the official lists, despite being only moderately placed in the excess mortality rankings for the famine year as well as the post-famine period.[26] Since relief operations were strongly influenced by these diagnoses, the discrepancies are of a certain amount of practical interest.

Finally, a remark on the excess mortality in Calcutta is worth making. Most people who died in Calcutta from starvation and from related diseases in the famine year were destitutes who had moved into Calcutta in search of food; the regular residents of Calcutta were protected by various public and semi-public schemes of food distribution (see Famine Inquiry Commission, 1945). Based on this observation it has been frequently stated that the residents of Calcutta escaped the famine.[27] This is largely true as far as starvation is concerned, but in the epidemics that were induced by the famine, Calcutta had its own share of casualties, reflected by the excess mortality figures after 1943, i.e. after virtually all the famine destitutes from elsewhere had left or been repatriated.

## 4. Which occupation category?

The death registration figures do not specify occupational backgrounds. We can, however, surmise something about probable death rates by examining the rates of destitution of different income groups. These were computed on the basis of a sample survey conducted by Mahalanobis, Mukherjea and Ghosh (1946), and are presented in Table v (from Sen, 1977, Tables VIII and IX). In the second column the destitution rates are added up with the transition to the occupation of 'paddy husking'—a typical destitution syndrome for rural women with children. On this basis it would appear that the most affected groups were fishermen, transport workers and agricultural labourers. In terms of absolute numbers, agricultural labourers as an occupation group were dominant.

One of the few direct surveys of the occupational basis of famine mortality was presented by Mukherji (1965) for five villages in the Faridpur district in East Bengal; the survey was conducted in 1944. The results are presented in Table VI. In these villages the highest mortality category is agricultural labour. The importance of agricultural labour among the famine victims is brought out also by the survey of destitutes in Calcutta conducted in 1943 by T. Das (1949).

Our information on this crucial aspect of famine mortality is limited and somewhat haphazard. And we have virtually no informa-

TABLE V

DESTITUTION RATES OF DIFFERENT OCCUPATION CATEGORIES IN BENGAL:
JANUARY 1943 TO MAY 1944

|  | *Proportion of destitution* | *Proportion of destitution and transition to paddy husking* |
|---|---|---|
| Peasant cultivation and share cropping | 1.3 | 1.5 |
| Part-time agricultural labour | 1.4 | 2.0 |
| Agricultural labour | 4.6 | 6.1 |
| Non-cultivating owners | 1.6 | 2.4 |
| Fishing | 9.6 | 10.5 |
| Craft | 3.8 | 4.3 |
| Husking paddy | 4.7 | — |
| Transport | 6.0 | 6.9 |
| Trade | 2.2 | 2.6 |
| Profession and services | 2.1 | 2.6 |
| Non-agricultural labour | 3.7 | 4.5 |
| Other productive occupations | 4.6 | 4.6 |

*Source*: Sen, 1977, Tables VIII and IX. These estimates are based on a randomly
selected sample of households from villages in famine-affected districts
in pre-partition Bengal surveyed in 1944 by Mahalanobis, Mukherjea
and Ghosh (1946).

tion at all on the occupational composition of post-famine mortality
in the epidemics.

*5. Famine mortality as magnified normal mortality*

Peculiarities in the pattern of famine mortality compared with
normal mortality have been a subject of discussion for a long time.
A supposedly lower impact of famines on women is one of the
regularities' that has received some attention in India. Sir Charles
Elliot, Famine Commissioner of Mysore in 1876 and Census Commissioner of India for the 1881 Census, summarized the general
belief regarding nineteenth century Indian famines: 'all the authorities seem agreed that women succumb to famine less easily than
men.'[28]

Was this the case with the Bengal famine? Das (1949) found in
his survey of destitutes in Calcutta in September 1943 that 'for every
dead woman there were nearly two dead men' (p. 93). In its Report
the Famine Inquiry Commission referred to Das's findings—then

14

## TABLE VI

### DESTITUTION IN FIVE SURVEYED VILLAGES IN FARIDPUR

| Occupation on 1.1.43 | Total nos. of families on 1.1.43 | Nos. of destitute families in each group on 1.1.43 | Proportion of destitution (%) | Nos. of families in each group 'wiped off during 1943' | Proportion being 'wiped off during 1943' (%) |
|---|---|---|---|---|---|
| Peasant cultivation & share cropping | 266 | 49 | 18.4 | 17 | 6.4 |
| Agricultural labour | 124 | 65 | 52.4 | 50 | 40.3 |
| Artisan | 20 | 7 | 35.0 | 2 | 10.0 |
| Petty trader | 107 | 34 | 31.8 | 15 | 14.0 |
| Cropsharing landlord | 16 | 1 | 6.3 | 0 | 0.0 |
| Priest & petty employee | 11 | 3 | 27.3 | 3 | 27.3 |
| Office employee | 20 | 2 | 10.0 | 0 | 0.0 |
| Landlord | 10 | 0 | 0.0 | 0 | 0.0 |
| 'Unproductive' | 18 | 8 | 44.4 | 3 | 16.7 |
| Total | 592 | 169 | 28.5 | 90 | 15.2 |

*Source:* Mukherji, 1965.

available in unpublished form—and also noted that there was a higher proportionate increase in male deaths compared with female deaths in 1943.[29] The Commission referred to the contrary result from Mahalanobis's survey of 2,622 families which found a higher percentage of mortality among women, but went on to comment on the 'considerable irregularity' in the various subdivisions covered in the survey.

The sex breakdown of pre-famine 'normal' mortality given by the average of 1941 and 1942 as well as that of the excess mortality in 1943 and in the period 1943–46 are all presented in Table vii, based on registration data. The ratios seem remarkably stable through the famine. While the proportion of men in excess mortality in 1943 is a bit higher than in the pre-famine average, the difference is small, and over the larger period of famine mortality the proportionate breakdown of the excess is just the same as for the pre-famine average.[30]

There may, of course, be biases in the registration system, but this should apply to registrations both before and during the famine. In fact, it is more likely that there was a serious bias in Das's sample survey of destitutes in Calcutta which contained a large proportion of families which had 'lost their male earning members', and this bias would be reflected in the results of the survey, which asked respondents to recall which members of the family had died.[31] To what extent this type of observation bias was present also in the accounts of the nineteenth century famines, I do not know, but certainly as far as the 1943 famine is concerned there is little need for going into the rather contrived explanations[32] that have been proposed to explain the supposed contrast of sex ratios.

Das (1949) also noted a much higher proportion of deaths among children, and opined that 'this will certainly cripple the next generation of the Bengalees'.[33] The Anthropology Department of Calcutta University had reported a similar bias in its press statement in 1944.[34]

Is this borne out by the registration data? The answer seems to be no. The data are given in Table vii. The proportion of children below 5 in average mortality in the immediate pre-famine period was 29 per cent, and that is also the percentage of children in excess mortality in the famine year (1943) as well as in the four-year period of famine mortality (1943–46).[35] The extraordinarily high level of mortality of children is, of course, an excruciating problem, but that is a charac-

## TABLE VII

### EXCESS MORTALITY OF MEN, WOMEN, CHILDREN AND THE OLD: WEST BENGAL

| | Average mortality 1941–42 | | Excess mortality 1943 | | Excess mortality 1943–46 | |
|---|---|---|---|---|---|---|
| | Numbers | Percentages of total | Numbers | Percentages of total | Numbers | Percentages of total |
| Men | 191,943 | 52 | 140,439 | 54 | 315,282 | 52 |
| Women | 174,310 | 48 | 117,774 | 46 | 285,434 | 48 |
| Children below 5 | 106,080 | 29 | 74,838 | 29 | 174,058 | 29 |
| Old people above 60 | 57,044 | 16 | 40,212 | 16 | 93,600 | 16 |

*Source:* Based on current registration data, reported in *Census of India, 1951*, vol. VI, part 1B. Note that 'men' and 'women' include figures for all ages, and 'children below 5' and 'old people above 60' include those for both sexes.

teristic not only of famine mortality but also of normal mortality in the absence of famine in this part of the world.

Table VII also presents the mortality figures for people above 60. Once again the proportions of famine mortality mirror the pattern of normal mortality.

I end this section with a final observation dealing with the monthly pattern of death at the height of the famine. Table VIII presents the

TABLE VIII

MORTALITY BY MONTHS DURING JULY 1943 TO JUNE 1944
(compared with previous quinquennial average)

| Month | Deaths during 1943–44 | Quinquennial average deaths: 1938–42 |
| --- | --- | --- |
| July | 126,437 | 78,816 |
| August | 151,126 | 83,968 |
| September | 171,755 | 85,253 |
| October | 236,754 | 105,529 |
| November | 289,723 | 128,454 |
| December | 328,708 | 142,033 |
| January | 228,128 | 112,263 |
| February | 170,955 | 89,594 |
| March | 162,933 | 98,428 |
| April | 167,368 | 98,615 |
| May | 145,812 | 85,176 |
| June | 106,032 | 74,774 |

monthly death registrations during June–July of 1943–44, when mortality was at its highest, and also the average monthly registrations in the preceding quinquennium[36]. The similarity between the two monthly patterns is striking.[37] This is brought out clearly by Chart II as well. (Regressing monthly mortality $y$ in the famine period on normal pre-famine monthly mortality $x$, by least-squares, yields a very high value of $r^2$. The estimated regression function, in fact, is $y = 3,175x - 122,535$, with $r^2$ having the convincing value of 0.95.) The famine seems to have worked by magnifying the forces of mortality each month, heightening the peak mortality relatively more.

## 6. Concluding remarks

While it is not possible to say at all precisely how many people were killed by the Bengal famine of 1943, there is evidence that an

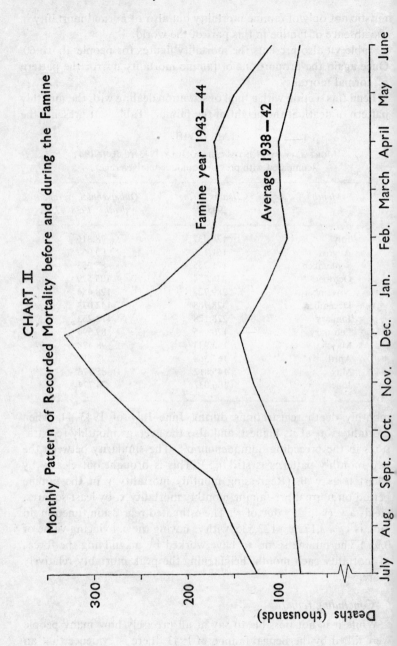

CHART II

Monthly Pattern of Recorded Mortality before and during the Famine

Famine year 1943—44

Average 1938—42

Deaths (thousands)

300

200

100

July  Aug.  Sept.  Oct.  Nov.  Dec.  Jan.  Feb.  March  April  May  June

estimate of around 3 million would be nearer the mark than the figure of 1.5 million arrived at by the official Famine Inquiry Commission (and widely quoted in later works). The difference is largely due to: (*i*) continued high 'excess mortality' for several years after the famine, caused by famine-induced epidemics the impact of which the Commission considered only for 1943 and the first half of 1944; and (*ii*) under-estimation by the Commission of the actual extent of under-registration of deaths in official records.

Both these largely reflect differences between the data available to the Commission and those available now. Apropos of (*i*) the Commission, working in late 1944 and early 1945, could hardly have gone beyond the first half of 1944 in its mortality coverage. Apropos of (*ii*), the Commission, not having any way of estimating it directly or indirectly, chose to use an arbitrary correction for under-registration. In contrast, we can use the results of 'reverse survival' exercises based on Census data of 1951 *vis-à-vis* those of 1941 and the results of a direct sample survey held in 1948. There is, thus, no quarrel, only a very substantial difference in the respective estimates based on *current* information (see Section 1).

While the gigantic size of excess mortality attributable to the famine is of a certain amount of interest, the *time pattern* of mortality is of possibly greater relevance. Very substantially more than half the deaths attributable to the famine of 1943 took place *after* 1943. The size of mortality did not return to the pre-famine situation for many years after the famine, and epidemics of malaria and other fevers, cholera, small-pox, dysentery and diarrhoea, that sprang up during and immediately after the famine went on raging for a long time (see Tables I and III and Chart I). This has obvious implications for health policy.

Regarding the regional pattern of famine mortality, the relative importance of different districts changed quite a bit between the starvation phase and the later epidemic phase (see Table IV). What is perhaps of greater interest is that the official diagnoses of the relative severity of the famine in the different districts differed substantially from the pattern emerging from the 'excess mortality' calculations, both for the starvation phase and for the later epidemic phase (see Section 3). Since governmental relief and rehabilitation work was based on these official diagnoses, the contrasts were of practical import.

Information on the occupational pattern of mortality is very limited, but some general impressions emerge from a broadbased 1944 survey covering the occupational pattern of destitution, and two local 1943 surveys directly going into deaths related to occupations (see Section 4). In absolute terms the most severe incidence of famine mortality during the famine itself fell almost certainly on the class of agricultural labourers. Their *relative incidence* was high too, but that applies also to other groups like fishermen, transport workers and non-agricultural labourers in rural areas. I have tried to analyse elsewhere (Sen, 1977) the nature and causation of the observed occupational pattern of destitution, relating them to the positions of the different groups in the structure of exchange in the economy.

Regarding the diseases that took most of the toll, they had the dual characteristics of being both (*i*) endemic diseases in the region, and (*ii*) epidemic diseases in past famines (see Section 2). Gigantic as the famine was, it killed mostly by adding fuel to the fire of disease and mortality normally present in the region. This possibly explains why the seasonal pattern of famine deaths even during the actual famine and its immediate aftermath was essentially the normal seasonal pattern—just linearly displaced severely upwards (see Table VIII and Chart II). The sex and age patterns of famine mortality also seem to show remarkable similarity with the normal pattern of mortality in pre-famine Bengal (see Table VII), contrary to some assertions.

As far as the nature of the epidemic diseases is concerned, perhaps the most interesting case is that of the dog that did not bark, viz. TB and other respiratory diseases. Widespread in pre-famine Bengal, reported mortality from these diseases hardly changed at all during the famine and the immediate post-famine period. This is not atypical of the experience in early Indian famines, but seems to go sharply against a prevailing expert opinion in the literature on famines and epidemics based on experiences elsewhere (see Section 2). Is this contrast real or illusory? If illusory, what causes the illusion? If real, what are the reasons for this contrast? These are among the open issues emerging from this paper.

# NOTES

1. 'The Death-Roll', editorial, *The Statesman*, 16 October 1943. See also Stephens, 1966.
2. Letter to Mr L. S. Amery, no. L/E/8/3311; document no. 180 in Mansergh (ed.), 1973, vol. IV, pp. 397–8. The earlier communication referred to by Rutherford is document no. 158 in the same volume.
3. Famine Inquiry Commission, 1945, p. 108. For the year as a whole the difference came to 688,846.
4. Famine Inquiry Commission, 1945, p. 109. See also *Census of India, 1951*, vol. VI, part 1B, pp. 1–2.
5. Famine Inquiry Commission, 1945, pp. 108–9.
6. See Aykroyd, 1973, p. 77.
7. Reprinted in Ghosh, 1944, Appendix G.
8. Chattopadhyaya and Mukherjea, 1946, p. 5.
9. There is something puzzling about the official statements on the minute size of mortality. Lord Wavell records in his 'journal' on 19 October 1943, when he became the new Viceroy, that the outgoing Viceroy, Lord Linlithgow, confessed to him that 'in July he expected that deaths in Bengal might be up to 1,000,000 or one-and-a-half million, and that we looked like getting off better than he had thought possible' (Wavell, 1973, p. 34). Presumably the Government had meanwhile persuaded themselves that the situation was *incomparably* better than had been 'thought possible'.
10. Aykroyd (1974) is candid in acknowledging the arbitrariness of his estimate: 'at all events, the figure of 1.5 million deaths is in the history books, and whenever I come across it I remember the process by which it was reached' (p. 77).
11. It is perhaps also worth remarking that for India as a whole, the ratio of registered deaths to the estimated number of deaths obtained by using the 'reverse survival method' for 1941–50 by S. P. Jain (1954) is 0.73, while the same method had yielded a ratio of 0.74 for 1931–40 (see Jain, 1954, p. 44). The estimates for earlier decades are of Kingsley Davis: 0.74 for 1931–40, 0.72 for 1921–30, and 0.70 for 1911–20.
12. A substantial *net* migration from East to West Bengal during the late forties would also tend to underestimate the actual death rate during 1941–50, and thus underestimate the under-registration of deaths, thereby underestimating famine mortality.
13. Note that the *absolute* number of deaths went on falling through the decades, despite the increase in the size of the population, which failed to increase only during the immediate famine years; see *Census of India, 1951*, vol. VI, part 1B, pp. 2–4.
14. Note, however, that the strictly monotonic decline of the number of deaths continued right through 1947 (see Table I). The death *rate* per thousand also underwent a strictly monotonic decline, since a declining number of deaths with an increasing population size implies a strictly monotonic fall of the death rate. Excess mortality figures beyond 1946 have, however, been ignored to avoid overestimating famine mortality, by biasing the procedures in the opposite direction.

15. This may be compared with the Famine Inquiry Commission's correction of recorded excess mortality in 1943 of 688,846 to one million, which amounts to a correction factor of 45 per cent. (For some inexplicable reason the Commission notes the correction ratio to be 'some 40 per cent' (p. 109).) For 1944, however, no correction was made by the Commission. A 'pilot survey' conducted by the Government of Bengal in 1948 found the correction factor to be 46.4 per cent (see Chaudhuri, 1952, p. 9).

16. See Famine Inquiry Commission, 1945, pp. 114–15.

17. *Census of Pakistan*, 1951, chapter 3, p. 30, The arbitrary nature of this estimate is emphasized, and reference is also made to the fact that 'according to popular belief, however, the deaths from famine in East Bengal were between two and two and a half million'.

18. The number of registered deaths in 1943 was 624,266 for West Bengal and 1,873,749 for Bengal as a whole (see Famine Inquiry Commission, 1945, p. 108, and *Census of India, 1951*, vol. VI, part 1B, p. 21).

19. Compare the problem of interpreting the large number of deaths from lethal scurvy during the Irish famine of 1845–47.

20. See Famine Inquiry Commission, 1945, on these disruptive consequences of the Famine and on the large scale trekking of destitutes, in search of food. See also Ghosh, 1944, and Das, 1949.

21. See Bailey, 1957. In fact, because of the spread effects of epidemics, the Bengal famine may also have contributed to deaths outside Bengal, especially in Orissa and Bihar. See Famine Inquiry Commission, 1945, pp. 144–5. See also *Census of India, 1951*, vol. XI, part 1, p. 41.

22. See the Reports of the Indian Famine Commissions of 1898 and 1901. Also the findings of S. R. Christophers regarding the nineteenth century famines, quoted in the Famine Inquiry Commission, 1945, p. 122.

23. On this see the Report of Indian Famine Commission of 1898.

24. Quoted in Mahalanobis, Mukherjea and Ghosh, 1946, pp. 11–14.

25. A sample survey of the destitutes in Calcutta conducted in September 1943 revealed that nearly 82 per cent of the destitutes surveyed came from this one district (see Das, 1949, p. 58).

26. Deaths occurring in Calcutta of people normally residing in 24-Parganas should, in fact, be attributed to the 24-Parganas itself. This correction would tend to raise somewhat the excess mortality rates of the 24-Parganas. The required corrections are difficult to estimate because of lack of precise data on 'normal residence' of those dying in Calcutta during the famine and post-famine years. But rough breakdowns would seem to indicate that the relative position of the 24-Parganas would not change drastically, especially for the period 1943–46. The contrast between the reality and the official perception will still hold, and the importance of being close to Calcutta in having one's distress officially observed will not disappear.

27. E.g. 'In the end not a single man died of starvation from the population of Greater Calcutta, while millions in rural areas starved and suffered' (Sir Manilal Nanavati's note to the Famine Inquiry Commission, 1945, p. 102).

28. For this and other observations, see *Census of India, 1911*, vol. I, part 1, Appendix to chapter 6, and also Das, 1949, pp. 93–6.

29. Famine Inquiry Commission, 1945, pp. 110–11. The Department of Anthro-

pology had noticed the same, and referred to it as 'a very sinister and significant feature' of the Bengal famine (see Ghosh, 1944, Appendix G, p. 183).

30. The male population exceeded the female population in Bengal, and the recorded death rate per unit of population was higher for women in every year during the decade 1941–50 through the famine (see *Census of India, 1951*, vol. VI, part 1B, Tables VII and VIII, pp. 29–30).

31. Das, 1949, p. 93.

32. My favourites are some of those proposed by Mr. W. C. Bennet, I.C.S.: 'Women find employment as maid-servants in the houses of rich men when men have no work to look for'; 'women possess ornaments of value which they may dispose for their own benefit whenever necessary'; 'the woman in a Hindu family always keeps the household stores, and has no scruple in availing herself of the advantage it gives her' (see *Census of India, 1911*, vol. I, part 1, Appendix to chapter 6, pp. 220–2).

33. Das, 1949, pp. 91–2.

34. See Appendix G in Ghosh, 1944.

35. The Famine Inquiry Commission, 1945 noted a decrease in the number of deaths for infants under 1 month, but attributed this to a decrease in the number of births as well as to a reporting bias (p. 109). Adjustments for this group would not affect the total proportions of children in excess mortality by very much.

36. The data comes from Famine Inquiry Commission, 1945, p. 213.

37. Cf. Jutikkala and Kauppinen's (1971) observation regarding 'catastrophic' and 'normal' mortality in pre-industrial Finland (1749–1850): 'The figures suggest that the seasonal distribution of deaths did not differ significantly between "catastrophic" and "normal" years' (p. 284).

# REFERENCES

Aykroyd, W. R., 1974, *The Conquest of Famine*, London.

Bailey, N. T. J., 1957, *The Mathematical Theory of Epidemics*, New York.

Banerji, D., 1975, 'Tuberculosis as a Problem of Social Planning in India', *NIHAE Bulletin*.

Blix, G., Hofvander, Y., and Vahlquist, B., 1971, *Famine: A Symposium Dealing with Nutrition and Relief Operations in Time of Disaster*', Swedish Nutrition Foundation, Uppsala.

Braudel, F., 1973, *Capitalism and Material Life: 1400–1800*, trans. M. Kochan, London.

*Census of India, 1911*, Government of India, Calcutta.

*Census of India, 1951*, Government of India, New Delhi.

*Census of Pakistan, 1951*, Government of Pakistan, Karachi.

Chambers, J. D., 1972, *Population, Economy, and Society in Pre-industrial England*, London.

Chattopadhyaya, K. P., and Mukherjea, R., 1946, 'A Plan for Rehabilitation', in P. C. Mahalonobis and others, *Famine and Rehabilitation in Bengal*, Calcutta.

Chaudhuri, D. G., 1952, *Vital Statistics Special Report on Pilot Survey: Incompleteness of the Birth and Death Registration in Urban and Rural Areas in the*

*Province of West Bengal during 1948 with Recommendations for Its Improvement*, Government of West Bengal, Calcutta.

Das, T., 1949, *Bengal Famine (1943)*, Calcutta.

Davis, K., 1951, *The Population of India and Pakistan*, Princeton.

Famine Inquiry Commission, 1945, *Report on Bengal*, Government of India, New Delhi.

Famine Inquiry Commission, 1945a, *Final Report*, Government of India, Madras.

Foege, H. W., 1971, 'Famine, Infections and Epidemics', in Blix, Hofvander and Vahlquist, 1971.

Ghosh, K. C., 1944, *Famines in Bengal 1770–1943*, Calcutta.

Government of India, 1958, *Health Statistics of India: Years 1951–52–53*, issued by the Director General of Health Services, Delhi.

Jain, S. P., 1954, 'Computed Birth and Death Rates in India during 1941–50', Annexure II, *Estimation of Birth and Death Rates in India during 1941–50–1951 Census*, Census of India, Paper no. 6, Government of India, New Delhi.

Jutikkala, E., and Kauppinen, M., 1971, 'The Structure of Mortality during Catastrophic year in Pre-industrial Society', *Population Studies*.

Keys, A., 1950, *Human Starvation*, Minneapolis.

Mahalanobis, P. C., Mukherjea, R., and Ghosh, A., 1946, 'A Sample Survey of After-effects of the Bengal Famine 1943', *Sankhya*, vol. VII, part 4; reprinted in P. C. Mahalanobis and others, *Famine and Rehabilitation in Bengal*, Calcutta, 1946.

Mansergh, N. (ed.), 1971 and 1973, *The Transfer of Power 1942–47*, Her Majesty's Stationery Office, London, vols. III and IV.

Mukherji, K., 1965, *Agriculture, Famine and Rehabilitation in South Asia*, Visva-Bharati, Santiniketan.

Post, J. D., 1976, 'Famine, Mortality and Epidemic Disease in the Process of Modernization', *Economic History Review*.

Sen, A. K., 1977, 'Starvation and Exchange Entitlements: A General Approach and Its Application to the Great Bengal Famine', *Cambridge Journal of Economics*, vol. I.

Stephens, I., 1966, *Monsoon Morning*, London.

Tranter, N. L., 1973, *Population since the Industrial Revolution*, London.

Wavell, Lord, 1973, *The Viceroy's Journal*, ed. P. Moon, London.

Wrigley, E. A., 1969, *Population and History*, London.

# 13

# The Relevance of Chayanov's Macro Theory to the Case of Java

SVEIN AASS

*Norwegian Foreign Service*

LONG before the renewed interest in the works of Chayanov that received such an impetus with the publishing in English of *A Theory of Peasant Economy* in 1966, his ideas influenced a whole generation of Dutch colonial scholars. The latter were brought to Chayanov's works by their own interest in the problems of non-capitalist societies. They themselves also made important contributions on these topics. The economic logic of the peasant economy in Java was discussed by Boeke in his doctoral dissertation in 1910 entitled 'Tropical–Colonial Economics: The Problem' (Boeke, 1910). This later became the foundation for his theory of 'dualism'. The clash between an imported plantation economy and a native small-scale subsistence agriculture was the point of departure of Boeke's probings. In order to explain the difference between the two economic sectors and particularly in order to understand the peculiarities of the peasant economy in Java, Boeke used Chayanov's 1923 article (included in Chayanov, 1966) in his very interesting *Economie van Indonesie* (Boeke, 1953). So did Vink in his important dissertation 'Foundations of the Indonesian Economic Enterprise', a treatise of the agricultural economics of the Javanese (and Indonesian) peasant household (Vink, 1942). The works by Chayanov and books written by authors supporting or criticizing Chayanov's theses were reviewed and discussed in professional periodicals such as *Landbouw* ('Agriculture') in the years between the World Wars (e.g. *Landbouw*, 1926, 1927, 1928).

To the Dutch scholars working on Java, it was Chayanov's micro theory that proved helpful. By contrast, I should like to discuss here the relevance of Chayanov's macro theory to the case of Java. In making a distinction between a micro and a macro theory in the work of Chayanov, I follow the analysis of Kerblay (1971, in Shanin, 1971). The micro theory concerns the economic logic of family labour and the allocation of resources in a household; the macro theory is one of demographic differentiation at the level of entire societies. I have previously discussed both aspects of Chayanov's theory (Aass, 1976).

Chayanov's concept of peasant economy as an economic system in its own right at the national level with its 'cyclical mobility' is opposed to the Marxist 'concept of class differentiation among the peasantry' (Kerblay, in Shanin, 1971, p. 154). As it concerns itself with whole societies, it would seem reasonable to consider this part of the theory as the one which poses the outlines of a specific peasant mode of production. This, for instance, is Kerblay's position. In spite of this, it has been the micro theory which has been most commonly referred to in order to contrast the economic behaviour of peasant household agriculture with that of capitalist agricultural enterprises.[1]

In an unpublished article Thorner effectively uses the micro theory in criticizing the attempts to apply the calculations of capitalist firms to Indian peasant agriculture (Thorner, n.d.). Considering peasant economy at the national level, however, Thorner separates himself from Chayanov in the use of the term 'peasant economy'. To Thorner:

In a peasant economy, roughly half of the total population . . . must be agricultural; and more than half of the working population must be engaged in agriculture. In a word we are saying that, to be termed 'peasant', an economy must be primarily agricultural. In a capitalist or socialist state which has been industrialized, there may remain thousands or even millions of peasants, but we would no longer apply the term 'peasant' to such an economy, taken as a whole. (Thorner, in Shanin, 1971, p. 203)[2]

This notion is much more descriptive than that of Chayanov, and not implying any assumption of 'demographic differentiation', it comes closer to an adding up of individual peasant farms (whose behaviour can be explained in terms of the micro theory) at the national level.

The thesis of 'demographic differentiation' implies a distinct theory of social mobility connected with the natural history of the family.

'Taking the sown area as a measure of peasant wealth and the volume of economic activity, Chayanov shows a clearly expressed dependence between development of a peasant family and the size of area sown by it' (Kerblay, in Shanin, 1971, p. 157). In the words of Chayanov, 'demographic process of growth and family distribution by size also determine to a considerable extent the distribution of farms by size of sown area and livestock numbers' (Chayanov, 1961, p. 67).

The phenomenon of 'demographic differentiation' as a specific form of stratification in a peasant society seems to be particularly valid for an agrarian regime where the peasant sector for one reason or another is being systematically 'levelled out'. This was the situation in both pre- and post-Revolutionary Russia due to the existence of the repartitional commune. As described by Shanin, after 1917 the levelling tendencies were further exaggerated through the egalitarian political revolution in the countryside making the peasantry into an even more than usual 'awkward class' (Shanin, 1972).

The question arises, however, to what degree the patterns of socioeconomic mobility, cyclical mobility, etc., pointed out by Shanin and Chayanov in the Russian case, lend themselves to 'possible inferences relevant to the general analysis of peasantry in the contemporary world' (ibid. p. 3).[3] Or, more to the point: how representative for peasant societies in general is the phenomenon that Chayanov labelled 'demographic differentiation'?

Chayanov thought his theory worked better for thinly populated countries than for densely populated ones. 'Where the peasants could not readily buy or take in more land, his theory would have to be seriously modified' (Thorner, in Chayanov, 1966, p. xxi). For the peasant farm in a land regime of impartible inheritance, Chayanov saw the land area as determinant (1966, pp. 112, 132). In Russia, on the other hand, as recognized by Chayanov, the land area was made extremely mobile through the particular land regime of *communal* repartitions, in addition to renting and purchase. This leads us to suggest that to the *ceteris paribus* in Chayanov's theory of the *family* farm, i.e. the non-use by the family of hired labour, there is a further *ceteris paribus* underlying the notion of 'demographic differentiation', i.e. a land regime of communal repartition. Thus in a positive appraisal in 1918 of Chayanov's work N. P. Makaroff states:

The adaptation of the size of the landholding to the needs of the peasant family is a complex process; it manifests itself not only in the selling or renting of land, as mentioned above, but also in a communal redistribution of land in peasant communities (the *mirs*). The communal redistribution of land is accompanied by the periodical and fundamental redistribution of land in the village communities by annual additions to, and subtraction from, each family's portion of land according to the increase or decrease of its size . . . (Makaroff, in Sorokin, Zimmermann and Galpin, 1931, p. 152)

## Russia and Java

It is interesting to note that the Dutch colonial scholars who successfully applied Chayanov's micro theory in order to explain the non-capitalist internal logic of peasant agriculture in Java, had serious reservations as to the validity of the notion of 'demographic stratification'.

Table I gives Meyer Ranneft's view of the relationship between family-size and income in Java (Meyer Ranneft, 1926, in Vink, 1942, p. 77). These figures, of course, do not speak for themselves, and were commented upon in the following manner by Vink:

It is likely that in Java the gross income is not determined by the number of family members. Rather the family size increases when the income is higher. (Vink, 1942, p. 77)

TABLE I

FAMILY SIZE AND INCOME IN JAVA 1926

|  | Family size | Income per family | Income per capita |
| --- | --- | --- | --- |
| Rich landowners | 8.4 | f.1090 | f.130 |
| Well-off farmers | 6.2 | f. 300 | f. 48 |
| Poor peasants | 5.0 | f. 148 | f. 30 |
| Share-croppers | 4.8 | f. 119 | f. 25 |
| Labourers in native agriculture | 3.5 | f. 101 | f. 29 |
| Coolies | 4.0 | f. 120 | f. 30 |

Scheltema likewise argued that 'in native society a larger number of children is to be expected by greater affluence' and also that 'an economically independent position causes family growth'. Finally Vink was of the opinion that Chayanov's 'law' is valid in a situation with a strong community; the weakening of the authority of the community in relation to the land made the notion of 'demographic differentiation' progressively irrelevant in relation to Javanese peasant agriculture (Vink, 1942, p. 77).

This seems all the more important as in Java we find a land regime of communal tenure in many respects resembling that of Russia (Lette, 1928). The dissolution of the communal regime in Java leads us to ask whether a regime of communal repartition can be said to be stable over time.

What follows is an attempt to outline some of the main phases in the development of Javanese peasant society leading to a situation different from one of 'demographic differentiation'. In doing this we will not try to suppress the many special factors behind the breakdown of the egalitarian village community in Java. The peculiar historical background, the traditional system of land tenure and the tremendous and premature impact both of foreign goods, money and colonial plantations make Java (as Russia for other reasons) a very particular case. Thus we are trying neither to dispute the relevance of 'demographic differentiation' in the Russian case nor to deny that even today for a considerable section of the peasantry the economic behaviour of the individual household can always be formulated in terms of Chayanov's micro theory. On the other hand, so far as the factors outlined for Java can be found in other historical settings one might imply that 'demographic differentiation' is no stable phenomenon, that the prerequisite for such a situation, communal land repartition, forever 'cannot withstand the disintegrating forces of trade and commercial development, the stealthy invasion of money economy' (Boeke, 1953, p. 27) without undergoing a change in the productive and social relations.

Mainly, then, we hope to show some important changes with respect to productive relations in Javanese peasant society over time. Although the thesis of 'demographic differentiation' does not entail any specific productive relations, and this is a main weakness, it does imply that the social units consist of individual peasant households and that most of agricultural labour is provided by family labour. Consequently, the model loses much of its relevance if this basic assumption is invalidated through the evolution of a situation in which an important part of the rural population is more and more dispossessed of land and on the other hand a substantial part of labour input is non-family labour.

15

## The historical background

In 1876 appeared the first volume containing the results of a vast investigation undertaken by the Dutch colonial government into the rights of the Javanese peasants to ownership of land (Bergsma (ed.), 1876–96). The conclusions of the massive reports (here called the 'Eindresume' for short) was that 'communal ownership' by the village was prevalent in Java. The most common form was that of regular and periodic (usually annual) redistribution of the cultivated land among the members of the village (see also Tydeman, 1872). However, the report also concluded that communal tenure had not always been there but was in fact a perversion of what had once been 'individual and hereditary' ownership ('Eindresume', vol. II, 1880, pp. 97, 123).

Under the impact of Dutch agrarian colonialism, so the argument went, the pre-colonial peasant communities were remodelled from within.[4] Especially from 1830 to 1870 during the time of the *Cultuurstelsel* or the so-called Culture System of forced labour and cultivation the villagers were deprived of their best land and forced to work in the colonial enterprises.

Before the Dutch . . . labour services had in general imposed no serious burden on the common people, and were rendered only by those who possessed land and were competent to bear them. (Day, 1904, p. 394)

Here not the exchange-value but the use-value of the produce predominated and there was no boundless thirst for surplus labour arising from the nature of production itself.

Under Dutch influence the services became vastly more onerous and were exacted from a constantly increasing number of people, including even those who had no land of their own. The peasants had to plant, cut and transport the products and in addition were forced to work in the sugar factories (Burger and Prajudi, 1962, p. 186). In theory the *Cultuurstelsel* called for only one-fifth of the peasants' rice fields being planted with a commercial crop decided by the Government (e.g. coffee, sugar, indigo). The peasant was to spend no more time cultivating this crop than he would have spent if the ground upon which it grew had been planted in rice. Upon delivery of the designated crop to the Government he was to be exempted from paying a tax (Van der Kolff, in Schrieke, 1929, p. 108).[5] In practice, the peasant was not only forced to continue payment of the land tax, but the restriction calling for the limitation of the Government's crop area was rarely observed. According to Van der Kolff 'one-third, half and even the whole of these fields were used for that purpose' (ibid. p. 109). 'So great were the demands on the landholder,' states Furnivall, 'that landholding was no longer a privilege but a burden which occupants tried to share with others' (Furnivall, 1937, p. 140). In the circumstances, in order to preserve the fragile balance between man and land, the result was communal tenure and a concomitant levelling of intra-village differences through communal regular and periodic redistribution of cultivated fields among the villagers (Wolf, 1957; Ter Haar, 1960, p. 93).

This process was encouraged by the government because, from the latter's point of view, supervision of crop growing and the most efficient use of irrigation facilities was much easier done if one could deal 'with compact blocs of land' and if such matters were regulated 'with a powerful village council rather than with the individual land-owners' (Van der Kolff, 1929, p. 111). On this background we ought to see Day's opinion that

communal land tenure in Java is not an aboriginal institution; it represents a modification of individual tenure by government influence, and hence resembles the Russian *mir*. (Day, 1904, p. 303)

## 'Communal' or 'private' property?

In spite of the conclusion in the 'Eindresume' that colonial economic policy had destroyed an agrarian regime where already 'land had become individual and private property', some peculiarities mentioned in the report or else observed by independent students, were throwing doubt on the very relevance of notions like 'property', 'individual tenure' and the like in the traditional Javanese setting.

Sollewijn Gelpke, who worked as an officer in the agricultural extension service and to whom we owe some remarkable reports of both agronomical and anthropological nature from the 1870s, has mentioned the fact that sale and purchase of land took place only rarely. He further noticed that the word for 'renting' of land was not understood by the Javanese peasants. When sale of land occasionally occurred, it happened in the following circumstances:

No one sells land before leaving a village entirely, leaving no relatives behind. But then when he sells, it is a *prix d'occasion*. (Sollewijn Gelpke, 1879, p. 36)

Tydeman equally noticed that land was sold 'far below its real value' and in this he saw proof that 'the native knows only too well that only the use right to the land is alienated', the final property rights thus resting with the Sovereign, that is the Dutch government (Tydeman, 1872, p. 14). Scheuer seemed to be closer to the truth when he noted how private tenure was 'crammed' by collective or higher-order rights, 'imbedded' in collective tenure so to speak.

The establishing of new villages earlier always needed the presence and supervision of a noble of higher or lower rank (Scheuer, n.d., p. 106). The latter did not get the new village as a fief. Rather, he incarnated in his person the fact that the land was 'tied in a magico-religious relationship with *the group of people living on it*' (Buchari, in Soedjatmoko *et al.*, 1965, p. 50). The opening up of new land simply on the initiative of a group of peasants was therefore a very modern phenomenon (Scheuer, n.d., p. 110).

Even in the case of garden plots, where the most individualized tenure reigned, 'the size of the plot was never measured when bought and sold. In hundreds of cases nobody knows the size of the surface inside the fences' (Sollewijn Gelpke, 1880, p. 26). Once more Tydeman observed the same thing and he commented that transactions like these are not accompanied by notions on the part of the actors involved that the land is bought and sold. Consequently, they do not have to measure the land (Tydeman, 1872, p. 17).

All this makes one ask whether in the case of traditional Javanese society there existed a concept of ownership in any Western sense, even in the case of the Ruler (Lyon, 1970). The main difficulty lies in our giving our own meaning of ownership to the corresponding Javanese object.

We overlook that ownership has a different significance and denotes several legal/economic relationships between which it is absolutely necessary to distinguish. (Malinowski, 1921, p. 3)

For one thing an 'individualist' interpretation does not fully see that we can have private labour process and yet there can be communal property. In concentrating on the 'technical tenure' expressing the nature of the labour process one easily misses the fact that producers produce *en passant par* the community. Neither does 'communal' land tenure imply that a village community all by itself is a mode of production when exploitation has the form of an exploitation of multiple communities.

In fact an inextricable tangle resulted from the use of such terms

as 'property rights' or the 'communal right of ownership' in the
Javanese case. Even if the conclusions of the 'Eindresume' were
correct one still had to ask exactly *how* individual tenure was converted into communal tenure. The end result must to a certain degree
depend on the nature of the precedent type of tenure. In this connection the development of the tenure system in Sunda (West Java) is
significant as here one could observe on the contrary a speedy transition to very 'individual tenure' and an early development of rather
large-scale and even absentee land-ownership (Scheltema, 1927–28,
pp. 271–305).

## The traditional Javanese 'desa'

An insight into the historical background to the agrarian question
in Java can best be gained by an understanding of the system of
Javanese customary law. In his path-breaking studies on Indonesian
customary law or *adat* (1918), C. Van Vollenhoven has accomplished
a real 'archéologie sociale' as regards traditional land tenure in Java
(e.g. Van Vollenhoven, 1918).[6] The *adat* in Indonesia was not only a
sphere of jurisprudence on the local level but 'customs' regulated the
whole relationship between the tillers of the soil and the State, i.e.
the King.[7]

Van Vollenhoven pointed out that the basic aspects of the life in
the *desa*s or villages could be explained in terms neither of the King
as the sole 'proprietor' (Rouffaer, 1918, pp. 305–99)[8] nor of the cultivators as proprietors or simple usufruitiers. It was the concept of
property that had to be reformulated in the Javanese context. Van
Vollenhoven raised the question: 'Does ... the Indonesian *adat*
know of "landed property"?' And he answered 'yes', it does know
of it if by 'landed property' is meant that a peasant or *petani* can say:
'This ricefield is *mine*.' On a closer look, however, we find that all
rights in the land are derived from rightful exploitation. The holding
rights are always 'crammed' in *adat* restrictions (Van Vollenhoven,
1919, p. 67).

In 1909 Van Vollenhoven had introduced the term *beschikkings-
recht* (Indonesian: *hak pertuanan*) or *'right of disposal'* to indicate the
central element in the village tenure system (Van Vollenhoven, 1909,
pp. 19 ff). There were several characteristic features of the right of
disposal, the most important of which was *the absence of any power
to alienate the land* (ibid.). Another essential feature lay in the interaction of communal and individual rights: when a person put his

individual efforts into a piece of land, he created something of an identity of self and soil. To the degree that he intensified this, it became a legal relation and the powers of the community with respect to that particular field were reduced. If he neglected his holding or permitted its usufruct to lapse through inactivity, then the powers of the community were re-established and the community right of disposal was once more freely asserted. The rights of the community permitted individual exploitation of the land only to the extent that the products of the land went to feed the peasant's immediate or extended family. If an individual overreached his right and produced for the commercial market he was treated as an alien.

The community usually exercised its right of disposal over fields, for the most part by an occasional recovery of such fields after the death of the occupant. It might prevent a villager from getting more than one field of normal size, in order to maintain an equitable distribution among the villagers[9] (Van Vollenhoven, 1918; Ter Haar, 1960; Supomo, 1970). We see that the 'right of disposal' does not imply the absence of precise and defined individual rights in land; rather this superior right indicates that the community has not lost control on the products of its labour (Godelier, 1971).

Material objects—land, water, crops, temples and buildings—were subject to the joint care of the collectivity (Ter Haar, 1960, p. 15).

The *desa* formed a law community (Van Vollenhoven, 1928, p. 32) ... and such communities are to be seen as legal personalities (Ter Haar, 1960, p. 16). ... It might be said that there is no sphere of activity that is not subject to the intervention by the collectivity. (Supomo, 1970, p. 15)

In summary we can list the following elements as constituting the main aspects of the 'right of disposal' of the *desa*:

(1) The community and its members have controlled access to cultivated fields.

(2) The community and its members have free access to uncultivated lands within the defined bounds of the village. (They can hunt, collect and exploit.)

(3) Strangers do not have the same rights and they can exploit resources only after having obtained permission to do so from the community.

(4) In order to profit from the exploitation of natural resources, strangers and sometimes even the members of the community have to pay a payment of recognition.

(5) The community is responsible for delinquencies committed within its boundaries.

(6) The right of disposal cannot be alienated.

(7) Important transactions need the co-operation of the community and transfer of land can often only be done between the members of a community.

(8) Abandoned land goes back to the community (Van Vollenhoven, 1919, p. 9).

Strict equality between the members did not reign and these differences 'went further than differences in age and sex' (Hilton, 1974). In most *desa*s at least the following groups could be encountered: (1) A group of *gogol* or nuclear villagers who were descendants of the pioneers who had once long ago cleared the land. They owned land, house and garden land and upon them fell the full burdens and rights as 'citizens'. (2) A group called *indung* who owned either a house or land, but not both. They had neither full rights nor duties. (3) The *numpang*s (which in modern Indonesian means 'passenger') had neither land nor garden land. Their house was constructed upon garden land owned by somebody else—or else they had an inferior status, living in with a family, being servants, etc. (Van Vollenhoven, 1918, p. 527, and others).

Outsiders and those of lower status might acquire a more favourable position in relation to land. On the other hand, outsiders might obtain a clearly fixed title to the land only after having lived in a community for generations. And even then their rights readily gave way to the rights of the community in time of crisis. Finally, the village chief (*lurah, bekel*) who was aided by a number of assistants, had rather autocratic powers (Kartohadikoesoemo, 1953, p. 63). The essential thing was that in every village there was a social group that had more rights than other villagers in relation to the land but that still did not constitute an independent social class. The villagers 'differed from one another in the abundance rather than in the quality of their possession' (Hilton, 1974). In the *gogol* and the *lurah* we rather have the case of an 'Asiatic' pattern of tribal continuities where 'clan and communal property exists in fact as the foundation' (Marx, 1973), the social privileges being due to a genealogical closeness to the founding fathers of the village and, which is identical, the village spirits.[10]

*The transition to individualized land tenure*

The situation in pre-colonial Java contrasts with the one in Russia where 'communal land tenure' can more easily be understood in terms of 'private property', that is, as a *direct* negation of the latter. Regardless of the disagreement as to the origin of the *mir*, the commune in Russia reached a high degree of stability over the centuries, coexisting as it did with the domainal sector (i.e. private property in some 'feudal' form). The 'social dualism' (Shanin, 1972) and the opposition between the two sectors (and later that of 'capitalist' domains) does not alter the fact that the Russian village community in the course of historical development gradually became one of the pillars of feudalism in Russia.

On the contrary, in Java the characteristic feature is the absence of property 'at least in any Western sense'. The property of the individual was here directly communal property, 'the individual has no property as distinct from the commune' (Marx, 1973). The tenure system in Java in its own manner reached a high degree of stability.[11] The repartitional commune found by the 'Eindresume' to dominate after 1850 can now be seen in relation to the traditional tenure system: Van Vollenhoven found that the former represented 'an abnormal strengthening of the village "right of disposal" '.

However, in contrast to the traditional tenure system, the outright communal structure 'created' by the colonial governmental policies was *not* a stable one. Running counter to the levelling effects of enforced communalism the conditions were created for an 'individualisme agraire', to use a somewhat anachronistic expression (Bloch, 1930). This tendency became apparent when in 1870 the *Cultuurstelsel* came to an end, and, with the new Agricultural Law of that same year, Indonesia was progressively opened up to private plantations using hired labour and renting land from the peasants on a large scale (Hardjosudarmo, 1970).

In the 1870s amendments were passed by the government in order to facilitate the transition from communal to individual and hereditary peasant ownership in land. In spite of the fact, as some authors have argued, that the renting policies of the sugar plantations perpetuated the communal pattern in the villages (Van der Kolff, in Schrieke, 1929), the tendency towards more individualized land tenure gradually grew stronger. This process can be seen from Table II which shows the decline in communal tenure in the region of Kediri

## TABLE II
### No. of Villages with Communal or Individual Tenure

| Year | Individual | Only communal | Mixed tenure |
|------|-----------|---------------|--------------|
| 1892 | 74 | 423 | 1017 |
| 1898 | 54 | 395 | 1064 |
| 1904 | 64 | 309 | 1165 |
| 1909 | 83 | 239 | 1135 |
| 1912 | 53(?) | 193 | 1264 |
| 1917 | 122 | 164 | 1255 |
| 1922 | 144 | 106 | 1262 |
| 1927 | 145 | 57 | 1095 |

*Source*: *Kolonial Verslag*, 1893, 1898, 1904, 1909, 1914, 1918, 1924, 1929.
*Note*: Villages where land titles are subject to special jurisdictions have
not been included.

in East Java, a core area for sugar plantations where in 1929 there
were villages in which 70 per cent of the land was under cane.
The result was a rural community where new productive relations,
however gradually, became prevalent.[12] This essential fact leaves
Geertz's affirmation below in need of qualification. Geertz wrote:

after about the middle of the nineteenth century . . . tenure systems
grew more intricate; tenancy relationships more complicated; co-
operative labour arrangements more complex—all in an effort to
provide everyone with some niche, however small, in the over-all
system. (Geertz, 1963, p. 82)

As has been pointed out by colonial scholars like Van der Kolff,
who has brilliantly described phases in the above-mentioned process
as well as its contradictory and roundabout nature (Van der Kolff,
1937), individualization brings about changes in the relations between
villagers that represent a break with the earlier pattern in spite of
resemblances in appearance.

The enforced communalism, while strengthening the village 'right
of disposal', is at the same time the first step in a process of *dissolution*
and the whole process can be conveniently termed 'conservation/
dissolution' thus using Bettelheim's notion developed in another but
not altogether unrelated connection (Bettelheim, in Emmanuel, 1970).
In order to see how all this happened we will mention only two of
the many factors in the 'economic revolution' brought about by
Dutch colonial rule. The two factors are the destruction of traditional

rural handicrafts and household industry on the one hand and the 'creation of the labourer' on the other.

## The destruction of household industry

In the exceptionally long history of colonization that Java experienced, the early destruction of household industry stands out as an important fact. This argument is not in opposition to Postan's remark that 'the rise of "money economy" is one of the residuary hypotheses of economic history: a *deus ex machina* to be called upon when no other explanation is available' (Postan, 1973, p. 28).

Here we are not primarily interested in showing a development away from 'economies *wholly* natural' (ibid.). Rather, the decline in handicrafts in Java is significant by being very premature and massive, thus ruining the primitive combination of industry and agriculture at a stage where the other preconditions for such a separation were not yet present.

This differs from the situation in other peasant societies where the destruction happened rather late and not so completely as in Java. As late as 1946, Fei wrote about China that, apart from industry in the big coastal towns, the chief industries, such as textiles, were 'mainly peasant occupations'.

The bulk of Chinese manufacturing industry is widely scattered in the homesteads of the peasants. The peasants work on their simple looms in their spare time. . . . [As a result] peasants live largely in a self-sufficient economy. (Fei, 1946, p. 153)

Likewise Jacoby remarked about Vietnam on the eve of the Second World War: 'Native handicrafts are still very common in the northern part of the country where land holdings are very small' (1961, p. 153).

In 1817 the situation in Java was still as described by Sir Stamford Raffles in his magnificent *The History of Java*:

The family of a Javan peasant is almost independent of any labour, but that of its own members . . . almost every article required for a family being prepared within its own precincts. In every cottage there is a spinning wheel and a loom. (1817, pp. 163, 96)

Java was 'a country without trade or manufactures' (ibid. p. 138) where 'not more than one-sixteenth of the inhabitants were employed in a branch of industry other than agriculture' (ibid. p. 107). The Javanese peasant laboured 'in a discontinuous fashion in order to meet the totality of his needs' (Godelier, 1966). But as already mentioned earlier, in 1830 the *Cultuurstelsel* was introduced. The growth in 'European' plantation crops took advantage of the peasant's 'seasonal labour' in those months of the year when he did not work in agriculture, thus making an hitherto unused potential surplus into an actual one (Godelier, 1966; Sachs, 1966). This could happen because earlier 'in the family labour farm, rates of labour intensity are considerably lower than if labour was fully utilized' due to seasonal variations, so that 'farm families possess considerable stocks of unutilized time' (Chayanov, 1966, pp. 75–6). The labour used in government works was taken at the expense of handicrafts etc. There was consequently a harder time for peasant home industry and a concomitant growth in cotton imports.

The first textiles had been imported in 1814 and by 1848 one-third of the clothing was of foreign origin (Mansvelt, 1924, p. 20). The price of European cloth fell significantly and in 1850 there were quite a few types of textiles whose price was already only one-third of the price 25 years earlier.

The annual reports of the colonial government sent to the Parliament in Holland, the *Kolonial Verslag*, mention the opening up of new local markets (*pasars*) and the increase in the sale of cottons, particularly after 1860. It is reported that clusters of tradesmen are to be found along all the roads in 1876 (*Kolonial Verslag*, 1876, p. 211). In 1878 cottons were widespread all over Java, most of them English, Dutch, German or Swiss made.

This is particularly the case with English textiles whose price is reduced to a minimum through reduction in quality and size. (*Kolonial Verslag*, 1878, p. 221)

The result was 'the elimination of textiles of native origin everywhere' (*Kolonial Verslag*, 1879, p. 218). 'Cheap imports smashed the native economic system and straitened the sphere of native arts' (Furnivall, 1937, p. 459). Sollewijn Gelpke contrasted with sorrow the new situation with that described by Raffles at the beginning of the nineteenth century:

Nowadays, as in every little market place can be found European cottons, one seldom any longer in the villages hears that strange clanging sound of the hand-loom. (Sollewijn Gelpke, 1880, p. 104)

An impression of the magnitude of the process can be gained from Table III which gives the value of imported cotton goods. Imported textiles were only 'the light artillery', however. After 1870

TABLE III

IMPORT OF COTTON GOODS

| Year | Import (in thousands of guilders) |
|------|-----------------------------------|
| 1825 | 1,696 |
| 1830 | 3,884 |
| 1840 | 13,100 |
| 1850 | 9,837 |
| 1860 | 20,943 |
| 1870 | 16,024 |
| 1880 | 34,333 |
| 1890 | 35,662 |
| 1900 | 35,744 |
| 1913 | 96,274 |
| 1920 | 315,573 |
| 1925 | 207,743 |

*Source*: Furnivall, 1937, pp. 105, 130, 171, 207, 335.

foreign direct investments came to the forefront. The importance of foreign investments (almost entirely concentrated in tiny Java and the Sumatran coast) can hardly be exaggerated. The scale of foreign investments is shown in the fact that in 1938 foreign investments in Indonesia were bigger than in China with a much larger population as can be seen from Table IV.

TABLE IV

FOREIGN INVESTMENTS PER COUNTRY

| Country | Foreign Investments (in millions of £) |
|---------|----------------------------------------|
| Indonesia | 400 |
| China | 300 |
| India | 600 |

*Source*: Burger, 1970, p. 194.

When peasant household industry was swept away, few alternative demands for labour appeared. The population was thrown back on agriculture, yet not entirely in the manner of an 'agricultural involution', that is by an overworking of the already established agricultural pattern (Geertz, 1963). This we hope to make clearer in the next and final section.

## The creation of the labourer

A consequence of colonial policies was to create the 'labourer'. This amounts to no less than an 'economic revolution'. In the nine-teenth century the necessity for forced labour was mainly the result of the near impossibility of getting people to work for wages in the colonial projects.

Wage labour was a very rare phenomenon. It was only performed to some extent by the free slum dwellers in Batavia where money economy was already common. . . . The Chinese were also active as wage labourers. (Burger and Prajudi, 1962)

But apart from this private entrepreneurs were dependent on a special group of vagabonds or 'trekkers', a very unstable lot who seemed to be more interested in spending their money on female dancers than anything else (ibid.). In 1820 it was reported that it was still an exception to get free labourers.

The difficulty was that of getting men who saw any chance to continue their independent existence to bind themselves to work for wages. Or, as one observer put it, the peasant 'can, by working for himself, satisfy all his needs; there is no reason why he should bind himself to work for others' (Day, 1904, p. 346).

Left to himself the peasant cultivates nothing but a tiny plot of rice-land sufficient for his needs, he is even abandoning the cultivation of indigo and cotton because he buys imported European goods, so that he is idle for eight months of the year. (ibid. p. 101)

In Java at that time the peasant lacked the incentive to undertake an intensification in production because of the 'smallness of his wants' (ibid. p. 345). As Seneca once said: 'If you desire anyone to be rich, you should not increase his riches, but decrease his wants.'

The contrast to the situation in Europe was summed up by an anonymous author in 'Indisch Archief' in 1850. The author called for the need to develop a specific theory of 'Oriental' economics:

Outside Java it may even prove impossible to get manual labour at money wages. Our Indian has few wants and satisfies them easily; to obtain some extra enjoyment he may be willing to work at times, but little and for a while only. . . . To get him to work one would have to compel him. (Cited in Boeke, 1953, p. 8)

According to Sollewijn Gelpke the Javanese peasant would sell products that had taken him a week of labour for one guilder (Sollewijn Gelpke, 1879, p. 71). 'Regarding himself the ordinary Javanese does not care about the time he wastes' (ibid.). And in order to illustrate the point of view of the peasants themselves Sollewijn Gelpke lets one of them speak for himself:

We will not do any *koeli* labour as long as there still is rice in the village. He whose supply is up will borrow from his neighbour and only when no one has any rice left, *then* we will go working for outsiders. (ibid. p. 72)

Sollewijn Gelpke comments: 'If you offer the native employment before this time has come—unless the pay is exceptionally high—his response is certain to be a negative one' (ibid.).

The break-down of household industry, the spread of money through 'plantloon', the necessity to pay *landrente* in money, the forced 'training' of the peasants to work in the colonial projects, gradually made it possible to overcome 'the stumbling-block of tropical colonization, the problem of labour' (Day, 1904, p. 344) and have work done by hired hands. The years just before and just after 1890 represent a watershed, after which in the region of Kediri, which we have already mentioned several times, people on 'their own behalf sought out wage work on the various colonial projects or private plantations' (Burger and Prajudi, 1962). A group of sufficiently 'free', mobile and 'landless' workers had been created. 'The natives were to some extent prepared for a system of free labour contracts' (ibid. p. 336).

This does not mean that a group of non-'proprietors' did not exist earlier. We have already mentioned the class of second-class villagers, the *instleute* or *numpang*s. At the beginning of the nineteenth century one observer noted that villages in Java were 'swarming with idlers'. However, as for the *numpang*s they were part of the family and 'paid' in kind, their subsistence fund simply being a part of the total produce of the land and only analytically distinguishable from the latter.[13] Further, with the prevalence of mutual labour-aid and communal labour like *gotong royong* and *sambatan* a situation was created where 'everybody worked for everybody' (Malinowski, 1921).[14] The labour reciprocity excluded the use of money or salaries (Van der Kolff, 1937) and 'the class of natives who had neither land nor a trade to support them and who served others for hire was not large in number' (Day, 1904, p. 355).

Of perhaps equal importance is the fact that this group 'was absorbed to a considerable extent in the internal organization of the village' (ibid.). Through the frequent ritual meals of *slametan*, through the village funds for elders and the disabled, *sjakal*, and particularly through the right for everybody to participate in the harvest and to receive a large part, *bawon*, thereof, all were at least secured a certain minimum.[15] In one way or another everybody had a right in the final produce of the land.

The essential thing to see is that no one in traditional Java was just a labourer and that work was no isolated activity. In various Indonesian languages the word for 'work' and 'feast' is the same. '*Gave* and *damal* in Javanese means feast as well as work. So is also the case with the Malay word *pakerdjaan* which is connected with the marital feast. In Gajo the word *boeat* signifies work and specifically field work done in connection with a ceremony' (Vink, 1942, p. 72).

The communal labour institutions of *gotong royong* and *sambatan* cannot be explained simply in terms of the needs for extra hands in peak periods in the agricultural cycle. Rather they were expressions of the fact that work itself was carried out in a communal setting:

mutual aid is such an established practice that help is asked for even when it is entirely unnecessary and the work can be easily done alone (e.g. when pulling the seedlings). . . . Labour aid happens in all kinds of situations . . . and is never refused. (Tydeman, 1872, p. 21)

Sollewijn Gelpke likewise remarked that 'one always is entitled to ask for labour aid'. Only in one instance would such a request be considered *koerang pantes* or improper, that is—significantly—for the cultivation of *palawidja* or secondary crops, i.e. often cash-crops (Sollewijn Gelpke, 1879). We see that to be simply a 'worker' was no status in its own right in the traditional Javanese *desa* and that 'the producing individual, appears as dependent, as belonging to a greater whole' (Marx, 1973, p. 84).

The positing of the individual as a worker, in this nakedness, is itself a product of history. [Formen] . . . Labour seems a quite simple category. The conception of labour in this general form—as labour as such —is also immeasurably old. Nevertheless, when it is economically conceived in this simplicity, 'labour' is as modern a category as are the relations which create this simple abstraction. . . . [This] example of labour shows strikingly how even the most abstract categories, despite their validity—precisely because of their abstractness—for all epochs, are nevertheless, in the specific character of this abstraction, themselves likewise a product of historic relations, and possess their full validity only for and within these relations. (Marx, 1973, p. 103, 105)

The increased possibilities of using hired labourers for the many colonial projects represented a stride forward on the path of 'individualization'. We have already indicated the massive scale on which Java was subjected to colonization by private enterprise after 1870. By paying money rents to the peasants the enterprises started a process, however stunted, whereby land became a source of income independent of any labour put into it. The converting of rent payment into 'credit bondage' was the source of a further 'means by which the Dutch solved the problem of "free" labour' (Day, 1904, p. 352).

The result of the process here schematically outlined and which really developed 'as a rich totality of many determinations and relations', was the partial separation of labour from land. This was an important step though, even today, a far from complete one.

The separation of land and labour comes at a comparatively late period in economic development and has scarcely more than begun in modern Java. (ibid.)

The new productive relations delineated above first began at the boundaries of the villages and had no existence inside the communities. But as soon as, say, wage labour became common in the external intercourse of a village, it also, by reaction, became so in the internal intercourse. In order to understand the importance of this movement we must consider the special nature, that is, the labour intensity,[16] of the cultivation of rice, by far the most common crop in Java. In contrast to the present situation of rural overpopulation the main labour problem in Java has traditionally been the lack of farm hands.[17] In the 1870s it was even reported that there existed a special word for ripe rice left rotting in the fields due to the lack of manpower for the harvesting.

The need for additional labour outside that of the single peasant family had been traditionally met through *sambatan* or exchange of labour. With the practices of the plantations, money circulation and the individualization of agriculture (and hence of the agriculturalists themselves), it gradually became possible to pay labourers a time wage.[18] This was done with reference to the old labour exchange institution, the money wage for the labour power sold substituting for the labour traditionally given in return. However, the similarity between the two situations was only apparent;[19] in the first instance one exchanged labour equivalents while the second case looked more and more like that of ordinary wage labour, with the coolie wages in plantation agriculture as a model. In the latter situation, then, the value of labour power was exchanged for its equivalent in money.[20] What really happened was the use of 'the traditional form of production, . . . a form "known and understood by all", in order to organize *new productive relations*' (Godelier, 1973, p. 90). Writing in quite a different connection about the integration of former independent 'primary communities' into the Inca 'Asiatic' mode of production, Godelier has eloquently defined the phenomenon referred to above in the following terms:

> Donc, d'une façon générale le nouveau mode de production prenait *appui* sur les rapports de production . . . éxistants pour les bouleverser. Il y a donc là un méchanisme d'éxtension de ces rapports au-delà de leur sphère d'origine, de fonctionnement originaire. (ibid.)

In Java the result has been the development of a peasant agriculture with widespread use of hired labour. This stands out in important contrast to the situation in Russia where, as Professor Thorner has pointed out, Chayanov considered his category of the labour farm 'as a real one drawn from life' (Thorner, in Chayanov, 1966, p. xiii). 'In Russia 90 per cent of the total mass of peasant farms are pure family labour' (Chayanov, 1966, p. 112). Similarly, citing a survey by Gadgil, Thorner noted that for India in the 1950s households supplied more than three-fourths of their labour needs and that 'the chances for alternative employment are slight' (Thorner, n.d.). On the contrary in Java in the late twenties and early thirties Vink found that 40–70 per cent of the total farm labour input in native agriculture was provided by hired labour (Vink, 1942, p. 87). In 1973 'an average of about 85 per cent of total man-days of labour used to produce the crop was made up of hired labour' (A.E.S, 1973).

As Thorner has pointed out, it is undoubtedly true that 'the fact that cultivation is carried out by hired workers does not necessarily mean that we have a capitalist farm oriented towards profitability, reinvestment and expansion' (Thorner, 1973, p. 19). Our argument does not entail such an assertion. We have tried to show that the development of new productive relations destroyed the 'repartitional commune' and this, we think, seriously modifies the workings of 'demographic stratification' (as well as that of 'agricultural involution' and 'shared poverty'). Instead, we think there will be a stronger

16

tendency towards a *more permanent* concentration (and stability in general) in landholdings.[21]

In Table v we tentatively try to illustrate the present situation by the structure of land holdings in three neighbouring villages that we surveyed in the region of Kediri in 1973–74. In villages A and B the percentage of landowners is clearly below 50 and more than half of them own less than 0.5 hectare of land. (One hectare is reckoned as the minimum to feed an average family.) The interesting feature, however, is the convergence in the tendency towards concentration/pauperization in all the three villages in the long run, and this in spite of different histories and backgrounds as to the original tenure system.

TABLE V

LANDHOLDINGS IN THREE JAVANESE VILLAGES

| Size distribution | Percentage of households | | |
|---|---|---|---|
| (in hectares) | Village A | Village B | Village C |
| Over 15 | 0 | 1 | 0 |
| 10–15 | 1 | 2 | 0 |
| 5–10 | 1 | 1 | 0 |
| 2–5 | 3 | 1 | 4 |
| 1–2 | 5 | 2 | 10 |
| 0.5–1 | 5 | 10 | 10 |
| Below 0.5 | 17 | 28 | 45 |
| Total | 32 | 45 | 69 |

Village C is partly an exception but nevertheless shows the tendency towards landlessness. On a closer look the tendency becomes even more obvious. At the time when Indonesia was still a colony, the area of village C 'belonged' to a Dutch company that used the land for sugar cultivation. At that time the peasants held the land in 'use-right' in communal rotation. The sugar factory was destroyed during the Independence War and a local 'land reform' was carried out among the inhabitants. Each family was given a plot of land according to need, the standard allotment being 0.350 hectare (twice as much to larger families). According to a survey undertaken by the regional authorities in view of the scheduled land reform, already in the beginning of the 1960s 37 per cent of the working-age persons interviewed had as their main occupation 'wage work'. Today, less than 30 years after the land reform, the uniformity is wearing out entirely. Although the percentage of land-holding households is over 70 per cent, 25 per cent own less than 0.5 hectare of land and only 4 per cent own more than 1 hectare whereas *30 per cent are completely landless*. The case of village C thus offers an excellent illustration of the history of an egalitarian community that polarizes under the impact of the development of private property in land. As Hinton puts it,

Their idea of the good society was one in which everyone had a plot of land, a roof overhead, clothes to wear. . . . The equalitarianism they dreamed of was noble, but it was also utopian—there being no conceivable way in which every family could enjoy a prosperous life on a long-term basis as long as production was atomized by small private holdings and cursed with primitive technique. Even if all the means of production could be equally divided, what was to prevent the . . . process of differentiation which . . . produced landlord and tenant . . . ? (Hinton, 1968, p. 55)

The history of villages A and B is different from that of village C. Village A was cleared by pioneers in the latter part of the nineteenth century and tenure in land has always been individual. However, earlier the population consisted of *gogol* landowners, *numpangs* (see above) and *santris* working and living in with families. The two latter categories of people have been reduced to the status of landless farm hands working for wages. Another source of manpower has been provided by late-comers who have been able to acquire land only very rarely. Village B earlier had communal tenure. This was originally of the 'periodic reallotments' type. Later it became of the 'communal-with-permanent-shares' and 'mixed communal/individual' type. In 1950, 30 hectares out of a total of 102 hectares was still under communal tenure but today all the land is individual and saleable property. A better impression of the social picture in villages A and B can be gained from Table VI, which shows the occupations of the heads of households in the two villages together.

The picture becomes even more gloomy if we note that the table shows the occupations of the heads of the households only. It is important to note that most households are supported by several of its members. In the poorer and landless families, the majority of women are also agricultural wage labourers. On the other hand, in the two topmost categories women are usually entirely unproductive

TABLE VI

Occupations of Heads of Households in Villages A and B

| Occupation | Percentage distribution |
|---|---|
| Independent farmer only | 15 |
| Independent farmer and other (prestigious) occupation | 12 |
| Farming and agricultural labourer | 10 |
| Agricultural labour only | 30 |
| Agricultural labour and other labour | 20 |
| Other labour | 13 |
| Total | 100 |

while the husbands only (and not always) supervise the labour pro
cess. On holdings above 1 hectare labour is almost exclusively don
by hired hands or by a special kind of labour-*métayage* arrangemen

In conclusion, in spite of the 'durability of the post-tradition;
economy' (Geertz, 1963, p. 28), with the individualization of labou
and land a situation has been brought about where the village com
munity 'has lost control of the products of its labour' (Godelie
1971). Regarding 'demographic differentiation', we think—to us
the words of the sharp-sighted 'Chayanovist' Boeke—that 'thos
happy days are past, gone for good, in all probability' (Boeke, 195;
p. 70).[22]

NOTES

1. Exceptions to this are Kerblay (in Shanin, 1971, p. 154), and Shanin (1972
2. The three other criteria mentioned by Thorner (1971) are the existence (
   the State, the presence of towns and the household as the unit of production
3. In his book on the Russian peasantry from 1910 to 1925 Shanin for his pa
   is not out to postulate any universal model of peasant societies. He write
   'Before turning to the relevance of our analysis it may prove useful to sa
   what it *does not* attempt to do. The analysis and concepts introduced are n
   intended to provide a master key to the understanding of peasant societies
   general, regardless of space, time and political and cultural framework. I
   the first place, it may shed further light on the history of Russia and, in par
   cular, contribute to clarification of the course of events in that major peric
   of Russian rural history which lies between the 1917 revolution and ma
   collectivization in 1929' (1972, pp. 3–4).

4. The argument was later generalized also to include the effects of sugar cultivation. See Van der Kolff (in Schrieke, 1929) and the later and inspiring article by E. Wolf, 1957.

5. An excellent summary of the process has been given by Kahin, 1952.

6. The expression is taken from the work on the Rumanian 'primary' communities by H. Stahl, 1970, p. 20.

7. '[The Javanese King's] administrative authority was limited. The ideal king refrained from interfering in the day-to-day administration of the countryside. ... The king was also limited by custom in taking decisions even within his own court' (Ricklefs, 1974).

8. In the author's opinion the key to the notion of the God-King and 'the king as the sole proprietor is that it is the negative expression of the absence of private property in land' (Aass, 1974, p. 13).

9. The passage above is taken from the English version of Ter Haar, 1960.

10. On the 'Asiatic' social formation, see the extremely original and brilliant article by Friedman, 1974. Some of the features of the particular society in Burma pointed out by Friedman, can also be detected in Java.

11. According to several authors there were very early in Java definite mechanisms for land equalizing also in the pre-colonial village community (see, for example, Slametmuljana, 1967, pp. 37 ff, and Lette, 1928).

12. Both 'individual' and 'mixed' tenure must be seen as a definite break with the village right of disposal. As Van Vollenhoven once pointed out, the essence of the latter right was that it was *total*; it could be weak or strong but in no circumstance did it leave room for another type of competing right, a superior right like itself *inside* the area of one and the same village community.

13. In his early and primitive 'agricultural' theory of profit Ricardo still assumed that wages were given in corn—a subsistence (see Dobb, 1973, pp. 70–1). The worker cannot yet at this stage be considered a commodity owner who sells his own commodity to another commodity owner, the capitalist. In the latter case the subsistence of the worker is not any longer an integral part of the capitalist's capital. The worker now also *buys* his subsistence in the market.

14. According to the laws of the Majapahit empire, a man was liable to punishment if he refused to allow a relative (probably meaning 'co-villager') to participate in the farm labour (Slametmuljana, 1967).

15. According to the estimates made by Sollewijn Gelpke in the 1870s the *bawon* represented from one-fifth to one-third of the harvest and the *sjakal* normally one-tenth.

16. 'A rice field produces a much greater quantity of food than the most fertile corn field, [but] its cultivation, therefore, requires more labour' (Adam Smith, *The Wealth of Nations*, 1776).

17. This is how E. Boserup explains the coexistence in Java over a very extended period of time of slash-and-burn cultivation (*ladang*) and permanent rice cultivation.

18. An official report noted, however, that even in 1924, 'in general all wages in native agriculture are received in kind' (*Verslag* . . . , 1924, p. 152).

19. In his excellent case study of the change from *sambatan* to work hire (and tenancy) Van der Kolff shows how the poorer villagers tried as long as possible to avoid being *paid* for their labour, thus also avoiding the status of

'labourer'. Instead they preferred to receive only the traditional meal at the end of the working day, which meant that the giver of the latter in his turn had to work on the other villagers' land when need arose. Van der Kolff writes: 'The [workers] were said to prefer the payment in the form of a meal, probably because the payment in cash tended to set up social differences, which the economically weaker brethren will always try to put off as long as possible. . . . By adhering to this system [the poorer person] protected himself from being declassed. He was free then when he needed help to ask it of his richer fellow villager whom he had formerly helped. The latter could not refuse him on pain of being able to get no help on some future occasion when he again needed it in a hurry' (Van der Kolff, 1937, pp. 14, 26).

20. Even the plantation wages, however, were not the *full* money equivalent of the value of labour power as the entire plantation system was based on the plantation workers for a large part being dependent on the village and the village economy for the reproduction of themselves and their families.

21. See the various reports and surveys undertaken by the Ministry of Agriculture in connection with the land reform (U.U, no. 5, 1960) in the early 1960s.

22. We are not asserting a tendency of concentration unbroken by counter-forces. For one thing, commodity production in agriculture is still under-developed. Secondly, many of the factors in 'cyclical mobility' mentioned by Shanin, 1972, are operative.

Fei (1946) observes for traditional China that 'Land breeds no land'. When people obtain wealth and acquire land in a village 'the pressure of population will be borne upon them and soon wear them out—and after a few generations the big house will break down into a number of petty owners again' (p. 6). In his history of *Les paysans de Languedoc*, E. Le Roy Ladurie has termed the pre-capitalist and *Malthusian* 'grand cycle agraire' (in a regime of private property) as one, going from 'morcellement' to 'remembrement' and back again (Le Roy Ladurie, 1969).

For a case study of the change in the village productive relations and the effect on social differentiation, see Aass and Aass, 1974.

## REFERENCES

Aass, P. and Aass, S., 1975, *Communal Rights and Rural Change with Particular Reference to Harvesting Methods* (PRIO-publication 26–32), Oslo.

Aass, S., 1974, 'The Agrarian Question in Indonesia: Its Historical Background', Oslo (mimeo).

——1976, 'Chayanov and Java: A discussion of Chayanov's Micro- and Macro-Theory of Peasant Economy', Institute of Agricultural Economics, The Agricultural University of Norway (mimeo).

Agro-Economic Survey, Indonesia (A.E.S.), 1973, *Research Note no. 8*, Bogor.

Bergsma, W. B. (ed.), 1880 and 1896, 'Eindresume van het Onderzoek Naar de Rechten van den Indlander op den Grond in Java en Madura', vols. II and III, Batavia.

Bettelheim, C., 1971, 'Theoretical Comments', in Emmanuel, 1971.

Boeke, J. H., 1910, *Tropisch-koloniale staatshuiskunde*, Amsterdam.

——1953a, *Economie van Indonesia*, Haarlem.

——1953b, *Economics and Economic Policy of Dual Societies*, Haarlem.

Bloch, M., 1930, 'La lutte pour l'individualisme agraire dans la France du XVIIIᵉ siècle', in *Annales*.

Collective, 1971, *L'anthropologie—science des sociétés primitives?*, Paris.

Burger, H. D., 1970, *Sedjarah Ekonomis-Sosiologis Indonesia*, vol. II, Jakarta.

Burger, H. D. and Prajudi, 1962, *Sedjarah Ekonomis-Sosiologis Indonesia*, vol. I, Jakarta.

Chayanov, A. V., 1966, *The Theory of Peasant Economy*, ed. D. Thorner, B. Kerblay and R. E. F. Smith, Homewood, Ill.

——1974, *La organizacion de la unidad economica campesina*, with a pre- and postface by E. Archetti, Buenos Aires.

Day, C., 1904, *The Dutch in Java*, London.

Dobb, M., 1973, *Theories of Value and Distribution since Adam Smith*, Cambridge.

Emmanuel, A., 1971, *Unequal Exchange*, New York.

Fei Hsiao-tung, 1946, 'Peasantry and Gentry', *The American Journal of Sociology*, vol. LII.

Friedman, J., 1974, 'Tribes, States and Transformations', in *Marxist Analyses and Social Anthropology*, ed. M. Bloch, London.

Furnivall, J. S., 1937, *Netherlands India*, Cambridge.

Geertz, C., 1963, *Agricultural Involution*, Berkeley.

Godelier, M., 1966, *Rationalité et irrationalité en économie*, Paris.

——1971, 'L'anthropologie économique', in Collective, 1971.

——1973, *Horizon, trajets marxistes en anthropologie*, Paris.

Ter Haar, B., 1960, *Asas 2 dan susunan hukum-adat*, Jakarta.

Hardjosudarmo, 1970, *Masalah tanah di Indonesia*, Jogyakarta.

Hilton, R., 1974, 'Medieval Peasants: Any Lessons?', *Journal of Peasant Studies*, vol. I.

Hinton, W., 1968, *Fanshen*, New York.

Jacoby, E., 1961, *Agrarian Unrest in South-East Asia*, London.

Kahin, G. Mc T., 1952, *Nationalism and Revolution in Indonesia*, Ithaca.

Kartohadikoesoemo, 1953, *Desa*, Jogyakarta.

Kerblay, B., 'A. V. Chayanov: Life, Career, Works', in Chayanov, 1966.

——1971, 'Chayanov and the Theory of Peasantry as a Specific Type of Economy', in Shanin, 1971.

Van der Kolff, 1937, *The Historical Development of Labour Relationships in a Remote Corner of Java as They Apply to the Cultivation of Rice*.

——1929, 'European Influences on Native Agriculture', in Schrieke, 1929.

*Kolonial Verslag*

Le Roy Ladurie, E., 1969, *Les paysans de Languedoc*, Paris.

Lette, J. R., 1928, 'Proeve eener vergelijkende studie van het grondbezit in Russland, zoals dit zich heeft ontwikkeld tot de russische revolutie, en op Java', Leiden.

Lyon, M., 1970, *Bases of Conflict in Rural Java*, Berkeley.

Malinowski, B., 1921, 'The Primitive Economics of the Trobriand Islanders', *The Economic Journal*, vol. XXXI.

Mansvelt, 1924, 'Geschiedenis van de Nederlandsche Handelsmaatschappij', vol. II.

Marx, K., 1973, *Grundrisse* . . . , London.

Ministry of Agriculture, *Land reform. U. U Pokok agraria. U. U Bagi Hasil. Peraturan pendaftaran tanah.*

Postan, M. M., 1973, *Essays on Medieval Agriculture and General Problems of the Medieval Economy*, Cambridge.

Raffles, Sir Thomas Stanford, 1817, *The History of Java*, London.

Ricklefs, M. C., 1974, *Jogya under Sultan Mangkubumi 1749–1792*, London.

Rouffaer, G. P., 1918, *De agrarische rechttoestand der Indlandsche Bevolking op Java en Madoera*, Bijdragen tot de taal-, land- en volkenkunde, deel 74.

Sachs, I., 1966, 'La notion de surplus et son application aux économies primitives', *L'Homme*, vol. VI.

Scheltema, A. M. P. A, 1927–28, 'De ontwikkeling van de agrarische toestanden in Priangan', *Landbouw*.

Scheuer, W. Ph., n.d. [1880?], *Het Grondbezit in de Germansche Mark en de Javaansche Dessa.*

Schrieke, B., 1929, *The Effect of Western Influence on Native Civilization in the Malay Archipelago*, Batavia.

——1955 and 1957, *Indonesian Sociological Studies*, Haag.

Shanin, T., 1971, *Peasants and Peasant Societies*, London.

——1972, *The Awkward Class*, London.

Slametmuljana, 1967, *Per-undang Madjapahit*, Jakarta.

Smith, Adam, 1776, *The Wealth of Nations.*

Soedjatmoko *et al.*, 1965, *An Introduction to Indonesian Historiography*, Ithaca.

Sollewijn Gelpke, 1874, *De rijstkultuur in Italië en op Java*, den Haag.

——1877, *De padi-cultuur in de afdeeling Ngrowo 1875–1876.*

——1879 and 1880, *Naar aanledning van Staatsblad 1878, no. 110*, vols. I, II, and III.

Sorokin, A. P, Zimmerman, C. C. and Galpin, C. J. (eds.), 1931, *A Systematic Source Book in Rural Sociology*, Minneapolis.

Stahl, H. H., 1971, *Les anciennes communautés roumaines*, Paris.

Supomo, 1970, *Hubungan Individu dan masjarakat dalam hukum adat*, Jakarta.

Thorner, D., n.d., 'The Relevance of Economics to Production by Peasant Households' (mimeo).

——1966, 'Chayanov's Concept of Peasant Economy', in Chayanov, 1966.

——1971, 'Peasant Economy as a Category in Economic History', in Shanin (ed.), 1971.

——1973, *The Emergence of Capitalist Agriculture in India*, Dakar.

Tydeman, H. J., 1872, *Was het grondbezit op Java oorsprongelijk communaal of individueel?*, Arnhem.

*Verslag van den economischen toestand der indlandsche bevolking*, vol. I, 1924.

Vink, G. J., 1942, *De grondslagen van het indonesische landbouwsbedrijf*, Wageningen.

Van Vollenhoven, C., 1909, *Miskenningen van het adatrecht*, Leiden.

——1918, *Het adatrecht van Nederlandsch-Indië*, Leiden.

——1919, *De indoneziër en zijn grond*, Leiden.

——1928, *De ontdekking van het adatrecht*, Leiden.

Wolf, E., 1957, 'Closed Corporate Peasant Communities in Meso-America and Central Java', *South-Western Journal of Anthropology*, vol. XIII, no. 1.

——1966, *Peasants*, New Jersey.

# 14

# The People's Commune of Ma Lo

CHARLES BETTELHEIM

*Ecole des Hautes Etudes en Sciences Sociales*

I VISITED the People's Commune of Ma Lo in the outskirts of Shanghai on 17 September 1975. What follows is an attempt to sketch my most important observations and to give an account of conversations I had with the leaders of this commune.

Ma Lo was founded in 1958 through the combining of ten or so co-operative farms; it now comprises 7,020 households and around 28,000 members. It has 14 production brigades organized into 144 teams.

Collectively farmed fields cover a total area of 2,261 hectares, which gives a density of over 12 inhabitants to the hectare. This is about average for the region, because the climate here allows people to grow two or three crops a year. The main crops are cereals (mainly rice, followed by wheat, corn and barley). These take up half the total cultivated land. Cotton accounts for a further 35 per cent. Remaining crops include oilseeds, vegetables, fruit and water melons.

As everywhere in China, people breed pigs and fowl (especially white ducks, of which we saw large numbers around the canals). The commune also breeds cattle and sheep and runs a series of fish-breeding ponds.

Agriculture and stockbreeding account for only one half of total income. In addition to the small farm-servicing industries one finds on all communes nowadays, Ma Lo has a condiment and Soya sauce factory and a handicrafts centre part of whose output (mainly wickerwork articles) is exported. One of the brigades is specialized in construction.

The commune is more than just a basic production unit; it also runs everything concerning education, health, communications and transport. All children living on the Ma Lo Commune attend secondary school. More than 5,000 pupils in all are taught in 24 primary and secondary schools. (Before the Liberation there were 5 primary schools, with slightly over 600 pupils.)

In 1974, the commune set up its own evening University for young workers who have already completed their secondary education. These 'educated young' are not necessarily natives of the commune; a good many of them are young people from Shanghai, who came to work in the countryside following the Cultural Revolution[1] and who have subsequently settled here. They want to stay on in the commune to work, but they also want to continue their education. It was at their request, apparently, that the evening University was set up.

Where health facilities are concerned, the commune has its own hospital, one health unit per brigade and 'bare-foot doctors'[2] in each production team. Commune members pay 2 yuan annually to the medical co-operative, in return for which they receive practically free medical care. Thanks to health measures taken, bilharzia, which was still a scourge fifteen years ago, has virtually disappeared.

Ma Lo possesses both trucks and boats for transport purposes. During our visit to the fields and the pumping stations we were able to see just how rapidly mechanization has spread in recent years. All irrigation and drainage is now electrified. There are 57 irrigation and drainage stations using 223 pumps of different kinds. 'Now,' we were told, 'local threats of drought and flood have virtually been eliminated.'

Ploughing is almost entirely mechanized, while the planting out of seedlings is 70 per cent mechanized. The commune also possesses a certain number of harvesters, decorticators and chaffcutters. The tractor station, set up in 1958 with two small tractors, now operates 190 motor-cultivators and tractors of different sizes. 150 large and 4,000 small sprayers dust crops for plant-diseases. The immaculately cared-for cotton plantations yielded 682 kg of ginned cotton per hectare, while cereal yields came to 140 quintals (1 q. = 100 kg) per hectare—several crops are harvested yearly—compared to the regional average yield of 110 quintals.

We also visited the piggeries, the handicraft workshops with their attractive cane-work and the condiment factory. Over the traditional cup of tea and bowl of fruit we plied our hosts with questions to which they answered carefully, consulting their records whenever they were in any doubt as to a figure.

*Question*: You told us that agriculture and stockbreeding account for 50 per cent of the commune's income while the remaining 50 per cent comes from industry and handicrafts. What is the proportion of workers employed in each type of activity?

*Answer*: During the peak periods practically everyone goes out to work in the fields. During the rest of the year, 76 per cent of the population is engaged in agricultural work and the remaining 24 per cent in industry and handicrafts.

*Question*: Do the transport and construction brigades form a separate sector?

*Answer*: Everything not involving agriculture or livestock is classified with industry.

*Question*: How have your main output indices changed since the Liberation?

*Answer*: In 1949 we produced 3,360 kg of cereals per hectare; in 1957, 4,612 kg, and in 1974, 13,950 kg. Ginned cotton yields averaged 80 kg per hectare in 1949; 315 kg in 1957 and 682 kg in 1974. In 1949 we reared 4,176 pigs; 6,780 in 1957 and 45,305 in 1974.[3]

*Question*: Is the stockbreeding run by the different brigades or by the commune as a whole?

*Answer*: Our stockbreeding activities are divided into three levels: commune, brigade and team. There are 165 livestock units scattered throughout the commune. But breeding also goes on at family-level; virtually every household has a pig[4] and roughly 30 per cent of the commune's pigs are reared by the families themselves. Pig-feed is drawn from three different sources at both community and family levels: (*i*) cereals; (*ii*) water-plants and second or third category vegetables; (*iii*) rice and corn stalks. The commune supplies households with part of their fodder, which is ground in a unit belonging to the commune. People may also use cereals supplied by the commune or else grown on their own plot of land.

*Question*: How big is the household's plot of land?

*Answer*: That depends on the number of people in the household. Individual plots already existed at the time of the higher type of co-operatives. In 1962, the size of these plots was reviewed and fixed at 0.1 mou[5] per head. Commune members merely have the right to the produce grown on their plots, but they do not own them. The size of the plots has remained settled since 1962; it is no longer modified according to births or deaths in the family. Nowadays it is left to the family to decide on the dividing up of plots as and when new households are formed.

We have also distributed small plots to the 'educated young people' from Shanghai, and they use them to grow vegetables. That way they can eat their own produce and don't have to go to the market to buy vegetables.

*Question*: What is the income of commune members? How is it distributed?

*Answer*: Income shares are distributed once a year. In 1974 they averaged 200 yuan[6] per head, this amount being distributed in the form of cereals and money. In addition, commune members also dispose of the produce from their plots of land as they see fit: they do not have to buy vegetables. They own their own houses. All of which means they spend little. Each household has its own cereal stock and its own savings account.

Shares are distributed in the following way: Each year, a portion of the commune's income is set aside for production costs (seed-purchases, chemical fertilizer, insecticides and so on). Another portion is earmarked for management overheads: supplementary points to cadres who are prevented from engaging in full-time pro-duction work; purchases of paper and office supplies. We also deduct the farm tax, accumulation fund and welfare fund contributions. The remainder is divided up among the members of the commune according to the number of work-points they have obtained.

*Question*: Are work-points calculated by the team or by the brigade?

*Answer*: By the team. We are currently making arrangements to shift this task from the team to the brigade, and it looks as though the change is going to occur without difficulty.

*Question*: How are points attributed?

*Answer*: Every day, the score-keeper records the amount of work done by each member. Every month, or every two months, an assess-ment is made of the amount of work done by the members and points are attributed. Three factors enter into consideration: (*i*) attitude to work; (*ii*) degree of technical and professional skill; and (*iii*) intensity of work.

There are three grades. The first grade is worth 12 work-points per day, the second 10 and the third 8. At the end of the year these points are totted up. Some people manage to accumulate 4,000 points, others 3,000.

*Question*: Are the score-keeper's decisions discussed by the members?

*Answer*: The score-keeper is elected by the team-members, and he records their presence at work every day. But it is the members themselves who judge their fellows' attitude to work; when they meet to discuss the month's work they select a 'standard' member, whose work they assess at 10 points. The other members then say whether they reckon themselves to be worth more or less than this standard.

Of course, we practise criticism and self-criticism during these meetings. Chairman Mao says: 'Management too is socialist education.' We put the principle 'from each according to his abilities, to each according to his work' into practice. So, a person who doesn't work gets nothing. However, we have five guarantees for aged, weak or invalid members of the commune: food, clothing, heating, medical care and burial. We also have a relief system for people whose earnings are very low. Generally the aged are cared for by their children, but people who have no children or whose children are not earning enough are taken care of by the commune.

*Question*: What price do you put on the cereals distributed directly?

*Answer*: The price paid by the State. Unhusked rice is sold at 0.22 yuan per kg. As to the distribution of cereals, first of all, the commune sets aside whatever is needed for seeding, animal fodder and household consumption. In principle, the rest is then sold to the State. The plan makes provision for the amount to be sold to the State. Last year we were supposed to supply 1,300 tons, but in fact, after setting aside the different items mentioned above, we were left with 2,000 tons. That gave us a surplus of 700 tons, which we used in the three different ways provided for in such cases: (*i*) increased distribution to commune-members; (*ii*) commune reserve; and (*iii*) increased sales to the State. Last year we distributed 269 kg of unhusked rice to each member of the commune.

*Question*: How are the people working in industry paid?

*Answer*: On a points system also. On average they earn 7 per cent more than the agricultural workers.

*Question*: What percentage of output is taken up by production costs, management overheads and the welfare fund?

*Answer*: If we take last year as an example we find: production costs, 38.4 per cent; management overheads, 0.1 per cent; accumulation and welfare funds, 14.4 per cent; taxes: 3.9 per cent; and personal incomes: 43.1 per cent.

*Question*: You have said that last year per capita income came to 200 yuan. What was the comparable figure for earnings just before the Cultural Revolution?

*Answer* (after consultation of records): 154 yuan in 1965.

*Question*: How is the commune's production plan drawn up? What are your relations with the District?

*Answer*: The commune's plan forms part of the State plan. The higher level, i.e. the District, proposes a plan to the commune which takes into account historical conditions, the present situation and the commune's habits. The commune then calls a meeting of representatives of the members to discuss the draft plan. Our remarks and suggestions are returned to the District which is then responsible for revising the plan and subsequently supplying us with the final version. Around the end of August or early September everyone knows the draft plan.

*Question*: Did the commune suggest any major changes in the initial plan this year?

*Answer*: The changes we asked for were not very substantial. For example, they concerned the amount of land to be devoted to wheat and rice, since we grow these alternately.

*Question*: Does the plan cover handicrafts?

*Answer*: Yes. You have seen our bamboo objects. Some of these are made from locally grown materials, but the bigger bamboo stalks are supplied to us according to a plan.

*Question*: Who teaches at the evening university, and what are the courses given?

*Answer*: Classes are given by teachers who have come from the towns to work in the fields. Also, we have sent a number of young people from the commune to study at the Shanghai Teacher Training College and at the Polytechnic College, thus providing the commune with trained teachers. At the moment we have 40 youngsters attending the teacher-training college.

The evening university is divided into 3 sections: theoretical study; agricultural mechanization; and plants and crops.

We invite experienced older peasants to come and give classes. In this way, the evening university combines experimental and theoretical knowledge. The university teachers too have learned something from these experienced peasants.

*Question*: What does 'theoretical study' involve?

*Answer*: We have study-groups in Marxism-Leninism, groups studying Marx's *Capital* and others studying political economy. We still have a lot to learn and much to do. When we look back we see that we have progressed, but when we look ahead, we realize that we still have far to go.

This last remark, made by one of the leaders of the Ma Lo Commune, reflects a very widespread feeling in China: while much has been achieved, a great deal still remains to be done, both in the field of production and in the field of the transformation of social relations and of men themselves, which the Chinese hold to be fundamental.

## NOTES

1. Young people are expected to work as factory workers or farm labourers for roughly two years following completion of their secondary education. Afterwards, if their fellow workers consider them to be fit, they may pursue their higher education.
2. 'Bare-foot doctors' are members of the brigade, and they tend to be young. They first attend a 6-month training course at a hospital under instruction from a qualified doctor. They then return to the brigade where they treat minor disorders, sending the more serious cases to hospital; at the same time they continue to work as productive members of the brigade. They also gather medicinal plants. Each year, they attend a two- or three-month hospital course to further their skills, and some of them go on to train to become qualified doctors.
3. This figure is superior to the regional average (5 pigs per family). This high number of pigs partly explains the high yields since pig dung is an excellent fertilizer and enriches the soil. Some fields on which green fertilizer (milk-vetch) was grown ten or fifteen years ago now grow wheat, with pig dung replacing the green fertilizer. Obviously the increase in the use of chemical fertilizers and irrigation has also played a major role.
4. Which means that each family rears roughly 2 pigs yearly. The pig dung is purchased by the team.
5. 1 mou = 1/15 hectare.
6. The official yuan–franc exchange rate is 1 yuan: 2.40 F, but the purchasing power of the yuan for essentials (food, clothing) is substantially greater than this. Unhusked rice costs 0.22 yuan per kg. It costs between 2,000 and 3,000 yuan to build a house. Bicycles, wrist watches and radios, on the other hand, are rather expensive.

# III

# Reflections on Development

# 15

# Energy and the Village

IGNACY SACHS

*Ecole des Hautes Etudes en Sciences Sociales*

IN the days following Independence the energy choice seemed obvious: India should leap from the cowdung to the nuclear age. Rapid electrification was the cornerstone for the modernization programme that would free the rural masses from poverty and squalor. Experts and political leaders were agreed on the prominence to be given in development plans to boldly conceived multipurpose river dams. Left-wingers recalled Lenin's quip: Communism equals electricity plus soviets. For the World Bank experts, the doctrine promulgated among the 'underdeveloped' countries was: use public funds to build an infrastructure in order to attract foreign private capital which will take care of the rest.

Soon India was to discover the escalating costs of the big river projects, the longer-than-expected gestation periods, the disruptive ecological effects of some irrigation schemes. Rural electrification was a slow and expensive endeavour, not to speak of the fact that in many electrified villages, the poor could not afford to use power. Already in the late fifties, many writers claimed that a better strategy would have been to concentrate first on small irrigation projects (such as tube-wells) which yield quick results, while leaving the mammoth multipurpose valley schemes for a second phase. The unspelled assumption of that counter-option was, however, the availability of energy for the diesel or electric pumps without which the tube-wells cannot be operated. In India, as everywhere in the world, people counted upon a steady supply of cheap oil. Despite foreign exchange limitations, oil consumption increased at an annual average rate of 8.6 per cent between 1953–54 and 1970–71, as compared to the rates of 11.5 per cent for electricity and 3.4 per cent for coal (Sankar, 1977, p. 210). During those years, questions of alternative and non-commercial sources of energy did not attract much attention. Biogas digesters (machines to produce methane from cowdung) were exhibited at the Delhi International Agricultural Fair in 1958, but serious interest in these gobar plants dates only from the seventies.

Yet, as late as in 1970–71 all the sources of commercial energy combined were supplying only 33.6 per cent of India's total energy consumption, which is evaluated at 387.12 mtce (million tonnes of coal equivalent). The share of non-commercial energy was 46.3 per cent (116.62 mtce of firewood, 35.58 mtce of vegetable waste and 26.91 mtce of cowdung) and that of animate energy (provided by beasts and people) 20.1 per cent (Sankar, 1977, pp. 208–9). Intensity of commercial energy consumption in agriculture, calculated in mtce per Rs billion of GNP has increased from 0.01 in 1953–54 to 0.07 in 1970–71. But, surprisingly enough, intensity of all energy consumption has been rather steady in the agricultural sector: 0.88 mtce in 1953–54, 0.96 in 1965–66, 0.77 in 1970–71.

The so-called 'energy crisis' of 1973 (in reality, the catching up of oil prices with the general price level after 20 years of stability in an inflation-ridden world) may not be a crisis at all for energy-rich industrialized countries like the USA or the USSR, boosting investment in non-conventional sources of oil such as deep off-shore, and in nuclear energy, coal gasification, etc., while bringing windfall profits to the US-based oil multinationals. It poses serious commercial problems to energy-poor industrialized countries such as France or Japan, forcing them into acute competition for foreign markets. The formerly poor oil producers of the Third World now have a unique opportunity to use the oil income for development, provided they resist the temptation to buy real estate in the most fashionable quarters of Paris, London and New York and to spend billions of dollars on semi-obsolete weaponry.

In contrast, for poor energy-poor countries who depended on oil imports, 1973 is a watershed. It marks the end of a persistent illusion: the possibility of an imitative growth, which would reproduce the stages through which today's industrialized countries (be they capitalistic or socialistic) have previously passed and ultimately catch up in terms of the GNP. Imitative growth based on indiscriminate transfer of western technologies and patterns of life for the rich minority is, of course, still possible. But the social price to be paid in terms of inequality would be more formidable than ever under conditions of a resource squeeze. If scarce resources such as energy are used on a priority basis to cater directly or indirectly for the solvent demand of the rich urbanites, the needs of the rural poor will never be satisfied. Moreover, growth through inequality breeds environmental disruption at both ends of the social spectrum: the rich waste resources through conspicuous consumption; the poor overuse the scarce resources to which they have access. Small cultivators and tenants are the main agents of erosion, but the blame should be put on land tenures and not on their victims who are compelled to live from hand to mouth. Day-to-day struggle for survival is certainly not conducive to taking a long-term, enlightened view of resource husbanding.

In a sense, thus, 1973 is a positive landmark in the search for development alternatives. These alternatives emphasize the concepts of self-reliance (i.e. autonomy of decision-making and not autarchy), endogenous development as opposed to imitative growth, need-oriented approach geared to the eradication of poverty, harmony with environment instead of the present predatory resource-use, and grass-root participatory planning oriented towards concrete institutional change. Harmonizing socio-economic objectives with environmentally prudent resource management calls for a mix of appropriate technologies and institutional measures ensuring that the potential social benefits of such technologies will not be intercepted by privileged elites.

What are the implications of this new approach to energy problems for a country like India?

As T. L. Sankar has pointed out, a low-energy profile must be assumed in realistic long-term development strategies. This is not tantamount to scaling down the rate of growth of the economy, and still less that of popular consumption.

But the planners must free themselves from the tyranny of the commercial energy elasticity coefficient with respect to GNP. Far from being a structural parameter, this coefficient should be treated as a variable to be minimized by an array of measures which will be discussed below. An analogy can be made with the import coefficient, for a long time treated as a parameter while in fact it constitutes a major strategic variable of the planning game (Sachs, 1965).

It may appear paradoxical that in a poor country like India with a comparatively low level of per capita energy consumption, there is nonetheless considerable scope for energy conservation, i.e. measures designed to reduce the demand for energy while maintaining the level of services performed. Yet, as Makhijani has shown, using the research done at the Hyderabad Engineering Research Laboratory, the redesigning of the cooking stoves traditionally used in rural India could reduce fuel consumption by 25 per cent. Improved stoves could be manufactured at reasonable prices by local artisans. Further economies of fuel could be achieved by redesigning cooking pots and utilizing a simple technique of cooking under pressure by loading the lid of the pot with a suitable heavy object: a stone, a bowl of water or a pot of food to be warmed (Makhijani, 1976a, pp. 26–8, and Makhijani, 1976b). These proposals should not be dismissed lightly since cooking takes a substantial share of all the non-commercial energy expended in India. According to Revelle (1976, p. 972), the estimated energy use in cooking per calorie of food energy consumed was higher in India than the energy use per calorie in the United States for cooking and home refrigeration taken together. Makhijani goes on to insist that heating requirements could be somewhat decreased by adequate clothing, blankets, beds and houses. J. C. Kapur (1975, p. 28) claims somewhat optimistically that more than half of the energy employed in modern Indian agriculture to lift water and manufacture fertilizers could be saved by resorting to organic farming. Makhijani (1976a, p. 46) seems to be on safer ground when he stresses the advantages of drip irrigation using earthenware pots and pipes. Since this method uses much less water, it would drastically reduce the energy required for irrigation.

The two most important factors shaping the demand pattern for energy will be the balance of power between rural and urban India and the income distribution in village and town. While we cannot deal with these questions here, they cut to the heart of the discussion on alternative development strategies.

Let us now look at the supply side. A lot can be done to rationalize the uses of non-commercial and animal energies, so as ultimately to increase the total supply of energy to the countryside. Gobar plants (which extract methane from cowdung and organic waste and return a valuable compost to the soil) have been at last carefully studied, and their performance has been improved (Prasad and Reddy, 1974). But a family-size biogas plant for providing cooking fuel is simply beyond the reach of most villagers. Only 12 million rural households in India are reported to have the four to five bovines which would be required (Sankar, p. 242 and Makhijani, 1976a, p. 25). Accordingly, the present crash programme to build 100,000 family biogas plants per year will, at best, benefit 1 to 2 per cent of the rural population. It will thus become one more factor of differentiating well-off *maliks* and the 'gentlemen farmers' described by Daniel Thorner (Thorner, 1976, pp. 2 and 15) from the rural poor. As for collective biogas plants, they pose difficult social and institutional problems which we will discuss in the next section.

The bovine population should be kept at the present level or slightly expanded, because of the multiple services it renders to the peasant economy. As K. N. Raj has put it, cattle, as an economic good, plays many roles, perhaps more than any other economic good. It is a consumer good (C-good) because it is eaten; it is a machine for producing consumer goods (I-good) because it yields milk; it is an intermediate good (R-good) because it can be used for traction (apart from the manure made available as a by-product); it is also a mother machine (M-good) because cattle produce cattle (Raj, 1967, quoted by Sankar, 1977, pp. 238–40). The fact is that, despite the received opinion regularly repeated by superficial foreign observers, Indian cattle do not compete with people for agricultural land; they are fed primarily on inedible by-products of human food crops (rice straw and husk, wheat bran, etc.). As Marvin Harris has put it, 'the shameless truth about the sacred cow is that she is an indefatigable scavenger' (Harris, 1975, p. 24). The same author quotes figures to the effect that, contrary to expectations, studies of energy costs and energy yields show more efficient use of cattle in India than in the United States. The gross energy efficiency of cattle (defined as the total of useful calories produced per year divided by the total calories consumed during the same period) was 17 per cent in India, as compared to less than 4 per cent for beef cattle in the United States. These figures reflect not a high productivity of Indian animal husbandry, but a wasteful luxury-style product utilization on the American side.

As the output of food crops grows, the average diet of Indian bovines is likely to improve and their contribution as draft animals and producers of milk and dung will increase. In contrast to the popular view in the West that the large cattle population in India is a liability, recent Indian studies insist on the important role of cattle in alternative energy strategies.

Another surprising conclusion arising from current research is the lasting role foreseen for firewood, charcoal and biomass liquid and gaseous fuels. This view contrasts sharply with the superficial conservationist position that whatever is left of Indian forest should be preserved in amber and defended jealously against any further exploitation. Derek Earl has shown that the unused increment of 3,500 million tons of coal equivalent in tropical developing countries amounts to 51 per cent of the world's forest increment and is more than three times their present total energy consumption. Placing only 10 per cent of rain and deciduous forests in Africa and Asia under ecologically sound management would be sufficient to produce enough fuel from low quality wood and wood wastes to sustain a 5 per cent annual growth rate in total energy consumption in the developing countries for more than two decades. According to Earl's estimates, the conversion of 100 thousand hectares of tropical forests (assuming an average yield of 85 tons per hectare) each year would provide firewood equivalent to 4.2 million tons of coal and jobs for 42,500 men. If the fuelwood were to be converted into charcoal the manpower input would be even greater (Derek Earl, 1976). Though less optimistic, Indian authors also emphasize the under-utilization of Indian forests and the possibility of increasing significantly the present yields over a long period on the basis of an intensive reforestation programme.

With proper silvicultural practices the Indian forests should yield about 240 million tons of wood, out of which 180 million would be available as firewood. The 'Report of the Fuel Policy Committee' (quoted by Sankar, 1977) estimates that 15 million acres of forests planted with quick-growing species could provide a regular yield of 90 million tons of wood per year, while the average exploitation rate of fuel and industrial wood in India has been only 0.3 ton per hectare. Table I reproduces alternative scenarios for 1990–91 prepared by Sankar and exploring the 'forest fuel' and two 'animal resource' options.

Considerable scope seems to exist furthermore for non-conventional energies like solar energy (other than through the use of the biomass) and windpower even if we limit our consideration to short and medium term technological options. Kapur (1975) rightly emphasizes the possible uses of solar energy for crop drying and probably also fish drying. Appropriate technologies are already available for space and water heating and cooking. They may be too expensive for individual use, but could find collective applications in hospitals, canteens, schools, military barracks, etc. Research is going on in

TABLE I

ALTERNATIVE PATTERNS OF ENERGY CONSUMPTION IN INDIA, 1990–91 (mtce)

| | Based on historical trends | As recommended by 'FPC coal option' | As per 'forest fuel option' | As per 'animal resource option' case I | As per 'animal resource option' case II |
|---|---|---|---|---|---|
| Coal | 188 | 202 | 165 | 172 | 172 |
| Oil | 122 | 89 | 69 | 70 | 70 |
| Electricity | 315 | 326 | 326 | 326 | 326 |
| Firewood | 116 | 116 | 173 | 116 | 25 |
| Dung cake | 21 | 21 | 21 | 51 | 142 |
| Vegetable waste | 44 | 44 | 44 | 44 | 44 |
| Animal power | 76 | 76 | 76 | 95 | 95 |
| Total | 882 | 874 | 874 | 874 | 874 |

the Birla Institute of Technology and Science (Rao and Rao) to produce a cheap solar water pump for irrigation. Windmills are being redesigned so as to improve their efficiency. The 1976 Indian Science Congress considered the possibilities of making windmills from inexpensive local materials. Such windmills could perhaps be linked to existing means of drawing water, such as Persian wheels (Indian Science Congress Association, 1976, p. 58).

The danger, however, is that appropriate technologies will end up by being yet another version of the 'technological fix'. We can safely assume that the technologies as such will be improved and made available to produce methane from organic waste, use solar energy for specific purposes and build relatively efficient and cheap windmills to lift water. But these technologies alone will not change the situation of the Indian poor, so long as they do not fit into a strategy of social and institutional change. The 200 million Indians below the poverty line are so poor that the cheapest technology is beyond their reach (Hanlon, 1977). Even if firewood is produced in sufficient quantity, they cannot afford to buy it (although in 1973, according to Derek Earl, the price of fuelwood in India was 9 times cheaper than electricity per calorie).

There is little point, therefore, in designing elegant supply systems based on a skilful combination of biomass, organic waste, solar and wind energy without addressing oneself to the whole question of technological change in a peasant society.

To obtain a sufficient supply of energy is a major daily task for the household economy. Gathering fuelwood (and cowdung) may involve from 50 to 200 or more workdays per family per year according to Makhijani (1976b, p. 21) or else costs of 20 to 50 dollars per family. Revelle (1976, p. 971 footnote) estimates that collecting wood, straw and dung for fuel may take perhaps 2 hours per day and 600 kcal per domestic worker, to which one should add about 45 minutes for fetching water, 2 hours for procuring and preparing food, cooking, washing, carrying cooked food to farm workers, and another additional 2 hours for other household activities. All these activities are performed by the family work force and do not entail any monetary expenditure. What would be the consequences of a massive shift to gobar-gas plants?

We have already seen that individual plants can at best increase the privileges of the top one per cent. If cowdung is purchased and the methane produced from it sold, there are good chances that the poor will lose on all fronts. They may be forced to sell their cowdung cheap, and almost certainly will be unable to buy much of the methane. Under the present conditions of the Indian rural scene, a move from the household sector to the market of an essential item of basic need satisfaction might give an additional opportunity to the local elite to increase their grip over the poor.

An obvious, but not entirely satisfactory, way of obviating this undesirable social effect would be to organize the energy supply on a co-operative basis. Hence the ingenious scheme of village public utility proposed by Makhijani (1976a) and described in the Appendix. This proposal goes far beyond the energy supply problem. Still it is open at least to two doubts. How is this scheme to be reconciled with the present land tenure patterns and relations of production outside the communal plot? What are the built-in guarantees against the control of the village public utility by the local elite, as has happened in many water management schemes and rural co-operatives so acutely analysed by Daniel Thorner (Daniel and Alice Thorner, 1962, pp. 14–20 and Thorner, 1964).

Even if we make due allowance for the impact of Gandhi's constructive and generous ideas on the organization of the rural life, it is hard to believe that Indian villages will be collectivized simply in order to improve energy production, water supply and sanitation.

The agrarian prospect of India depends now as ever on institutional change. The agrarian problem to which Daniel Thorner devoted his talent and a lifelong study looms large behind the present day discussions of appropriate technologies and energy profiles.

## APPENDIX

### The Village Public Utility
*as proposed by A. Makhijani (1976a)*

The village public utility would be responsible for the physical and fiscal integrity of the facilities in its charge and ensure that all villagers have access to its services. This utility would be managed by an elected committee whose members would be individually subject to recall. Village-wide meetings would be called to which accounts and reports of progress would be submitted every two months. The accounts would be kept by the committee and they would be public. A supervisory committee (also elected) would handle grievances and be responsible for auditing. Overlapping membership between the managing and supervisory committee would be prohibited—i.e. no family member of a person on one committee could be a member of the other. Except for *ex officio* members, all committee members would be from the village.

The funds for the projects could come from four sources:
1. Individual villagers;
2. Existing community funds (some villages have them);
3. Voluntary labour;
4. Loans from sources outside the village (banks, governmental rural development agencies, etc.).

Inevitably, in poor communities most of the seed money must come from sources outside the communities, as a loan, Often poor people do not eat enough to be able to donate labour: they must be paid for it so that they can at least compensate, immediately, for the additional food intake required as a result of working. The money available in village community funds is likely to be a small fraction of that needed. However, its effect in mobilizing and maintaining the community's involvement and interest in the village utility can be great.

Plans for water supply, fuel supply, cooking stove supply and installation, sanitation and composting would be prepared by the managing committee with the help of the (outside) development agency. Such plans would be modified or approved by the village as a whole.

Payment by the people for the goods and services supplied by the utility would be in the form of labour. The utility would acquire a small parcel of land on which the labour would be used. The compost produced from the sanitation facilities would be applied to the utility land, or sold directly, or some combination of the two. The utility could repay the loan in cash obtained from the sale of compost and produce, or directly in crops produced on the utility land. The facilities would be maintained almost exclusively by loan labour. A fund would be set up for acquisition of parts or replacement of worn-out equipment.

The utility would also provide the village with fuels. A village of 1,000 people (200 families) would need 200 tons of fuelwood each year for use in cooking. This assumes that cooking fuel needs would be 50 to 60 per cent of current levels due to the use of efficient stoves and cooking methods. A village woodlot would require 10 hectares land to supply this quantity of wood with a renewable yield of 20 tons per hectare per year. A substantial portion of this land requirement could be met by lining the village streets, approach roads, windbreak areas, etc., with trees. The rest of the land could be obtained from the village commons or some other piece of land not now being used for cultivation. Management of the woodlot by the villagers themselves would considerably reduce illegal felling of trees.

Establishing a woodlot to meet the entire fuelwood needs at the rate of 200 kilograms per year per capita will be a difficult matter in areas such as the Gangetic plain where little land is available for such a purpose. Every effort must be made in such cases to use stoves and cooking methods that are as efficient as possible and to meet the fuel needs from the trees established on village streets, etc. Such efforts will pay for themselves in terms of the increased food production that will result from using surplus manure as a fertilizer instead of fuel.

While the woodlot is being established, the village fuelwood supply could be organized by the community. This would not require any additional investments. A store of wood for the entire village for several months could be harvested during the off-peak labour periods. Since installation of efficient stoves would be one of the first actions of the villagers and the utility, the amount of labour expended in gathering fuelwood would be substantially reduced. Organizing the fuelwood for every village in the area in this manner would allow the integration of regional afforestation and reforestation schemes with people's fuel needs.

Coppicing—the practice of cutting trees in short rotation and allowing the sprouts to reappear from the stumps of the trees—can significantly reduce the time of maturation of a village woodlot. While full growth of trees may take ten or more years, coppicing could enable harvesting in five years or less. Coppicing can increase yields because certain tree varieties grow very much faster in the first years than later on. The tree varieties must, of course, be properly selected (generally, broad-leaved trees). Adequate steps must be taken in time to replant since repeated coppicing can cause a stand to deteriorate.

I have calculated the tentative economics as well as a loan repayment schedule for a village public utility for an Indian village of 1,000 people (200 families). My figures show that for an initial investment of about $12 per capita the utility could be generating substantial funds of its own, having paid off the entire starting loan, within five years. Each family would obtain water for household use, fuelwood, a stove, and the use of community sanitation facilities in return for 30 to 35 days work (6 to 7 days per capita). Note that this is considerably less than the amount of labour which the poor spend today on gathering fuelwood alone. This work would be directed towards producing one or two crops per year on the three hectares of agricultural land acquired by the utility (three hectares is of the order of 1 per cent of the cultivated land in a typical Indian village of 1,000 people), maintaining and managing the facilities of the utility, and establishing and maintaining the village woodlot.

## REFERENCES

Earl, D., 1976, 'A Renewable source of fuel', *Science and Public Policy*, London, vol. III, no. 6 (December), pp. 497–503.

Hanlon, J., 1977, 'What Prospects for Appropriate Technology', *New Scientist*, London, no. 1055 (9 June), pp. 594–5.

Harris, M., 1975, *Cows, Pigs, Wars and Witches*, Vintage Books, New York.

Indian Science Congress Association, 1976 (Sixty-third session), *Science and Integrated Rural Development—An Agenda for Action*, Calcutta.

Kapur, J. C., 1975, *India in the year 2000*, India International Centre, New Delhi.

Makhijani, A., 1976a, *Energy Policy for the Rural Third World*, International Institute for Environment and Development, London.

Makhijani, A., 1976b, 'Solar Energy and Rural Development for the Third World', *Bulletin of the Atomic Scientist*, Chicago, Illinois, vol. XXXII, no. 6 (June), pp. 14–24.

Prasad, C. R., Prasad, K. K. and Reddy, A. K. N., 1974, 'Bio-gas Plants: Prospects, Problems and Tasks', *Economic and Political Weekly*, Bombay, vol. IX, no. 33–34, Special Number.

Raj, K. N., 1967, 'Investment in Livestock in Agrarian Economies: A Theoretical and Empirical Analysis' (mimeo).

Rao, D. P. and Rao, K. S., 1975, 'Solar Water Pump for Lift Irrigation', Pilani (mimeo).

Revelle, R., 1976, 'Energy Use in Rural India', *Science*, Washington, D.C., vol. 192, no. 4243 (June 4), pp. 969–75.

Sankar, T. L., 1977, 'Alternative Development Strategies with a Low-energy Profile for a Low GNP/capita Energy-poor Country: the case of India', in Leon Lindberg (ed.), *The Energy Syndrome*, Lexington Books, Lexington, pp. 205–46.

Sachs, I., 1965, *Foreign Trade and Economic Development of Underdeveloped Countries*, Asia Publishing House, Bombay.

Thorner, A and D., 1962, *Land and Labour in India*, Asia Publishing House, Bombay.

Thorner, D., 1964, *Agricultural Cooperatives in India: A Field Report*, Asia Publishing House, Bombay.

Thorner, D., 1976, *The Agrarian Prospect in India*, second edition, Allied Publishers, Bombay.

*What now?*, 1975, The 1975 Dag Hammarskjold Report on Development and International Cooperation prepared on the occasion of the Seventh Special Session of the United Nations General Assembly, Uppsala.

# 16

# Agriculture and the Birth of Classical Economics: The *Docteur* Quesnay

## LOUIS DUMONT
*Ecole des Hautes Etudes en Sciences Sociales*

THE *Docteur* Quesnay and the movement that issued from him under the name of Physiocracy and was influential in France for some ten years (1760–70), represent for the student of economic thought a critical stage in the transition from tradition to modernity. Quesnay's influence was one of the ingredients that went into the making of Adam Smith's *Wealth of Nations* (see E. Cannan in his introductions to Smith, 1896 and 1904).

The following is part of a book in which I study the genesis of economic thought against the background of the contrast between modern and non-modern, or traditional, ideas and values. Actually the few simple concepts I use to express this contrast have emerged from a sociological study of India. They must be briefly introduced here before being applied to the understanding of Quesnay's history of economic thought.

First comes the contrast between individualism and holism to designate systems of ideas and values centred respectively on the individual human being (the modern case) and on the society as a whole (the traditional case) (Dumont, 1967, § 3). Second, and of central import for the present topic, is the vast and complex difference in the conception of wealth, itself part of a more general contrast. I posit that there is a basic difference in the ordering of human relations (or relationships, but I prefer the more abstract term) between modern and non-modern civilizations (or, indifferently, here 'traditional societies'). Relations between men have always and everywhere been more highly valued than relations between men and things. Relations to things were subordinated to relations between men. The moderns have reversed that primacy, and the rise of economic thought is an aspect of that revolution, as is the emergence of our category of 'wealth'. In traditional societies, what we call 'wealth' is found under two segregated forms. Landed (immovable) wealth, or what is called in English *real* estate, was associated with power over men, and as such highly valued. Movable wealth (money, chattels) was disparaged or subordinated as a mere relation of men to things. The modern revolution has consisted of: (1) breaking the link between immovable wealth and power over men; (2) emancipating and enfranchising movable wealth, which thus became 'wealth' *par excellence*, while immovable wealth became an inferior aspect of 'wealth' (as less mobile, etc.). Thus did 'wealth' emerge as a major idea and value. It should be clear from its genesis that this category embodies the primacy of the relation of men to things as against the relations between men.

The *Docteur* Quesnay confronts us with a paradox.[1] By common consent, economic thought made a great step forward through the genius of this man. Yet he lived, not in the economically most progressive country of the age, England, but in France, then relatively less advanced. The fact can be partially explained if one thinks of the intense interchange between the two countries and insists, as does Schumpeter in his *History of Economic Analysis*, on the continuity from Petty through Cantillon to Quesnay. But the paradox is found again in the content of the doctrine: industry and trade are disparaged, and agriculture is extolled. The emphasis is on capitalist agriculture, and the farming entrepreneur is the central figure. As Marx remarked as early as in the 1844 'Manuscripts', there is in Quesnay a combination of feudal survivals and of modern or bourgeois features:

. . . Physiocracy is in a direct sense the *economic* decomposition of feudal property, but for this reason it is equally directly the *economic transformation*, the re-establishment, of this same feudal property, with the difference that its language is no longer feudal but economic. All wealth is reduced to *land* and *cultivation* (agriculture). 'Manuscripts', 2nd. MS.; trans., p. 121)

Is this a matter of chance? Quite the contrary. I shall argue that there is a necessary relation between the traditional elements in Quesnay and his basic contribution. Marx and Schumpeter are in almost complete agreement in identifying the central merit of Quesnay. Marx stresses and praises Quesnay's famous and puzzling chart, the 'Tableau Economique'. Here is an extract from his notes for the fourth book of *Capital* (*Theorien über den Mehrwert*):

... this attempt: to represent the whole process of production of capital as process of reproduction, and circulation as the mere form of this process of reproduction, the circulation of money only as an element (*Moment*) of the circulation of capital; to encompass within this process of reproduction the origin of revenue, the exchange between capital and revenue, the relation between reproductive consumption and definitive consumption; to encompass within the circulation of capital the circulation between consumers and producers (actually between capital and revenue); finally to represent the circulation between the two great divisions of productive labour, production of raw materials and industry, as moments in the process of reproduction; to group all that, in the second third [Marx: 'first third'] of the eighteenth century, in the infancy of political economy, in a table of five lines with six points of departure or arrival, this was an extremely genial idea, no doubt the most genial idea that economics has put to its account until now. (Translated from *Werke*, vol. XXVI, i, p. 319)[2]

As for Schumpeter, he distinctly separates Quesnay's general theory from the 'Tableau' itself (1954, p. 239). But after all, from the present point of view, this is only a minor difference, for both authors agree that Quesnay has given the first idea of the economic domain as a consistent whole, as a whole made up of interrelated parts. With him for the first time the economic viewpoint brought forth, not a series of more or less disconnected observations, correlations or aspects, as in Mercantilism, but the idea of an ordered whole, of a system of logical interrelations extending to the whole domain. Schumpeter expresses this precisely when he credits Quesnay with the first 'explicit formulation of interdependence'.[3] He adds that Quesnay gave a 'picture' (the 'Tableau') of the 'fundamental problem' of economics—(static) equilibrium between interdependent quantities —where only much later Walras was to give a set of equations (Schumpeter, 1954, pp. 242–3).

Now, my contention is that such a holistic idea could not be reached initially from within the economic point of view itself— in so far as the latter can be said to have existed before Quesnay's invention—but had to be derived from outside it; it had to result, so to speak, from the *projection on the economic plane of the general conception of the universe as an ordered whole*. This is what happened with Quesnay, and it accounts for the presence in his thought of a very marked traditional component, which I shall briefly stress.[4]

18

What Quesnay explicitly presents is a particular development of 'Natural Law' theory—a general socio-political theory *with strong emphasis on the economic aspects*, which are constructed into a logical system. One could almost say that Quesnay describes the old society from a new viewpoint: his sociology-cum-politics is quite traditional in many important respects, and within it he fits a properly economic system that is almost modern.

The traditional aspect is obvious, barefaced, when the stability of China is given as a model and as an argument against the historical relativism of a Montesquieu: there are eternal, metaphysical principles; they need only to be recognized. And, first of all, as in traditional systems in general, (real) wealth consists of land as distinguished from movables, and is inseparable from power over men.[5] More properly, land is the only source of (real) wealth, and Quesnay's landowners, 'les propriétaires', are at the same time in charge of the political functions, including the administration of justice, with all the responsibilities and liabilities that it entails: the taxes should fall exclusively upon their income. Only agriculture is 'national', trade in particular is conceived as an international, that is to say anti-national, interest. The monarch is something like the first among the landowners, having a right of co-ownership (an eminent right) in the land; the taxes he levies are a revenue attached to that right. He is properly a sovereign (priest together with ruler) and the Physiocrats are not afraid of calling the political regime they support a 'legal despotism'. It is true that Natural Law rules supreme over all. The State should not interfere with it, and it should make Natural Law the object of compulsory public education (Quesnay, 1958, vol. II, p. 741; Weulersse, 1910, vol. II, pp. 65–6).

Within this polity, wealth circulates in a regular and harmonious fashion. The only source of it is nature, or rather the soil aided by human activity and initiative. The basic condition of this economic order within the political order is private property, the corollary of which is freedom as the absence of any interference or regulation, whether direct or indirect, on the part of the State. We find combined here holism and individualism: holism in its traditional religious-and-political form, individualism on the economic level. As a distant but striking parallel, one would think of Leibniz's metaphysics. But my present concern is to insist on the fact that economics reaches the status of a logically consistent system though propped up by a strictly traditional social theory or put in the framework of a holistic view.

Two aspects of this relation may be distinguished: on the one hand the State, the kingdom, affords the physical as well as moral boundaries of the system: the circulation of the annual produce that is represented in Quesnay's 'Tableau' is, in its utmost extension, a picture of the circulation of nourishment through the whole kingdom, as blood circulates in the human body. On the other hand, the Natural Law, moral as well as physical, which Quesnay thinks he is expounding, is that of the order of the world as preordained by God. Thus, the economic order, or system, depends both upon the body politic and upon a general teleological orientation bearing on all aspects of human life. Here I may seem to contradict Schumpeter's findings, but the difference is in the point of view. Schumpeter insists (1954, p. 233) that Quesnay's theological beliefs do not enter into his *analysis*, which is thus, according to him, scientific. I am not disputing this statement, I am only observing that the analysis does not deliver its own framework, and I am tracing the origin in Quesnay of this framework.

It is clear under the circumstances that on the one hand the domain can be thought of as a whole, while on the other hand it is not autonomous. This is in conformity with Quesnay's conception of order as expressed in his definition of Natural Law:

Natural laws are either physical or moral. We understand here by physical law *the regular course* (cours réglé) *of any physical event of the natural order obviously the most advantageous to the human genus.* We understand here by moral law *the rule* (la règle) *of any human action of the moral order in conformity with the physical order obviously the most advantageous to the human genus.* These laws together form what is called *the natural law.* (Translated from 'Droit Naturel', chapter 5, Quesnay, 1958, vol. II, p. 740)

As Schumpeter observes, we are here in line with the scholastics: within the teleological order man as a free agent is not separated from nature, and his assent is necessary for the order to extend to his affairs. Only if men act in accordance with Natural Law will the order be realized. The 'Tableau' depicts an ideal, and Quesnay traces the deplorable consequences of any departure from its requirements. The right policy on the part of the State is a necessary condition of the economic order. This is a point which Adam Smith could not leave unnoticed: he argued, in substance, that the economic order was more independent of human decisions than Quesnay had made it (1904, vol. II, p. 172). It must be added, though, that according to Quesnay the right policy of the State is by and large one of abstention. The State has few positive duties: external protection, the maintenance of a network of communications, the care of the poor, the levy of its income exclusively from land, and education of the people in Natural Law. Yet again, as Schumpeter observes, Quesnay was concerned with reforming the bad practices of the State, and that meant that the State had to act upon itself in order to become non-active in economic matters.

On the whole, here is our paradox: the consistency of the domain is 'explicitly formulated' for the first time, not by someone who separates it from politics, morality, and religion, but, on the contrary, by a man who argues from the over-all consistency of the world, including human or moral affairs, to the *conditional* consistency of the particular domain. And I may add: not by starting from the individual agent and arguing in terms of cause and effect, but by starting from a teleological order including and warranting the freedom of the individual agent. No doubt Adam Smith went further than that.

There is perhaps one more fundamental feature that classical economics owes to Quesnay, which Marx underlines and which Schumpeter does not ignore. To paraphrase Marx very briefly: it was essential to separate production from circulation etc., for no progress was possible as long as 'surplus value' could be searched for in the sphere of circulation and was not considered independently from circulation. To begin with, it was possible to do so only in agriculture, where 'surplus value' is clearly visible apart from circulation, and this is one reason why agriculture is prominent in the place where this separation was made for the first time (*Mehrwert*, French translation, vol. I, p. 44 ff).

It is a fact that Quesnay neatly separates two processes: the *production* (or reproduction) of the 'annual produce', which includes, over and above the equivalent of the total investment, the 'net produce' which in Marx's view can be roughly equated with what he calls 'surplus value'. Then, in a second stage, Quesnay studies, in his 'Tableau', the circulation or *distribution* of the produce among his three classes of economic agents. A similar dichotomy, it is well known, rules in Smith, Ricardo and Marx, and the classics in general. Schumpeter at bottom deplores it, but he does not explain its prevalence, even if we may gather from him some hints for gaining some understanding of it. Quesnay represents here, actually, an initial step in a process that is easier to grasp in its later development, but with hindsight we can characterize Quesnay's step.

Opposing the mercantilist view, it was essential for Quesnay to state what constituted 'real wealth', or rather—Schumpeter has the word—the 'creation' of real wealth. He saw it in agriculture, and called it 'production', and he called therefore all other pursuits unproductive or 'sterile'. In doing so, he was making a value judgement (to which we shall return), and he was also modifying a tenet of Cantillon, and of Petty before him, who had isolated land and labour as the twin sources of wealth. Where they had thought of a 'par' or a rate of correspondence between the two factors making it possible to express both in terms of one of them, i.e. land, Quesnay hierarchized them: land was the productive factor, the natural fertility of the soil alone accounted for the increase of real wealth from seed to harvest, and human labour and initiative were merely necessary adjuvants in the process, in keeping with the idea of Natural Law as natural-cum-moral law. On the whole, the economic process was essentially a process of increase in wealth, that is, *production*, and the secret of this increase lay in land, or the set of natural powers: a single, self-sufficient entity enshrined the *rationale* of the economic process. Economy was production, and production was land. Through a quite traditional hierarchization—nature commands morality, land commands labour—we have here the first step in the identification of the economy with a single essential factor, a *causa sui*, a substance. The subsequent development leaves no doubt on the point. To anticipate, I can adduce one of the passages of Marx where the word 'substance' is used in that connection. It shows that, for him at any rate, the process was of the kind I suggest. He says that with the Physiocrats surplus value does not yet take its proper form because 'they have not yet reduced *value* itself to its simple substance (*einfache Substanz*)', that is, labour (*Mehrwert*, from *Werke*, vol. XXVI, i, p. 14).

To Quesnay's characteristic combination of economic individualism encompassed within traditional holism corresponds his peculiar conception of economic value. According to Schumpeter, Quesnay, who defines economy as the greatest satisfaction for the smallest expense, has a psychological view of value as linked with enjoyment and wants, which will remain alive in the French tradition, with J. B. Say as its leading exponent. Let us look at it more closely. As others, Quesnay distinguishes between value in use and value in exchange:

air and water have use value, they are 'goods' (*des biens*), they have no exchange value and therefore they are not commodities, or wealth (*des richesses*) (Quesnay, 1958, vol. II, p. 526). What is special to Quesnay is the relation he posits between the two kinds of value. At bottom lies a value judgement: the essential commodities, the only 'real wealth', are those provided by nature for the subsistence of men, with corn, the staple, as the prototype. For a kingdom to be prosperous, foodstuffs, and corn in the first place, must be abundant, and their production must be rewarded, that is to say that their price, or exchange value, must be high (ibid. pp. 690–1, 972; cf. pp. 661–2: the amount of the State tax is proportional to the exchange value of corn). 'Low value (*non-valeur*) with plenty is not wealth. Dearness with scarcity is misery. Plenty with dearness is opulence' ('Grains', ibid. p. 507, and Maxim XVIII, p. 954).

Let us observe what Quesnay does here. He has recognized that some of the commodities, that is some of the goods having exchange value, have a *superior use value*. They are the commodities essential to the subsistence of men. From this 'physical law' he passes quite naturally to the corresponding 'moral law', namely that this superior use value must be expressed in a high exchange value. At the same time he relies on observation: there is a value, or more exactly a price, a 'fundamental price' of the commodity (ibid. p. 529), below which its production would be abandoned. Therefore, it is salutary that wheat should maintain a price high enough to encourage its abundance. That is its 'good price' (ibid. p. 508 ff)—an expression that transcribes Quesnay's normative orientation, illustrating the fact that for him economic values are dependent on absolute values. Observation and Natural Law converge, and in this particular sense use value commands exchange value, which is a mere corollary of it. There is thus in Quesnay, properly speaking, no theory of exchange value as such. The relation will be reversed in the classics: Adam Smith, for instance, will get rid of use value in a few words, as a mere condition of exchange value, and will reserve his attention for the latter. In Marx's terms, he will 'reduce value to its simple substance'.

There is another facet to the relation between Quesnay and the classical economists, which does not seem to have been much noticed and which is interesting from the present point of view. At first sight, Quesnay is aberrant in his judgement bearing on industry and trade but on closer inspection this obvious difference reveals a similarity. In Quesnay's theory, only agriculture—plus the extraction of raw materials from the earth—is productive. He distinguishes three main classes of economic agents, namely the 'landowning class' or 'sovereign class', the 'productive class' made up of the farmers, and what he called 'the sterile class' comprising all the people engaged in non-agricultural pursuits. Industry and trade are not useless, they are useful within limits, but they add nothing to the sum of wealth issuing from nature. Industrial labour in particular only incorporates in the product the value used up by the worker, or necessary to maintain or reproduce him. It results only in a transfer, not in a creation of value. This was so already in Cantillon, and in Quesnay it accords with his conception of value, or real wealth. Yet it is a striking, indeed a puzzling feature, and it remains, all in all, unexplained. It is of course not, in its arbitrary demoting of a part of the economy, a mere traditional feature. It cannot be explained simply by the contemporary state of France, for there too industry was developing. Nor can it be explained as just a reaction against the efforts of the State to bolster industry and industrial exports at the cost of agriculture, that is against a mercantilist policy of long standing—although such was certainly a preoccupation of Quesnay. It is characteristic that Turgot, a great administrator and an impeccable, if concise, economist in Schumpeter's judgment, while not sharing the Physiocrats' hostility to industry, yet adhered to their thesis regarding the creation of wealth ('la formation des richesses') and was content to replace the offensive word 'sterile' by speaking of 'the retributed class' ('la classe stipendiée') for all those who derived only indirectly their livelihood from agriculture. Is it enough to see in the feature in question, as Marx apparently did, an extreme consequence of Quesnay's feudal or traditional conception, and a sign of the immaturity of his theory of value?

I see in that point of Quesnay's doctrine a manifestation of a built-in constraint of high historical and ideological significance which is manifested in all the classics as well, albeit in a quite opposite form. All along classical economics there runs like a red thread an incompatibility between land ownership and land rent on the one hand, and industrial capital and profit on the other. We may say that it is a matter of either/or: either the one or the other element is acknowledged and built upon, and the opposite element is invariably rejected, disparaged or marginalized. In this regard, Ricardo offers a mirror image of Quesnay: land is not a source of value, there is no absolute rent, there is only a relative rent which is explained by the law of decreasing returns, that is—and the fact is very remarkable in contrast with the general inspiration of the system—through a marginal consideration. Even Marx, who diverges most from Ricardo on this question, admitting the existence of an absolute rent and explaining it through an ingenious device, refuses to acknowledge the existence of private property in land as such (*Capital*, vol. III).

Two observations are in place here. First, I have stressed in the example of Quesnay the fact that the economists' search at this stage is for a *substance* responsible for the creation of wealth or value—I mean a single, self-sufficient factor that enshrines the essence of the economic process. As a creative factor, it must be actually a living agent: nature in Quesnay, the labourer in Smith, Ricardo and Marx. This substantialist mode of thought is in keeping with the individualistic tendency of the whole movement, but this is a point I must leave out here. At any rate it is incompatible with the recognition of a multiplicity of factors (see the fate of the 'triad of factors', in Schumpeter, 1954, pp. 557 ff). In that regard, Petty's and Cantillon's pair of factors, land and labour, has branched out into two alternatives; hence the parallelism between Quesnay and Marx (ibid. p. 238).

The second observation bears on the transition from the traditional to the modern ideological set-up. The incompatibility between land and capital, rent and profit, agriculture and industry clearly mirrors the historical change in the conception of wealth, better called the emergence of wealth as a major category or the emancipation of movable wealth, that I mentioned at the outset. The historical transition between two modes of thought explains that it has been a matter of either/or. Either the traditional view was maintained (mastery over men and over land went together) which meant that, whatever ingenious shift could be effected in the direction of property, freedom and production, wealth consisted only of the means of human subsistence, and capital could be enfranchised only in the hands of the farmer. Or, the emancipation of wealth was adhered to, and then it was inevitable that the one aspect of wealth which, as a legacy of the previous order, was antithetical to that emancipation should be looked down upon or impatiently put to one side. The difficulties, hesitations and contradictions of Adam Smith in the matter are an example of this. In classical economics in general, land and land rent cry out their extraneousness, whatever particular form it takes in one particular author. On the whole, land was a natural element like air and water that had become a 'monopoly', that is to say that had been arbitrarily confiscated or arrogated by certain people. Land ownership represented a kind of usurpation or at least the intrusion into the economy of an extraneous fact. Marx has the distinction of having neatly transcribed the incompatibility under the form of a class antagonism between landowners and industrialists bearing on the price of agricultural products.

The 'sterility' of industry in Quesnay expresses the same incompatibility in reverse.

## NOTES

1. The following is a slightly expanded version of chapter 3 of my book, *From Mandeville to Marx: The Genesis and Triumph of Economic Ideology*, University of Chicago Press. The last part of the text draws from other parts of the book. The French version (Paris, Gallimard) evokes briefly the French climate of opinion in relation to Physiocracy.

2. There is more in Marx on the subject in the 1844 Manuscripts and later in *Mehrwert*, etc. On the latter see Meek, 1963, p. 266. In a letter of 1863, Marx proposes to Engels a model of the capitalist process explicitly as a renewed form of the 'Tableau Economique', 6 July 1863, cf. Oeuvres, vol. II (pp. 1510–15).

3. Schumpeter speaks precisely of an *explicit* formulation. A little earlier he has shown how much Quesnay owed to Cantillon, including the idea of the economic process as a circular flow of 'the produce of the earth' as represented in the 'Tableau': '. . . The fundamental features of Quesnay's analysis set-up . . . are unmistakably foreshadowed in Cantillon's work' (Schumpeter, 1954, p. 218).

4. It should be clear that what follows in the text is no picture of Quesnay's thought but insists unilaterally—and very schematically—on one component of it. A complete picture should restore the balance between traditional and modern aspects and in the first place show the close association between ideal aspects and the painstaking empirical and statistical inquiry (cf. the very detailed questionnaire in Quesnay, 1958, vol. II, pp. 619–67). Meek, 1963, gives the main texts in English and adds valuable essays.

5. Bonar makes the point in relation to Harrington: 'the domestic empire . . . is founded on dominion, or proprietorship', 'he who owns the land is master of the people' (1927, p. 88); and he quotes Harrington's forceful words: 'Men are hung upon riches of necessity, and by the teeth; forasmuch as he who wants bread is his servant that will feed him. If a man thus feeds a whole people, they are under his empire.' Harrington deduces subordination from subsistence, he gives a modern view of a traditional situation.

# REFERENCES

Bonar, James, 1927, *Philosophy and Political Economy in Some of Their Historical Relations*, 3rd edn., London.

Dumont, Louis, 1967, *Homo Hierarchicus*, Paris; English translation, London and Chicago, 1970.

Marx, Karl, 'Manuscripts' (Oekonomisch-Philosophische Manuskripte aus dem Jahre 1844, *Werke*, Ergänzungsband 1, pp. 467–588; trans. by T. B. Bottomore, in Eric Fromm, *Marx's Concept of Man*, New York, 1961).

——*Mehrwert* (*Theorien über den Mehrwert*, in *Werke*, vol. xxvi, i–ii; French trans. by Molitor in *Histoire des Doctrines Economiques*, Paris, Costes, 1925-).

——1965–68, *Oeuvres* (Karl Marx. *Oeuvres, Economie*, ed. Maximilien Rubel, 2 vols., Paris, Bibliothèque de la Pléiade).

——1957-, *Werke* (Karl Marx/Friedrich Engels, *Werke*, 39+2 vols., Berlin, Dietz).

Meek, Ronald L., 1963, *The Economics of Physiocracy: Essays and Translations*, University of Glasgow Social and Economic Series, N.S. no. 2, London and Cambridge, Mass.

Quesnay, François, 1958, *François Quesnay et la Physiocratie*, 2 vols., Paris, INED (Works of Quesnay in vol. II; commented bibliography in vol. I).

Schumpeter, Joseph A., 1954, *History of Economic Analysis*, Oxford (quoted from the 1967 edn., London).

Smith, Adam, 1896, *Lectures on Justice, Police, Revenue and Arms, 1763*, ed. Edwin Cannan, Oxford.

——1904, *An Inquiry into the Nature and Causes of the Wealth of Nations*, ed. Edwin Cannan, 2 vols., London.

Weulersse, Georges, 1910, *Le Mouvement Physiocratique*, 2 vols., Paris; reprinted 1968.

# 17

# Economic Growth: Income or Welfare

BERT F. HOSELITZ

*University of Chicago*

ECONOMIC growth is a long-standing concern of social scientists but although economists and others have written numerous works on the subject and, especially in the years since the last war, have paid a good deal of intensive attention to it, no generally accepted definition of what is meant by economic growth or economic development has been elaborated as yet. Although many writers feel that they know what they are writing about when they discuss economic growth, and feel that their readers understand them, no *one* definition of the term has been put forth which commands general assent, and whenever any one tries to propose such a definition numerous dissenters raise their voice. However, there seems to be general consensus in the theoretical and, above all, in the practical literature on economic policy, which permits us to identify quite clearly the main characteristics of economic growth. Economic development or economic growth—two terms which in the course of this essay will be used interchangeably—involves a process in the course of which the real income of a given social group experiences positive change.

This description requires further refinement and explanation. We must specify more clearly what kind of social group is involved and we will have to say a few more words about the way in which income as a variable enters the picture. Let us first turn to a consideration of the first point, i.e. to a discussion of the social unit experiencing economic growth.

In principle, economic growth may be experienced by any social unit; i.e. the real income available to any social group, no matter how large or how small, may undergo positive change. Thus, we can speak of the economic growth or development of a family, a clan, a village, an urban centre, a province, a nation, a regional bloc, or all of human society. Some of the most general propositions on the conditions of economic growth may doubtless be applied to any of these units, or to any units somewhere between any two in this enumeration. Yet, at the same time, there can be no doubt that for practical and theoretical reasons the size and complexity of the unit must be taken into account. In fact, some theories of economic progress, as, for example, the various theories of stages of economic evolution, worked out by several economists of the German historical school, make the growing size and complexity of the unit under study the criterion of economic progress.

At first sight it might appear that from a theoretical viewpoint the unit to be chosen for consideration ought to be a society bound together by a common culture. This choice might be justified in many instances, but there are numerous other instances in which this might lead to the selection of too large or too small a unit. For example, all Western Europe had a common culture during most of the middle ages, and yet it would be more useful to discuss the economic development of certain parts of Western Europe separately from others. Similarly we may find presently countries on a very low level of development in which many tribal groups have a common culture, but their actual contacts are so scarce that each separate tribal group would more appropriately be regarded as a unit of study. In contrast, we have countries, such as India or Indonesia, in which peoples with differing cultures share a common political bond and in which the impact of this common membership in a political entity appears to have overwhelming significance for the study of development. These instances are however not all too frequent and as a rule political boundaries, at least in societies on a somewhat advanced level of economic activity, coincide roughly with cultural limits. Thus, although on purely theoretical grounds the unity of culture should be regarded as the determining factor in the choice of a unit, political divisions and combinations may impose in some instances an important modifying influence.

In addition, in many instances practical considerations have prevailed in the choice of the unit, and the nation state or some analogous administratively separate and clearly circumscribed political unit, such as, for example, a colony, a province, or some other sharply delineated portion of a country, has been selected. The reasons for choosing such a unit rather than any other are predominantly practical, although some theoretical arguments in favour of this choice could also be listed. We will first examine the practical arguments and then turn to theoretical considerations determining the choice of unit of economic growth.[1]

The first and perhaps chief practical reason for choosing the nation state as a unit of study is the fact that all data which are collected and which together are regarded as supplying indices for the degree or level of a society's economic advancement are availablle usually for nation states and similar clearly defined political units, and for these units only.

In the second place, major interest in problems of economic growth is evinced by policy makers who regard it as their task to elaborate plans and programmes for the economic development of their own countries, or policies of technical assistance for the economic development of other countries. These plans are addressed usually to national governments who are expected to implement them.

Thirdly, much of the interest in economic development, especially in plans and policies designed to bring about an elevation of real incomes in the poorest countries of the world, is generated in the United Nations and its specialized agencies as well as in foreign and colonial offices of national governments. All these agencies, for obvious reasons, have dealings only with nation states or similar territorial units, and think in terms of such units. In fact, the preoccupation with individual countries on the part of policy makers, members of technical assistance missions, and persons concerned primarily with the practical elaboration and implementation of development programmes, sometimes makes them blind to the fact that, in many instances, a country is neither the most efficient, nor, in the long run, the optimum unit for a development plan.

This observation suggests itself forcibly if one attempts to draw parallels between the development plans of countries like India or Brazil on the one hand, and Lebanon or Honduras on the other. The various countries, customarily classified as 'underdeveloped', range in population from less than one million to over eight hundred and fifty million. In a similar degree such countries vary with respect to the distribution of skills among the members of their populations or the endowment of non-human resources. Large as these differences may be, they pale in comparison with differences in culture, traditional values, and socio-political structures.

These last mentioned factors are the most significant in determining our selection of a unit of economic growth on theoretical grounds. If we are interested not in development plans and programmes, but in the theoretical analysis of the conditions and path of economic growth, our unit should be so chosen as to exhibit certain features which all parts of that unit have in common, and at the same time other features which clearly distinguish it from other units. A nation state, especially one which has been in existence within relatively fixed boundaries for some time, provides a suitable unit also on theoretical grounds. It usually has a common language and culture, its members are tied together by participation in a common political structure and a common economy. They adhere to a shared set of traditions and the sentiment of a common loyalty provides a framework whose interrelatedness and structural unity make the choice of such a sharply self-contained social unit a meaningful one.

For example, England is a good unit for analysis though she never presented a completely closed economy or society: she interacted from her origins with other political units, and maintained an open, free-trade economy for almost a century, making for a constant movement of men, goods, and capital funds across her frontiers in both directions. Yet it is possible to speak of the economic growth of England. For, despite these forms of interaction with the outside world, the national community of Englishmen found itself tied together so closely by a common history, common loyalties, and a common world view, as to endow this community with a clear and sharply drawn identity whose economic and wider cultural activities formed a set of variables with a common core and purpose.

It is, of course, true that at one extreme of the process of economic growth we find primitive societies among which the sentiment of nationhood is absent and which form small highly particularistic kinship groups who view even their close neighbours as foreigners. Even a common language and subjection to a common government do not, in the view of these people, bring them into close contact with similar co-ordinated groups and evoke the sentiment of mutually shared goals.

This holds not merely for the most primitive and economically underdeveloped aboriginal groups in Australia and parts of Africa, but even for such relatively more advanced peoples as the Indians of the highlands of Guatemala. In spite of intense economic interaction with members of other village communities and of contact with Europeans and their descendants for four centuries, the Indians in each community regard their own village as an exclusive entity with its own ceremonies, forms of speech, types of clothing and other symbolic manifestations of separateness. What matters in this context is not this symbolism, but the beliefs behind it, for which it is a symptom. Each village in Mayan Guatemala is a world in and of itself, and although contacts with outsiders are necessary for the sheer survival of the community, one's loyalties are only to the in-group.[2]

Attitudes such as these are prevalent to a greater or lesser extent in many economically underdeveloped countries in which particularistic loyalties are still prominent. To some extent inroads into these sentiments of particularistic loyalties are made by the prevailing nationalistic ideologies which tend to replace this attachment to the local community or, at best, to the district or region, by attachment to the nation as a whole. But, usually, the effective social group in such societies is not the nation state, but a smaller group of persons associated with one another on the basis of local contiguity or familial relations. As a rule, these simple particularistic societies are characterized by a relatively little developed division of social labour and the complexity of economic relations is far less advanced than among the greater, more highly specialized societies.

The consideration of the appropriate unit of study of economic development thus draws our attention to the fact that two closely associated trends must be distinguished. One is the change in the overall size of the social group among which effective interaction takes place, and the other is the change in the complexity of economic organization, and with it of occupational and social roles of the members of the group.

These two processes are usually closely interwoven although in principle each may take place by itself. For example, the effective size of a social group may increase without any change in the economic complexity and the role structure of the society. At the same time a society which is stable in terms of size may experience a change in economic complexity and increasing differentiation in social roles. In practice, however, such developments are rare and an increase in the size of the effective social group is usually associated with an increase in differentiation of its role structure and with greater complexity of economic organization. This process, moreover, is usually not a smooth and gradual one. Even superficial inspection of socioeconomic conditions in developing countries of today shows what great 'jumps' must be made in order to transform a still largely particularistic community into one in which there exists a high degree of economic and social interaction between the members of the society.[3]

Although it must be admitted that, on theoretical grounds, the appropriate unit for the study of economic growth may sometimes be a group smaller than a state or an analogous political unit, it should be pointed out at the same time that these cases will refer usually to societies with as yet very little complexity in their economic relations and with a rather simple form of economic organization. Economic growth among such small highly particularistic social groups takes place primarily by extension of the effective interaction between such units. Although this is often associated with increasing specialization and complexity of division of labour, the highly particularistic character of social relations is little disturbed. In the terms proposed by Robert Redfield, the first step in the economic growth of social groups with strong characteristics of folk societies does not disturb the prevalent folk character of the group. It may move in a folk–urban continuum somewhat farther away from the extreme on one side, but in many of its aspects it still displays the typical features of a folk society. Although the economic integration of these simple folk societies into larger social units may lead to the formation of urban centres, these 'cities' are predominantly cult centres and not places of orthogenetic cultural transformation.[4]

These processes are doubtless instances of economic growth, but the crucial type of social transformation is that in which a predominantly folk-oriented culture gradually—or suddenly—is changed into one in which features of urban society predominate. It is this step in the historical development of a social group which is of greatest interest from the viewpoint of economic development, but this process almost invariably takes place in societies in which a fair degree of complex socio-economic organization has already been reached and in which the size of the effectively interacting social group is close to or contiguous with a nation state.[5]

It is the common practice in discussions of the problems of economic growth to deal primarily with societies of such a level of complexity and of such size as to be roughly conforming to countries or states. In doing this, to treat any one such unit as a unified fully interacting society and a closed system may often oversimplify the case, and allowances must be made for different forms and degrees of interaction with other systems. This last problem takes on significance chiefly in the discussion of contact between different cultures and between the members of these cultures or the movement of commodities and services between different societies. Since certain aspects of economic development must be regarded as adaptations on the part of one cultural group to the demands and inroads made upon it by another culture, a clear conception of the unit of economic growth with which we deal at any one time is of great importance.

Next to achieving clarity on the unit of economic development to be studied, it is also necessary to state in precise terms what aspects of real income are involved in the study of economic growth and in what manner changes in real income may be employed for our purpose. Is change in real income a measure or the result of economic growth? What is the relationship between real income levels and welfare levels? And, finally, is the growth of total real income or per capita real income the more significant factor?

These considerations have brought under scrutiny such complex problems as the measurement of a community's welfare and, above all, the question of whether any real meaning can be assigned to comparisons in the level of welfare or between societies with very different consumption or aspiration patterns, i.e. between societies which are widely separated in space or time or greatly different in culture.

Unfortunately a lot of mischief has been done in the use of the real income concept. Some writers and, most unfortunately, some official agencies of international organizations and national governments have tended to endow various published series of comparative per capita income figures with more meaning and more validity than they deserve. Even worse, in some quarters a close correlation between these figures and levels of living or levels of welfare were tacitly assumed or openly stipulated. The reaction against this somewhat indiscriminate use of real income figures as indicators of welfare levels has been prompt. It resulted in their becoming discredited and their usefulness being seriously questioned. Perhaps the most outspoken attack against the use of real income data as a measure or resultant variable in the estimation of economic growth has been made by S. Herbert Frankel.[6]

The main point in Frankel's criticism, and it is well taken, is that owing to differences in productive and consumption patterns, as well as due to differences in aspirations and cultural conventions, comparisons between real income have only limited validity, and certainly do not reflect accurately relative standards of welfare. Quite

19

apart from the essentially statistical difficulties of finding accurate weights, and the empirical difficulties of determining accurate value relationships in different societies—both of which difficulties are, of course, also primarily a result of the differences in culture between different societies—there is the basically more important objection that income is not a culturally neutral concept and hence, as Frankel insists, any meaning attached to it becomes coloured by the particular cultural and philosophical predispositions of the persons using it.

But there is another point which Frankel omits to mention, which is that many of the widely popularized national income data, such as those supplied by the United States government, the United Nations, or even those computed by Colin Clark or Simon Kuznets, take on a life of their own. By this I mean that whatever caution may have been expressed by the original authors or compilers of such data about their accuracy and comparability, and hence their applicability as guides for problems of measurement and ultimately for policy, is forgotten and the data employed brazenly as if they were ineradicable symbols of some social reality. Colin Clark was the first to publish a set of bold per capita income figures, expressed in International Units (which however are only poorly disguised dollars of constant purchasing power). Since then the relative ranking of countries and, more importantly, the absolute differences between countries which these figures express have been taken as valid descriptions not merely of actual differences in levels of productivity in the various countries, but also as indicators of differences in living levels and levels of welfare.[7]

But, although we must exercise caution in using the concept of real income, it would be wrong to throw it out altogether. The concept of real income, or as I would prefer it, of real output, has above all the quality of being all-embracing and being capable of encompassing all types and kinds of goods and services produced under the most varied conditions and for the most widely divergent ends. It has, moreover, the advantage of being closely correlated with a series of other indicators which can be used, with a high degree of validity, as indicators or measures of living levels. For example, there is a fairly high correlation between real per capita income and such variables as life expectancy at a given age, infant mortality, death rate from tuberculosis, daily food intake in calories, per capita per day protein consumption, illiteracy rates, average amount of schooling per person, per capita number of telephones, railroad mileage and similar indicators of communication and transport facilities, and certain indexes measuring the per capita consumption of housing, textiles, and certain other goods of common usefulness.[8]

Merrill K. Bennett elaborated an index of consumption levels based exclusively on non-monetary indicators. He applied this index to thirty-one countries and compared the resulting ordering of countries with the monetary indicator of real national income. The comparison between these two classifications is exhibited by Bennett in a lucid and well-constructed chart. As could be expected there are some discrepancies in the two classifications, but the most striking impression gained from the chart is the generally high degree of correspondence between the ordering of countries on the basis of non-monetary indicators computed by Bennett and their ordering on the basis of average real income.[9] Moreover, one may justly assume that some of the discrepancies between the two classifications might be markedly diminished if the reliability of the monetary, as well as the non-monetary indicators could be improved.

Although, on the whole, the actual estimates of the data making up the non-monetary indicators are more reliable in some little developed countries than national income estimates, they are sometimes subject to serious doubt and possible grave inaccuracies. Bennett explains himself that he rejected a number of well-known and widely popularized non-monetary indicators because they appeared to him defective or biased. Yet, it may be questioned how accurate are, for for example, estimates of school attendance or the consumption of non-grain calories (both indicators were used by Bennett) in some of the statistically less well-surveyed countries. Moreover, the very composition of Bennett's index (he includes, for example, movie theatres and motor vehicle registrations as indicators) imposes a cultural bias, and though this is explicitly recognized, it does not make the estimates any more neutral from a cultural point of view.

Nevertheless, the general overall correspondence between Bennett's classification based on non-monetary variables and real income per man-hour worked as computed by Colin Clark in the first edition of *The Conditions of Economic Progress* is striking. Since then, Clark has published a second edition with considerably improved and more up-to-date figures. At the same time, under the influence of the United Nations and its specialized agencies, the statistical organizations charged with the collection and estimation of data for monetary and non-monetary indicators have been much improved in countries in which previously they were poor or altogether absent. As a result, social scientists today have at their disposal more accurate data than were available to Bennett. It would be of great interest to make new comparisons using the more refined and more complete data in order to see whether the overall correspondence of the two scales improves or worsens. Until and unless it is shown that a general ordering of societies according to non-monetary indicators and the monetary indicator of real income yields very different results, the use of income as a measure of the general level of growth and, with appropriate caution, as a level of living, seems justified.[10]

Although the general order of living levels in different countries seems to be relatively well represented—at least in a crude form—by real income figures, they apparently exaggerate the overall difference in living levels between countries. According to the data published by Clark, the income per employed person per year in the richest countries was roughly ten times that of the poorest countries. For example, the income per worker in the United States in 1947 is computed at 2,566 International Units, whereas that of the Indian worker in 1944/5 is estimated at 246 International Units. For China, Clark computed an annual income per worker in 1933 of 138 International Units, and found the income of the American worker in the same year to have been 1,561 International Units.[11] Bennett, on the other hand, found that consumption levels in the richest countries were only roughly ten times those in the poorest countries.

Although this difference between the classification based on monetary and on non-monetary indicators may be explained, at least in part, by the relatively greater proportion of total resources devoted to capital formation in the richer countries, the discrepancy may also result from a bias in the measures used by Clark. Simon Kuznets compared American and Chinese real per capita income and attempted to eliminate those factors creeping into the computations of the national income of the two countries which have their basis in the particular forms of exchange and economic organization in an economically highly developed country. On the basis of this recalculation Kuznets arrived at a per capita consumption of China in the period 1931–6 of $62.5—as against $37 before the recalculation—whereas the United States, in the same period, showed an annual average consumers' outlay of $433 per capita. Thus the American figure was roughly only seven times higher than the Chinese, and Kuznets believed that further refinement would bring the two figures even closer together.[12]

The comparison of different countries by per capita income was believed to be the only valid basis of distinction between them because other magnitudes could not be measured. But in the early 1960s many underdeveloped countries became independent and to compare their per capita incomes with those obtained in the advanced countries was misleading because a large number of exchanges in the newly independent countries was not against money but against other goods and therefore per capita income could not be used as an objective measure. For this reason, in the late 1960s and in the 1970s a number of authors chose not to compare countries merely by real income but also by other factors, social and political.[13] The authors of these distinctions are not yet recognized but I have no doubt that in the next twenty to thirty years other factors will be elaborated to such an extent that countries can not only be compared with one another on the average per capita income figure but also on a figure which we can call general per capita welfare.

Thus, per capita real income data or derivatives of them are not very good indicators of welfare levels. Granting that economists are often motivated in their work by considerations of welfare and the desire to contribute to knowledge by means of which welfare can be improved, the quantitative measurement of welfare levels, even within a culture, has so far been believed to be impossible and promises to remain so, for some time to come, but not, I think, for ever.

Whether a higher level of welfare will be attained depends not merely on such entirely or partially economic variables as income distribution, level of employment, and division of social product between consumption and investment, but even more on political, socio-structural, and cultural factors—in short, on the prevailing values and ideology of a society. But in view of the wide variety of cultural values all over the world, complete objectivity and avoidance of some ethnocentric bias is difficult and perhaps unattainable in sociological writing. Purists in matters of cultural valuations may demand procedures which would make research in the area of international comparisons of levels of economic development and levels of consumption an impossible task. Moreover, Western values, especially as they relate to production and economic organization of society, are gaining acceptance in less advanced countries, although more fully among their educated classes and the political leadership groups.[14] One impact of modern mass communications has been the spread of information on the kinds of goods and services which make up western consumption patterns. Although many of these items are beyond the means of most persons in economically less advanced countries, there is a growing desire, even in relatively tradition-bound societies, to approximate in several ways western consumption patterns. The introjection of a certain bias stemming from a generalization of western European consumption patterns, therefore, may be regarded as a relatively small violation of strict objectivity.

## NOTES

1. A reasoned defence for the choice of nation states as the unit of observation was presented by Simon Kuznets, 'The State as a Unit in Study of Economic Growth', *Journal of Economic History*, vol. XI, no. 1 (Winter 1951), pp. 25–41. Although Kuznets was one of the first to compare countries by per capita income, his direction was followed by many general textbook authors, among which I mention only two: Benjamin Higgins, *Economic Development* (revised edition), W. W. Norton, New York, 1968, and Everett E. Hagen, *The Economics of Development* (revised edition), Richard D. Irwin, Homewood, Ill., 1975.

2. See Sol Tax, 'World View and Social Relations in Guatemala', *American Anthropologist*, vol. XLIII (1941), pp. 29 ff.

3. In this field there have appeared many books of new views and in general these views are represented in Jason L. Finkle and Richard W. Gable (eds.), *Political Development and Social Change*, John Wiley, New York, 1966, and John H. Kautsky, *The Political Consequences of Modernization*, John Wiley, New York, 1972.

4. See Robert Redfield, 'The Folk Society', *American Journal of Sociology*, vol. LII (1947), pp. 293–308, and Robert Redfield and Milton B. Singer, 'The Cultural Role of Cities', *Economic Development and Cultural Change*, vol. III (1954/55), pp. 53–73.

5. One instance in which apparently significant economic growth occurred although the social units experiencing this growth were still organized on a level close to folk-like kinship groups was the rapid economic advancement of the Maori in the early nineteenth century. Instances such as this, although not impossible, are, however, rare. On the Maori, see Robert W. Merrill, 'Some Social and Cultural Influences on Economic Growth: The Case of the Maori', *Journal of Economic History*, vol. XIV (1954), no. 4, pp. 401–8.

6. S. Herbert Frankel, *The Economic Impact on Underdeveloped Societies*, Harvard University Press, Cambridge, Mass., 1953.

7. The earliest comparative data in systematic and comprehensive form are due to Colin Clark, *The Conditions of Economic Progress*, Macmillan, London, 1940, second edition, 1951.

8. United States Department of State, *Point Four*, Washington, D.C., especially pp. 113–24. For a further and more detailed discussion of these indicators and their relevance to the determination of standards of living, see Public Administration Clearing House, 'Definition and Measurement of Standards of Living' (report of a conference of United States experts convened 30 January–1 February 1953), Chicago, 1953 (mimeo).

9. Merrill K. Bennett, 'International Disparities in Consumption Levels', *American Economic Review*, vol. XLI, no. 4 (September 1951), pp. 632–49. The chart referred to in the text is on page 643.

10. Another attempt at providing a classification of various countries on the basis of non-monetary indicators, which was undertaken independently of Bennett's work, and which used several more variables than those employed by Bennett, was by Father Lebret and his collaborators. Although Lebret insisted that his models display comparative levels of welfare, it is difficult to see how this can be maintained in a rigorous way. However, the circle-shaped models of Lebret are of interest and further refinement may transform them into indices of living levels. Cf. L. J. Lebret and R. Delprat, 'Niveaux de consommation et de production dans les dix zones du monde', *Economie et Humanisme*, vol. XI, no. 74 (July–August 1952), pp. 22–53, and an English summary of the views expressed there in L. J. Lebret, 'Applications of Circular Diagrams in the Study and Comparison of Standards of Living and Patterns of Development', *Indian Economic Review*, vol. II, no. 2 (August 1954).

11. Colin Clark, op. cit. pp. 46–7, 124–6.

12. Simon Kuznets, *Economic Change*, W. W. Norton, New York, 1953, pp. 180–91.

13. Whereas in the 1940s and in the early 1950s the difference in per capita national income between the most advanced and the most underdeveloped countries was approximately 1 to 10, this difference has vastly increased in the last twenty years, e.g. between the United States and India it is now 60 to 1, and in the third world countries it has increased at a comparable rate. In part this has been attributed to a difference in prices and exchange rates, but it is very difficult to assess to what magnitude this enormous difference is due. Among publications of studies on social and political differences are the following two books: Irma Adelman and Cynthia Taft Morris, *Society, Politics, and Economic Development*, The Johns Hopkins Press, Baltimore, 1967, and D. V. McGranahan, C. Richard-Proust, N. V. Sovani, and M. Subramanian, *Contents and Measurement of Socio-Economic Development*, United Nations Research Institute for Social Development, Geneva, 1970, Report no. 70.10.

14. These transfers of pieces of cultural valuations sometimes lead to somewhat incongruous results. For example, the leaders of the religious socialist parties in Indonesia have developed an ideology in which the teachings of Islam are reconciled with positions of Marxism and values of economy and efficiency characteristic of western liberalist thought.

# 18

# Has Land Reform Become Obsolete?

ERICH H. JACOBY

*University of Stockholm*

FOR more than three decades, land reform as an instrument for rural development was used as a political slogan by reformers and revolutionaries alike. It was a recurring theme of discussion on the highest level in the United Nations as well as in national governments; it was analysed in scholarly books and propagated in pamphlets, and in many countries it was considered a cure-all by the common man, particularly in the villages. Land reform as a slogan was thus to be heard everywhere; but except under revolutionary conditions actual land reform programmes were never thoroughly implemented. The evolutionary type of land reform, in fact, showed a unique tendency to wither away and add disappointment to the existing misery. During the first post-war decade, land reform in India, the largest democracy in the world, occupied the minds of a whole generation of Indian and Western scholars. Outstanding amongst the latter was Daniel Thorner with his clear and precise analysis and his deep sympathy with the fate of the Indian peasants. With a rare sense of realism he and his wife Alice wrote their book *Land and Labour in India*, published in 1962 by Asia Publishing House, Bombay.

Very early Daniel recognized the ambiguous character of the Indian land reform and of the Indian co-operative organizations. He came to the conclusion that the technique and concepts applied would never change the prevailing balance of power and that the landlords, both as individuals and as a class, would remain the decisive factor in the villages as well as in the governing bodies. He was amongst the first to recognize the narrow limitations of the Indian reform efforts and proved right in his assumption that, after the relatively easy abolition of the Zamindaries, they would soon taper off. In many parts of rural India, in fact, the much celebrated tenancy reforms were implemented so half-heartedly that instead of improving tenancy conditions they led to a mass eviction of tenants. Daniel Thorner's keen analysis of the Indian land reform has become a paradigm for the analysis of land reform programmes in under-developed countries in general. During the last decade of his life, Daniel Thorner turned his attention to the problems involved in the modernization of agriculture. As an economic historian he now looked with some sympathy on the new forms of capitalist farming in India which gradually developed in the rural areas around the larger urban centres.

Developments in India and elsewhere seem to prove that the con-cepts and views of rural development during the first three post-war decades have been rendered outdated by modern technology and neo-capitalistic practices. It is high time, therefore, that the problems of agrarian structure and agrarian reforms be re-examined in a new light. It is true that feudalism and semi-feudalism is on the retreat in the rural areas of Southeast Asia and Latin America. But this is certainly not caused by changes in the agrarian structure through land reform but merely by the advance of technology, by the penetra-tion of money transactions into the rural areas and, above all, by the development of a new form of capitalism which is based on the many-sided activities of transnational corporations.

In the traditional peasant economies, and particularly in the densely populated areas agricultural production was extremely labour inten-sive though with a very low productivity per man and per working hour. As a matter of fact, agriculture in these areas was actually based upon the super-exploitation of human labour. With the intro-duction of new genetic and engineering technologies, however, the entire picture was changing. Within a relatively short time, the value of good irrigable land increased so much that the frequently inferior land of small peasants lost its competitive capacity. Almost every-where, in fact, technological progress proved to benefit only those who already owned the better natural resources and disposed of the necessary financial means, credit facilities and technological know-how. The first serious blow against the peasant economy was the 'green revolution' with its packages of new technologies which soon trebled the price of land, and greatly reduced the use of tenant culti-vators and agricultural workers. Gradually landlords are turning into industrial entrepreneurs and the traditional patriarchal landlord-tenant relationship is becoming superfluous in the new economic environment in which rising land values, large capital investments and progressing mechanization widen the gap between rich and poor.

In the large areas of Asia and Latin America where the 'green revolution' has accelerated productivity and growth, tenancy as an institution is thus about to disappear—though certainly not in the manner visualized by land reform. In the Punjab and in Bihar, in the fertile plains of Central Luzon, Peru, Argentina and Mexico, tens of thousands of tenants have been ejected and hundreds of thousands of small peasants have been economically ruined because they have lost their competitive capacity. In a never-ending stream they are moving towards the urban centres where, however, only a tiny fraction have a chance to be integrated as industrial workers and the great majority are left to fend for themselves in the slum districts and shanty towns. True, orderly statisticians register the ever increasing number of petty-traders, ill-paid household workers and shoe-cleaners as 'persons employed in the service sector'; but this is only a face-lifting statistical operation which does not create meaningful employment; with rare exceptions the migrant peasants remain displaced persons. Mainly because of the increasing exodus from the rural areas large cities like Calcutta, Bombay, Lima, Buenos Aires, Mexico City, Manila have grown immensely within a relatively short period. Take only Mexico City whose population between 1950 and 1968 grew from 3 million to well over 7 million and today probably has reached the 9 million mark.

In other words, the new type of agriculture which in many regards resembles an industry leaves no room for the peasants in the traditional sense. Large-scale cultivation, in fact, excludes peasant farming and mechanized agriculture severely limits the employment possibilities of the landless agricultural workers. After years of negligence the World Bank now tries to provide credit schemes for small peasants. But it seems very doubtful whether the peasants in underdeveloped countries with their usually tiny plots of land will be able to adjust to the new production pattern and at the same time carry a heavy debt burden. Rural credit alone cannot bring about the needed changes in the prevailing agrarian structure; experiences in developed and under-developed countries alike have proved that the modernization of agricultural production is gradually leading to the liquidation of the small peasantry.

In the present age of uncontrolled technological advance and productivity-fanaticism, the traditional concept of land reform seems no longer valid. The redistribution of land to small peasants or the sub-division of large estates do not correspond to the requirements of modern technology for large-sized fields for cultivation, and to the individualistic development strategy that rejects any kind of group solution. No wonder, therefore, that the technocratically minded economists of today speak of the need for a reform of the land rather than for land reform. One can of course defend this new attitude in countries where economy and society offer the landless workers alter-native employment opportunities and the self-owning peasant has the possibility of reaching a level of living comparable to that of industrial workers. But this is hardly ever the case in underdeveloped countries where the 'informal sector', as it is called in Kenya, with its masses of unemployed landless agricultural workers and ruined small peasants, is growing rapidly in the shanty towns of the urban centres.

Considering the prevailing structural and institutional set-up in the rural areas of most underdeveloped countries, the introduction of advanced technology is almost bound to impede economic and social progress. This is not the fault of the technology as such; it is the natural consequence of the very economic and social system. Just as the application of fertilizers without sufficient water results in serious crop failures and irrigation without drainage causes salina-tion of the soil, the indiscriminate introduction of modern technology in underdeveloped countries without concomitant changes in the agrarian structure will force the peasants to leave the land and thus ultimately lead to the disintegration of the peasant communities. The ill effects of this process, however, are not limited to the rural areas. The exodus of the peasants to the urban centres and all that goes with it represents in fact the formidable social price which underdeveloped countries have to pay for accepting the uncontrolled transfer of advanced foreign technology while preserving their out-dated and distorted agrarian structure. It is safe to predict, therefore, that only countries which have reached a certain degree of structural maturity will be able to absorb the shock caused by the transfer of advanced technologies on neo-capitalistic terms. Although it should be feasible in theory to harmonize technological advance with ade-quate institutional changes, this is impossible in practice, since the very fact of such a harmonization is incompatible with the objectives and business calculations of the transnational corporations which conduct the transfer of modern technology.

When transnational corporations penetrate the agriculture of an underdeveloped country by the vertical integration of the process of agricultural production, they repress the small peasant and deprive him of his decision-making capacity and economic responsibility. They adjust his economic activities to their own requirements which are determined by world market conditions and the cost–benefit calculations of their processing industries.

Contrary to the large colonial enterprises of the past, transnational corporations are interested primarily in the control of activities rather than in the control of property, for example land. The real basis of their powerful position is the 'ownership' of the technical process which is difficult to attack by the normal procedures of expropriation and nationalization. Consequently they cannot be frightened by the menace of agrarian reform and the peasant merely becomes a part of their inventory and is hardly more than a tool in their process of production. Even if he actually owns his land the price of his produce is arbitrarily determined by the transnational corporations and his income may hardly exceed the miserable share of a tenant. In the majority of cases a peasant is losing his freedom when he becomes part of a transnational contract system which controls his inputs and the marketing of his produce, that is to say his expenses and his earnings.

In large areas of underdeveloped countries, the transnational corporations are directing the prevailing land utilization patterns towards the production of primarily industrial crops and luxury food items for export to the rich countries. Such a change in land utilization, of course, deflects land and labour from the traditional peasant farming which concentrated mainly on the cultivation of domestic food crops with only a limited marketable surplus. The reduction of the domestic crop area combined with the ruthless use of the usually scarce water resources for intensive capitalist farming, multiplies the effects of drought on the remaining peasant and pastoral communities which, in turn, increases their dependence and weakens their bargaining capacity.

This change in the relationship between land, labour and capital affects by necessity not only the agrarian structure but also the social and political organization of the rural communities in the countries concerned. The increasing power of capital favours the already privileged groups whose very position gives them access to co-operation with the transnational corporations and their bank connections at home and abroad. Members of these groups now become capitalist farmers who apply modern management principles and machinery instead of traditional farming methods and labour relations. The very ownership of land is fast losing its economic meaning unless it is combined with the capital resources needed for the modernization of agricultural production.

True, the modernization of agriculture does mean progress; the question only is: progress for whom? In the fifties and early sixties, the advocates of land reform were convinced that changes in the agrarian structure would enable the rural masses to move upwards on the so-called agricultural ladder, i.e. from landless agricultural workers to tenant farmers and further up to owner cultivators. But since the beginning of the seventies this agricultural ladder has broken to pieces once and for all. Today, landless agricultural workers do not have the slightest chance of becoming tenant cultivators let alone successful owner cultivators. The agricultural ladder, in fact, has been replaced by a descending escalator on which small and even medium-sized farmers, be they tenants or owners, rapidly move down to the level of landless agricultural workers. Only those cultivators who have access to the natural resources and the financial means required by the new technologies can compete with the new class of capitalist farmers which is composed not only of traditional large landowners but also of newcomers to agriculture like retired military officers, professionals and civil servants for whom modern farming has proved a worthwhile capital investment.

In the rural areas of many underdeveloped countries in Asia and Latin America the modernization of agriculture has led to the economic ruin of peasant farming and to the social and economic degradation of the small cultivator. Everywhere, the human factor in agriculture is losing out by the uncontrolled and abrupt introduction of sophisticated technologies. Whereas the free market forces allow the producers to divide the markets by agreements in order to keep their spheres of interest under control, the peasant and pastoral communities have been denied any protective regulations. In the final analysis, therefore, it was a grave error that governments did not safeguard the economic survival of the rural population through an effective control system that could avoid the emergence of rural slums which are as bad as were the city slums during the time of the industrial revolution.

There is hardly any doubt that time is running short for using land reform as a means of preventing the imminent collapse of the peasant communities. Does this mean that land reform is about to become obsolete? Personally, I do not think this will be the case provided that the ultimate objectives of land reform, i.e. an equitable distribution of income and an improved equality of society, are incorporated into the entire development policy. Land reform must no longer be considered a water-tight compartment containing a variety of programmes to be applied when needed. More than ever, land reform is a development concept and, in fact, development is identical with land reform. The implementation of land reform, therefore, is a continued up-hill battle in which every step forward must be guarded not only against traditional prejudices and the opponents of social progress but, above all, against the increasing strength of the free market forces due mainly to the widespread activities of the transnational corporations.

Moreover, the ideas and values of land reform will add moral strength to the countervailing power which is bound to emerge during the fight against the power of the transnational corporations, which is as fatal as feudalism for the agrarian structure in underdeveloped countries.

The development of agriculture loses its meaning if it is not identical with rural development and the improvement of life and work of the rural population. At every stage during the implementation of technological development projects, the question must be asked: *cui bono?* If the answer implies that it may benefit only the privileged few, the direction must be changed or the entire project discarded. There must be an end to the typical United Nations projects which during two development decades have improved and strengthened the position of the few while the rural masses have remained as poor as ever.

Certainly, land reform has not become obsolete; on the contrary, there is a growing need to recognize land reform as a permanent process in order to provide the development strategy with a measure of social responsibility which is strong enough to counteract the economic effects of transnational corporations and capitalist farmers. Conditions in Mexico are a sad example of a national development strategy which did not continue to defend the achievements of a revolutionary land reform. Once the *ejidos* were formed, the government left them to fend for themselves within the framework of a rapidly developing capitalist economy. Unable to control the aggressive market forces, the peasants were soon losing the larger share of their surplus production to traders and moneylenders and, consequently, their political influence in Parliament and even in the villages. Although they never had to give up an inch of *ejido* land they are today almost as impoverished and indebted as before the revolution of 1917.

In view of the growing strength of transnational agro-business and capitalist farming, traditional peasant farming hardly has a chance of survival even though it is now supported by some credit programmes and modern gadgets. The very fact of an outdated agrarian structure with small farm units is an obstacle to modern management methods and the large-scale operations required by modern technology. It is unrealistic to believe that development programmes which do not include land reform but are focussed on the artificial establishment of service institutions can possibly still bridge the widening gap between capitalist and peasant farming. Neither co-operative land use nor block farming alone has substantially improved production and life in rural areas.

If we assume that it is an essential objective of land reform—seen from a technical point of view—to establish a system of viable farm units sufficiently flexible to handle production problems even in periods of large demographical changes, then it is hardly wise to suggest to underdeveloped countries a kind of peasant economy in the traditional sense. From a general development point of view, land reform should rather establish a system which combines equality with increased productivity of land and man. Such a system would call for large centrally-farmed units which are in a position to harmonize technical advance and social progress. Such an objective, however, can only be realized by state or collective farms and not by capitalistic estates, since their profitability depends on keeping labour cost at a minimum and gearing their production to the demands of the most profitable markets in the developed world.

The great superiority of collective and state farms in comparison to peasant farming is in the field of the adoption of advanced technology, since one of the most difficult problems of peasant economies —besides fragmentation—is to organize the transfer of the needed technical knowledge to millions of individual cultivators. By definition, underdevelopment implies the lack of trained people and this holds true particularly in agriculture. Consequently underdeveloped countries cannot provide the immense number of local staff needed for an effective extension service.[1] Obviously the requirements with regard to numbers, composition and supervision of the agricultural extension staff service will be much larger in peasant economies than in areas where collective and state farms are the prevailing types. Of course, those farms also need careful extension workers and skilled guidance in management and operation; but this seems a manageable task compared to the efforts that would be needed in order to increase the efficiency of millions of often undersized individual farms.

If we seek to determine the role of collective farming in agrarian reform, we must answer two fundamental questions. Firstly, whether the principle of co-operation can be applied at all in agricultural production and, if so, in what form and to what extent, And, secondly, whether co-operation is likely to influence the power structures in the villages and thus affect the agrarian structure too.

There is no doubt that collective farming as a tenure system should not be treated as a monopoly of the socialist countries; it is a rational means for increasing agricultural production and creating a less depressed society in underdeveloped countries. Provided that there is no discrimination against collective farming, it can happily co-exist with individual tenure types, as is the case in Israel and Tanzania. The co-existence of capitalist and socialist tenure types in agriculture should, indeed, be as feasible as the mixed economy in industry, banking, services and communications in Western Europe.

The time when individual tenure types could monopolize agriculture is at an end. The continued subdivision and fragmentation of holdings and the growing rate of landlessness is making millions of peasants increasingly aware of their state of isolation and frustration. Working their minute plots with outdated implements for returns hardly exceeding mere subsistence, they are becoming increasingly less susceptible to the argument that collective farming will reduce them to a state of still greater frustration and exploitation. The increasing evidence of the success of collective farming in the socialist world, and China in particular, is making them aware of the obvious advantages that can be gained from working the land collectively in larger units with a growing influence of the organized peasants at the village level.

As for the labour-displacing effect of collective farming, the Chinese experience proves the contrary. The collectivization of Chinese agriculture mobilized the huge army of idle labour for the construction of irrigation and drainage works, for terracing and other forms of capital formation.[2] It has been assumed, quite rightly, that the impressive progress in Chinese agriculture in a relatively short period of time would have been impossible without the capacity of collective farming for mobilizing labour and substituting labour for capital.

No doubt, there exists considerable scepticism about the productivity aspects of collective farming among western agricultural economists. The reasons for this attitude are the difficulties of the Russian *kolkhoz* and Soviet agriculture in general, although the defects in Soviet agriculture can easily be traced back to a conscious neglect of agriculture through many decades in the interest of the development of heavy industries. It can well be argued that under the prevailing price and investment conditions in the Soviet Union individual peasant farming would not have been more successful than the collective farming units. I would like here to refer to the investigations of the Israeli Agricultural Research Institutions, which after thorough investigations have stated that under equal production conditions collective and individual farming have on the average the same results even though no collective farm will be as good as the best individual farm, nor so bad as the worst individual farm.[3]

At the present stage therefore, when development is sliding back in large parts of the underdeveloped world and time-tested devices can no longer cope with the task in hand, we have to discard all prejudices and to re-examine the situation in the light of the new social and technological developments. We will then recognize that the concept of land reform in its very substance remains valid, even if some of the former programmes and conclusions can no longer be retained.

## NOTES

1. Erich H. Jacoby, *Man and Land*, Appendix III, Andre Deutsch, London, 1971 in connection with the *Provisional Indicative World Plan for Agricultural Development*, C 69/4, FAO, Rome, 1969.
2. W. F. Wertheim, 'Recent Trends in China's Population Policy', para. 17.
3. Jehuda Lowe, 'Kibbutz and Moshav in Israel: An Economic Study', in *International Explorations of Agricultural Economics* (Iowa State University Press, Ames, Iowa, 1964).

# Daniel Thorner: A Bibliography

1. 'India and Pakistan' (with Alice Thorner), in Ralph Linton (ed.), *Most of the World*, Columbia University Press, 1949, pp. 549–653.

2. *Investment in Empire: British Railway and Steam Shipping Enterprise in India, 1825–1849*, University of Pennsylvania Press, 1950.

3. 'Problems of Economic Development in India', *Annals of the American Academy of Political and Social Science*, vol. 268 (March 1950), pp. 96–103.

4. 'Prospects for Economic Development in Southern Asia', *Foreign Policy Reports*, vol. XXVI (15 April 1950), pp. 18–28.

5. 'Rapporteur's Report of Round-Table Discussions on Economic Forces', Twenty-fifth Harris Memorial Institute, University of Chicago, published in Phillips Talbot (ed.), *South Asia in the World Today*, University of Chicago Press, 1950, pp. 142–50.

6. 'Anglo-Russian Rivalry over Sinkiang, 1800–1917', 'Sinkiang and China's First Foreign Loan', and 'International Boundaries on the Pamirs', three sections in Owen Lattimore (ed.), *Pivot of Asia: Sinkiang*, Boston, Little, Brown and Co., 1950.

7. 'India: Economic Development', in *Encyclopedia Americana*, vol. V (1951), pp. 5–9; also published as chapter II in W. Norman Brown (ed.), *India, Pakistan, Ceylon*, Cornell University Press, 1951. Reprinted in *Land and Labour in India*.

8. 'Sir Henry Maine: Analyst of British India', chapter V in *Some Modern Historians of Britain: Essays in Honour of R. L. Schuvler*, New York, Dryden Press, 1951. Reprinted in *The Shaping of Modern India*.

9. 'Great Britain and the Development of India's Railways, 1849–1947', *Journal of Economic History*, vol. XI (Fall, 1951), pp. 389–402.

10. 'Land Reforms in Kashmir', *Economic Weekly*, Bombay, vol. V (12 September 1953), pp. 999–1002. Reprinted in *The Shaping of Modern India*.

11. 'The Village Panchayat as a Vehicle of Change', *Economic Development and Cultural Change*, University of Chicago, vol. II (October 1953), pp. 209–15.

12. 'Land Reforms in India: Some Speculations', *Economic Weekly*, Bombay, vol. v (5 November 1953), pp. 1217–20. Reprinted in *The Shaping of Modern India*.

13. 'Land Reforms in India', a review article, *Indian Economic Journal*, Bombay, vol. II (July 1954), pp. 27–36.

14. 'An Agrarian Handbook for India', *Agricultural Situation in India* (Tenth Anniversary Souvenir Issue), New Delhi, November 1954, pp. 60–4.

15. 'Pattern of Railway Development in India', *Far Eastern Quarterly*, vol. XIV (February 1955), pp. 201–16. Reprinted in *The Shaping of Modern India*.

16. 'The Fate of the Census of Landholding', *Economic Review* (Fortnightly Journal of the Economic and Political Research Department of the All India Congress Committee), New Delhi, vol. VII (15 August 1955), pp. 75–8. Reprinted in *Land and Labour in India*.

17. 'Long-Term Trends in Output in India', in Simon Kuznets *et al.* (eds.), *Economic Growth: Brazil, India, Japan*, Duke University Press, 1955. Reprinted in *Land and Labour in India*.

18. 'Feudalism in India', in Rushton Coulborn (ed.), *Feudalism in History*, Princeton University Press, 1955. Reprinted in *The Shaping of Modern India*.

19. *The Agrarian Prospect in India: Five Lectures on Land Reform*, Delhi School of Economics, Delhi, University Press, 1956.

20. 'The Agricultural Labour Enquiry: Reflections on Concepts and Methods', *Economic Weekly*, Bombay, vol. VIII (23 June 1956), pp. 759–66. Reprinted in *Land and Labour in India*.

21. 'India's Agrarian Revolution by Census Redefinition', *Indian Economic Review*, Delhi, vol. III, no. 2 (August 1956), pp. 1–21. Reprinted in *Land and Labour in India*.

22. 'Casual Employment of a Factory Labour Force: The Case of India, 1850–1939', *Economic Weekly*, Bombay, Annual Number, January 1957, vol. IX, pp. 121–4.

23. 'Demarcation of Agrarian Regions of India', in *Rationale*

*Regional Variations in Agrarian Structure of India*, Indian Society of Agricultural Economics, Bombay, *Seminar Series* no. 1, 1957, pp. 46–67.

24. 'Types of Employer–Labourer Relationships in Indian Agriculture' (with Alice Thorner), *Indian Journal of Agricultural Economics*, Seventeenth Conference Number, vol. XII (April–June 1957), pp. 84–97. Reprinted in *Land and Labour in India*.

25. 'Agricultural Manpower in India: Labourers' (with Alice Thorner), *Economic Weekly*, Bombay, vol. IX (9 November 1957), pp. 1443–9.

26. 'Agrarian Regions', in A. R. Desai (ed.), *Rural Sociology in India*, Bombay, Popular Prakashan, 1959.

27. 'Economic Concepts in the Census of India, 1951' (with Alice Thorner), *Indian Population Bulletin*, New Delhi, April 1960.

28. 'Land Reform in Bombay: An Agonizing Appraisal', *Economic Weekly*, Bombay, vol. X, January 1958, pp. 117–19.

29. 'Dropping the Pilot', a review article on the community projects, *Economic Development and Cultural Change*, Chicago, vol. VII, no. 3, part I, April 1959, pp. 377–80.

30. 'Ploughing the Plan Under: Ford Team Report on Food "Crisis" in India', *Economic Weekly*, Bombay, vol. XI, Special Number, July 1959, pp. 901–4. Reprinted in *Land and Labour in India*.

31. 'Economic Recommendations for the Census of 1961' (with Alice Thorner), *Economic Weekly*, Bombay, vol. XI, 5 September 1959, pp. 1230–42.

32. 'India's Elusive Agricultural Output Figures', *Economic Weekly*, Bombay, vol. XII, Annual Number, January 1960, pp. 199–200. Reprinted in *Land and Labour in India*.

33. 'The All-India Rural Credit Survey Viewed as a Scientific Enquiry', *Economic Weekly*, Bombay, vol. XII, Special Number, June 1960, pp. 941–55. Reprinted in *Land and Labour in India*.

34. ' "De-Industrialization" in India, 1881–1931', in *First International Conference of Economic History, Contributions and Communications, Stockholm*, Paris, Mouton & Co., 1960, pp. 217–26. Reprinted in *Land and Labour in India*.

35. 'L'Inde d'aujourd'hui: le problème agraire', *Annales: Economies*,

*Sociétés, Civilisations*, Paris, vol. XVII, janvier–fevrier, 1962, pp. 65–74.

36. *Land and Labour in India* (with Alice Thorner), Bombay, Asia Publishing House, 1962. A translation in Polish was published in 1966 by the Maison d'Editions PWN in Warsaw.

37. 'Context for Cooperatives in Rural India', *Economic Weekly*, vol. XIV, Annual Number, February 1962, pp. 251–66. Reprinted in *The Shaping of Modern India*.

38. 'Peasant Economy as a Category in Economic History', *Economic Weekly*, vol. XV, Special Number, July 1963, pp. 1243–52. Also in *Second International Conference of Economic History, Aix-en-Provence, 1962*, Paris, Mouton & Co., 1965, vol. II, pp. 287–300. Reprinted in Teodor Shanin (ed.), *Peasants and Peasant Societies*, Harmondsworth, Penguin Books, 1971, pp. 202–18. Reprinted in *The Shaping of Modern India*.

39. 'Les Coopératives agricoles aux Indes', *Archives Internationales de la Sociologie de la Coopération*, Paris, Numbers 13 and 14, 1963 and 1964.

40. 'L'Economie paysanne: concept pour l'histoire économique?', *Annales: Economies, Sociétés, Civilisations*, Paris, vol. XIX, mai, 1964, pp. 417–32.

41. 'The Twentieth Century Trend in Employment in Manufacturing in India as illustrated by the Case of West Bengal' (with Alice Thorner), in *Essays on Econometrics and Planning, presented to Professor P. C. Mahalanobis*, Oxford and London, Pergamon Press, 1964, pp. 301–8. Reprinted in *The Shaping of Modern India*.

42. *Agricultural Cooperatives in India: A Field Report*, Bombay, Asia Publishing House, 1964. A Marathi translation appeared in 1966: Poona, Samaj Prabodhan Samstha.

43. 'A Post-Marxian Theory of Peasant Economy: The School of A. V. Chayanov', *Economic Weekly*, Bombay, vol. XVII, Annual Number, February 1965, pp. 227–36. Reprinted in *The Shaping of Modern India*.

44. Edited in collaboration with Basile Kerblay and R. E. F. Smith, *The Theory of Peasant Economy*, by A. V. Chayanov, Homewood, Illinois, Richard D. Irwin Inc., 1965.

45. 'Une théorie néo-populiste de l'économie paysanne: l'Ecole de

A. V. Cajanov', *Annales: Economies, Sociétés, Civilisations*, Paris, vol. XXI, no. 6, novembre–décembre 1966, pp. 1232–44.

46. 'Marx on India and the Asiatic Mode of Production', *Contributions to Indian Sociology*, Paris, no. IX, December 1966, pp. 33–66. Reprinted in *The Shaping of Modern India*.

47. 'Coastal Andhra: Towards an Affluent Society', *Economic and Political Weekly*, Bombay, vol. II, Annual Number, February 1967, pp. 241–52. Reprinted in *The Shaping of Modern India*.

48. 'The Social Framework of Agriculture: Studies by Dr Harold H. Mann', *Economic and Political Weekly*, Bombay, vol. II, no. 13, 1 April 1967. Reprinted in *The Shaping of Modern India*.

49. Edited, *The Social Framework of Agriculture: India, Middle East, Africa*, by Harold H. Mann, Bombay, Vora and Co., 1967.

50. 'India's New Farms', *The Statesman*, New Delhi and Calcutta, 1, 2, 3, and 4 November 1967. Reprinted in *The Shaping of Modern India*.

51. 'L'Inde: obstacles sociaux au développement rural', *Paysans*, Paris, vol. XI, no. 67, août–septembre 1967, pp. 69–74.

52. 'Predatory Capitalism in Indian Agriculture', *Economic and Political Weekly*, Bombay, vol. II, no. 43, 26 October 1968.

53. 'Peasantry', *International Encyclopedia of the Social Sciences*, Macmillan Co. and Free Press, 1968.

54. 'The Emergence of Capitalist Agriculture in India', paper presented at the Conference of European Scholars on South Asia, Cambridge, July 1968. Reprinted in *The Shaping of Modern India*.

55. 'Marx et l'Inde: Le Mode de Production Asiatique', *Annales: Economies, Sociétés, Civilisations*, Paris, vol. XXIV, no. 2, mars–avril, 1969.

56. 'Old and New Approaches to Peasant Economies', in Clifton Wharton (ed.), *Subsistence Agriculture and Economic Development*, Chicago, Aldine Publishing Co., 1969.

57. 'Capitalist Farming in India', *Economic and Political Weekly*, Bombay, vol. IV, no. 52, Review of Agriculture, December 1969.

58. 'Le Monde Indien' (with Alice Thorner), in M. Crouzet (ed.), *Le Monde depuis 1945*, Presses Universitaires de France, Paris, 1973, vol. II, pp. 763–803.

59. 'The Principal Modes of Production of Karl Marx: Some Preliminary Notes', in Ashok Mitra (ed.), *Economic Theory and Planning*, Calcutta, Oxford University Press, 1974, pp. 151–6.

60. *The Shaping of Modern India*, Bombay, Allied Publishers Ltd., 1980.

61. Introduction to the second edition of *The Agrarian Prospect in India*, Bombay, Allied Publishers Ltd., 1976, pp. 1–6.

62. Edited, *Agrarian Regions of South Asia: A Benchmark Study of British India centred on the 1930's*, by Chen Han-seng, J. Arballot *et al.*, Allied Publishers Ltd., 1980, for the Indian Council of Social Science Research.

# Index